Working Lives

The forgotten voices of Britain's post-war working class

David Hall

CORGI BOOKS

TRANSWORLD PUBLISHERS
61–63 Uxbridge Road, London W5 5SA
A Random House Group Company
www.transworldbooks.co.uk

WORKING LIVES
A CORGI BOOK: 9780552162234

First published in Great Britain
in 2012 by Bantam Press
an imprint of Transworld Publishers
Corgi edition published 2014

Copyright © David Hall 2012

David Hall has asserted his right under the Copyright, Designs and
Patents Act 1988 to be identified as the author of this work.

A CIP catalogue record for this book
is available from the British Library.

This book is sold subject to the condition that it shall not,
by way of trade or otherwise, be lent, resold, hired out,
or otherwise circulated without the publisher's prior
consent in any form of binding or cover other than that
in which it is published and without a similar condition,
including this condition, being imposed on the
subsequent purchaser.

Addresses for Random House Group Ltd companies outside the UK
can be found at: www.randomhouse.co.uk
The Random House Group Ltd Reg. No. 954009

The Random House Group Limited supports The Forest Stewardship Council®
(FSC®), the leading international forest-certification organisation. Our books
carrying the FSC label are printed on FSC®-certified paper. FSC is the
only forest-certification scheme supported by the leading environmental
organisations, including Greenpeace. Our paper-procurement
policy can be found at www.randomhouse.co.uk/environment

Typeset in 11/14pt Minion by Falcon Oast Graphic Art Ltd.

Printed and bound in Great Britain by Clays Ltd, St Ives plc

2 4 6 8 10 9 7 5 3 1

To Nina

Bracknell Forest Borough Council	
5430000031990 4	
Askews & Holts	2014

Contents

Introduction

BRITAIN WAS THE birthplace of the Industrial Revolution. Throughout the eighteenth and nineteenth centuries the country led the world in harnessing the power of coal, water and steam to drive the heavy machinery that made mass production possible. New inventions enabled British manufacturers to increase their output while cutting their costs, making Britain prosperous on a scale that no other country in the world could match. It was a time when Britain was described as the 'workshop of the world'. By the twentieth century, although increased competition from Germany and the United States had challenged this supremacy, Britain remained a major industrial power.

In 1951, within a working population in Britain of some 20.3 million people, the proportion doing what were recognized as manual, working-class jobs was 72.2 per cent.[1] From the women operating three or four looms at once in a hot, noisy weaving shed to the men hewing coal on a dirty, cramped, claustrophobic face deep down in a coal mine, or manhandling sheets of white-hot metal in the searing heat of a steelworks, all these jobs, almost

[1] *Austerity Britain 1945–1951*, David Kynaston, Bloomsbury, 2007.

without exception, involved a degree of physical effort. The work was hard and the hours were often long as people put in the overtime to make up their wages and give their families a reasonable standard of living.

The industrial landscapes that formed the backdrop to the working lives of the millions who laboured in the industrial areas of Britain were dominated by great, gaunt mills and smoke-blackened factories, dirty black slagheaps and the giant skeleton-like pithead gear of countless collieries, the fiery glow of furnaces lighting the sky and glimpses of glowing, white-hot metal flowing through the smoke of foundries and rolling mills. All were mighty centres of filth and pollution with hundreds of chimneys belching out thick, black smoke over endless rows of terraced houses clustered around the pitheads and the mill and factory gates.

It's the sort of landscape that I remember vividly from growing up in inner-city Manchester. In the late 1940s and early 1950s I lived in Bradford, a district two miles north-east of the city centre. Our house stood in the middle of a row of terraces surrounded by railway lines, canals, a chemical works, pithead gear, a gasworks, a coke works, and dozens of mills, foundries and engineering works. We lived with the sound of metal clanging against metal in the forges and engineering works, and the smell from the chemical works made the atmosphere rancid. In the winter it always seemed to be foggy and we rarely saw the sun from one week to the next. But for a young boy growing up in the midst of all the smoke and the fire and the hiss of steam, there was something exciting about it.

When I was little I used to go for a walk with my dad on a Saturday or a Sunday morning past the coal mine and the engineering works that surrounded our house. We'd go past the Lancashire Hygienic Dairies grocer's shop on our corner, where the sugar and butter and other essentials like dried peas were all sold loose and bacon was cut on a great big slicing machine with a dangerous-looking blade. At the traffic lights we'd turn right along Ashton New Road and walk past a pub on every corner towards Clayton Aniline. The Clayton Aniline Company manufactured textile dyes which were exported all over the world. It had been there for nearly eighty years by the side of the Ashton Canal, which gave a plentiful supply of water – the key raw material in dye manufacture. All I knew about this place, though, was that it was some sort of chemical works and the horrible smell from it used to hang over the whole area. It was like rotten eggs or the stink bombs you could buy at the joke shop in town.

Opposite the Aniline we'd turn down Bank Street towards Philips Park, with the dirty waters of the River Medlock flowing through it. We called it the Red River because its banks were covered in red brick and because it sometimes ran bright red. But it would also run purple or yellow or green because of the effluents discharged from the Aniline and from numerous dye-works, bleachworks and chemical factories along its banks. After a short walk along the river and through the cemetery, the excitement really began when we came out on to Forge Lane – a dark corridor of mining and engineering. On one side, just down a short side street, was the great pithead gear of Bradford Pit, with the wheels at the top whirling round as the coal was hauled up from the depths of the earth. On the other side stood a place that I thought hell must be like. Johnson's Wireworks stretched all along one side of the street, with big double doors opening up on to the road to reveal a gloomy, machine-filled interior illuminated by the flickering light of fires set at intervals across the vast shop floor. There was something fascinating about the sight, but it was also a bit scary and I was always reluctant to walk close to it. I felt much happier along the other side of the road at what I saw as a safe distance from the flames.

In the industrial communities of the 1950s there was very little greenery or fresh air, no beauty in the environment, but there was warmth and friendliness and a real sense of community. I remember how on warm summer evenings all the kids would be out playing, inventing their own forms of amusement. The girls would throw their skipping ropes around the gas lamps to make swings and the lads would kick a tennis ball against the gable end of a house. Women sat on the doorsteps with cups of tea, chatting with neighbours and catching up on gossip. Life was poor in money but rich in love and affection; few material possessions, but a wealth of concern and warmth. The places people lived in may have been dirty and run down, but there was a collectiveness, a cohesion between everybody in those communities and there was an understanding that if you didn't stand with one another you wouldn't survive. Relationships and the dramas of working people's lives were played out against a background of Ewan MacColl's 'Dirty Old Town', a lyrical portrait of Salford.

The last verse of the song talks about chopping the town down like an old dead tree, and in the 1950s that was starting to happen. Many of the people whose stories are told here recalled how housing and living conditions improved dramatically for them when they moved from the inner cities to new council housing estates. It was the time of massive slum-clearance programmes. Throughout Britain industrial workers and their families moved out from the inner-city slums to new houses on council estates on the edge of the countryside. By the time of the Coronation in June 1953 we'd moved from Bradford with its pit and wireworks and terraced houses to the brave new world of Wythenshawe, a massive housing estate on the southern outskirts of the city. It was created as a so-called 'garden city', where an overspill population could be re-housed away from what was regarded as the slum squalor of inner-city areas like Ancoats, Ardwick, Bradford and Beswick. We got a brand-new house with a bathroom and a toilet. No more baths in the tin bath in the kitchen and no more sitting in a cold, draughty toilet in the back yard. Instead of the yard we had a garden at the front and the back, and miles and miles of the Cheshire countryside starting at the end of the road.

Soon after moving we crowded into the living room of a neighbour's house to watch the flickering images of the Coronation on a black-and-white television. It is regarded as the beginning of the modern age, but it was also a time when the country could still quite legitimately be regarded as an industrial power because we were 'still good', as Fred Dibnah used to say, 'at making things'. Workers throughout industry had a real sense of pride in the work they were doing and they were well regarded in their local communities. Miners were supplying the country's energy needs, while engineers, steelworkers, shipbuilders, mill hands and factory workers gained satisfaction from investing their skill and energy into making things that were not only needed but also generated wealth for the country. 'The old industries were the beating hearts of the communities they sustained,' says Owen Jones in *Chavs*,[2] his seminal analysis of the demonization of the working class. 'Most local people had worked in similar jobs and had done so for generations. And of course, the unions, whatever their faults and limitations, had given the workers in these communities strength, solidarity and a sense of power. All of this had sustained a feeling of belonging, of pride in a shared working class experience.'

Working in heavy industry had always been dangerous, but in the post-war years workplaces were becoming safer and between the start of the twentieth century and the 1950s there was a dramatic drop in the number of fatal accidents at work. In spite of the improvements in the first years of the Queen's reign, however, a lot of work was still heavy, dirty and dangerous. Conditions for workers, particularly for those employed in the many family-owned, backward-looking manufacturing enterprises that filled Britain's industrial heartlands, were still almost Dickensian. Health and safety was virtually non-existent in many smaller workplaces, and deaths and horrific accidents were frequent. Employers were reluctant to re-equip with modern machinery that would have reduced the risk of injury and complained about the expense of implementing health and safety legislation.

Whatever the legislation, some workplaces, like coal mines and steelworks, remained inherently dangerous

[2] *Chavs: The Demonization of the Working Class*, Owen Jones, Verso, 2011.

environments. Peter Phillips grew up in the heart of Scotland's steel-producing area in Lanarkshire and went to work at the Clydebridge Steelworks in Cambuslang. 'It was a very dangerous place,' he recalls. 'At Clydebridge in the mid-1970s there were three guys killed, one week after another, in three totally separate incidents. One guy fell off a crane, another guy got decapitated when they dropped a hot plate and another lost his life when the floor fell through where he was working. And that was all within the space of a month.' Despite the danger of the work and the appalling conditions, working in manual labour was regarded within the community as proper man's work. The whole business was tied up with self-image and manual workers would look down on any man who didn't earn his living from his strength and toughness and the sweat of his brow. Taking risks at work, putting up with hardships and living with danger were regarded as manly attributes.

The men who worked in the shipyards were intensely proud of what they did. The shipwright, the fitter, the rigger ... they were the 'worthy' occupations, not comparable in any way with the 'wimpish' occupations found in the office or outside the shipyard. It was the same for the melters, the rollers and the forgemen in the steel industry and for the coal cutters, drillers and fillers in the mines. Working men took pride in their ability to perform hard, physically demanding tasks.

Family ties were of vital importance for getting a job and an apprenticeship was regarded as a father's legacy to his son. In *Making Ships, Making Men*[3] Alan Mackinlay describes how the personal relationship between a boy's

[3] *Making Ships, Making Men*, Alan Mackinlay, Clydebank District Libraries, 1991.

father and the foreman – 'someone he trusted; someone he had dealings with' – was considered by many shipyard workers to be directly related to their introduction to the trade. Apprenticeship was the key to gaining acceptance into the community and the challenge of the work, the dangers and the appalling conditions brought with them a strong feeling of comradeship. They are values that are summarized perfectly in the autobiography of Govan's most famous son, Sir Alex Ferguson.

I remember the people I was raised among. The great holiday adventure of my childhood was to go to Saltcoats on the Ayrshire coast for the Glasgow Fair fortnight. Some families in Govan couldn't afford even that and would go to the local Elder Park or Bellahouston Park in order to be surrounded by a little greenery. For the men, it was respite enough to be spared the noise and grime of the shipyards for a couple of weeks, to escape the hammer of the Clyde. Ambition had nothing to do with their lives. Survival was the essence. Yet there was an incredible warmth of fellow feeling among them, a loyalty that was as deep as the marrow. I wish I could revisit, however briefly, the sense of community that existed in the Govan of my childhood. It could be a rough world but there were wonderful values at the heart of it. Loyalty has been the anchor of my life and it is something that I learned in Govan.[4]

Toughness, hard graft and knowing your place in the

---

[4] *Managing My Life*, Alex Ferguson, Hodder and Stoughton, 2000.

hierarchies of family, work and community were essential qualities for survival. An apprentice soon learnt that the ideals of 'hardness' won respect for you not just in the brutal environment of the mine, the steelworks or shipyard but in the wider community outside work.

The years immediately after the Second World War and well into the 1960s were a time of full employment. Many people began to believe that they'd got a job for life, but in some industries workers were still hired and fired at short notice. Under these old 'contractor' systems one skilled worker would hire his own gang, be paid a lump sum by the employer and share out the pay at the end of the week. Many coal mines still operated on the old 'butty' system, which involved the mine manager negotiating a rate of pay for a particular piece of work with a collier, who then recruited his own men. There were similar arrangements in most of the old industries. When economist Alec Cairncross tried to get shipyard-owners interested in management studies in 1951 he was met with a complete lack of interest. Management in the industry was almost non-existent. In a large yard the organization of the work was in the hands of the yard superintendent and that work was devolved to the foreman on the job. There was no planning staff and each ship was built as a one-off job with workers employed on a hire-and-fire basis.[5] For the ordinary shipyard worker and his family it meant that times were often hard.

In spite of these throwbacks to an older way of taking on labour, conditions were improving throughout industry in the 1950s and life was getting better for millions of workers. The whole method and basis on

[5] *Austerity Britain 1945–1951*, David Kynaston, Bloomsbury, 2007.

which most people were paid and employed was becoming fairer, more standardized and secure, and over this same period the nature of the work that had to be done was changing. In the old industries some of the sweat and sheer back-breaking effort of human labour started to be replaced by machinery. In the shipyards pneumatic and hydraulic-power hammers began to replace hand-riveting and caulking. In the steelworks the furnaces in the melting shops started to be charged by machines rather than by hours of shovelling and in the mines coal came to be cut and moved not by human muscle power alone but with ever more powerful cutting machines and haulage systems. But none of this happened overnight, nor did it happen in all works and all industries at the same time.

The steel industry involved production on a massive scale. But even in a huge industry like this much of the work still had to be done by hand. For many years there was a limit to what machinery could do and it was only in the 1960s and 1970s that the key processes in steel-making began to be automated. Even then there were many works where outdated plant meant that working conditions were even tougher than they needed to be. It was an industry in which the work was always demanding, where muscle and physical endurance were as important as skill. All this meant that for many their working lives continued to be ones of hard graft – a life you accepted without too much questioning because, if your dad said that's what you had to do, you did what you were told.

One of the things that distinguished the workforce was a strong trade union movement to represent it. During the war the appointment of trade unionist Ernest Bevin as

Minister of Labour in Churchill's coalition government signalled the arrival and acceptance of the unions at the national top table and by the end of the 1940s there was a broad consensus that organized labour had permanently arrived as a force to be reckoned with. Union leaders were consulted by government on a regular basis and by 1951, against a background of full employment, union membership stood at an all-time high of 9.3 million. In the late 1970s over half of all workers were trade union members.

To many observers one of the most striking features of British industrial life was the social divide between managers and the workforce. Summed up by the phrase 'Them and Us', evidence for it could be seen everywhere. There were separate canteens and separate toilets and pension rights; holiday provision and the way people were paid all highlighted the differences between management and workforce, white collar and blue collar, skilled and unskilled. Because groups of workers were anxious to protect their own crafts, there were widespread restrictive practices and a great deal of inter-union rivalry, which meant that managers in many industries were compelled to deal with as many as ten or twelve different unions within one factory. A great deal of management time had to be spent on labour difficulties and demarcation issues rather than on getting on with their proper job of organizing production efficiently. But if labour was inflexible and found it hard to change its ways, so too was management. The stereotype of the British manager as the conservative, paternalistic businessman who used the insecurity of the workforce as a tool of control, hired and fired at short notice, and kept welfare provision and consultation with the workforce to a minimum persisted well into the 1950s and 1960s. But then management began to understand that looking after their workers and consulting with them was in their best interests.

Today our urban and industrial landscape has changed dramatically as whole industries have disappeared and with them the communities that had grown up around them. The great industries of iron and steel, coal mining, textile manufacturing, and ship and railway-engine building on which our industrial supremacy was built have disappeared. Entire communities used to be based around a particular mill, coal mine, steelworks or shipyard. Most of the men would have worked in the same place, but as industries disappeared their workforces were broken up and scattered. Skilled jobs of which people had been proud were done away with. Some of the people who were interviewed for this book believed that union militancy was responsible, but the majority had no doubts about who was to blame for this state of affairs. 'Maggie Thatcher came along, took our jobs and destroyed the communities we lived in' was the common refrain. In *Chavs*, Owen Jones sums up the view that many people expressed: 'Margaret Thatcher's assumption of power in 1979 marked the beginning of an all-out assault on the pillars of working-class Britain. Its institutions, like trade unions and council housing, were dismantled; its industries, from manufacturing to mining, were trashed; its communities were, in some cases, shattered, never to recover; and its values, like solidarity and collective aspiration, were swept away in favour of rugged individualism.'[6]

[6] *Chavs: The Demonization of the Working Class*, Owen Jones, Verso, 2011.

In interview after interview we heard how communities were left ravaged by unemployment, poverty and the social problems that accompany them. 'We were a close-knit community,' Bob Clark from Padiham in Lancashire said. 'But since Margaret Thatcher it's been different.' For the people who lived and worked in our industrial communities, making things, as far as Thatcher was concerned, was a thing of the past; finance and service industries were the future. With the Thatcherite offensive against industries, working-class communities, values and institutions, the central reference points of working-class identity disappeared. The communities that grew up around our traditional industries were fragmented and had to adapt to new types of employment or, in many cases, to no work at all, neither of which fosters the same sense of community that the traditional industries once did. The old community bonds that came from industry have been destroyed. Coal, steel, textiles, shipbuilding and engineering were the things that had given life to communities. Once the heart of the community had been taken away they began to wither and die. 'The old smokestack factory skyline has gone,' Owen Jones says in *Chavs*.[7] 'With it has disappeared (or is rapidly disappearing) the largely male, industrial working class, with jobs for life passed on from generation to generation, and whole communities based around the workplace. A new movement has to speak to a more fractured, largely non-unionized workforce marked by job insecurity and growing numbers of part-time and temporary workers. The jobs they are doing are generally cleaner and involve less physical exertion, but they come

[7] *Ibid.*

without the same sense of pride and fulfilment that many of the old industrial jobs had. Skilled jobs with prestige have, in many cases, given way to shelf stacking.'

A whole way of life has gone and the voices of those who laboured in the 'workshop of the world' in its last days are now largely ignored and forgotten. *Working Lives* gives a few of them a voice as it takes us to some of the great industrial centres of the 1950s, 1960s and 1970s to meet men and women who worked in our major industries when they were still at their peak and talk to them about their working lives, working conditions and the communities they lived in. The book is about a way of life that has now disappeared in many places; about the way that industries influenced the character of a region; and the way in which working in these industries shaped people's lives, giving them a sense of identity and belonging.

1

The Industrial Community

IN THE YEARS that followed the Second World War the great industries of iron and steel, coal mining, textile manufacturing, shipbuilding and engineering on which Britain's industrial supremacy rested were still at the heart of the working communities that had grown around them in the nineteenth century. Entire communities were still based around a particular mill, coal mine, steelworks or shipyard and these places of work provided the bread and butter for the majority of people who lived in that community. Most had worked in the same places, doing similar jobs, as their families had done for generations. There was a sense of continuity in these working communities, a feeling of belonging and of pride in a shared working-class experience.

Throughout Britain, the landscape of the major industrial regions was shaped by its industries. Skylines were dominated by hundreds of smoking chimneys, and filthy, rat-infested rivers wound through landscapes in which ugly, smoke-blackened industrial buildings stood among heaps of spoil and scrap. Everywhere was the hiss of steam and the clank of machinery as lives were lived to the constant accompaniment of steam hammers, the ring of metal meeting metal and the clatter of line-shafting driving machinery in the mills and factories.

In Lancashire and Yorkshire smoke from the mill chimneys filled the air – dozens of them belching thick, black clouds day and night. They had to be tall not just to carry the smoke and noxious fumes up into the atmosphere but also to create a draught for the boilers in the mills and factories down below. In Bolton there were so many chimneys that around seven tons of soot would fall on each square mile of the town every year. Thick smogs, or 'pea-soupers' as they were known, would envelop all the towns around there for days, making them unhealthy places to live. The endless rows of terraced houses surrounded by railway lines, canals and wastelands left derelict by earlier industries added to the factory emissions as they puffed out smoke from their own domestic fires to form a dirty grey canopy that hung over the cobbled streets. Everywhere the smell from works and factories made the atmosphere fetid and toxic, creating a semi-permanent greeny-yellow smog. But it was an environment that was largely taken for granted by the inhabitants of our great industrial regions – one in which they, like their parents and grandparents, lived, worked and died.

Kath Dunne, who grew up in an inner-city district of Manchester before the war, remembers the pea-soupers that would cover the city for days on end.

We used to have a lot of fog then because of all the chimneys and the soot and if you'd been to town and it had got foggy while you were there the buses would still be running but the guard would walk along the edgings with his little lamp to show the driver where it was. We used to live in a cul-de-sac and when it was very foggy, you could hardly find your way out of it even with a torch because it would be that thick, and when you got back home you'd be black all round your nose with the soot.

Talk to anybody about living in an industrial area at this time and one of the first things they mention is the smoke and the smog. Neville Wilkinson lived in Siddal, near Halifax. 'With all its chimneys,' he said, 'it was horrible.'

It were a very bad place for smog and muck and I was getting bronchitis pretty bad so the doctor said I had to move. So we moved up the hill to Illingworth. But I can remember walking down from Illingworth and halfway down you'd walk into this wall of fog, and you couldn't see more than about three foot away. We were going to Scouts and you had to go to this hall down the hill. We was all running and we ran into it and within seconds we had to stop for the last two hundred yards.

Back across the Pennine Moors it was just the same. Alan Crompton, who grew up in Bolton, remembers going to the cinema with his mum and dad, and when they came out the smog was so thick that they got lost and couldn't find their way home. It was so bad they couldn't see the street name four or five feet above their heads, so they had to knock on doors asking what street they were in. Dorothy Pomfrett lived in Padiham, a small mining and weaving town three miles west of Burnley, and her memory too is of the whole place being covered in chimneys and fog.

You could go up to Hapton and look down over Padiham and all you could see was the smoke. You could see perhaps an odd chimney or two, but you could hardly see the houses. It only cleared when the mills shut for Wakes Week. Then people would say, 'Oh look – you can see for miles.' But all the rest of the time the fog was there. I think people seemed to have a lot more coughs and colds then but you just got used to it. You didn't know any different really, unless you went to Blackpool where there were no mill chimneys.

Eric Beaghan, from Rishton near Blackburn, also remembers the annual week's holiday as the only time they got a break from the grime of all the industry that surrounded them.

Most people went to Southport, Blackpool or Morecambe and the posh people went to Bournemouth. It was good to get away for a week because near us the landscape was grey and murky and at night there was always a haze. You'd climb the hilltop, perhaps a few hundred feet, and you looked out over Blackburn or over Burnley and there was an orangey-brown haze that looked to be a few hundred feet thick. It wasn't exactly a pea-soup fog, or anything like that, but it wasn't pleasant. You were constantly in this layer of industrial pollution. The mill chimneys were belching smoke out from early morning until teatime, and then when two-shift and three-shift working came along they were going night and day. Everybody lived in this and we just put up with it.

The sights and sounds of heavy industry formed a constant backdrop to life in many of Britain's major cities. Sheffield's hills provided the city with raw materials for the industry that led to it becoming known as 'Steel City': coal, iron ore and millstone grit for the grinding wheels of its workshops. Mike Lomas was born in Darnell, quite close to the city centre.

The whole place was just dominated by steel and factories and noise and smoke belching away. If you looked north you were looking at a pool of smoke, a big dark cloud. As a kid on a quiet day you might wake up in the early hours of the morning and there was always this presence; some furnace doors had opened and the night sky was glowing red, or you could hear drop-hammers, forging, banging away in the middle of the night. It was always there, always around you. You'd see wagons, lorries loaded with steel ingots and things like that, to-ing and fro-ing from one side of the town to the other. They were twenty-four-hour operations.

Things were much the same in industrial Lancashire. Tony Cummings was born in Burnley and grew up surrounded by mills, though most of his family worked in the mines. His dad was the only one of four brothers who didn't go to work down the mine. The youngest was one of nineteen men who lost their lives in a disaster at Hapton Valley Colliery in 1962. He was just seven years older than Tony.

I can remember the areas that certain members of my family lived in, and they were very poor. Not me, though – I was very blessed really. My parents weren't wealthy, but they worked very hard. My mother was a cook in one of the mills and a house came with the job. It was quite palatial compared with a lot of the miners' and mill workers' houses. It was a two-bedroom terraced house with a bathroom, and me and my brother's bedroom overlooked the mill, so we'd wake up to the sound of the textile mill. It was just day shifts – they didn't do nights there – and I remember the engines starting in the morning. If they opened the gate the difference in volume with the weaving looms going was immense. We could hear it with the doors closed, but it was duller. Once they were opened in hot weather it was very noisy.

My paternal grandparents lived not very far away in what is now known as the Weavers' Triangle. It's an area near the Leeds–Liverpool Canal and they say that at the turn of the twentieth century it was one of the most industrialized areas in the world. I can remember when I stayed there with my grandparents the miners going to work and the sound of the people in the textile mill going to work very early, because a lot of them, even in my living memory, wore clogs which you could hear on the cobbled streets.

Burnley had a lot of working men's clubs and there was quite a drinking culture to it. But there was also a cultural dimension that Burnley always had. There were brass bands and there were always a lot of opportunities for cultural involvement in terms of amateur dramatics, choirs and music. There was also a very keen walking fraternity. These walking clubs evolved from people working in the textile mills and finishing work at lunchtime on Saturday. When they finished work they'd go for a walk in the countryside on the Saturday afternoon.

Jimmy Crooks, a miner from Wigan in Lancashire, also remembers the sounds of people going to work in the mornings in the 1950s.

Everybody had clogs on as they went to catch the six o' clock bus from the centre of Wigan. Fifty or sixty men all walking down with clogs on must have woken everybody up if they weren't already up and on their way to work themselves. The mill girls used to start at six as well. It was like the middle of the day, especially on Market Square where all the buses were. There would be hundreds of people knocking about. Not like now; they're all still in bed.

More than any other industry, coal mining left its marks all over the landscape. Harry Meadows grew up in the little town of Atherton, near Wigan, surrounded by the slagheaps and the pithead gear of the collieries that were dotted all round the area. For a child in a mining community like this the landscape created by the pits became an adventure playground.

We didn't have a lot of money but everybody had a bit of a friendship. People seemed to bond better then. Where I lived there was a disused mine shaft down the side of Leyland Park. You could get over the wall and there was a sleeper across and some of the kids used to walk across it. And if you dropped something in the mine, you would wait for it and you couldn't hear it hit the bottom. There were two fatalities, young lads who were too adventurous.

At the side of the shaft there was a hill made up of waste from the pit from years back. This waste had all heated up from being there years and one fella bought it. Eli Brindley his name were, and he used to take this red shale and he made a good living out of it, doing tennis courts and things like that. Then there was a place where they dropped a bomb in the field at the back during the war and it had made a pond where kids used to go swimming. There was one fella who used to pass the park every day with a bike and he'd a sack of coal underneath the crossbar and another on the top. He'd been to a local pit that had closed down, picking up coal that was lying around to earn a crust, and he had a job to walk with that bike.

Things were rough, they really were. But they were good. You could leave the door open and leave anything lying handy.

Nowhere was a landscape changed more dramatically by its industry than in South Wales. Two centuries ago the series of valleys running down from the Brecon Beacons was an area of great natural beauty, but exploitation of their natural resources at the time of the Industrial Revolution made this one of the most heavily industrialized regions in Britain and names like Rhondda, Rhymney, Mountain Ash and Ebbw Vale are linked with the ravages of coal, iron and steel. Welsh coal had been known since Roman times and small ironworks had long dotted the landscape, but the demands of Britain's new industries were to be responsible for an explosive growth in population and a rapid disfigurement of the landscape.

The great period of industrial growth in the valleys began in the eighteenth century, when huge ironworks began to appear alongside the collieries, and continued in the mid-nineteenth century with the discovery and mining of high-quality steam coal. Over these hundred years the sparsely populated rural wilderness was transformed by the slag from furnaces, the spoil tips from the mines, the winding gear of the deep pits and the sights and sounds of heavy industry. This was Britain's only mountainous coalfield. Roads along the valley bottoms were lined with ribbon developments of closely packed terraced houses built along the valley sides to accommodate the influx of huge numbers of people from rural areas to work in the mines and the ironworks.

Wyndham Jones, who grew up in the small mining community of Gilfach Goch close to the Rhondda area in Mid-Glamorgan, remembers the environment created by the pits.

One of the things I remember most when I was growing up was that it was always very dusty. I suppose the air pressure was low and the whole valley in Gilfach would be covered in smoke from the chimneys of all the houses. Coal was all around the mountain and it still is. I could go up there now and pick up coal – a whole bucketful, because I know where to go. I remember one day a big hole just appeared in the ground overnight. It was so big you could put a double-decker bus into it, so the whole face had to shut down because we didn't know what was there. There must have been old workings underneath. But there wasn't only deep mines; there were a lot of drift mines[8] littered around the mountains. All around the mountain is scarred with coal levels. Just dig into the mountain and you come to them. There are old workings everywhere. The old coal-owners used to take coal from under farms and they wouldn't report it, because they had to pay out money for it. Up at Gilfach on top of the hill I know a man who bought his council house and in his garden about four feet down there was a coal seam but he wasn't allowed to touch it. They told him he could dig his garden but the coal that was there was not his.

The geographical shape of the South Wales valleys had their effect on working life and culture. To this day roads stretch along valleys connecting the settlements that are strung out along them. As a result the separate towns in a valley are more closely associated with each other than they are with towns in the neighbouring valley, even when the towns in the next valley are closer on the map. Even so, some men would go from one valley to the next for work. Wyndham James remembers how some of the men from the Rhondda got to work in the pits of Gilfach Goch.

[8] A form of underground mining which is done where the coal deposits are below the surface of a mountain or hillside. The mines are cut into the side of the mountain and, rather than going downwards, the tunnels that are dug are horizontal and called drifts.

That mountain there divides us from the Rhondda and men used to walk over that mountain to go to work. We'd see them because we lived on the top of the colliery on the right-hand side of the valley where they would walk. There were about five or six of them would walk every day, go down, do a shift and then walk back home, because the buses weren't that regular and it saved the fares. One woman the other day rang me and said, 'I remember as a little girl seeing my grandfather coming in with icicles on his eyebrows and his whiskers. They had walked the mountain and that was at a time when they lost two men there. They'd walked over and sheltered behind a wall and just froze to death.' But they walked rain or shine over that mountain. You'd walk it in any weather and then do your eight hours. I remember Glyn Owen and he had a council house up in Ton so he used to walk over the top. Once in the wet he couldn't walk because his trousers froze on him. My father was an official overman and every Sunday morning he had to go out looking for men to go in and work on Sunday night. So me and him, and I was only a youngster at the time, would go, with him clutching my hand, up over the mountain down to Penygraig, around Tonypandy and Tonyrefail and back again. And the men would be waiting there, thinking, 'I hope they pick me this week.'

While the natural landscape of South Wales affected the way people lived and worked, the industrial landscape created by mining meant that communities existed with the shadow of death hanging over them. Not only were fatal accidents underground common in all coal mines, but Merthyr Vale Colliery will for ever be synonymous with one of the greatest tragedies ever to hit such a community. For many years millions of tons of mining waste from the colliery were deposited on the side of a mountain directly above the village of Aberfan on the opposite side of the valley. On the morning of Friday, 21 October 1966 the waste tip slipped and engulfed the Pantglas Junior School and other buildings in the village, killing 144 people, 116 of them children. At the school the children had just returned to their classrooms after morning assembly. Up on the mountain a tipping gang was working and saw the slide start, but their telephone cable had been stolen and they couldn't raise the alarm in the village below. A thirty-foot-high wave of black waste swept across the Glamorgan Canal and engulfed the school, a farmhouse just above it and about twenty houses in the village before coming to rest. Around half of the schoolchildren and five of their teachers were killed. The very landscape that had been created by the region's industry brought death to the valley and wiped out a generation. It was the most tragic day in the history of British coal mining and a stark reminder that an industry that sustained a community and gave it its identity could also destroy it.

*

Throughout industrial Britain, a large part of the population still lived in the small back-to-back houses that had been put up in the nineteenth century to get the largest number of people into the smallest amount of space near the mills, collieries, foundries, rolling mills, shipyards and engineering works where they earned a living. With its mills and factories and its mile upon mile of terraced houses, the Manchester of the 1930s still looked like the city from which mass industrialization had spread across the world. The city centre was the grand district of great Victorian warehouses where the actual business of buying and selling Lancashire's cotton took place. The main cotton-mill areas, where all the spinning and weaving was carried out, were clustered around the city on the east and south sides of the centre, in Ancoats, Chorlton-on-Medlock and Hulme, while the main dyeing and bleaching works were in the northern suburbs of Collyhurst and Harpurhey. In these inner-city districts workers' housing was built back to back in little rows crowded together in narrow streets. Kath Dunne was brought up in one of these areas until she was moved out in a slum-clearance programme before the war.

I was born in Manchester, down Oldham Road in Collyhurst, and was brought up there till I was about eight years old. The houses were just two up and two down and there was five of us girls, my mother and father, my grandma, my aunty and my uncle and a lodger, and we all lived in that house. Don't ask me where we all slept because I don't know. Then we moved to Moston in the slum clearances. When you moved out of them slum areas they used to take all your furniture and your clothing and everything to be fumigated at Monsall Hospital before you could take anything into a council house, because every-thing you had was buggy. Then they used to fumigate the houses before they knocked them down.

In his book *Chronicles of a Lancastrian Boilermaker* Alan McEwen recounts how he was born into a desperately poor family who lived in a slum dwelling in Blitz-ravaged Ardwick, a mile or so to the east of Manchester's city centre. It was dirty and run down and, according to a survey that had been done in the 1930s, this part of east Manchester was judged to be the unhealthiest place in Britain. Alan's house was in the middle of a row of terraces and he paints a vivid picture of the area as it still was when he was growing up there in the 1950s – the cobbled mean streets lined with little two-up two-down slum dwellings, tiny textile factories, engineering workshops, beer houses and off-licences.

Although slum clearances began in many areas between the wars, a great number of appalling Victorian slums and large pockets of inadequate, overcrowded houses remained in all our industrial areas until well after the Second World War. About seven million dwellings lacked any hot water supply and some six million had no inside toilet or bath. Peter Phillips was born in Halfway, a district of Cambuslang in Lanarkshire, and his family were all involved in the steel industry. His grandfather, a steelworker from Redcar, moved to Scotland for employment and lived in Hallside Village, which was originally built to serve the nearby Hallside Colliery and expanded in the early 1870s to serve the Hallside Steelworks. The houses were hardly fit for human habitation but families were still living in them, as Peter recalls.

My father was born in the Hallside Village and then moved out to Halfway to a council house when he got married. Hallside Village was terrible, it was so run down. When I was a boy, in the early 1960s, there were outside toilets but it was only one toilet between four houses. The place was riddled with rats and I remember as a young boy doing the rat hunts. The men would be beating the rats as they came out of the cellars. I used to go and play in the scrapyards there and find old army shells. The war was well over, but a lot of the stuff like steel helmets was coming back in [to the steelworks] to get crushed and melted back down again. There were tossing schools then – that's gambling with two pennies. You'd toss them up and spin them and bet whether it'd be two heads or two tails. This was big gambling and there were specific areas for it. Behind the Miners' Welfare there was a big tossing school and every Sunday they'd come from Blantyre and Glasgow for it. They'd have the kids posted [to watch] for the police. The police used to come on his bike and blow his whistle so everyone knew he was coming and they'd run like hell.

In the mining villages of the Durham coalfield things were also slow to change, and a lot of families still lived in the traditional pitmen's cottages that had been built by the mine-owners in the nineteenth century. They were small and cramped and living conditions were quite primitive, with no bathrooms or toilets. Bob Willis was born in Trimdon in 1937 and grew up in one of these cottages.

There were standpipes, one at the end of each street, and you got your water from there and we had middens[9] outside for toilets. The houses had the old

[9] Pits used for sewage.

black-leaded fireplaces with the water heated in the boiler next to it. When we were kids, nobody locked the doors. You had nowt to steal. When I got married in 1958 things round here were still very basic. Our house had no hot water. We just had cold water inside the house and the toilet was outside in the yard. Women were always busy. They had their families to look after and they didn't have washing machines. They had posset tubs and then when they got the old washer on legs, you just had to stand there to do the washing. I've seen me come in at quarter to twelve if I'd been on the three o'clock in the morning shift and my wife would say, 'Give us a hand with this,' and you used to have to mangle the washing before you went to bed. It was all pits round here, so many that the air was terrible. The collieries all had big chimneys and everything used to get covered in coal dust, including when the women put the clothes up on the line.

Jim Grigg was born in one of the first council houses to be built in Trimdon in 1937, and his memory of them is that they weren't much better than the old pitmen's cottages they replaced.

The council houses were terrible. They were in what they call the Plantation and there were no proper streets, just rough dirt tracks. I remember them because I used to go round with a butcher's van as a kid. My wife was born and bred here as well but her family squatted after the war because there were no houses. A lot of these old houses had been closed up.

So, after the war and into the 1950s, when there was such a shortage, people squatted in these houses that had been closed. They just opened them, put a chair inside the house, and claimed it. It was like a barn what my wife lived in. They had no electricity, just a coal brazier type of thing. Other people lived in old wooden railway cottages and colliery houses. I remember at that time there were people who used to live in bell tents in a field because they didn't have houses.

Tyneside was dominated by the towering hulls and cranes of its shipyards, giving the region its own distinctive character, but for those who lived and worked there, housing conditions were much the same as in other industrial regions. Ken Findlay describes the house where he was brought up in Jarrow on the south bank of the Tyne.

The house I lived in was in a terraced row of single-storey cottages. We went in the front door into a passageway and on the left-hand side there was the main bedroom. It was called the front room and this is where my parents slept, but the furniture in there was better than anywhere else because as well as being a bedroom this was the good room that visitors were taken into. Then when you went further into the house we had a big kitchen which was the hub of the house where we ate and did everything. If my father was mending the clock it was done on the kitchen table and if you had anything to do for school you did it there. We had a black, cast-iron range there, where the kettle was boiled, with an oven at the side, where my mother made bread. At the side of the kitchen there was another secondary bedroom where I and my older brother slept. I had an older sister as well and for the life of me I cannot remember where she slept.

You went through the kitchen and we had a rather large scullery and it was at that point that we came across our water supply. There was only cold water in the house, no hot; just a big square sink with a cold-water tap. We only had this because my father had made an illicit connection from the standpipe in the yard to bring water into the house. We also had a gas cooker in this scullery and the boiler for boiling clothes. My mother had a day for washing and the fire had to be lit underneath the boiler to produce hot water and after she had washed the clothes I was very often put in there as well to be cleaned up.

Outside we had a back yard with a coal house and a toilet and a tap in the yard. In the toilet outside we usually had a candle to stop it from freezing up and no electric light – just a gas light. But we were quite sophisticated because I had a father who was always making things and in our toilet he had fixed a little bracket up on the back of the door and fitted a bicycle lamp on it.

Following a big slum clearance in Jarrow in the late 1930s, new housing estates were built in a semi-rural area just outside the town. Ken Goss and his family were moved up to the Primrose estate in 1938 when he was two years old.

They were all brand-new council houses there, but initially they just had gas lights in and it wasn't until later that the electricity was installed. We had a bath-room and a proper toilet inside the house and upstairs bedrooms. We also had a kitchen range with a fire and an oven on one side of it. It wasn't until the 1950s that people started taking these out and getting modern fireplaces put in.

When we were playing out we had certain areas that were taboo. There was a railway line nearby and we were told not to go over the railway bridge; we had to keep to our side of the lines. Bolden Colliery was in the other direction and we were told not to play there because there were bad lads there – they'd duff you up. But apart from that there was very little restriction and we got up to all sorts of antics. There were farms nearby and in the summer holidays we'd work on them, potato-picking.

I went to a little local primary school. I can remember the cold winter of 1947, going to school in all the snow and we never missed a day. The roads were almost always open and if we couldn't get the bus, we walked. Most schools just had what we called the pipes – four-inch cast-iron pipes running round the outside of the classrooms – and a big pot-bellied boiler next to the teacher, so the teacher was always nice and warm and the kids were freezing. If you sat on the pipes you got into trouble. One unfortunate thing was they were generally near the window and they didn't want you being near the window because you would look out.

Tommy Procter was born and bred in South Shields on the Tyne. He spent his early years in a house on an estate that had been built to replace some of the worst of the town's Victorian housing, but he too remembers conditions were not much better in these new houses than in the slums they replaced.

I lived in a house on what was called the Deans estate and it was built between the wars for the slum clearances of the old houses down by the river. Our house had two bedrooms and a bathroom with a toilet in it. We had a kitchen with a stove in it that was the backside of the coal fire in the little sitting room. One of my indelible memories of the place was the cockroaches – getting up in the night and finding great big piles of them. My memories of the town were very industrial; all the cranes down by the riverside and a lot of smoke. We used to have the steam tugs and steam ships, so there was always that smell of smoke and steam in the air. There were still a lot of the old terraced houses in the town and the women used to scrub their front doorstep with a scrubbing brush so they were nice and white, and they would polish the door handles. They took pride in the appearance of their houses. Inside your house you didn't have wallpaper. You had distemper on the walls, which was the early form of emulsion. I remember it being pink – it was all the same colour. We didn't have carpets. It was just canvas on the floor and linoleum. In the winter I can remember topcoats being put on the bed to keep you warm.

John Bage was born in South Shields in 1947 and spent his early years in one of the old houses built for workers beside Readhead's shipyard. Living conditions were not good but John remembers his childhood as a happy time and one where he never had to go without.

I was born in a one-bedroom, one-living-room and scullery flat. South Shields Council had built lots and lots of rows of these flats close to the shipyard and they were considered to be modern houses at the time. We had a tin bath and you used to have to boil water and fill the bath with a kettle and a pan. It wasn't terrible there – it wasn't dirty or anything, but in these places you got mice and we could hear them and other things like that running around the floor. The streets were all the same and they all had back lanes which is where we played. That's all we knew. It looks terrible now but that's the sort of places where we were brought up and we didn't think anything bad of it. I had a happy childhood. I always had clothes on my back, shoes on my feet and there was always food in the larder so we never, ever went hungry. We didn't have a lot but we were happy. We always got new clothes at Easter and a brand-new pair of leather shoes. I remember it well because they used to hurt and you used to get blisters wearing them. The clothes would be summer clothes to last throughout the summer, but you had to wear them at Easter and Easter quite often was early in the year and you used to freeze when you went to see the marching down at South Shields.

When John's parents had a third child, they qualified for a three-bedroomed terraced house at Whiteleas, a new council estate outside town. He remembers particularly the newfound freedom that came with moving out into what, for him, was the countryside.

> When we moved to this other place where there was fields and grass and freedom and space, what a difference it made to our lives. I think it was mainly families with young children who went into [the new houses] so there were lots of kids our age and we pretty soon gelled with them. We used to have cricket matches and football matches and then wander across the fields and go to the local farms. We would wander around all day long without any-body being bothered. In that house we had a bath with hot and cold water. It was amazing. We had an upstairs and downstairs and a front garden and back garden to play in. Incredible.
>
> When we first moved there I remember seeing piles of soil and heaps of sand because there was still lots of building going on, so we just went out playing on the building site. We climbed over the scaffolding and sat on the dumper trucks and there was a watch-man we became friends with. Parents didn't say, 'Keep away from him – he might be a dirty man.' Nothing like that. We just went and befriended him and we followed him around as he went round the site.
>
> Marvellous freedom we had as children. We'd just go down to the beach and play all day. It was accepted there were dangers, I suppose, but no one looked at them in the same way as they do now. I used to go down to my cousin's house. I must have

only been about eight or nine, and we used to go down to the coast at South Shields. There are cliffs there and we used to just climb on them. Now they have got them all fenced off. But that railing wasn't there in those days and when you used to climb down on to the beach the tide might be coming in and people sometimes got trapped. I broke my leg down there once and when I woke up I was in hospital.

As soon as we moved to that house my dad got into gardening straight away. He loved it. We kids used to help a little bit, especially harvesting all the stuff he grew in there. I still remember getting some fully grown onions out and frying them up. It would be a nice summer night, probably, and the back door would be open and the smell drifting around was mouthwatering.

After we'd moved to that estate they built some shops and a couple of pubs and there was also a social club where they had leek shows, chrysanthemum shows, vegetable shows and that sort of thing. These shows were always a big event on the estate. It was an annual thing in the autumn when the crops had been brought in. It was a really big thing to win something and the prizes were quite good as well. They were money prizes, and for the people at the time it would have been big money. But the main thing, if anybody won something, was the honour of being the one who grew the biggest leek or the biggest onions. It was something that had started with the mining community because the area the estate had been built on was still very much a mining area and the committees in the clubs were always miners. The pits were still operating at the time and Bolden Pit and Harden Pit were very close by. Next to the club was a long row of mining houses and it meant there was still a really strong village-type atmosphere in the whole place. We could tell the miners because every so often a lorry would pull up and tip a great heap of coal on the road outside their house. They just left it in the road and nobody stole it. That wasn't a problem. There was no thieving or anything like that. And then they would give it away or sell it to neighbours, so we'd all go over with our buckets and get so many buckets of coal because we all had coal fires in those days.

I got a motor scooter when I was seventeen or eighteen and I used to leave it outside the house on the path. There was no fencing or anything around in those days. It was just open plan – the lawns in front of the houses went straight out on to the main road. I used to leave this scooter outside the house and there were no locks on it at all; no key to start it or anything. You just turned the petrol on and kick-started it and you were away. It stood there for as long as I had it. Nobody took it. That's what it was like in those days.

The communities were based around the ship-yards, in the same way that the mining communities had their villages around the pitheads, so people were able to walk or cycle or bus to work in the 1960s. In fact there weren't many cars owned by shipyard workers. It was mainly managers that had a car and it was interesting when one of our older draughtsmen bought a car and we all went out to look at it at lunchtime. The draughtsmen were regarded as a staff job in between management and the workforce in the shipyard, so they were able to get mortgages and buy cars. To buy a car in those days on hire purchase you had to get a signature or you had to be a house-owner to get credit. It was very difficult, not like nowadays. So a draughtsman tended to have a mort-gage and a slightly better job that was probably less temporary than some of the workers in the yard, who were finished when a ship finished. They were finished and had to go to another yard to work and wait for that yard to get another ship.

The cramped conditions in which many workers lived were often made worse by the size of their families. Freda Swarbrick, who was born in 1922 in the great cotton town of Rochdale a few miles north of Manchester, was one of eight children.

I lived in a house of ten, including my mum and dad, in Basil Street. I were the youngest girl. I'd a brother younger than me but t'others were all older. It was just an ordinary house like all the others on the street. They were all two-bedroomed. Nobody built any extensions on top of them or out at the back. Everybody had big families then and there were no televisions. I don't even remember us having a radio. We didn't need one – there were enough of us to whistle and to sing. We had no bathroom, just a tin bath that we used to fetch in out of the back yard and put in front of the fire. My mam used to bath the

47

kids and put them to bed and then somebody else would jump in because she couldn't keep emptying it. The youngest kids were always first and then when everybody else had gone to bed one of the older ones could have a bath.

No matter how hardworking parents were, if they had a large family, providing enough for their children was sometimes simply more than they could do. Dorothy Pomfrett from Padiham was one of twelve.

The only entertainment we had when I was a child was playing out – playing hopscotch and skipping, hide and seek and tig. It was mainly outside, but I had one friend called Freda and her parents had an attic and we played in that attic when it was raining. She had loads of toys and it was warm and it was wonderful up there. But most of the time we'd just play outside. Straight after breakfast my mother would say, 'You can go and play out now.' She knew you would be safe enough and it would give her a bit of peace. Everybody on the street knew each other. We used to be in and out of each other's houses and children would call for you. A lot of younger children would call for me because I used to play games with them. They'd be at our door saying, 'Is Dorothy playing out?' even when I was getting to eighteen.

I lived on Station Road and there were about four families on our street that had large families. Our family had twelve children, next door but one, the Colons, had nine and at the opposite end of the street the Farnworths had eight or nine. There were a lot of children, but all the houses were small. In our house there were three bedrooms but one was only a boxroom. All the girls slept in one room and all the boys slept in another. It was horrible; always somebody's foot sticking in your face or you'd just doze off and somebody else would get into bed. Because they were all different ages they would come to bed at different times. I hated that. You were just going to sleep and the light would go on while they got undressed. It was awful. My mum and dad slept in the front room downstairs with the baby because my mother was having babies for twenty years so there was always a baby with them. But the oldest child in the house had their own bedroom in the boxroom. It was a stone terraced house opposite the Padiham cinema and the police station, so there was always something going on and that was my mother's social life, sitting or standing at the door on a summer's evening. She'd watch people going in and out of the cinema, watch the police cars going backwards and forwards. Not during the day, though, because she was too busy.

When I was about nine I had to go to a convalescent home in Blackpool and that was the first time I saw the sea and the sand. It just felt so clean there. I can't remember anyone else from the family going with me, but different siblings went at other times. My mother said I was going on my holidays. I can remember this lady coming for me and I had a coat on and my name on a ticket and a little suitcase. She came for me and took me on the train to St Anne's.

The lady said, 'We're going to this convalescent home to get you strong.' And it was absolute magic there. I wasn't ill, but I don't think we were right well nourished because we'd come through the war. I was always hungry, but so were my brothers and sisters. You just didn't get enough to eat, so most of my brothers and sisters eventually went there for a week or two weeks. When you were there you got three meals a day and you got a bed of your own with clean sheets and pillow slips. I remember the dormitory matron taking me in for the first time and she said, 'This is your bed, Dorothy.' I said, 'Just mine? Anybody else sleeping in it?' She said, 'No, this bed is just yours.' Then she showed me the baths. They were really deep baths and I'd never been in one of them before because we had a tin bath at home, so I was a bit scared, especially when they put the taps on. I'd never used taps before so they made me feel nervous.

I loved it at the convalescent home. I didn't want to go home. I had a nurse and she was called Dorothy too and she was delightful. She was always holding my hand and listening to me. I'll never forget that lady. The most impressive thing for me, though, was getting food. When we woke up there was the smell of bacon and fried bread and tomatoes and egg, and we had that to eat every morning, and orange juice and syrup porridge. I just couldn't believe it. We had these long tables covered in green tiles and they passed all the meals down. You had a knife and fork and a place of your own and a chair. At home we didn't have chairs. Only the ones that worked had chairs because there wasn't enough money for chairs for all of us, so those who weren't working stood around the table. When we'd finished our meal at the convalescent home we all passed the plates down to a trolley and then we'd all clean the green tiles and then after breakfast you went out.

They had a big garden and they grew a lot of their own fruit and vegetables and I got friendly with the gardener. I've always been interested in gardening and growing things, so I used to help there. Then at about ten o'clock you'd have a cup of cocoa with honey in. You sat on a veranda in the garden to drink it. I thought, 'I love this.' Every time you turned round somebody was bringing you food.

They had a big playroom with a rocking horse and we were always queuing up to go on that rocking horse. I loved it because we didn't have any toys at home – not many people did; you just used to play with sticks and stones. So we played on that rocking horse as much as possible and then it was lunchtime so you got a dinner and a pudding. We used to have puddings at home, but it was just on Sunday, when we had stewed apples and custard. But here they had a different pudding every day. With all the food I was getting there I just felt stronger and stronger.

At home we had porridge for breakfast every day, and school dinners. I think it was school dinners and school milk that kept a lot of children alive in those years. Then we had jam butties or syrup butties for tea. I used to go to the Co-op for the jam. They sold it in big earthenware jars that weighed about five pounds and I used to push a pram up the hill to get two of these jars and two large loaves and that would last just a couple of days. They paid wages so low to people in the mills and the mines that people couldn't make a living, so a lot of the children were malnourished. Our parents worked hard enough, but there just wasn't enough money to feed the children.

Stanley Bolton and his sister Mabel Ryding grew up in Horwich, Lancashire, in the 1930s. They remember it as pretty drab place. 'It were a very tiny town,' Mabel recalls, 'hardly a town, more of a village. And there were loads of children, because nearly everybody then had a biggish family, five or six children.' With so many mouths to feed and so little money around times were hard. As a child you knew your place and discipline was strict at home and at school, as Stanley recalls.

There were twelve of us, but two unfortunately died. It was only a two up and two down we lived in with a very big back yard. We used to go to school in the morning and at dinnertime when we come home we didn't even go in the house for our lunch. My mother cooked a pan full of chips and she put them in a newspaper and screwed the top up. Then she used to give us one each of those and we had to go down to the bottom of the street where there was a field. We used to call it the meadow and we used to go there and play and eat our chips, and then we used to go straight back to school. We never went indoors at all, whatever the weather; never played indoors at all, all the time we were young.

We always had holes in our shoes so we used to

have to put cardboard in them. But we were more fortunate than a lot of people because my father used to work as a panel beater at a paper mill. They made thick paper there on big machines and where the paper was dried the rollers were covered in thick felt and every so often they used to cut this felt off the rollers and that was put to one side for scrap. But the workers could help themselves to it if they wanted and my dad used to fetch this felt home and we used to cut it and put it in our shoes.

When we went to bed we slept tops and tails, all twelve of us. We used to get the bed sheets and fasten them on the bed knobs with our garters and make tents and we used to play all sorts. But my dad used to come in and leather us, so we put a catch on the inside of the door so he couldn't get in. One night he woke up in the middle of the night and smelled gas. We used to have gas mantles for our lighting and what had happened was that the one in our bedroom had gone out because the gas had run out. My mother had put a shilling in the gas meter but we didn't know, so gas started coming out from the mantle in our room. But we were all asleep so nobody lit it. When my dad got up he could smell the gas coming from our room but he couldn't get in because we'd put the hook on the other side of the door. So he wet his handkerchief through and wrapped it round his head and broke in and we were all unconscious. He couldn't wake any of us up, so he carried us downstairs and out of the house and lay us down in a line along the street. He laid us across the footpath with our heads overhanging the kerb in the road. Then he got a big bucket of water and put half a packet of salt and a cup in it and my mother went along the row of us pouring a cup of salt water in all of our mouths. This made us all sick and then we all fortunately recovered.

Another time we set the house on fire. My mum and dad never used to go out, but one Christmas they decided they would go to the pictures. We'd been making paper lanterns at school and, after my mum and dad had gone out, our eldest brother, Clifford, was putting decorations up. He put these lanterns up and said, 'Eee, wouldn't they look nice with a little candle in?' so we put little candles in all of them and lit them. It looked lovely but the candles burnt the decorations, the decorations fell down, set fire to the curtains and soon the whole room was on fire. The big sideboard with horses on top caught fire and all the varnish on the dresser started to melt, so we sent for the fire brigade. When the fire brigade arrived we had to go into the picture house and call for my mum and dad and when they got back we were all in big trouble.

If we ever misbehaved we were fastened to the bottom of the bed and we were belted. We used to have a belt that were double at one half and single at the other end and my dad used to get this out and crack it when you did anything wrong. You got this belt and then you were fastened to the bottom of your bed rail and you were left there for twenty-four hours without any food at all. So we used to sneak a bit of jam and bread up our jumpers and go upstairs and give it to whoever was in trouble. Then you got a leathering if you were found out for that.

The countryside started just across the road from our house and they used to call it the Plantation because there was a row of great big thirty-foot trees there. There was a pond, and one day there was a whole gang of us there and a lad of about fifteen came down with his younger brother, who was about eight. He said to his brother, 'Here, get in this sack.' I think he'd seen something about an escapologist at the pictures. The younger one got in the sack and his brother tied it up and threw it in the pond. But the little lad couldn't get out and he drowned.

This was in the early 1930s, because I know in about 1935 or 1936 I went from primary school to the newly opened senior school. There was a teacher that was horrible. He used to thump you and hit your hands with the cane across your fingers, hit you with his knuckles on your muscles and make you stand with a pile of books on your outstretched hands. Twisting your arm was another thing he used to do. And it wasn't just the boys he'd do it to, it was the girls as well. They had great big blackboards in those days on two arms and the blackboard was swivelled at the centre and they had a space at the bottom of the board with a trough where they put the chalk. One day I was being mischievous and he came to me and got hold of the hair above my ear and dragged me out by my hair because I'd been mimicking him. He more or less threw me in the corner by the blackboard and said, 'Right, you can stay there for the rest of this lesson.' So I stayed there and while he was teaching and writing on the board,

I carried on mimicking him. He couldn't see me but the class could and they were all giggling. Of course he cottoned on, so he came over to the board, but instead of chalking he put his other hand at the bottom of the board and pulled it quickly to make it spin round and hit me on the head. But I automatically put my hands up to stop the big heavy slate board crashing down on my head and it bounced up off my hands and spun back to him and cut his forehead. It caused uproar and he really laced into me afterwards in front of all the class. Punishment was instantaneous in school in them days.

As teenagers we used to walk along the lane near our house. To pick your partner we had what they called the 'monkey run'. There were three main roads in Horwich, forming a triangle, and we used to walk continually round that triangle from about seven o'clock at night until eight or nine o'clock at least. You'd pass a girl you liked and chat them up and say, 'Ah well, next time round we'll ask them will they come out with us.' That was how we used to make dates. Gangs of us used to go in temperance bars and we had sarsaparilla and dandelion and burdock. Then at the weekend we went to Blackpool, dancing at the Tower Ballroom. We used to go to Horwich station to catch the train and there would be two locomotives side by side waiting to go out, with at least 250 or 300 people standing on the platform waiting to board these trains.

Ian Richmond spent his early years in the small market town of Oswestry in Shropshire but when he was twelve years old he moved with his family to a very different environment and community – the steelmaking city of Sheffield.

[Our house] was literally next door to the flour mill on one side and Bridgehouses railway depot on the other. Sheffield Rolling Mills was bang across from us over the other side of the river, so from a little market town in the countryside that was all clean I'd suddenly arrived in Sheffield, which in those days before smokeless fuel was virtually a black city with the most tremendous fogs at times during the winter. Of course it was a major culture shock for me. I used to stand at my bedroom window and look across the street, where I could see the red-hot steel bars going through the rolling mills. All you could see was the red. You'd look at it and it would start off looking only about two or three feet long and as they passed it through various rollers it extended and extended until you were looking at huge red ribbons of glowing hot steel in the night. I suppose it was almost romantic in a way, and it was fascinating to watch.

It was difficult to keep things clean when the air was so thick with dirt. You could go out with a nice white shirt and tie on, and jacket, all dressed up, and by the time you got back home all your collar was speckled, especially when you got into autumn and winter when the fogs were absolutely appalling. Coming from an extremely quiet place, where the only thing you ever heard would be animals, it was a massive change coming here with the trams running outside. Because Nursery Street was narrow the trams changed from two lanes to a single one just going past, and the points were bang outside the pub. The trams used to run quite late and also very early in the morning for the people to go on the morning shifts. You could hear the rolling mill across the river too. I don't think my poor mum got to sleep properly for about three months because we had never been used to that sort of noise.

As you walked up Nursery Street you could actually feel in the pavement when the really big hammers in the forges were thumping. They shook everything around. You could hear them inside the pub. It didn't get madly intrusive but you could feel the thump of them because they were very noisy. The street was cobbled all the way up and there were always three-wheeler Scammell trucks running up and down to the railway depot. They were like small carts and they used to pull trailers full of goods, so they used to rattle terribly up and down the slope. Then the thing with having a flour mill next door was the fact that it didn't half encourage the rodent population. The place was full of rats, mice and pigeons because lorries used to come and tip the wheat into the hoppers underground. I really think Sheffield finished my mum off because she got lung cancer. She died in 1958 and left me and my dad. My sisters had more or less left by then, but my dad got remarried and I stayed here.

I used to play darts for the pub team from when I was about thirteen or fourteen. I used to toddle in when we had these darts matches and nobody ever used to mind. The people were absolutely wonderful and when Dad and I were on our own just after Mum had died they used to take me home. Joe Llewellyn lived with his mum in a back-to-back house up on Pits Moor and he'd take me home for Sunday dinner. They used to look after me wonderfully and we used to go to the football matches on Saturday. One week they'd go to the Sheffield United game if they were at home and the next week they'd go to Sheffield Wednesday. They always used to take me with them and they took me fishing. The area around the pub was extremely poor. Pits Moor, which ran up behind us, was full of the old back-to-back houses and the great thing about it was the beautiful way so many of them were kept. There weren't a lot of mums who went out to work in those days and I can remember how Joe Llewellyn's mum kept her doorstep pristine white and inside the old metal grates were all blacked. The houses were absolutely immaculate even though they didn't have much money. And you'd go down the yard to the outside loo and that would be absolutely immaculate as well.

Our pub was a real working-class pub and you used to get these guys who came in from either the steelworks or from the flour mill next door, or from the railway depot. There was also what we called a doss house across the road, which is where people who had got no homes used to doss down overnight. So we used to get some wonderful characters in. When we took that pub it had sawdust on the floor and these guys used to come in and because it was such a dirty area and because a lot of people smoked, many of them had lung problems and they used to think nothing about spitting on the fire. Their language was a bit ripe, but to their eternal credit when my mother used to be in the bar they would never swear.

We had an upstairs function room in the pub and we used to have all sorts of things in there like the Judo Club, because my dad was always looking to try and make some extra income. And we used to have small animal shows when people used to come with their hamsters and guinea pigs. We also started to let it out for weddings, and the weddings were phenomenal. I've seen bridesmaids carry other bridesmaids out, and bridegrooms taken out horizontally. They were so paralytic drunk they didn't have a clue where they were. We used to get quite a few scraps, because you'd have her family sitting on one side of the room and his family on the other and sometimes there was a bit of a history going back. In the pub we used to have quite a range of characters who certainly were heavy drinkers. All that the guys from the doss house along the road really seemed to exist for was to get in the pub and have a drink. They were in almost as soon as you opened the door. They would stay in there as long as they could possibly manage to stay. A lot of them were very keen on card games and domino games, crib and all that sort of thing. There was an awful lot of that played in the pub. But they never caused us any problems and you never saw the level of violence you tend to see nowadays. Okay, there was the odd case of fisticuffs, but there wasn't anything major. Usually in those days it seemed to be if you had an argument and you whacked one another that was the end of that and you didn't go in for wholesale kicking them all over the place.

We had one or two characters there who used to go to prison at regular intervals, but not for anything particularly nasty. We had one who was a lovely bloke when he was sober, but he refused to pay his maintenance to his wife so they used to come to collect him and take him off to prison for about three months. When he went off to prison he was absolutely dishevelled, beardy, scruffy, the whole thing. Then lo and behold there'd be a knock on the door one morning about ten o'clock before I opened up and there he'd be standing on the doorstep. My dad used to let him kip in the pub overnight and he'd always say, 'I'm going to get myself a job.' He could drive, so sometimes he would get odd jobs driving a lorry for somebody, but eventually he would deteriorate and go back inside. Then unfortunately one day he got too drunk and he pulled a knife on my dad. He didn't stab him, and I still don't think to this day he would have, but that was the end of the association.

Pub hours were a lot shorter and stricter in those days; it was, as I remember, eleven o'clock till three o'clock and half past five till ten o'clock, although this eventually went to half past ten. Lunchtimes were busy because when my mum was still alive she would cook meals and so we used to get a lot of people in from the flour mill and some of the lads in from the Bridgehouses railway depot. They would come in and have a lunch and have a pint as well.

The flour mill was good. They were mostly girls who worked there – absolutely cracking bunch. I'd been brought up that you didn't swear, but then you got with a bunch of girls who all worked together in that environment who could cuss a bit and you tended to get the wrong idea of them. If the fact that they cussed a bit made you think they were perhaps a little bit loose in their morals, they soon jumped on you if you said something out of place. But they were wonderful lasses to be around and they really taught me the fact that just because somebody's rough and ready it doesn't mean to say that they aren't a good person.

Lots of people would be on shifts and those who were on six in the morning till two in the afternoon would try and get in and have a pint before closing time. We had to be careful because the main police station wasn't very far away up the road and they were quite keen if you hadn't got your bar cleared off and the pub doors shut in time. Then at half past five when we opened again some steelworkers who worked day shifts would come in.

Keeping up appearances was important. However little income was coming into a household, children had to have new shoes and clothes for Easter or for the Whit Walks and away from work people had to look smart, even if it was only for a night out to the pub or the club. The answer for many was the 'credit draper'. Ian got his first job with one.

I went to work for a wholesaler less than a quarter of a mile away from the pub up in what we call West

Bar. There were several companies there, like Sheffield Wholesale and Bradford Woollen. Then there was Lacey's, which was down the road and occupied what had previously been a Salvation Army home. That was known for its ladies' underwear. The one I worked for was called Western Seniors. All of these places were big warehouses, because at that time an awful lot of people used to buy their stuff through 'credit drapers', as they used to call them in those days. This would be somebody who had set up a small business selling clothing and things like that. Instead of having a big shop full of clothes, and also because a lot of people were still pretty poor, he'd come round to people's houses and offer things like bedding bales for perhaps a bob a week or whatever it was you could pay. If you wanted some new clothes and you hadn't got enough money to go and buy a suit, or clothes for the children to start school or whatever, then he would give you a note authorizing you to spend up to X amount. He'd say, 'Right! You pop down to Western Seniors and get yourself sorted out.' The wholesaler would mark the note and let the credit trader know what it was you had bought and how much it was and then he would collect his money from you week by week. They were what we used to call CCs; in other words the credit trader was our customer and the people who came to the warehouse to buy things were his customers. It was a very lucrative business and some of these credit traders were very well off and had big businesses.

Someone at the place I worked had a horrible

habit of wandering around the ladies' department and whipping the curtain across and saying, 'Oh, I didn't realize you were in there.' He had a terrible reputation. Quite often they would have a fashion show for their credit trader customers and they would get some models in for this and he would never leave them alone.

Whitsun was a phenomenally important part of the year in Sheffield and everybody wanted their children decked out in their Whitsun best. We used to have racks and racks of hundreds of little suits with short trousers for the boys. They would almost always be navy blue or charcoal grey, because that's basically what suits were in those days. You'd have to wrap it up because everything was done in brown paper there and [there was] no Sellotape in those days; it was all string. Then I went into the floor-covering side. Fitted carpets were only just about to start properly then, so most people had a carpet square in their room and lino around it, and that's if they were doing quite well. The most economical ones of those used to be the Belgian cotton ones, which were relatively cheap, and so we used to have huge piles of those in all sorts of sizes, and then rolls of carpet that were twenty-seven inches wide. This narrow width was used for stair carpet, or it was sewn together to make up a big carpet.

Provident was one of the largest credit companies around in those days before people had credit cards. Of course we used to get phone calls in from various credit traders saying, 'For God's sake, if Mrs So-and-So comes in you're not to serve her.' Obviously Mrs

So-and-So had not been paying, but she might still have a note. The trader would have issued her with one for, say, £60 and she might still have £20 she could spend. But if she'd not made any payments to the credit trader he didn't want her to spend any more. So we would always have a list and if somebody came in who was on that list you had to duck and dive because you couldn't turn around and say, 'I can't serve you, love, because you haven't paid your credit.'

Ian met his wife Pauline while he was working at Western Seniors. She remembers her parents being customers of the credit drapers.

We shopped at places like that because my parents didn't have money and sometimes my mum was one of those who would get a job and straight away get all this stuff on credit. Then she'd decide she hated that job and would stop going, but she'd got all this stuff to pay for and she had no job. We never had anybody nasty coming round, and a lot of the people who were employed by the middle man to collect the money were people you knew anyway, like somebody who was one of the mums who went to school with my mother when they were taking the children there. She used to collect the money and if you didn't have it she'd just say, 'Oh, it's all right. We'll see you next week.'

*

People thought of themselves as working class because of the communities they grew up in and the shared values that came from their upbringing. Tony Willis lived in Ancoats, in Manchester, just a short walk from where I lived, and I talked to him about growing up round there in the 1950s. He remembers there was a collectiveness, a cohesion between everybody in that community and there was an understanding that if you didn't stand with one another you wouldn't survive.

> When we were kids we had an invisible support net-
> work. You had the woman next door to come in and
> help if your mum got ill, but God forbid that ever
> happening because your mum couldn't afford to be
> ill. It was the women who got us through, not the
> guys. Your auntie took you to school and picked you
> up and done the old fella's cut up [lunch] because he
> could never have done it on his own. Then there was
> Mrs Simpkins, who was almost like a soothsayer,
> giving good advice and delivering kids and laying
> out and washing the bodies when somebody died.
> All of these things were part of the network and the
> tapestry of life that kept us going.

Mining areas in particular were known for the strength of their communities. As a miner you always had to live with danger, and in such a hazardous and hostile working environment workmates had to be able to rely totally on each other. Because of this a strong sense of comradeship developed – probably more than in any other job – and this spilled over into their daily lives. An example was Brandon, in the heart of what was the Durham coalfield, just a few miles south-west of the city of Durham. It was originally one of seven small townships within the ancient parish of Brancepeth, which grew from a sparsely populated agricultural area into a populous mining district in the 1850s when the expanding iron, shipbuilding and manufacturing industries of the North East needed coal and coke in ever-increasing quantities. Entrepreneurs moved into the area and developed three coal mines and a coke works. In a mining community like this toughness, hard graft and knowing your place in the hierarchies of family, work and community were essential qualities for survival. Ron Grey was born in Brandon in 1939 and was familiar with all these qualities.

Pre-1947 the mines were privately owned and the miners were so under the thumb of the owners they were virtual slaves and were paid peanuts. My dad worked down the pit for fifty years and I remember him telling me about a deputy who was visiting part of a pit that was flooded. He said, 'I wonder how deep it is?' and one of the men waded in, right up to his waist, and said, 'Oh Mr Thompson, it's this deep.' He was so subservient he just went wading in. Pit work was really hard work, but these old pitmen used to come home and go on their huge allotments and dig them over. That was straight after they'd just put in a rough shift in the pit, and they would always keep these bloody big allotments all neat and tidy. They'd grow their vegetables there and flowers as well. They used to have a yearly flower show, so they'd grow chrysanths and big dahlias and show things like leeks. Every village had a flower show with a beauty queen and in my village there were two picture houses and quite a few clubs and pubs.

When I was five my mam used to send us down on a Sunday morning to get a cabbage off one of the fellas at the allotment. She'd give us threepence or something like that. So I went down and said to somebody there that my mam wanted a cabbage. 'So who are you then?' he would ask. Grey, I told him. Now round here everybody knew each other so he would say, 'Is Geordie Grey your dad?' I said, 'Aye,' and he said, 'Well tell your dad I can beat him at dominoes any time and next time I see him I'm going to give him a big hard thumping.' But I knew he was just joking and he said, 'Here, give us that carrier bag,' and he filled it up full of so much stuff that I could hardly carry it back. I offered him the money but he said, 'No. Get some bloody sweets with it.' That was respect. I knew they must have respected my dad immensely.

Where I lived we used to walk twenty yards to the netty or midden. That was the outside toilet and it was disease-ridden. I had meningitis when I was two, and I had diphtheria when I was eight. That was rife, because it was very unhealthy living as a result of the lack of sanitation, especially in the summer. We had no sense of hygiene – as kids we never washed our hands when we went to the toilet in them days. Same with smoking. I was smoking and inhaling when I was eleven years old. If you went in the club there'd be blue smoke everywhere, hanging down a metre below the ceiling. We used to breathe that in when we were playing dominoes or darts. That was the social life.

Brandon club was always full, every night for thirteen years when I was living in the colliery road.

There were some real comedians working down the pit. One of them was a fella called John Morrissey. He was one of those people who always saw the funny side of everything. His humour was deadpan and usually delivered as a throwaway remark. One day he was sitting in the bar at the club with a friend of mine when two lads appeared in running gear. John shouted over to the steward to get these two lads a shandy and while they were drinking them he said, 'So you've been running, have you? I used to do a spot of running myself when I was younger. They used to nickname me "The Flash". But for sheer speed you couldn't beat my uncle Tommy. He did two hundred yards in ten seconds.' One of the runners shook his head and said, 'That's impossible. Nobody could run as fast as that.' John paused and took a draw of his Woodbine before saying in a toneless voice, 'Runnin'? No, not runnin'. He fell down the pit shaft in 1947.'

The club, or the Miners' Welfare to give it its official title, was the focal point of a community. Trimdon is a former pit village nine miles west of Hartlepool and Jim Chater remembers the Welfare Hall there.

They had a dance floor that was so good they used to come on the train from the surrounding villages to the dances there. Then there was a reading room where you used to get all the papers delivered, a card room and a little library. You'd get money taken off your wages to pay for this. In the club during the week the conversation would be mainly about things like pigeons. Saturday night was the night out with the wife. Friday night was the lads' night out. That was the biggest drinking night. On Saturday they would have turns on. There was a lot more entertainment then and more places to go to, so them people who didn't drink, chapel folk and people like that, went to the pictures.

Close-knit mining communities, with firm loyalties and a great sense of tradition, were a particular characteristic of the valleys of South Wales. Wendy Simms, who has lived in Merthyr Vale all her life, remembers what it was like growing up there.

I was born in 46 Bryntaf on 11 July 1940. I was one of seven children, four girls and three boys. We were ten in all at home as my gran also lived with my mam and dad. It was a three-storey house with three bedrooms – my gran, younger sister and myself in one bedroom, two older sisters in another and three brothers in the small bedroom. My mam and dad slept in what we called 'the parlour' on the middle floor. That never stopped Mam putting up relatives from London and Oxford when they wanted to come down. My cousin David would come down from Enfield to stay for the school holidays. He would cry when he had to go back because he wanted to stay to play in the dirt! He didn't get dirty in London.

I didn't realize it then, but oh how hard my gran

and mam worked in the house. No mod cons, no electric upstairs, no gas cooker. All cooking was on an open fire and an oven at the side – what was known as a 'black-lead grate'. But what good meals they cooked. Before breakfast was prepared they would rake out the ashes from the day before and relight the coal fire. Sticks were chopped by them the day before from the wood Dad would bring home from the colliery where he worked. The big heavy 'blackhead kettle' would then go on the fire to make tea, and toast was made with a toasting fork held directly in front of the fire.

There was no bathroom. We would wash under the cold tap in the coal house with a bucket to catch water and when full the bucket would be taken to the outside toilet for flushing. Monday and Tuesday were wash days and when we left for school the big wash tub would be placed on two kitchen chairs by Mam and Gran. Water was on the boil for the family wash, the scrubbing board and carbolic soap was got out and washing would be started. There was no spinner or even a mangle; the washing would be on an outside line to dry. It was ironed in the evening then hung to air on a line across the kitchen.

Mam had no social life, but was happy as ever. Pubs were different then – mostly men after a hard day in the mines would go. Very few women went. Mam never went outside the door apart from getting food in the shop in the middle of the street. Gran did go out once a week to 'Cork Club' – a group of women who met in a neighbour's house – and what gossip she came home with! Then once a month she went to the Labour Party meeting to put the world right and as she was a war widow she was a member of the British Legion.

We lived in Bryntaf and what a street it was. One hundred and thirteen houses and everybody knew everybody. I remember my mother telling me she was going to town and if Mrs Price over the road needed tea or sugar she knew where to find it in our house. There was great neighbourliness, but there's none of that now. If neighbours across the street needed to catch the bus, which was behind the canal bank on the back of our side, they would come through our house to save walking right around the street. We never had to lock our doors because there was nothing to take as we were all in the same position.

All the miners would have their allocation of coal delivered and tipped outside. We were lucky because where we lived the coal was just shovelled in through the grating into the coal house below. Across the street had to have theirs carried through the houses. A committee was formed by a number of fathers and they would riddle the coal on delivery and store the 'small coal'[10] in the quarry in the middle of the street. This would be sold and once a year the whole street would be taken free in coaches to Barry Island. Every child would have ten shillings [50p] to spend – that was a lot of money in those days. The night before the adults would hang flags across the street and children would sweep the street clean. We always

[10] Small pieces of coal that have been separated from the larger pieces by screening.

had new clothes every Anniversary Sunday and we would keep them for the Barry trip. The street would be full of coaches. The first held the adult Bryntaf Usherettes Jazz Band. They used to practise in the Old Quarry and my two older sisters were members. In later years a children's usherette band was formed and my younger sister and myself were members. We went most weekends competing and often won prizes. There was also a men's band called the Coons. They had white outfits, black patent shoes and their faces would be blackened. We were the first street to organize a carnival, choosing a queen and attendants from names entered and placed in a hat. And what carnivals we had – people came from everywhere to them.

One memory of my childhood was we would be playing out in the street, be it skipping, chasing, hop-scotch, marbles or whatever, and Mr Hughes who owned the little sweet shop in his front room would come out and say, 'Go and get your chairs, kids,' and he would put music on and we would play musical chairs. He would then go in the shop for a prize for the winner. Our parents had no fear of leaving us out to play after school as long as they knew where we were going. There wasn't the danger then that there is today.

We didn't have a television, but we were lucky as my sister's friend's family had one and we were invited along with a lot of other neighbours to watch the Coronation. It was like a cinema in there. Dad liked to go to the local cinema and when he was ready we would put our coats on and tag along. It cost him 7d [3p] but because the usherettes lived near us he would get us in for nothing and we would sit in the 'one and nines' seats.

We could never afford holidays as a family, but I did have a treat when I was at the Grammar School and I went to Boverton Camp for one week for ten shillings [50p]. That was a lot then for Mam to find. We had to do our share of work when we were there, though – wash dishes, clean dormitories, clean veg – but to me it was a holiday.

Teenagers would gather along Aberfan Road on a Sunday night, calling in Manueli's café for a glass of hot Vimto, and then parade up and down the road between Aberfan and Troedyrhiw. It was what was known as the 'monkey parade' – boys looking to meet girls and girls looking to meet boys, all dressed up in their Sunday best. The local dance hall opened in my teenage years. It was underneath the cinema. No alcohol was sold, only soft drinks. If you went on the Friday you would get a free pass for Wednesday. A live band would play and the popular dance then was the jive. It was at this dance that I met my husband. He came over to me at 10.20 p.m. and asked me if he could walk me home. He didn't ask me to dance then as he said later that he couldn't!

The mining community of Gilfach Goch was once the home of author Richard Llewellyn, who set his novel *How Green Was My Valley* in a fictional town based on the village. Ruth James and her husband Wyndham were both born in Gilfach Goch and remember growing up there in the 1950s. 'The houses we lived in,' Ruth says, 'were built in 1913.'

They were built as a garden village in lines of little terraced houses and this is where I was born and where Wyndham was born. These were an improvement on the older houses because they had a bath and they were built with a tree in each garden, like Welwyn Garden City. When we first moved into one we had a bath for the first time and an indoor toilet. There was always plenty of coal about and they gave you a coal allowance. We had a little coal boiler in the corner of the kitchen and we had a bath alongside it. Most people put wood over the top to make the bath into a table. Life was hard and money was short for a lot of people, so you do hear a lot of the older people saying, 'Oh, there was a family living in there and the next morning they had done a moonlight flit.' You knew they must have owed money and a van had come and taken them and they'd gone by the morning.

Somebody said the other day, 'It's a good job the pits have gone because we've got clean washing now.' Well I don't ever remember my mother complaining that the washing was all soiled. What we did have to live with, though, was the colliery noise, the hooters and the engines and that's what would keep us up at night. But we never noticed the thump, thump, thump of the fan until it stopped and then we'd know instantly that something had happened. But we wouldn't notice that because we lived there and were brought up with that noise, but somebody else coming in, visitors to see us, would say, 'What's that bumping all the time then?'

When the holiday came, the whole place would shut down as everyone took the miners' fortnight. It was the last two weeks in July and most people went to Porthcawl with tents. It was all they could afford. There were sand dunes there and you could get a lot of people in a big bell tent or an old army tent. People used to take their sideboard with them to live down there.

All the chapels used to be going then. There were eleven in Gilfach, all so full to the brim you wouldn't get a seat. Chapel used to provide quilting classes, penny readings, concerts, choirs and they even had table tennis. So they were hubs of the communities. There was much more that went on at chapel than just worship. All the men used to give a few coppers and they built a workmen's hall which had a reading room underneath, snooker tables, a library and a cinema with a stage. I used to act on the stage in the pantomimes and things they did. They used to have drama weeks, where they'd invite other societies and they'd all put their own play on during one night and then at the end they'd have an adjudicator who'd decide who was the winner for that week.

In the 1950s and early 1960s the valley was alive with lots of shops, two cinemas and a dance hall in Tonyrefrail. Even though Gilfach Goch has now been transformed back to the green valley it was before coal was discovered there, people miss the community spirit of the days when everyone worked and played together and they speak fondly of how friendly people were and how the doors were always open for a cuppa. Michael Cowdrey remembers it as a time when everybody knew each other's business and recalled some of the characters who lived there.

A lot of people had allotments and some had their own little smallholdings. We had chickens in our back garden and my father had pigeons too. No lawns or patios in those days. I remember Morg Evans kept pigeons as well and I used to go to let them out for him because he had a bad back. He'd broken it in an accident and he'd got £3,000 so he bought a pair of pigeons from Ireland with the money, a cock and hen. He said, 'If Rene [his wife] knew that I done this she'd kill me.' Anyway he spent the money on this pair of birds from Ireland because they were the best. He didn't care, because for Morg it was his life. But old Morg was a character; a hard man but a real character. I think he had about nine children. Mrs Kerry who lived next door had twenty-one. The only joy she had was that she used to go the pictures on a Wednesday. One Wednesday there was a little one missing in the street so everybody went looking for this little Reggie Evans, the blond boy. Mrs Kerry's husband, George, used to put their kids to bed and he came out to see what the problem was. 'Half a minute,' he said, 'I've got one up there crying like hell. He's not resting at all.' Well, he'd put the wrong boy to bed. Because he had twenty-one of his own he'd chucked the wrong boy in as well.

Families were large, living conditions were poor and times were generally hard, but they are remembered fondly by many people as happy times. It was the same throughout industrial Britain. Bob Clark, who was born in Padiham and worked as a coal miner, remembers what it was like when he was growing up.

Where I was born in Padiham it was, I would say, very hard times. It was just after the war, 1951, and during my childhood it was a happy place, but it was a very impoverished place. Where I was born there would have been at least six mill chimneys, but I think my main childhood memory was the Padiham tripe-works which was a terrible smelly place. There was another factory where they made carborundum grinding wheels, but mainly most of the men were employed as coal miners and the ladies in the textile industry.

Padiham had many rows of terraced houses and everyone in those little streets knew each other. There was no gas in the houses, no gardens, no TVs and no motor cars. As kids we played games in the streets. The girls played hopscotch and ball games, the boys played cricket or football and there were a lot of chasing games that we all played. Everybody had very little, but the traditions we had were special and you looked forward to things like Christmas and Easter. But the biggest day of the year was the Whitsuntide Walk, when all the children walked with whichever church or school group they belonged to. When I was young I was in the Cubs and then in the Scouts, and I played in the Scout band. Then in later years I was in the town brass band, so I always looked forward to the Whit Walks when I marched with the band. The population of Padiham hasn't altered much since then – it's still about ten thousand, but it would double for the Walks. The big thing was that the police turned a blind eye and the pubs were allowed to open all day, which was very unusual then because they were very strict on licensing hours.

The Wakes Weeks were the time that all the mills and factories here closed down. It was a time that was earmarked for maintenance work. Over these two weeks the machinery would be overhauled. It was a traditional thing for people to go to Blackpool at this time. A lot of the miners went year in and year out and they'd always go to the same guest house and the same pub. All they were doing was having a fortnight where they weren't down the pit. But they were the same people together. Most people didn't have motor cars, so they'd go by coach and the big places to stay were the holiday camps, Butlins and Pontins.

The social activity around here was good. There were the working men's clubs where there was always plenty on. There was always a bit of competition between them on a Saturday night for who could have the best club artist on. The clubs were also very good on the sports side. The younger men played cricket and football and they nearly all had very strong swimming teams. They used to hire the local swimming pool and then the older chaps would teach the children how to swim. Then of course there were all the old favourites. They had numerous teams of darts and dominoes and cribbage, all the pub games. They had pigeon clubs and a lot of them were allotment people. People were very proud of their allotments, growing everything from dahlias to cabbages for competitions.

With its cotton mills and collieries it was a time of full employment in Lancashire. 'All hustle and bustle' is the way Alf Molyneux remembers Bolton at that time. 'You went out to work in the morning, walked to the bus stop and two buses would go past full. You'd no chance of getting on them. Of course there weren't as many cars about then. But it was very busy – a time when you could knock on any door and get a job and they'd say, "Can you start now?"' Graham Dibnah also remembers what it was like living there in the late 1950s.

Oh Bolton was a brilliant town when we were lads. We used to enjoy it. There were still a lot of mills. And some of the girls who were our age who worked in the mills lived down Croft Lane. They used to do shift work. There was a six to two and a two to ten shift and sometimes they would be on days. At the end of the shift they'd come home past our house with white socks on, all covered in cotton, and their clogs and their pinnies. They always used to be friendly and we used to talk to them all at the end of our street.

I used to go to night school then for my trade as a bricklayer. We finished at nine o'clock. We used to go and meet the lads at the pub and then we were off to Bolton Palais. One and sixpence, I think it was, jiving and rock and roll, Tuesday and Thursday. Then we used to go on Saturday night and that was the night for ballroom dancing. But we had some good times, believe me.

One of the girls who used to go down there was Barbara Yates.

Bolton was a wonderful town to grow up in. We had so much. We had about fifteen cinemas in the town, lots of dance halls, the Albert Hall which had all the big bands coming in on a Saturday night and on a Sunday night teenagers could go and have a sing-song in the Albert Hall and we'd lots of coffee bars. It was a superb place to grow up in. We still had a lot of industry around at the time in the town. We had all the cotton mills, we had a lot of engineering places and small machine-making industries.

In the North East, Tommy Procter from South Shields remembers what a good place it was to live, particularly when you were a young man who had just started work and had a few bob in your pocket.

We had dances every Friday and Saturday night. A shilling to get in – that's five pence now. There were about half a dozen dance halls in the town and they used to have the local bands on there. There was no drinking, just soft drinks and a packet of crisps. It was the 1960s, the Beatles era and the Liverpool sound, and it was just brilliant. I met my wife at a bus stop. There was one night I had off and I had been out taking photographs and she was at the bus stop with a couple of pals I went to school with. In fact she had been courting one of the lads who used to be in my class at school. So I started chatting to them and one thing led to another. I quite liked the look of her and she must have liked the look of me, so I asked her if she fancied going to the pictures. I'll never forget the first time I took her. I lived at one end of the town and she lived at the other and I can remember going to pick her up. It was the Gaumont Cinema we were going to, to see a Rock Hudson film about fishing, and I can remember her coming down the stairs and she had this yellow coat on with three-quarter sleeves and she had her hair down in flicks. She had jet-black hair and she had white shoes and white gloves. And I thought wow! Hey, you've clicked here, son – you are one lucky boy. I had my collar and tie on, because whenever you went out you made the effort. You didn't go out in jeans all ripped to hell. I bought her a small box of Cadbury's Milk Tray and we went upstairs in the pictures.

As well as cinemas and dance halls there were plenty of pubs and night clubs in a place like South Shields. John Bage remembers nights out in town and also on the estate where he lived.

We'd start off in the pubs in town and then go off to a night club afterwards and it was a great scene. In the mid-60s they built a new night club and every week they had a big-name act on, like Tom Jones. It would always be crowded and people would be queuing up to get in. We sometimes used to go there two or three nights a week because there were differ-ent events on each night of the week. They would have a fun night on a Thursday night when those that could used to drink a yard of ale and there used to be daft games on stage.

I was still living at home then and there was a

great community spirit on the estate. The pubs always used to be packed. You could go in during the week and probably get a seat in the lounge, but the bar would always be full. I used to go in the evening about nine o'clock and just have a couple of pints and gradually, by just going in, I got to know people because people would just talk to you, and before I knew it I would be sitting at several tables with a big crowd of people. That's how friendly they were. There were no problems at all, no fighting or anything like that.

I met my wife, Irene, there. She came in with her friends. First time she'd ever been in that pub. Her cousin dragged her along there because she wanted to show her me and my brother, because she fancied my brother! She hadn't really wanted to go, because it wasn't her scene sitting in pubs, but she did and that's how we met. When we got married, though, we went downhill. We went back into one of those one-bedroom flats in the town with the down-the-yard toilet. It was only for about eighteen months till we saved the deposit for the house we live in now, because you had to have 5 or 10 per cent for a deposit. But while we were in the old place I put a shower in and a new kitchen, so it was quite nice when we did it all out, and we knew we were just there temporarily.

John was not on his own in doing jobs in the house. Do-it-yourself, or DIY, had taken off in a big way and there were several popular magazines devoted to it. Self-improvement in all its forms became something of the credo of the decade – improving yourself, your job prospects and your home. It was a time that promised life would get better if you were prepared to work hard, and for those who were prepared to put in the effort there was no shortage of work.

*

The years immediately after the Second World War and well into the 1960s were a time of full employment. Jobs were generally easy to find and many people whose stories are told in these chapters recall being able to leave a job one day and walk into another the next. But in the 1960s the post-war boom gave way to the recession of the 1970s and 1980s. For many it was an all too familiar story that they, their parents and their grandparents had seen before as they shared in the changing fortunes of British industry. After the brief post-First World War boom came the Depression of the 1930s, followed by the pressure for all-out production during the Second World War. Then in the 1950s the British people, as Prime Minister Harold Macmillan remarked in 1957, had 'never had it so good'. But memories of boom and bust were still fresh in the minds of many, colouring their attitude to work and especially to job security. Peter Phillips, who grew up in the heart of Scotland's steel-producing area in Lanarkshire, went to work at the Clydebridge Steelworks in Cambuslang. 'The only thing about the steel industry in Lanarkshire,' he said, 'was that from the day you started everybody told you it was closing. "You'll no be here long, son, this will shut," they always used to say.' Even at a time when jobs were plentiful there was always this nagging feeling of insecurity and throughout Britain's industrial communities the bad times of the Depression were still remembered very clearly. Alf Carr grew up in West Bromwich in the 1930s and was just old enough to remember his dad being out of work for two years.

He lost his crane driver's job just after I was born and it was two years before he got another regular job. It must have been a terrible existence scratching around. He went out every day searching for a job. That was a regular thing in the 1930s in the Depression. There were hundreds of people out of work. Eventually he got his name on a certain list at a foundry. It was a notorious place called Rudge Littley. Some time later the door went and there was a fella from Rudge Littley. He knocked at the door and when my mother answered he said, 'Tell Fred to start at Rudge Littley's on Monday morning.' So, after the two years out of work, he got his foot in the door. It had made him so desperate he never offered to leave Rudge's until the end of his life. He was afraid to leave it in case he was out of work again. It was a way of life – once you got your foot in the door you stayed there. You couldn't take the risk of leaving a job.

His job was clearing the excess metal off the finished job, what they call the 'flash'. It was damned hard work. His tools were just a pneumatic gun and a pneumatic chisel and a grindstone. It was real fettling. It wasn't cutting, it was actually knocking the metal off with the pneumatic chisel edge. He was quite a brawny chap, but still his physique developed enormously with that particular job. He'd come home at five o'clock and there'd be a huge dinner ready for him which he could eat without any trouble. They needed it, them workers. Before you knew it they'd have gone to sleep in the chair in their foundry dirt, too tired to go and have a wash and change. They just slid away into sleep for an hour. About eight o'clock he'd go and have a good wash, change and then go off down the pub. The kettle was always on the hob in those days but he'd go down to the pub.

Then when the war started almost everybody had work and they were doing extra hours, so you were having to take dinner down. So me being the oldest, that fell on to me. I'd run home from school at twelve o'clock and my dad's dinner would be ready in the basin, so I'd get cracking with it. I was always running and I had about half a mile to go across the field. They'd see me coming and say, 'Fred, your young one's here with your dinner.' And he'd come and take it off me, after I'd walked through the foundry. It was a horrible place – absolute darkness, and there was a cloud of burnt sand everywhere. How he stuck the job all them years I do not know. But you'd got no option. He stuck at it but I don't think there was any joy in retirement, because by the time they got to sixty-five they were clapped out after the foundry work. They were just done for. I reckon it helped to finish my dad off. He really died a horrendous death and I think that foundry work contributed to that. When you come to think about what must have gone down into their lungs over the years, it's a wonder their lungs weren't solid. Out of four parents from me and my wife, three never got to retire.

During the Depression jobs were hard to find wherever you lived. Doris Lloyd was born in Rochdale in 1916 and left school when she was fourteen.

> They sent me from the labour exchange for a job at a shirt factory. You had no choice; you'd to go where they sent you and that's where they sent me. The first job I did there, I worked all morning for a penny. I had to fold a shirt and put it in a box and all I got were one shirt to do. I went home at dinnertime and said to my mother, 'I'm not going back. I've worked all morning for a penny.' So she came down to the factory with me after we'd had our dinner and said, 'Can't our Doris work?' They said yes, and after that I started to get more to do and I made sixteen shillings the week after. But I wanted to get work at a mill, so every Monday morning I used to go down to Dale Mill. I had to go there every week for twelve months before I could get in. That were in 1930 and you couldn't get jobs then, so when I did get a job there my father said, 'She's gone in, she stops in, whether she likes it or not.' I were the only one in our family with a job so I stopped at it and never disliked it.

With the advent of war in 1939, most men between the ages of eighteen and forty-one (later fifty-one) were conscripted to serve in the armed forces. But some jobs, including mining and working on the railways, were protected or reserved occupations, meaning that the men doing them were exempt from being called up. Amy Carr's father worked in a foundry in West Bromwich and his job was one of those. 'When they were called up in the war,' she recalls, 'Dad's job was one of those jobs that took priority over being called up. My mum was ever so worried about Dad because he wanted to go in the navy but he couldn't swim. So we were terrified that he would be called up. But his job was important for the war effort so he wasn't. He was ever so upset about it.'

In those early months of the war many men were still waiting for their call-up papers. Jean Harpur from Leeds remembers very clearly the day her father's arrived.

My dad had to go in the army straight from the beginning because he was what was called a reservist. I remember picking this letter up that the postman had left and me dad were in bed, so I went up and took him it. When he opened it he said, 'Oh, I've been expecting this.' I thought he was going to get killed and I was frightened to death.

I remember the war, but I were only young. I remember bombs falling and, as we'd only a one-bedroom house, we went down the cellar. We all had cellars in them days, so that's where we went when sirens went. We took me brother – he were only a baby – and me and my twin sister and me mam went down. Some people had shelters but that were later on in the war. I'm talking about when it first began, and I've thought about this as I've got older: if anything had hit that house it would have come down on top of us. I was always scared and I went

under the table on the bucket because I got
diarrhoea every time the sirens went.

During the war the industrial importance and contribution to the war effort of major cities like Manchester
and Birmingham meant they were heavily bombed. Ray
Barrett was born and brought up in Aston close to the
centre of Birmingham and lived there throughout the war.

When I was living there during the war my thoughts
were always with the young mums. It must have been
awful for them. Most of them had their husbands
away and they didn't know where they were in the
world; they weren't allowed to know. And then
they'd be possibly working in factories during the
day, getting bombed every night and they'd still got
their children to look after. I knew young men in the
army who'd say that they'd spent the whole war in
workshops. One of them was a motor mechanic
in Cairo. So it meant nothing to him, but his wife
was getting bombed in Birmingham. It was the
women who suffered the most, in my opinion.

As so many men were called up to serve, Britain depended
on women to carry out much of the war work. During the
war women worked in all manner of production, from
making ammunition to tanks, aircraft and electronics.
Kath Dunne had been working at Moston Mill in
Manchester but when the war started they closed it down.

When the mill closed you had to go on munitions, so
myself and my sister that worked in the mill with me

went to Ferranti's at Hollinwood. I enjoyed it there because it was all bench work and conveyors and you all had your own little part to do on these radios we were making for the aircraft. You did your own part and then it carried on down the conveyor to the next person till it was finished.

When you went there you had to go to training school first before you could go on these belts. You had to learn different parts and you had to learn soldering with an electric soldering iron. All the electric wires then were all brown and what I had to do was to paint the ends of these leads in different colours so you knew exactly which colour went on to which part of this little component. Then you had to solder it on and then after you had done your part it carried on down the belt to about six other people, then it would go to a passer and he would examine it and if it wasn't right or it had too much solder on or summat like that, he'd know who'd done it so it used to go back to you. So you had to make sure you did it right otherwise you got all your work back.

At the mill I never used to see any of the bosses but at Ferranti's it was different. The bosses there would have a walk round and look to see if everything was all right. When Mr Ferranti was coming round you all had to clean your bench up and make sure there was no rubbish around.

In the room where we were there were the long benches that we worked on and on the other side there were bigger machines, what they called capstans, and it was mostly the men that worked on them. They were mainly the ones who were too old to go in the forces. We used to have targets there and it used to go up on a big board whether you had met your target and they used to have flags and streamers all across the room. It was really lovely; with the war being on it kept spirits up. And they had the radio, *Music While You Work*. You'd be talking all day long and passing jokes. Mind you, I didn't know what they were talking about when they were joking. I was right naïve. You didn't know anything about sex or anything like that then, unless you'd seen it written on a wall and even then you didn't know what it was.

During the war my father worked outdoors in the building trade, not building but demolishing, because we had the Manchester air raid in 1940 and a lot of the buildings in town were damaged and had to be knocked down, so he worked on them. But if the weather was really bad and they got rained off they didn't get paid. When that happened they got a meal ticket that you could change at a certain grocer's shop. People say it was a scary time, but it was also exciting. It was terrible when somebody got hurt and when you went down into Manchester it was terrible to see all the buildings that had been destroyed.

We used to have an Anderson shelter in the back garden and my father put forms around the walls and wood on the floor, but it always used to get all water-logged. We used to go in there before the air raid started and got settled down. There were loads of people fitted in our air raid shelter. I don't know how we all got in, but my father never used to come in. He wanted to make sure there was space for everyone else.

So he'd be outside saying, 'Ooh, I can hear that. That's coming over us.' And you could tell it had got bombs on it because of the sound of the engines. Then he used to shout in, 'It's not over here now. It's over Blackpool. It's all clear now.'

Then in 1941 he was working on one of the buildings that had been destroyed in the Blitz the year before and it collapsed and he got killed. So we had two girls who was still at school and there was three of us that were working and my mother. She was only forty-one when that happened and she got a pension, ten shilling [50p] a week, and I think she got 2/6d [12½p] for each of the girls who were still at school, so she had to go to work. We all had our jobs to do in the house when we got home from work and when you was working you had to turn your money up. You didn't have it yourself – you turned it up and you got spends, perhaps £1 or something like that if you were lucky, to buy stockings and your own underwear.

During the war I know it was terrible, but everybody had a good time. You didn't stay in just because there was a war on. You used to go to dances and you used to go to the pictures. You could go and see a different film every night if you went to different picture houses and if you had the money. You had to be in for a certain time, mind you; you couldn't be coming home in the middle of the night or early morning because the buses used to be finished by eleven o'clock. I used to go dancing in town to the Plaza and I always had to come out before the end to get the last bus home. If you missed the bus that came to where we lived in Moston you'd get the bus going up Oldham Road and then you'd have to get off at Dean Lane and walk. But there were anti-aircraft guns you had to walk past and you'd always say to yourself, 'Please God, don't let that gun go off while I'm passing here.'

Horwich Loco Works was one of the country's major locomotive-building businesses. During the Second World War it became a munitions factory and nearly five hundred tanks were built there. Many of the local women were taken on for the war effort, including Stanley Bolton's sister Mabel Ryding.

I worked at the railway works during the war on munitions. The job involved examining the shells and rejecting any that were faulty. They always picked soldier's wives to do this, because if a faulty one went through they would have exploded as they were loaded on to the anti-aircraft guns and the soldiers operating them would have been killed. So you'd always be extra careful because it might have been your husband who was firing it. They were very heavy and when you'd inspected them you had to lift them on to a truck and push these trucks on to the next job.

At the works they made tanks in place of railway engines during the war. It was easy to change over to tank production because the mechanics shop was set up with overhead cranes and all the equipment they needed. There was a test course for the tanks up on the moors near Rivington Pike and all the local children used to run to the works gates to watch the tanks coming out for testing.

The history of the 1940s is full of romance amid pain, suffering and uncertainty. Many women arranged wartime weddings at very short notice to accommodate fiancés coming home on twenty-four or forty-eight hours' leave before being sent to some distant posting. Irene Wharton was a war bride.

I got married in 1940 when I was nineteen. He were a local lad I met in the pub. I used to love to go dancing, but on Saturday night I used to go for a drink because my mam and my dad both played the piano in the local pubs. So I used to go with my friends and Jack and his mates used to be all sat where my mam played the piano. He thought my mother were lovely because she used to play for them. And then one Saturday night he sent me a drink over, did this young fella. It were a bottle of stout, so I said to the waiter, 'Who sent this?' My mate said, 'I think it was that lad over there.' I lifted the glass and had a sip and it were quite nice to drink, so I looked over to him and he blushed to his hair roots. I said, 'Oh he's bashful, isn't he?' I knew his mates and I knew his cousins but I didn't know him, but there were a group of them all used to go together.

When we were leaving he said, 'Would you like to come and meet me on Sunday night?' I said, 'Why don't you come to our house? You know my mam and my dad.' My brother was an evacuee in Doncaster and I used to go and see him every Sunday morning and that Sunday night I were a bit late getting the bus after going to see him, so he got to our house before I got back. My mate across the road fancied him and she was there with him when I got back. She said she'd fetched him from the end of the street and was just keeping him company because the lad didn't know my family really. Anyway we went out for a drink and it was the same night as we had the first air raid in Leeds and the sirens went while we were out. We went to the fish shop and when we were coming out the air raid started, so we hid in a shop doorway. We must have been there for an hour just huddled together with our fish and chips. We daren't go out because there was what we called shrapnel falling all over the place. But when it calmed down I said to Jack, 'Come on. Let's make a run for it.' We had air raid shelters but at our house we used to go down to the cellar. My mam used to have a little camp bed there and she had a big old-fashioned wooden table that she had moved down to the cellar when she got a new dining suite and she used to make a little bed on there for us.

When we got married in 1940 I went on working in tailoring until I had our Malcolm in 1941. Then Jack's mother said, 'I'll have him.' So I went to Clayton's boilermakers and I went on rivet-heating when I first went there.

At the end of the war there was a huge influx of workers back on to the labour market. The vast majority went into manual work. Depending on where you lived, where your family worked and on the expectations attached to class that came with that, you didn't have very much choice about where you went to work. At a time when money was tight, if your parents said you had to leave school and get a job to help support the family, that's what you did.

Bob Clark from Padiham followed his father down one of Burnley's pits in 1956. When he started at Colva Colliery he was one of the last batch of lads to go underground at fifteen. He went down for a few months and then the law changed, so he had to come back up to the surface for a few months until he was sixteen, when he was allowed to go back down again.

Going down the pit was pre-determined because of family. When I was born, Bobby was going down the pit with his dad. End of story. You never fought against it. My dad was a colliery overman.[11] Within the mine structure the mine manager was number one, the under-manager number two, and the overman was number three, so, because of my dad's position, we as kids used to go into the mines. We used to go to the canteen and all over and maybe from time to time underground on a Sunday morning.

When I left school at fifteen I had to go for a short course that lasted for sixteen weeks and then they split us all up. Because of transport problems and the fact that none of us had motor cars they tried to fit us in at the nearest colliery to where we lived. I went to a local colliery, Colva, that's just down the road from where I lived. When you started they found you

[11] Men who showed managerial qualities would become overmen. They were responsible for managing the shifts and directing who worked where in the colliery. Along with the deputies they had responsibility for ensuring safety underground and were required to keep a daily record of work done, wages paid and any incidents that occurred.

Heavy industry shaped and dominated the landscape of Britain's major industrial regions. Coal mining left its mark more than any other industry with its slagheaps and towering pithead gear.

Above left: In the terraced houses of the inner-city slums, women took great pride in the appearance of their homes; scrubbing the front doorstep was part of the daily routine.

Above right: The only form of entertainment for most children was playing outside. With few cars on the road, mothers knew their children would be safe on the streets.

The kitchen: the hub of the home.

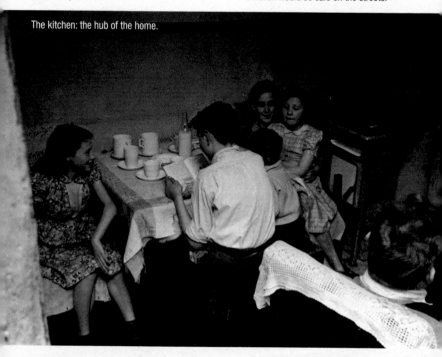

In the 1950s a large part of the population still lived in back-to-back terraced houses, though slum clearances were making way for new council-housing estates away from city centres, such as the Manor Estate in Sheffield (*below*).

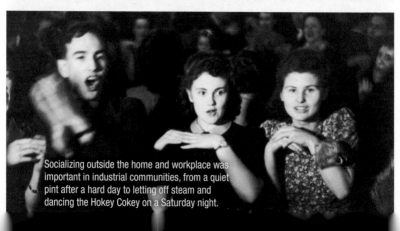

Socializing outside the home and workplace was important in industrial communities, from a quiet pint after a hard day to letting off steam and dancing the Hokey Cokey on a Saturday night.

Holidaymakers on the beach at Blackpool during Wakes Week, the annual holiday for workers in the industrial north when all the mills and factories closed down for maintenance work.

There were opportunities for workers to engage in cultural activities. Here shipyard and factory workers play in a flute band in Belfast (*above*) and the Ollerton Colliery brass band (*below*) leads a procession of miners at the Cinderhill pit in Nottinghamshire.

Above: Mills and factories often had subsidized canteens where workers could go for good meals at affordable prices.

Below: Big works such as the Sheffield Twist Drill and Steel Company had their own leisure facilities where workers could join in sports from cricket and football to gymnastics and hockey.

The oil tanker *World Unicorn* dominates a street in Wallsend during its construction at the Swan Hunter shipyard, Tyne and Wear.

a 'chapper' and they called him your pit dad. They were there to make sure you didn't get hurt. You tagged along with him and did what you were told – not for very long, maybe a month of settling-in period, and then you had your own work to do.

If you lived in the valleys of South Wales, the mines provided the main source of employment. In a lot of families a boy had no choice when he reached school-leaving age: if your dad worked down the pit, that was where you went. But some parents didn't want the life of the miner for their sons, as Wyndham James recalls.

When I was fourteen I went to the shoe factory first because my mother said you're not going underground. But I went for a walk one day down to the local colliery and the manager came past me and I said, 'Mr Morris, have you got a job for a young boy?' 'Yes, my boy,' he replied, 'but you'll have to wait now until the August holidays are over. Come down after that.' So I carried on at the shoe factory for a few weeks, then I went down the mine. After I'd finished work there I used to have a wash in the river coming out from there. Mother didn't know at first and I did that for a week before she caught on.

For those who did go down into the pit, it could be a sudden, sharp introduction to the adult world, as Roy Davies found when he went to work at Coedely Colliery.

My first wage pay packet was £2.3s.7d. [£2.18]. Before I could take it out my father and the time clerk had come to an arrangement to put fifteen shillings [75p] in the Post Office savings. I wasn't allowed to touch that. When I started work as a measuring boy at fifteen I had to work mornings and afternoons on Fridays to get the measurements in. And then we used to go to a pub for the overman to sign the book. So the first week I went there and this foreman took me in the kitchen because I was too young to go into the bar. The overman came in, signed the book and asked me all about what measurements I'd got. 'Have a little drink, Roy?' he asked. 'Yeah, orange juice,' I said, so he fetched orange juice but there was a short in it as well. I was only fifteen and I'd never had a drink, so they had to get two fellas from the bar to take me home. They led me through the door but instead of going to the house I went into the coal house. I was still in my working clothes and I went to sleep. My father came down in the morning and said, 'What are you doing here?' I said, 'I couldn't come in. They give me drink last night.' He said, 'Get to bloody work.' I was still black, but I went off to work. My mother was a big chapel woman and when I came home she said, 'Where was you last night? You wasn't in bed.' But my dad said, 'Leave the boy alone. He's only doing his job.'

Money was still short in many working-class communities after the war. It meant that Francis Newman from Dunston near Newcastle had no option but to leave school when he was fifteen to help the family earnings.

I got the job on the railways through a friend I was at school with. He said there was a job going at Dunston Staithes where he worked. These were wooden structures which were built out into the River Tyne so that coal could be dropped directly into the holds of the colliers. I got the bus down and they took me on immediately. It's not really what I wanted to do. I wanted to be a journalist, but they were the days when the kids came second. I remember my mother the day I was going to school to take the exam when I would have moved on to grammar school. She said, 'Don't get any fancy ideas about passing this exam and going to grammar school, because your job's to get out there and get some money to help support this family.' I thought nothing of it at the time, but when I look back now I could never imagine we would say that to our daughter. But things were different. We were a big family and my father was on a low wage, so you just went and done it automatically. The kids didn't count then and didn't have any say in things. The eldest daughter was usually the lackey. Her job was to cook and clean and give the mother an easier time.

I had one brother and three sisters and we were born in a slum. It was one-up one-down, and there was a little outhouse that had one cold tap in. We lived there till I was about eleven years old. It was mice-ridden and the toilet was up in the middle of a field – the 'ash middens' we used to call them. I can remember being frightened of going to the toilet because it was pitch black, but my father was very strict, a real disciplinarian, and he wouldn't take us. He called us cowards, so we had to go up on our own, sit in the pitch black on the toilet and then walk back down to the house. Can you imagine doing that with your children today?

All the children slept upstairs. We just piled into two beds and my mother and father had a single bed under the stairs. Being such a slum you used to get problems with fleas and things like that. I remember how my father used to have a big pot of DDT powder which he used to spread on the bed and on the blanket. We used to have to get into it and sleep on that. If we did that now we'd be done for cruelty.

There was just one cold tap in the house and there was this grotty little gas oven in the back. In the morning when my mother was making breakfast – that's when we could afford it – she'd get this frying pan that was full of dripping. You'd keep the dripping because you used to have it on bread with salt. And when she picked it up there'd be mouse prints all over it, but it would still be used. It was never thrown out. You were just glad to get fed. That was the way life was.

It was so bad that an uncle went to the council and said it was wrong the way we lived. My father wouldn't go himself. 'I'm begging from nobody,' he'd say. But when my uncle went down to the council they sent a man up. My mother was up at the shop when he came and I was looking after the little ones. He wasn't a nice guy and when I showed him round he was tut-tutting all the time. But it wasn't so bad, because within a month or so we moved to a three-bedroom house, which was luxury. It had a toilet and hot and cold taps. We couldn't believe it. People deride council houses now, but they shouldn't. It was a good house and a massive improvement for us.

The main employment round here was in the mines, but I didn't really fancy that. I wasn't scared of the hard work, I just didn't fancy coal mining. All my family, with the exception of my father, were miners and they weren't very complimentary in what they said about it. But they did say the mining fraternity was great to work with. It was great working underground and you were all mates. That was true, and you could see it in the pubs and clubs how they stuck together. If you went to a club on a Saturday morning it would be full of miners, off for the weekend, all having a pint. You could see them all over the bar, their arms going as they told each other what work they'd done. By the time you left you were worn out. You'd worked the shift. That was the only topic of discussion, the work. And they'd use all these terms like having a 'good keble', which meant they had some soft coal to get out. I used to love being with the miners at the weekend. I can't remember as a little lad down there being treated unkindly by any adult coal miner. They were helpful, friendly, wanted to know you, to be friends.

When I started work on the railway my job was messenger boy, which meant I took all the mail up to the office. I had to be there by six, then I had to distribute the mail, walking along the railway track from Dunston Staithes to Blaydon, dropping the post off at each signal box. While I was there I had to pick up their mail and bring it back to the offices where I collected more mail to take to Marley Hill, where there was a big pit. All of this was supposed to be done on foot, but what I used to do was hook a lift from an engine. If an engine was passing in the direction I wanted I would jump on and jump off when I wanted to. The train drivers didn't like it, but I don't think they were that bothered. Then I used to use the gravity haulage system to get from Dunston up to Marley Hill. The system was quite simple. A cable passed round a big drum at the top of the hill. At one end there were all the full trucks of coal and right down the bottom end were the empty trucks. The brakesman took his brake off, the wheel started rotating and the weight of the full trucks coming down pulled the empty ones up to the top. So I used to jump on either the back or the front and get a lift up. I often used to sit on the front with the bank rider and when I look back it was horrific. I don't know how we got away with it. The bank rider just sat on the front with a big handle and I used to sit next to him – me, a fifteen-year-old lad. We used to sit there chatting all the way up. If you'd fallen off it was instant death. When you reached the top of the incline and it started dropping down, he would pull the pin out that held the cable on and hit the clamp with a hammer. The rope would go one way and then we both used to jump off. I suppose the men would have had a problem if anything had happened to me, but that's what we used to do.

When I got back to the offices at Dunston I'd pick up mail and walk along the Tyne Bank, up and across the Tyne Bridge and drop the mail off at Newcastle Central Station. That was the end of the day and I was allowed to get a bus from there home to Sunniside where I lived. The job wasn't what I would have wanted, but it paid a wage: £2.19s.1d. [£2.96]. And with that I even bought a bike to help me get about with the postage job. That was 1955. Then after a few months they put me up on the Staithes as a switch lad. My job then was to send the sets of coal trucks to the relevant bay for them to put on the ships. I had to alter the rails going from one bay to another. It was horrendous in blizzards – it was absolutely freezing cold. I didn't go much on that, so I decided it was time to leave and find fresh fields.

I stayed on the railway about eight months before I moved on to Marley Hill Colliery. My father came in one Sunday night and said, 'You're not happy doon there, are you?' I said, 'Well it's a job.' So he said, 'Be at the pit gates eight o'clock Monday morning. Billy Kendal, one of the managers at the coal mine, has said he'll take you on.' Billy was a great guy – safety officer – and he got me a job at Marley Hill pit which was one of the deepest coal mines in the North East and one of the biggest. It covered acres and acres and had two shafts. I would have preferred not to have gone to the pit, but when your father said 'Do!' you did – simple as that. He was ex-army and still acted as a sergeant major.

At work and at home you knew your place and you did what you were told. Durham miner Bob Willis says, 'If you were cheeky to anyone down the pit, to your elder ones, they'd tell your father. And you were frightened. If you back-answered anybody in the street, they'd go and tell my mother and father. That was it, and you got a clip across the earhole and a boot up your backside.' Margaret Taylor from Rochdale remembered how strict things were at home in the 1950s and early 60s and how much work she had to do there after she had already done a day's work.

My mam and dad had split up and me and my sisters lived with my dad. All of us used to be on the same pay and we used to have to take our wages home unopened. Out of my first wage of £3.15s [£3.75] I used to get five shillings [25p] spends. At home we had to do all the household chores. We cooked, we cleaned, we did the big old mangle with the posser and dolly tub, dolly blueing and starching. It was the same in a lot of houses. Not a lot of people had washing machines. It's what we got used to and that's the way we were brought up, but we were taught to cook. My dad taught us to cook. But he was very, very strict. We had to be back in at home at eight o'clock at night; we hadn't to be out after that, so we always had to do the first session at the pictures. He wouldn't let us wear tights and he wouldn't let us wear high heels. I had to wear Cuban-heeled shoes, very low-heeled shoes, and white socks, and he wouldn't let us wear make-up. That's how I used to have to go out. I weren't allowed to go dancing or anything like that, so I used to say I was going to the church Girls' Brigade which I was a member of. We lived in a ground-floor flat so I used to go out in certain clothes and climb back in through the window to get into my other clothes to go dancing in and my dad had gone out when I got home. I reckoned to be asleep when he'd get in and he used to say, 'What time did our Margaret get in?' My sister used to say, 'She's just come in, Dad,' so I used to get leathered.

I left home at sixteen because my dad was so strict and I went to live at my married sister's. It all came about because I'd been out on a bike ride down the lanes to Hollingworth Lake one night after work. While I was out I met the lad who was to be my future husband and I were in bother because I got back a bit late that night, so I was grounded for a week. Even though I was working I had to stop in, so I left. My dad didn't speak to me because I had left home but I had to get his permission to get married.

Today, in a world of service industries and computers, central heating and washing machines, it's hard to imagine the sheer hard graft of working life and the toughness of home life – waking up in a bedroom that was so cold thick ice had formed on the inside of the window; walking to school or work in the pouring rain; doing heavy manual work in a freezing workplace that was exposed to the elements. John Williams is from Cefn Coed in South Wales and it is having to walk everywhere that he remembers most.

When we were young we'd do a lot of walking. We always walked to school and we'd walk miles on a Saturday mainly because we couldn't afford to do anything else. In fact most people used to walk everywhere. There were only two cars in the whole of the village and that was at a time when there were about two thousand people living there. One of the people who had a car was Colonel Jones, whose chauffeur drove him about. He was very posh and he would give us all a new penny coin. On New Year's Day the bank would issue brand-new pennies and all the youngsters would go and knock at the colonel's door and get a penny each. Then they'd all be swapping scarves and caps and going again for a second coin! But I suppose he didn't mind. So the colonel had a car, and then there was a grocer at the bottom of the village who had the other car. The grocer's shop was right opposite 27 High Street and he had a car because he used to go fishing in the reservoir.

There were trams running then from Merthyr. It was only a penny to travel on them, but sometimes my mother couldn't even afford a penny so we used to walk down the Pandy Road. She would go and see her mother and I'd go with her. I can remember my mother would go Saturday evening to Merthyr and look in all the butchers' shops. It was because there was no refrigeration then, so, as the evening went on, the price of meat dropped because they didn't want to keep it over the weekend. So she was waiting till the right price came before she bought her meat for the Sunday dinner.

I had four brothers. My elder brother was killed in an air crash in 1942. He had joined the air force before the war in 1936 as there was no decent work round here. There was plenty in the collieries and he'd had a job in one of the drift mines, but he disliked it intensely so he volunteered for the RAF.

There was another grocer's shop in Cefn and as a young lad I went to work there on a Saturday, doing their deliveries. There were only six people that I delivered to but one of them was up at Pontsticill and I used to walk from Cefn Coed to Pontsticill in order to deliver to one farm. I also used to carry large baskets of freshly baked bread up from the baker's down the road. My wages were 7/6d [37½p] and this was one of the first paid regular jobs that I had. Another was at a limestone quarry just up the road called Calcium Products and Fertilizers Ltd. I worked there in the summer holidays where I weighed all the lorries on the weighbridge.

Later on in my school career I had another job, which was marvellous as far as I was concerned. I got a job with the Post Office delivering post to the northern row of houses. Up on the way there was a quarry and after that there were seven farms and cottages, ending up way up on the Brecon Beacons. I was getting up before school to get over to the Post Office for about six o'clock in the morning, sort the letters and then deliver them, all on foot of course. For that I got £1.17s.3d. [£1.86]. The headmaster gave me a lecture about it before I started. He said he didn't want me to use it as an excuse for being late for school, 'especially on a Monday morning when you've got German and I know you don't like it'. So I made sure I was never late. I was there bright-eyed at nine o'clock when the other children were only just getting out of bed, because of course I'd already been

walking on the mountain. I'd walked about five
miles or so before I went to school.

Throughout the Depression of the 1930s and the war
years life had been hard and for the majority of working
people this continued into the 1950s. This experience had
a major influence on their attitudes to life and work. Life
with its ups and downs was still seen as a struggle but
most people accepted it without too much questioning
just as their parents and grandparents had done before
them. Work was hard and the hours were long but people
were prepared to put in the effort to make life better for
themselves and their families. If there was any overtime to
be had, most people wanted it – the extra money in the
pay packet would pay for new shoes for the children, a
new dining suite or even go towards a holiday.

In spite of the hardships, though, it was also a time of
an increasing optimism that came with full employment,
rising wages and greater opportunities to get on. People
had lived through the war and the slump that had
preceded it and in post-war Britain there was a feeling
that things could only get better.

2

Making Things

T HE DESCRIPTION OF Britain as the 'workshop of the world' generally refers to the time during the reign of Queen Victoria when Britain's industrial and economic power was unchallenged. The Great Exhibition of 1851 was a showcase for the work of British engineers. No other country in the world could match their skills in designing and building the machine tools and steam-powered machinery that drove the Industrial Revolution forward. Just over a hundred years later, when Queen Elizabeth II came to the throne, Britain was still the most urbanized and industrialized nation in the world, accounting for a quarter of world trade in manufacturing. The country was the foremost world producer of ships and the leading European producer of coal, steel, cars and textiles. Engineering workshops manufacturing everything from nuts and bolts to massive engines and generators covered vast swathes of our industrial cities. Coal was still the main source of heating and energy, providing the fuel that drove the wheels of industry. Science-based industries like electronics and engineering were growing rapidly, as were oil and chemical refining. Britain led the field in civil aviation with the world's first jetliner, Comet, and Rolls-Royce was a worldwide symbol of excellence in aero and motor engines. Even the textile industry had been revived by the introduction of synthetic fibres. Most people used trains for long journeys and the railway network reached to almost every part of the country.

Trafford Park, just to the west of Manchester's city centre, was the world's first and biggest industrial estate. It was a place where dozens of factories, large and small, made things – everything from Kellogg's Cornflakes to huge boilers, turbines and generators for the power industry. Originally parkland, it was purchased in 1896 for £360,000 by Ernest Hooley who created the Trafford Park Estate Company. In the 1950s, although Manchester is thirty-five miles from the sea, its port was ranked as the fourth most important in the UK, thanks to the Manchester Ship Canal and the direct access it allowed to the sea. The canal ran through Trafford Park, making it well suited to the import of raw materials and the export of manufactured goods to the world. The Park was a major economic success story for Manchester. Among the biggest employers there was Metropolitan-Vickers, known to everyone as Metros, or Metro Vics. It was here that Alcock and Brown had first met each other and talked the company into building and supplying the Vickers Vimy aeroplane in which they flew across the Atlantic in 1919. Throughout the 1950s and 1960s the Park was a major provider of jobs: it was the industrial home of the Co-operative Wholesale Society, which had a large food-packing factory and a flour mill there, and to over forty other companies, many of them connected with food processing and with engineering. Workers came in from all over Manchester and the surrounding area. Jim Bottomley was born and brought up close to Trafford Park and in 1955 he started an apprenticeship at a wireworks there.

I was born and bred in docklands, Salford, and I wouldn't have swapped it for the world. I was surrounded by pubs and houses. My granddad would take me for a walk on a Sunday in Stretford and that was when I'd see grass that I could go on. The only grass and trees where I lived was in Ordsall Park and there were railings round them – you were not supposed to go on the grass or climb the trees. So going out to Stretford for a couple of hours on Sunday meant I could run around on grass. Where I lived was less than half a mile from Trafford Park gates and, depending on which way the wind was blowing, you got all kinds of different smells. If it was an east wind you'd get Guinness coming from Pomona Dock, which is where the bottling plant was. If it was the other way you got a smell of corn because of all the corn ships being unloaded. There were all sorts of smells, some of them horrible, some nice.

Trafford Park was an amazing place. Until Victorian times it was the estate of the de Trafford family who had lived there for centuries and it was all woodland. Then the Manchester Ship Canal was built to bypass Liverpool, because Liverpool was charging the earth to berth ships for Manchester cotton. So Manchester said, 'Up yours – we'll build a canal!' It was all done with pick and shovel and Irish navvies. They built the canal, built the docks, and then they got rid of all the woodland and started building factories. It was probably in its heyday in the 1930s, 1940s and 1950s, and it was the biggest industrial complex in Western Europe at one time. And it was so diverse. The whole place was built on a grid system. You had First Avenue, Second Avenue and so on and there was streets 1–12 going across it at ninety degrees.

Across the road from Trafford Park on the Manchester Ship Canal, at a point near Mode Wheel Locks, there was always a ship moored called *City of Salford*. It used to be known as the 'shit ship' because it took all the effluent out. All the toilets being flushed in Salford went down to Mode Wheel Lock where [everything was] pumped on to this ship to be deposited on the other side of the Mersey Bar. But when the tide came in it would bring all these deposits back in. It always put me off going to New Brighton, because you'd see it on the beach there.

In the middle of Trafford Park there was a village and I used to go there before I left school because they had a swimming baths. It was better than the one we had in Salford, so we used to walk there across Trafford Bridge. Round the village there were thousands of different factories, but the main one was what we then called Metro Vics, or Metropolitan-Vickers to give it its full name. When Trafford Park was built it was called Westinghouse, which was an American company. They always made electric motors there, from small things to massive generators. They had to use huge Pickfords lorries to transport them from the factory and they would clog up the roads for days on end because of the size of them. Later on the company became AEI [American Enterprise Institute] then eventually GEC [General Electric Company].

Jim moved from Salford in 1954 when he was fifteen and went to live on the other side of Trafford Park in Stretford. He had been a pupil at Salford Grammar School from the age of eleven, but was keen to leave school and begin work.

I didn't do well there and came out with three O-levels, which really wasn't that good. I hadn't a clue what I was going to do and you didn't get much help from school. But there was the Youth Employment Office, so I went there and when I told them I'd got maths and science O-levels they said I'd be all right in a laboratory. They helped me a lot more than school did.

I got an interview for a job as a lab assistant at Frederick Smith's wireworks in Trafford Park and I started there on 19 August 1955, working mainly in the electroplating department. The wages were £2.15s [£2.75] a week. My friends at Metro Vics earned £2.2s.1d [£2.10½], so I was pleased with that, but I wasn't even allowed to open my wage packet. I had to give it straight to my mum, who gave me pocket money of two bob [10p]. The man who interviewed me was called Arnold Ashton. He was the boss there and he was a brilliant man who really influenced my life. He guided all of us very well and made sure we went to day release [classes]. He wanted us to do the best in life and most of us did. So I had day release and two nights a week until I qualified as a metallurgist. I went to college in Newton Heath, then to UMIST [University of Manchester Institute of Science and Technology] in Manchester. That took from 1955 to 1962.

Frederick Smith's made copper wire and strip. They used to take copper wire bars from the docks; the ships came in with them from South America, South Africa, Sweden and all over the place. They'd unload these copper bars and put them on to railway wagons. Trafford Park had its own railway system, part of the Manchester Ship Canal Railway, and the trains used to go everywhere, down every little side road. It was fantastic. So the copper would come by rail from the docks right into the company yard. The copper bars were about 370 pounds each in weight – massive things. They would be put in a furnace and put up to red heat, which is about 900°C. Then they'd roll them down and, as you put them through the rollers, it reduced the cross-section, so it increased in length. You'd keep doing that through a series of rollers till you came out with a ⅜-inch diameter rod. That was then drawn into wire or strip and supplied to people like Metropolitan-Vickers, because it was the copper wire they used in windings for their motors and generators.

[Frederick Smith's] had three sites: Trafford Park, Salford and Leyton in London. Trafford Park was where all the heavy stuff was done, breaking it down from wire bars into wire. Salford used to make very fine wire; they'd take the wire from Trafford Park and break it down till it was finer than a hair. At Leyton they used to put a coating of enamel on it to insulate it. That enamelled copper was then wound into electric motors. That was the basis for electric motors at GEC or AEI and for most electric cables.

There were two rolling mills on the Trafford Park site. One was an old Victorian mill; the other was automated and was only two years old when I first started there. It was state of the art then – automated by control boxes in the middle of the rolling mill. The old mill was dirty black and you couldn't see the other end of it for smoke and steam and copper dust in the atmosphere. That was probably used more, though, because the modern one was always breaking down. You'd get faults that would take two or three days to fix, but the other mill would just keep going. It was run by a big steam engine somewhere in the factory. In fact, a lot of the factory was still run on the old belt and overhead-cams system. I had an uncle who used to mend the belts. If a belt snapped he used to put something on it where he could get two teeth meshing together and he'd put a pin through it. He'd repair all these and he'd oil all the machinery and put grease on axles and such. He was the oil-and-greaser for the factory and that's all he'd do.

There was also a guy who looked after the engine and his engine room was like a clinic. You could have eaten your dinner off the floor, it was so pristine. There were massive belts and thick ropes going round the big wheel in there. For someone starting work at the age of sixteen it was a magical place. We used to go in the engine room and talk to the guy who ran it, because you could go anywhere then. Health and safety wasn't a big factor the way it is now.

In the actual drawing shop, where they'd draw the wire, coils of ⅜ wire that had been through the rolling mill would go through the drawing machine and go down to less than 1/20 inch. There were banks of machines, hundreds of them, and the noise was colossal. All these machines were there running all day long, with pumps pumping lubricant round. I now suffer from tinnitus because of the rolling mill and the noise in the factory. No one would be allowed in there today without earplugs, but we were never given any then. One man would look after two or three machines, much like a textile mill. If one of the machines broke down or the wire ran out the operator would have to thread them up, and threading up could take a couple of hours so that was downtime with no production on that machine. A couple of hundred people worked in the drawing shop and there were four or five hundred in the whole factory. Everybody worked shifts because the machines had to be kept going all the time. The only time they stopped was the two Wakes Weeks when the whole factory shut.

I worked in a laboratory that was part of the chemical control of the process. That meant I was staff, which was a big thing then. If you were on the staff you were a cut above everyone else. You'd still clock in on an old-fashioned clocking-in machine, but you didn't start till nine o'clock and you had better benefits than people on the shop floor. The company had four canteens – or at least one canteen with four different serving hatches and four different places to sit. All the food would be the same but there was this segregation. Company directors and top-notch bosses had what was called the Directors' Room, then you got the Foremen's Canteen. Below that you had the Staff Canteen, then the Workers' Canteen. They were all separate rooms; they'd just got hatches all leading on to the same kitchen. In fact, you could wave at each other through the hatches. The Directors' Room had tablecloths and water on the table but the same food and the same people serving you. The workers and the staff went at one o'clock for lunch, and then there was a fifteen-minute gap before the elite came for theirs. So all the workers got served first and they had an hour for lunch. The elite had longer – they didn't go back till half past two.

One of my friends went from staff to foreman. This wasn't a normal move and it was a long time before they would take him into their elite company. He'd been foreman for about two years before he got the key for the foremen's toilet. They used to wear the key round their necks on a string. It was a status symbol. I don't know whether there was a presentation ceremony! All of this was dead serious.

Occasionally, if there was a problem, the bosses would come on the shop floor. You'd always call your bosses 'mister', but it was first names coming back down the line from them. On the shop floor some of the foremen were addressed as 'mister'.

Because I was staff it meant that generally I didn't work shifts. The only time I did was if we were working on a prototype, which happened quite a lot because it was a very forward-looking company and there was always lots of development work going on. One example was printed circuit boards. We were one of the first companies in the world to make copper foil that you could make printed circuit boards from. So on the prototypes for those you sometimes had to work through twenty-four or even forty-eight hours.

I got my qualifications and it did me a favour because I got out of National Service.[12] As a metallurgist it was a stepping stone for me to other companies, not just working in copper but also in steel. I did actually stay in copper and cabling for quite some time, but I also got involved in gold and silver, which is where I am today.

When you started to go to night school and day release you got talking to other people doing an equivalent job to you and you'd start comparing how much you were earning. They got to the point where they'd have a survey each year. You didn't put your name to it but you'd put down what you were getting, then they'd put them all together and say the highest salary is this, the lowest is this and you knew where you stood in that league table. We were always bottom! None of us had the nerve to go and see Mr

[12] People who were studying were exempt from National Service because the government didn't want their studies to be interrupted. By the time Jim had completed his course in 1962, National Service had finished.

Ashton. He was a nice guy, but he could wrap you up in a ball and throw you out of the window he was so powerful. So I decided we should join a union. All the rest of the lads were behind me, so we contacted the union and a representative came down and we met in the pub after work, because he wouldn't have been allowed on the premises. I've got a feeling he bought us all a drink on the union and it was all like, 'This is how it is, fellas!' All camaraderie. Anyhow, we went away and talked about it and decided to go for it, so we joined the Association of Scientific Workers (AScW) run by Clive Jenkins, who was one of the highest trade unionists in the country at that time. Because it had been my idea I got elected and I was the first representative for staff. The shop floor was well represented in different unions. Anyway, we went to Mr Ashton and told him. It sort of put a wedge between us but it didn't matter. We were there to earn money at the end of the day.

When we joined I remember one of the girl laboratory assistants coming to me and saying, 'Us girls have got together and we want to have the same money as you men.' I said, 'Why?' 'We work the same as you,' she replied. 'But you're a woman,' I said. I was being extremely sexist, but at the time I knew no better. I actually meant it. But the women talked to me and in the end I thought, they are absolutely spot on. I thought, 'How am I going to tell this to Mr Ashton? He'll just laugh.' So I approached him and . . . he just laughed! So that was it.

But the union was good for us. We paid our dues and got a card and tried negotiating pay increases, which I seem to remember we got. But we also shot ourselves in the foot when we set it up. The management said, 'All right, we'll run things the way we want as well. If you're late so many times in a week we'll fire you,' whereas it had been a bit lax before that. You could be a few minutes late a few times, have an afternoon off to go to the dentist and so on. That all stopped. There were no terms of employment then, but you knew start times and finish times and they made sure you adhered to them after that.

Starting time was half past seven in the morning and people got there by bus or bike. There were ten times more bikes then than you see now. People didn't go in cars at that time and, even if they did, there was nowhere to park them. Companies didn't have car parks; they had cycle sheds. You'd put your cycle on the same peg and lock it so no one could nick it. There wasn't much theft, but you never went to work with new mudguards or anything. There were hundreds and hundreds of red Manchester buses in the morning. They used to stream in, packed with workers, then go out empty or with a few night workers on them, then they'd come back at half past four. Everybody at Trafford Park finished at five o'clock except at Frederick Smith's; we finished at half past five. People would fall asleep on the bus. After a day's work, sitting on the bus for maybe an hour, people would just nod off, so you'd shout to someone, 'Eh, it's your stop.' Everyone knew where everyone else got off.

Because everyone finished at around the same time it took ages to get out [of Trafford Park] and no one thought of staggering start and finish times. Metro Vics alone employed twenty-eight thousand people at their Trafford Park site. Going into a place like that was a bit like going into a cathedral and going 'Wow!' It was just so big. When you went in and saw the aisles there, they'd go on as far as the eye could see – massive, cavernous places with hundreds of people all working. I didn't work there, but because my company was associated with them and made a lot of their wire I had to go there occasionally. The place was like a town on its own and you could walk where you wanted. No one stopped you. In fact, I used to use it as a shortcut, because the road that went through came out near where I lived in Stretford. The gates were always open – nobody asked you for a pass or anything. At Metro Vics there used to be stories of people who went round with clipboards. They said they were time-and-motion people, so everybody would start being busy if they saw somebody with a clipboard. The rumour was Metro Vics employed these people because it kept the workforce busy! How true it is I really don't know.

Frederick Smith's owned two semi-detached houses next to the works. One of the people who lived there was the superintendent of the rolling mill so they could get him out any time of the day to make a decision on repairs. The other was a caretaker. One of them kept pigs, so you'd look over the fence from the factory and see pigs. But there were just these two houses in the middle of all the factories; no neighbours or anything. It must have been dreadful to live there because if you went out any time other than the working day there were no buses running.

There was no health and safety to speak of. The first day when you came as a lab assistant they gave you a white coat; that was your status symbol. It had to last you twelve months, but it would soon be full of holes, barely any use at all, because you would have had acid burning it and all sorts of things. I even got set on fire once. In the old Victorian rolling mill the floor was made of shiny steel sheets. It had lubricant on it, mainly to facilitate the movement of the rods across it, but also to stop it rusting. One of my jobs was to go down a few times a day with a pyrometer to take the temperature of the wire bars to make sure they were at the right heat. One day they'd opened the furnace door and I was down on my haunches when one of the guys flicked a red-hot rod over and it went under my lab coat, which was trailing on the floor. I smelt fire and someone shouted, 'Do you know you're on fire?' When I looked down I could see I was in flames! So I had to get my coat off, stamp on it to put it out and I still had to wear that coat for a few weeks before I got a new one.

One of the more serious things that happened to me was when I had an accident and nearly lost my sight. We were always joking and playing tricks in the laboratory, but this one backfired on me. Two of us were listening to a bloke talking to us and he'd got a boiling tube full of liquid ammonia and started to shake it up. As he did so it blew his thumb off the end and I got showered in all this ammonia. If you've ever tasted raw ammonia, it takes your breath away, and this was concentrated. It went all over my face, in my ears, in my mouth and in my eyes. I couldn't breathe and as I was flailing about trying to get oxygen inside me I started knocking glassware off the benches. My mate said, 'Stop it! You're going to get us in trouble.' He didn't realize how bad I was; he thought I was joking and I was more or less unconscious by the time they decided I wasn't. So they took me to the ambulance room and they realized there that it was my eyes that were the problem. The nurse washed them out for hours and hours it seemed, then dashed me off to Manchester Eye Hospital. They told me there I would probably lose my right eye as I had burnt a hole through the cornea. I was in hospital for over a week and they didn't think it would grow again, but it did. Accidents like that happened all the time. The ambulance room was a very busy place and there was always blood on the floor. But the nurse there was very good.

Where we worked we used to do a lot of pioneering stuff on wire, including making silver-plated wire. You'd have a reel of copper wire at one end and by the time it had gone through the plating machines you'd have a reel of silver-plated wire at the other end. There were capstans that used to drive the reels round. One of the lads who used to run these machines was about our age; his name was Paddy Nolan. He was trying to straighten the wire one day and got his fingers caught in it, and it went round the capstan and took his finger off. So we had to get him to the ambulance room and it was about a day later we found his finger. We put it in one of the sample packets that went to the laboratory for analysis and put a note with it for the girls in the spectrographic analysis department asking what the copper content under the nail was.

The lads were always playing pranks on each other, including once when I was suspended on a chain above a huge vat of acid for fifteen minutes. When the copper came from the rolling mill it was about two hundred yards long and was in a round coil. Because it had been oxidized it was bluey-black and it didn't look like copper at all. It couldn't be drawn down like that, so the rolls were put on great big booms and ducked into sulphuric acid baths which dissolved all the copper oxide off. These were in an open shed to let the fumes and gas escape. One day I wanted to look in a nest of pigeons I'd seen up in the roof of this shed, so my mates lifted me up in the hoist. But while I was looking at the baby pigeons suddenly they started traversing the hoist and took it right over the middle of the bath. Then they said, 'See you later!' and off they all went. There was nothing I could do. I was stuck on this chain over the acid bath, I couldn't shout, couldn't do anything, because if anyone found me there I'd have got sacked. So I just had to hang till they came back and let me down. The thing is you never saw danger at work when you were young.

Going to work was going to meet your mates. They were all my age and we all had the same interests. We're still mates. You felt you were part of a family. At lunchtime you'd get two or three blokes who'd supplement their income by doing haircuts.

They didn't have electric clippers, but they'd do a proper job. If you wanted a bet there would be a bookie's runner there to take bets. He'd be running his machine and people would come up and say, 'I've just left a bet on there for you' and he'd put it in his book when he had his break. Then at lunchtime he'd take it to someone who used to go round all the factories taking all the bets. The bosses knew all about it, but it wasn't something they frowned on; it was just part of working life. Wherever you worked in Trafford Park there was always a camaraderie. Somebody would say, 'Have you heard this joke?' and they'd just stop their work and tell the joke. People don't seem to have the time now.

When I started to work in 1955 it was the heyday of West Indians coming over for work. Frederick Smith took on a massive amount of West Indian labour and because they were cricket mad we had a cracking cricket team. It was such fun playing with them; win or lose, it was a cracking time.

It was at Frederick Smith's that Jim met his wife. She worked in the personnel department at the Simon Street site in Salford. They used to go to the Ritz Ballroom on Whitworth Street in Manchester where Phil Moss and his band played, and sometimes to the Locarno in Sale after going to the pubs along Washway Road. They got married in 1961 and decided it was silly both working at the same place. 'When you get home at night,' he said, 'there's nothing to talk about. You've both experienced virtually the same day. And when you're married and got children on the way you need more money so I moved on.'

*

If one British city above all others could claim to be at the very centre of the Industrial Revolution, that city would be Birmingham, and for most of the nineteenth and twentieth centuries hundreds of industries, large and small, were based there. Beginning with small workshops turning out a variety of products, from nails to fancy goods, Birmingham and its surrounding areas developed rapidly and as early as 1791 it was described by the economist Arthur Young as 'the first manufacturing town in the world'. It became the hub of the English canal system in the eighteenth century, and the coming of the canals, the railways and then motor vehicles, together with metalled roads, accelerated Birmingham's industrial growth to make the town – later city – into one of the world's greatest centres of manufacturing producing the most diverse range of goods imaginable.

Birmingham's economy was characterized by high wages and a wide range of specialized skills that were not suited to wholesale automation. For most of the nineteenth century, industry here was still dominated by small workshops rather than large factories, which became common only towards the end of the century. Birmingham became known as the 'city of a thousand trades' because of the wide variety of small, high-value metal items manufactured there: buttons, cutlery, nails and screws, guns, tools, jewellery, toys, locks and ornaments were among its many products, together with the tube industries[13] which made Birmingham ideally

[13] Specialist branch of metallurgy engaged in the manufacture of steel pipes and tubing.

placed for the manufacture of bicycles, motorcycles and cars. By the middle of the twentieth century it had become the centre of the UK's metalworking, engineering, manufacturing and automotive industries. The city's economy flourished in the thirty years that followed the end of the Second World War. Birmingham led the way in two of the British economy's major growth areas – motor vehicle and electrical-equipment manufacture – and was second only to London in the creation of new jobs between 1951 and 1961. Unemployment in Birmingham between 1948 and 1966 rarely exceeded 1 per cent, and by 1961 household incomes in the West Midlands were 13 per cent above the national average.

Ray Barrett was born and brought up in Aston, close to the centre of Birmingham. He started his working life in the 1950s in a small workshop where they made parts for the motorcycle industry and finished up at Austin's Longbridge car plant in the 1970s when it was a hotbed of union militancy.

Where I lived in Aston it was back-to-back housing built in the nineteenth century and I believe it was condemned in the 1930s as being uninhabitable, but we lived there till 1951. It was a very busy area, with houses and factories all mixed together. It's a bit hard to understand now, but the factories were all in among the houses. They were just small ones, making nuts and bolts and small parts for the motor, bicycle and motorcycle industries. Everybody round there seemed to work in them. My father wouldn't move from where we lived. He'd say, 'I'm not catching a bus just to go to work.' He wouldn't live in the suburbs and go on a bus for two or three miles; he preferred to live where we were with the work on the doorstep. The factory he worked in was so close I used to go round there and ask him for a penny for the gas meter when we ran out. You could just walk into any of the factories. But it was dirty. No sun ever came through; you'd just get haze. As a boy I can only remember haze and a permanent hum of machinery. Everybody you knew was pale and I had my own little theory about this. I reckoned the atmosphere was so filthy the germs couldn't live in it. So we were pale but fit and healthy.

My first job was where my dad worked, at a place called Shelley's where they used to make Norton motorbikes. My first day was on my fifteenth birthday. Before that I'd worked shovelling sand. It was much easier to get jobs then than it is now. You had your overalls under your arm and your working boots on and you'd knock on the factory door and say you were looking for a job. 'Can you do this?' they'd say, and you always said yes whether you could or not. 'Can you operate this machine?' someone would say and you'd always say, 'Yes, I've done that job.' But you hadn't and the thing was you couldn't always fool the foreman. He wasn't somebody who'd come from university; he was somebody who'd been there before you and if you couldn't operate that machine, he knew it. He'd sack you on the spot sometimes.

There used to be a bloke in Hercules Bicycles in Aston Cross, five minutes from where I worked, and he told me how in the 1930s the foreman used to come out on a Monday morning and there'd be a little crowd there waiting to see if there were any jobs. He'd go into the factory and he'd sack half a dozen blokes for no reason. Then he'd go outside and say, 'Right, I'll take you, you and you,' and he'd been known to take back somebody he'd just sacked that same morning. He didn't even know who he'd sacked. He was just saying, 'I am the boss, I make the decisions.' It must have been terrible times then. But in the 1950s it was a prosperous time. It was easy to get a job.

Nobody really taught you what to do. They'd stick you on a machine and say, 'Here, watch this man,' and then you'd have a go yourself. I worked on a broaching machine. This is a machining process that uses a toothed tool called a broach to remove material. I broke a couple of the broaches and I scrapped a couple of flywheels. When I did the first one I told the foreman that I'd scrap it. He had a little moan at me but said, 'Okay, don't do it again,' so the next time I thought, 'How am I going to tell him again?' So I put it under my overalls and went down to the toilet. If you opened the window in the toilet there was a little brook, Aston Brook, running beside it. So I threw it out of the window into the brook. When you looked out of the window, you could see all these rusty motor-bike parts all along; everybody was doing it.

When I first started work all the blokes in their early to mid-twenties were my heroes. They'd just fought and won a war. I think their attitude was, 'We've done our bit and we aren't going to be pushed around like our fathers and grandfathers were.' Nobody was going to intimidate them. I suppose I must have been impressed with their attitude, and I wanted to be one of them.

I was keen to get into the union as soon as I could so I joined when I was fifteen years and two months. You didn't have to join at that stage, but I joined because I wanted to be on a picket line during a strike. There was an engineers' strike coming up at the time and I wanted to be on it. Boys were exempt from striking, but I wanted to be with the blokes. I remember going [to join the union] with the works convener, who was a mate of my dad. Before we went into the meeting hall he started walking into the pub, so I followed him. But he turned round and said, 'Where are you going? Get out and wait outside.' So all the shop stewards and the convener went into the pub for a pint and I stayed outside. Then they took me round the corner to the meeting hall, where I joined the union. You had to state the wage you'd earned that week and what you were doing. It was a very formal matter and you were welcomed into the union. So I went on that engineers' strike. It was about February 1952 and it was a general engineers' strike. I was on the back gate of Shelley's with George Canning. He was shop steward then and later became Lord Mayor of Birmingham. I remember being threatened by somebody who was going in to work. Somebody nudged me and said, 'Call him a scab.' And I did. He was the other side of the road so he said, 'I'll come over and give you a thick ear.' But George Canning used to be a boxer and he just said, 'Come over and try it.'

Wages at Shelley's were £1.1s [£1.05] a week. I

stayed there for about two months, then I went to British Hub where they made all sorts of different hubs for bicycles and motorcycles. It wasn't like a factory as such; it was like a whole load of little sheds all knocked into different departments. Intermingled in this were the gunmakers. In them you'd have an old bloke sitting making a piece for a gun. They'd probably work on two or three shotguns a year. It was amazing to see them. The skills they had were unbelievable. One man would make the lock, another the stock and another the barrel. The whole area was like a labyrinth of little alleys and back yards and there were tiny little workshops all over the place. In them you'd have a drill press, a lathe and a work bench. There were very few machine tools; it was all hand-made.

I was at British Hub for about eighteen months. They had one huge electric motor there and the workshop was no wider than a kitchen. There was a row of eight centre lathes by the windows and another row of eight centre lathes up the middle. You've got to remember this place was very old, built about 1760. There were only men and boys up to the age of eighteen there, because young men were away doing National Service. Each machine had its own belt driving the lathe and it had three gears. To change gear you had a lump of wood and you just knocked the belt over with this while it was still moving, then you went to the belt men when the belt broke, which they did often. They were soaked in oil and they caused blue smoke as well, so you couldn't see from one end of this place to the other. There were tiny windows, like you see in Georgian houses, but they'd never been cleaned in two hundred years so you couldn't see out of them. So in a workshop that was only about thirty feet long you couldn't see properly and it was full of fumes. A machine would be set up for a certain size and you'd stay on that all day. You'd turn the phalanges on the end and across the middle. The faster you went, the worse the job was. If you made a poor job of turning the hub and sent it to the polisher, though, he'd come to you and throw it at you because it was more work for him. We were paid five shillings a gross, so the faster you went the more money you made. I could earn £1 per day, which was very good money in 1952.

I've had lots of jobs. I just went for the best money; I've done it all my life. If somebody said there's more money down the road, I would be off. For me it was just earn money and enjoy. I never had any ambitions. I never even thought about it. I just always went for the highest pay. They used to give us our wage in tin cans with your name inside it. You only got paid for what you'd done; you didn't get paid for attendance. I think I told fibs to my mother about my earnings. I used to pay my keep, but I used to keep most of my wage.

Car manufacturing was central to the economy of Birmingham and the Longbridge plant was the city's major employer. Opened in 1905, it was once the largest manufacturing plant in the world and in the 1950s and 1960s the site still employed thousands. At the time its most famous product was the Mini and from 1959 onwards tens of thousands were manufactured at Longbridge. On the production line the car bodies moved past ceaselessly. Ray worked there at that time.

I was working on much more modern machinery than anything I'd done previously. I was on a grinding machine doing the journals[14] on crankshafts. The crankshaft is where you turn the power of the engine into the actual momentum and the journals were on the end where it fits into the engine. Here you just did your little bit and passed it on. So I'd be grinding the journals and then it would get to the next man who would do the pins, which was another part of it, and it would go along like that. So you were just doing one thing all the time, very boring, very repetitive. But it was high wages. It was for all of those repetitive jobs. They were all very simple – a monkey could have done them. You had to be brain dead to do it, or your mind had to be somewhere else. But you were getting about £20 a week, which was good money. Not many were getting that then, but I hated it. You couldn't chat or anything because it was too noisy. When you stopped for lunch was the only time you got to talk to anyone.

I was among a few communists at the time. Red Robbo,[15] who was very famous then, worked two

[14] Sections of the crankshaft which ride on a thin layer of oil coating the main bearing surfaces.

[15] Derek Robinson was a well-known AEU (Amalgamated Engineering Union) convener and shop steward at British Leyland who led a long-running campaign of strikes in the 1970s.

machines up from me, and Dick Etheridge[16] was there. They were both communists who were big in the trade union.

Things seemed reasonably prosperous until they made us all redundant. I had been there about a week less than two years, so I didn't get any redundancy payment because you had to be there for two years for that. I was made redundant seven times altogether in my working life but I only got redundancy pay twice. When I was made redundant from Austin there were eight thousand of us all in the same area, all looking for a job. They were talking about having redundancy parties. You'd go in the pub and it was packed, everybody spending their redundancy cheques. It had a devastating effect on the whole community. You were all right till your redundancy money ran out, then disaster. You just looked out for yourself and took whatever you could. It was something you got used to. Every Christmas I'd always been on short time for as long as I could remember – a four-day or three-day week. So you learnt to do other things: scaffolding, construction, anything to fill in. It was like this for two years, then I got a job at Cummins Diesel Engines in Daventry.

The West Midlands has always been regarded as the home of the motor industry. It was here that Herbert Austin created the Austin empire, Vickers made buses and cars

---

[16] Another leading union official. Derek Robinson's predecessor as convener and shop steward at Longbridge, Etheridge was often described as the most militant union official in the car industry.

and Morris made trucks originally. The 1970s and its associated strikes decimated the industry, but recent years have seen a turnaround in the fortunes of car-making in the region. Land Rover, Jaguar and Peugeot all produce cars here and there are more than five hundred car component suppliers in the region.

Derek Meeking was born in the Small Heath area of Birmingham and spent most of his working life with Land Rover.

Small Heath was the suburbs, really; we had fields and farms just up the road. I had to stay on at school because the leaving age went up from fourteen to fifteen [in 1944], then I went straight into work. I went to the Ministry of Supply factory run by the Rover Company at Clay Lane, where they used to make tank engines. I was an apprentice there. It was general engineering and I went all round the works and I had to go to technical college one day a week. There were different departments we went into. One was a sort of experimental machine shop where they made the prototypes for any different type of engine that they were going to build and then they made the one-offs. I was machining and fitting, turning, milling and grinding. Then I went in the tool room after that, toolmaking.

When I finished the apprenticeship I had to do two years' National Service and when I finished I went back to Clay Lane. I did some machine-tool fitting, which was repairing machines, lathes and milling machines. If they broke down on the shop floor you had to go down and try and fix them. I was there about a year but after that I was made redundant because after the war the Ministry of Supply didn't require it any longer. Most of it was shut down, but Rover took some of it over and took in some machinery and made some of their parts there. One of the things I can remember them making were parts for axles.

I went for some other jobs, but I didn't get them. Then my father, who used to work at Lathe Lane where they made Land Rovers and Rover cars, asked if there were any vacancies there and they said that there were. In Solihull back in the 1950s Land Rover was the main employer in the area. So I went to an interview there and I got the job, building prototype vehicles. When I first got there they were building what they called 'forward controllers'. These were army vehicles that towed field guns. I was a sort of general fitter, so [I was involved in] building bits of body for the forward controllers and making brackets, fitting engines and all that type of work. All of the vehicles had to go out for testing. They used to go out Nuneaton way, where they had a high-speed test track. They ran over what they called French roads, which were all bumpy, and they had a cross country. I also used to go out to the army bases, usually with one of the engineers.

We were pretty isolated from the rest of the factory most of the time. We just did our bit. We used to go out around the factory to get parts or try and scrounge something, but we didn't have very much to do with the rest of the factory and the general car-building side of things. The only thing we did was when they brought in the production line for one of the gearboxes we went over there a few times and tried to assist in sorting out how to build it.

When I first went there the Land Rover shop was pretty grotty and crowded. You had a line in there with the vehicle moving up along and people were all crowded in very close. Then you had all the cans of nuts and bolts and bits and pieces to go on and you hadn't got much room. It was quite dark too.

It was a very friendly place, though, with good people working with you. The men used to get up to a lot of tricks and you could always buy anything; there was always somebody somewhere selling things like cigarettes. We had a couple of chaps there who used to tell jokes and they could tell them all day. There was always a bit of competition to see who could tell the most. In some parts of the works they even had toy train sets running around just for fun – that was something the management just let happen. The company had a big social club with a dance hall and a bar. The dance was very popular – you had to get in early if you wanted tickets for that because it was always full. It was a dress-uppy affair. They used to have the big bands at the time, proper bands. They also had a caravan section that had caravan rallies and they had cricket and football clubs and bowls.

To the north and west of Birmingham lies a region that was once one of the most intensely industrialized in Britain. In the nineteenth and early twentieth centuries the south Staffordshire coal mines and the iron foundries that used the coal to fire their furnaces made the area one of the most polluted in Britain and led to it being called the Black Country. It was renowned for its production of iron and steel goods, including chains, nails, tubes, forgings, rolled products and castings. Nail-making was the earliest of the region's 'metal-bashing' industries. It had been well established here by the Middle Ages, and at its peak in about 1820 there were over fifty thousand nailers at work in the area. Then as the trade in hand-made nails declined due to the mechanization of the industry, the Black Country turned to the production of chains, for which it was to develop an international reputation. At the end of the nineteenth century 90 per cent of all the chain workshops in England and Wales were in the area, most of them in the back yards of workers' houses.

The heavy industry which once dominated the region has now largely gone and clean-air legislation has meant that the Black Country is no longer black. The last coal mine, Baggeridge Colliery, was closed in 1968, but the biggest economic blows came in the late 1970s and early 1980s, when many of the area's large factories closed and unemployment rose drastically as the Black Country became another victim of Margaret Thatcher's plans to modernize Britain's industries.

Les Dunn, from West Bromwich, one of the principal towns of the Black Country, worked in the office of a forge called Brock House. 'There was a machine shop,' he recalls, 'and a shop where they just made heavy axles and a place that made windscreens for caravans. Then there was another site where there was a boiler shop where they made big boilers for heating greenhouses and factories.'

When I started all my family were factory workers. My dad was a roller in a factory just down the road. They made hot wire that was coiled into rolled wire. He worked in an open shop, summer and winter. It just opened on the side of the canal. I could go down and stand by the side of the canal and I could see my dad working in the mill on the other side. My mum worked in the foundry industry and she was a coil-maker.

In West Bromwich it was good for employment. You could go from one job into another without any problem. Originally my dad's main ambition for me was that I shouldn't work in a factory. At school, when you went into the third year you had a choice: you either went into engineering, commerce or art, and I went into commerce. I did three years of commercial work, which was primarily where we specialized in bookkeeping and shorthand. When I left school they said, 'What job do you want?' and I said I wanted to be a compositor in the printing industry because my sister had said it was very good pay. But when the employment-exchange people came to the school they said, 'No. Not with all the training you've got. You're not going to be a compositor, you've got to be commercial.' They gave me a list of jobs and I chose Brock House, where I got a job in the office, in the estimating department. It was a technical department because all the prices for the trailers and the road sweepers and everything that was made there all came through that one department.

Working in the office the pay was poor. There were benefits, though. You had things like the pension and you worked less hours, and if the office workers were late they didn't lose their money. If you worked on the clock in the works you were only allowed three minutes before you were classed as late for one stoppage. So if you started at eight o'clock and you clocked in at four minutes past eight you lost fifteen minutes' pay. And if you were late for a third morning you had to go home for the whole day.

The chief estimator suggested that I should become an apprentice, so I left the department and started an apprenticeship. I worked in the machine shop, in the inspection department, in the tool room and in the laboratory. As an apprentice I had a day off a week to go to college and I went three nights a week extra as well. Then there was all the homework to do after that on top.

Then they had a problem with the estimating at another works within the group. It was in the coil-rolling factory and because I'd got experience in the estimating side they sent me to sort it out. I was only about seventeen or eighteen at the time. In the forge at the place they sent me to they clocked on and clocked off when they were on a job. If there was any breakdown they clocked off and went off on a break on waiting time. They'd just started a union and they wanted someone to time the jobs and that fell on me. I'd no experience – I was just thrown into the deep end. Before I started the forge superintendent took me around the forge and told me what people to be careful of and how to handle them, because, he said, 'Some of these men will hit you and think nothing of it.' He also told me to be careful if I saw any of them outside. 'If you're in a pub and that person is in there and he's drinking,' he said, 'go out, don't come back, have nothing to do with him. Here in the forge they might be as docile as anything, but in the pub anything can happen.' Overall, though, I got on really well with them. I think it was because I appreciated the job they did; because my dad worked in that trade I knew what it was like. I know when my dad came home at night he'd be absolutely exhausted.

The biggest hammer at that time was the four-ton hammer. They used it to make handbrake levers for Leyland trucks and they were solid. On a full shift, if they had no breakdown, they used to do 120 of these. They wanted the job to be timed properly to work out the price for these handbrakes so I went and timed half a shift. I timed the job right up until the breaktime and they didn't stop working one minute. At the rate they were going they could have done 144 over the day. I asked them why they were only doing 120 when they did more than half of that in the morning. They said it was because they were so tired they couldn't do that much work in the afternoon. The thing is, these men, working as a team, used to be handling steel up to 168 pounds. They used to have to get it out of the furnace and cut the steel while it was red hot and then they put it on the hammer.

The conditions were terrible, filthy. They had little oildrums they used to sit on and they'd have a bottle of water. When I went in there were no gloves and no safety glasses. They had boots but no steel toes and no safety helmets; they just used to wear caps. Some, like the smiths, had a leather apron, so if a spark blew out it would burn that and not the trousers. And there were quite a lot of sparks flying around. It was hot, and dangerous and smoky as well and we weren't as clean then as we are now.

[Over the years] I saw a lot of changes in terms of the machinery that was used and safety procedures. They got gloves and safety glasses. They might not wear them, but at least they got them. They resisted when helmets were introduced in the forge because they said it was too hot. There were a lot of minor accidents and there was a lot of grit in the eyes. They never bothered going to the nurse for this; they just used to get it out themselves.

I was working in this factory and my wife was working in another factory. Before we were married we'd ride home on our bikes, have a wash, have our tea and then we'd meet and go and ride to Kinver, which is sixteen miles away. It would take us an hour. We used to have a little walk on the Edge and we used to ride back and it would take us an hour and a quarter to get back because it was more uphill. And that was our night out.

In the Black Country there was a long tradition of women working in the 'metal-bashing' industries. They were employed in nail-making and chain-making workshops and factories making hardware, kitchen appliances and other small domestic items. Les Dunn's wife Marjorie was born and bred in West Bromwich and got a job at a spring-makers.

We had the smogs because everybody was burning coal, but they let you off work early to get home when it was smoggy. It wasn't a very rich area, but we had about seven cinemas in West Bromwich and they were cheap enough for you to go two or three times a week and the dance halls were as well. But in the summer we used to go out on our bikes and we used to go swimming. I think it was a good time to grow up.

I worked in a factory from the age of fifteen until I was married. It was George Salter's the spring-makers, who also made bathroom scales and kitchen scales. My mum worked there and she got me the job. I left school on the Friday in ankle socks, which is what girls wore at the time, and I went to work on the Monday without them. Mother said, 'You've grown up now.' I worked on a hand-press doing plait springs. You worked in a team [and] everybody would be doing a different operation. If it was a big job – say forty thousand ordered from somewhere – you'd be on it for a couple of weeks. Then after that it might be a couple of hundred, so you might just be doing that job for a day. It was piece work and we were supposed to be able to make about £1 a day. You'd have a piece of chalk marking down how many you did and if anybody came to talk to you, you'd have to put your number down so you wouldn't forget. It was the lowest pay, but at that time you earned more money in a factory than you did in an office – it was very poor pay for office work.

Working on the press you always covered your wedding ring because you invariably got your fingers under the press. They used to say you're not a hand-press worker until you've had your finger under. So there were some nasty accidents. I got my finger caught in there but I was fortunate, it was just cuts and bruises I got.

It was like a big tin shed we worked in, freezing in the winter, boiling in the summer. It was a huge factory with about four thousand working there. When the bell went to go home they just used to stop the traffic because there were so many coming out of the factory gates. It was so big it had roads running through for the trucks and the lorries to drive in and out. But it was a happy place and everybody would be singing – the management were quite happy to let people have a chat and a sing. Everybody used to have tea together and we all took it in turns to make it. They always had a sports day and there were football, cricket, netball and tennis teams. It was a good firm to work for.

Factories making small items and component parts often had large numbers of women and girls in their workforce. Amy Carr from West Bromwich started work at a firm that made bottle tops when she was fourteen. Her father died not long after the war, leaving her mother with eight children to bring up. Life was hard and the family relied on the wages brought in by those children who were old enough to work.

When I started work I was fourteen on the Friday and I was in work at half past seven Monday morning. I didn't have any choice. I worked at Metal

Claridge's where they made bottle tops – screw-on tops. I had to stand on a box because I didn't start to grow until I was about sixteen. I started off in the press shop where they punched out the shapes. I used to have to grease the sheets for the guys to feed through the machine. I was only fourteen and I was only a little bit of a girl and the smell of the grease made me feel sick. I hated it, but I wasn't allowed to leave the job.

The noise [in the factory] was terrific. I've got tinnitus now because of it. I would be talking away all day and I used to read a book as well. I still really mouth my words when I'm talking now – it was a habit I got into. We knew exactly what each other was saying, but couldn't hear anybody.

As for money, I'd work every hour because it was piece work. I'd work on until seven, half past seven at night and I'd work my fortnight's holiday just to give Mum extra money. At dinnertime we used to have an hour but I couldn't afford to go and have meals in the canteen so Mum used to do us packed lunch. We used to have a £5 note at Christmas on top of our wages, a big white £5 note, and we used to have a dinner and dance. That's how I met my husband, Alf. It's ever so funny because his mum and dad met at Metal Claridge's and Alf and I met there as well.

Factory girls were very crude and I didn't like it. They'd be coming showing you dirty photographs and they liked to see you blush. I'd go like beetroot. I wouldn't look at them because I was totally naïve about boys. Our manager was a bit of a ladies' man and he'd slip his arm around you and things like that. I was ever so prim and proper in those days. I didn't like it. He only had to come and stand by me and I'd go red. But he respected his workers. He was a good worker himself and he did his best for you. We had a period of time where we had time and motion men in. And they'd come in timing you for piece work, but it was really to cut you down in money. The machine I was on at the time had a big handle and you could turn the speed down. So this manager would come round to us and say, 'They're coming around with a clipboard, so turn your machine down.' So say for argument's sake it would produce a hundred tops in an hour, you turned it down and it might produce seventy. So they'd time it at that and when they'd gone you'd turn it back up again.

If it had anything to do with metalworking there would be firms doing it in the Black Country. Chains, anchors, tubes, boilers, machinery and machine tools, hardware, home appliances and parts for road and rail vehicles were all manufactured here. John Thompson, one of the largest firms in Wolverhampton, produced boilers and pressure vessels. Alan Perry did a student apprenticeship with the company and subsequently went through various positions, including works manager, before becoming a director of the company at the age of thirty-one.

When I left Queen Mary's Grammar School, Walsall, in 1951 I joined John Thompson Ltd at their Bilston factory as a student apprentice, which meant I had to travel about eight miles a day by bus. Thompson's employed getting on for thirteen thousand around the world and had companies in Australia, South Africa, India, Argentina and Canada. The company made all sorts of different boilers – Lancashire boilers for the cotton industry, small boilers for canal boats and big steam-generating plants. The company had three different apprenticeships: a craft apprenticeship, a commercial apprenticeship and a student apprenticeship. Commercial was to do with the financial side of the business and craft was to do with working on the shop floor full time. With the student apprenticeship, which I did, we went through the different departments of the works. We had six months in each doing different jobs, sometimes in the works, sometimes in the offices.

I had a little bit of experience because my father had a small factory that I had worked in, so I got on quite well in the training school. One of the problems I had was understanding the people there. The Black Country was made up of lots of little villages and each one had its own language, virtually. I'd been to the grammar school and they tried to teach us to speak properly, but when you got into the environment of Bilston it was like a completely foreign language. But you soon got into it. We always had all sorts of leg-pulls there, like sending you to the stores for something daft. When new lads came in they'd send them to the stores to fetch something like wooden electrodes.

In the training school we had work benches with four or six lads on them with two or three either side. We had to do what they call a filing test, making one piece of metal fit to another. But one lad kept pinching my tools and another fella's. I put up with this the first week, then on the Monday morning the following week I said to this other fella, 'If he starts again, we'll get him.' Anyhow, it started again so when the tea break came at ten o'clock we got this lad and put one arm in his overalls and his legs in the other armhole. Well he started squealing and screaming and the supervisor came out of his office to find out what was going on. 'You don't do things like that,' he told us. 'I'm suspending you for a week.' So I put my coat on and off home I went. But the other fella's father went down to the company in the afternoon and explained what had happened. So he went back to work on the Tuesday, but I lived so far away that nobody could be bothered to get in touch with me. So I didn't go back till the following week. As far as I can remember I didn't get any pay for that first week. I'd earned three shillings from the time I was there and the National Insurance at that time was 2/11d so I had a penny in my pay packet. It taught me a lesson, I suppose, and it didn't do me any harm in the long run.

I went into the stoker's shop, manufacturing automatic coal-fire stokers for shell boilers and big water-tube boilers. John Thompson's trademark was La Mont boilers and to broaden my training within the group I was moved to La Mont works and assigned to a team building a marine package boiler for Esso. Then I went on to the pipework fabrication, which didn't seem very interesting initially, but it's where I spent the rest of my life. There was a lot of technical know-how involved and welding technology became a very big part of what I was doing. We were working in all sorts of exotic materials, and manipulating or bending thirty-inch diameter pipes. Bundles of straight tube came in and that would be manipulated into all sorts of things. We bent it, welded it and put attachments on. The first big job I had in the pipeworks contracts department was acting as project engineer on work for the Dounreay fast breeder reactor tubework. Then in 1957 I was put in charge of the workshop building heat-transfer tube bundles for Berkeley Nuclear Power Station.

In 1961 I was appointed deputy superintendent of the La Mont works and in 1964 I went out to Argentina for a short period to sort out the layout and manufacturing facilities for the production of tubework in a shipyard that we were associated with, just outside Buenos Aires. They decided that they would start to make power-station boilers out there, so I went out to sort the manufacturing facilities for the factory and demonstrate certain manufacturing techniques.

Back in the UK the water-tube boiler industry was under immense pressure from the Central Electricity Generating Board to increase manufacturing facilities to meet their projected 8 per cent increase in the demand for electricity. We had ground available at our Bilston factory to put further workshops up, but we could not get industrial development certificates because the government then was trying to persuade people to move out to development areas. So we were offered the old English Electric works site at Larne in Northern Ireland, but that was never a practical proposition. Then we were offered a place at Skelmersdale in Lancashire, which again was not really worthwhile. We finished up taking over the main hangar of Gloucester Aircraft Company, which gave us ninety thousand square feet of manufacturing space. At this time, because of the size and number of power stations the CEGB was planning to build, pressure was put on boilermakers to share contracts and expertise. This led to an association with Clarke Chapman of Gateshead. They had never designed or built the sort of big boilers that we did, but they were based in a development area.

Boilermaking was a major industry in its own right and one of the main crafts within a number of other industries, most notably shipbuilding and the construction of steam engines and railway locomotives. Horwich Loco Works was one of the country's major locomotive-building works. Opened in 1886 by the Lancashire and Yorkshire Railway, by 1907 it had already produced its thousandth engine. In 1923, when the railway became part of the London, Midland and Scottish (LMS) Railway, its chief mechanical engineer, Geoffrey Hughes, was responsible for the design of a highly successful mixed-traffic locomotive which became known as the Horwich Crab. Ken Berry was born in Horwich in 1930. He started work in the telegraph office at the Loco Works in 1944 when he was fourteen years old. As he worked his way up through the company, he encountered the huge range of jobs and skills that were involved in that one business.

There were about seven thousand people there during the war and it was all war effort. They had a bullet shop and they made tanks and flails for tanks and for mines. The women worked on what jobs women could work on. I don't think there were any women working on tanks in the erecting shop; that work was too heavy for them. At the end of the war there were possibly five thousand people still working there. Some of the women stopped on for quite a while after the war; others left, others moved out of the workshops into the offices.

When I was sixteen year old, I started a seven-year apprenticeship in the machine shop. But I wanted to become a millwright, so I eventually got a transfer. In the millwright's shop there were at least twenty-five to thirty apprentices at that time and there must have been a few hundred apprentices in total at the works. There were patternmakers and joiners, fitters and turners – every trade had its apprentices there. To me, it was fantastic. I started my apprenticeship as all the lads in the millwright shop did with a little fellow called Robin Marsh. He was in his latter days but he was brilliant for apprentices. You'd go stage by stage doing different jobs, maintenance jobs and anything that came in that needed work doing on it, like well pumps and jiggers for the cranes. There were some good lads there. You enjoyed your work in them days. We had a good foreman too, Mr Leach. He had an assistant called Cecil Crewe and Cecil looked after all what we called the outside gang, which did all the maintenance of the whole of the works. You could go anywhere on the works to maintain cranes, hoists, lathes, shaping machines, milling machines, the whole lot. It was a great experience.

After nationalization in 1948, locomotive building at Horwich Works continued at a high level for another ten years and British Railways continued to overhaul steam engines there until the mid-1960s. Ken worked there throughout this period.

When I was twenty-one I could have gone in the offices, either the drawing office or the plant office, but I wanted to do my National Service. So I did two years in the Royal Navy and when I came back I started back in the millwright shop and gradually worked my way up the ladder. They put me back on the outside gang and I used to deal with every manager when I was doing that – it was a terrific experience. You might get something that wanted a repair that needed a casting and you had to pro-gramme the whole job, all that the pattern shop were going to do and what the foundry was going to do; you could progress the job all the way along.

In that works everything was based on getting practical experience. Even my mates, who were just fitters working in the erecting shop, progressed through all the engines stage by stage and, at the end of the day, when they finished their apprenticeship it didn't matter what they had to do on an engine, they could do it.

Horwich had its own foundry and we had the millwright shop next to us, which was a maintenance shop for the whole of the works; then there was the joiner's shop and the pattern shop. In the joiner's shop they would make ladders and also the beams for the old derrick cranes. In the pattern shop they would make patterns for everything that was needed to build or repair a steam locomotive – big cylinders and everything that was cast iron on a locomotive was started off in the pattern shop. In the machine shop they had every type of machine. It didn't matter what you wanted, you could get it machined. Then there was the smithy. Hooks for cranes and anything that a blacksmith made you could get made there. And there was a boiler shop where they made all of our boilers on site. In the boiler shop I think there would have been at least 150 people working – and not just making boilers; they would be making frames for the locomotives as well and these would be finished off in the erecting shop. When you think there was a Boilermakers' Union and it hardly exists now. All these skills and trades that we had there have gone almost completely now.

From there I moved on to examining the cranes and lifting tackle for the whole of the works. Then I was given responsibility for the outdoor machinery, things like the coaling plants and turntables, for a region that stretched all the way from Birmingham to Glasgow. On that outdoor machinery job I dealt with every shop on the works, every foreman, everybody in the main offices. I had to deal with the stores, the production people, people in the drawing office, because looking after all that machinery covered everything. That was a good job.

Then in 1963 I went up to Carlisle to be mechanical

foreman. That was at the time they were upgrading the West Coast Line. They had a Chief Civil Engineers School in Watford and British Rail wanted me to go down there as a lecturer. I did it temporarily, but I couldn't move down to Watford because it was too expensive. Anyway, this job cropped up at Horwich so I moved back there. When I came back I was the maintenance superintendent for the whole of the works, apart from the foundry. I'd only done it for about eighteen months when I got made manager, but we weren't doing any locos by that time.

The railways themselves were still big employers. After the war locomotive building continued to flourish and with so many things being made in works and factories throughout the country the railways provided the main means of transport. Great long goods trains pulled by dirty black locomotives belching out clouds of smoke clanked their way along the pre-Beeching[17] railway network that crisscrossed the country. At nationalization in 1948 British Railways had nearly twenty thousand route miles. Reg Sawyer was based at Hereford and worked on the goods trains that ran from Birmingham to the Welsh border.

I left school in Hereford in 1937 when I was fourteen and there was a vacancy in the locomotive department

---

[17] Richard Beeching, commonly known as Dr Beeching, was chairman of British Railways in the early 1960s. His report *The Re-shaping of British Railways*, commonly known as the Beeching Report, led to the closure of over four thousand miles of Britain's railway network on grounds of cost and efficiency.

at the Hereford Barton engine sheds on the other side of town. I and eight others went for a sit-down examination – maths, arithmetic, spelling and dictation. I didn't pass, so the examiner said to me, 'Come back, son, when you've grown a bit more.' Then a vacancy arose for a telegraph messenger at the railway station at Hereford Barton when one of the lads left to join the Grenadier Guards. I applied for it and went to Chester for the interview and my mother came with me on the train. This time I got the job.

When I started it was really interesting work. I had several duties to perform – taking out messages to various offices around the station and the goods department and to the refreshment rooms as well, and also we had to learn the Morse Code instruments. There was one called the single needle. It was a black instrument with a handle and a needle which you pushed to one side for a dot and the other for a dash. Then the other instrument was a sounder[18] to Birmingham Snow Hill, Worcester and Gloucester. I used to like the sounder, and this clerk I used to work with, Mr Modge, was a bit nervous of this instrument so he said, 'Son, will you send this message for me to Birmingham?' So I used to do everything. I used to operate the telegraph exchange, the signalling instruments and the sounder.

One of the chief clerks said to me, 'I'd like you to apply for a clerical job here.' When I did they wrote back from Chester wanting to know if I'd had a

---

[18] Receiving instrument for Morse Code.

secondary-school education. Well I hadn't, and that was it. So then I had to go as a shunter instead, up in the yard at Hereford. I started there, and what a difference this job was to telegraph messenger. It was dirty and you were out in all weathers, twelve hours, seven days a week and seven nights a week.

While I was a shunter at Hereford I also joined the Home Guard. I was only about seventeen and a half and I had a Canadian rifle which was nearly as tall as me. I kept it at home in the living room with ten rounds of ammunition. We used to guard the telegraph office, two of us on at a time, and also a railway bridge over the River Wye just outside Hereford at night.

On the late shift in the telegraph office you also had to work the telephone exchange. One night we heard enemy aircraft approaching, so I said to the telegraph clerk that I was on with, 'I don't know about you, Charlie, but I'm off.' He said, 'I'm coming as well,' and we ran up the platform over the road and into the air raid shelter. Just as we did a German plane flew over – it was only passing over, probably on a bombing raid for Liverpool. A week later we had to go before the stationmaster for deserting our post. All he did, though, was just tell us off; we weren't disciplined or anything.

One night there were three of us on the sidings and I had terrible pains in my stomach so the head shunter said to me, 'Go and get your head down in the cabin.' Well this cabin was only a small wooden hut, enough for four people; no light, no nothing, just a little coal fire. I went there but the pain was getting worse. I managed to get home, but the next thing I was rushed into hospital at Hereford with a burst appendix. I was off work for quite a while and before I started back I went to a convalescent home in Par in Cornwall for two weeks. This home used to be free because we used to have to put so much money from our wages each week towards it. When I eventually got fit I started back on the railway but they put me on light duty in what they called a 'ground frame' – just a few levers to operate some of the points on the siding.

From there I applied for a job at the goods yard the other side of the town at Hereford Barton and I went over there when I was twenty years of age in 1943. I was a goods guard on freight trains. The hours we used to put in were long. I've done as much as eighteen and twenty hours at a stretch. During the war all the journeys took a long time. It was only fifty-three miles from Hereford to Shrewsbury but it took twelve hours to get there. And then you had to get home as well and the ruling was you had to have twelve hours off as rest.

A goods guard has much more to do than a passenger guard. It's different work altogether. All a passenger guard does is blow a whistle to start the train off and wave a green flag. But a goods guard has got to take a tally of his train, see that it is all coupled up properly and that all the doors are closed. He's also got to make sure that the class of engine is right for the load it's pulling. Only about five or six of the wagons would be coupled to the engine and the rest were all loose-coupled, so when the train went through a dip the guard had to know where to put the brake on that he had in the guard's van to keep the couplings tight and when to take it off when it started going on the rising gradient. He also had to know where all the catch points were as well. There were thousands of rules and regulations on the railway and I studied these from A to Z every day.

One day I had to go on a train that had come from near Chester and the driver had been drinking so much that me and the fireman had to help him up on the engine. We were going to Shrewsbury on this goods train and the fireman had to do the driving! But I've gone to work drunk, as a guard. There were times when I couldn't even sign my own name to book on duty, but you couldn't get the sack for it. The fella in charge just said, 'You've been having a few, haven't you? You'd better go and have a lie down and sober up.' It was well known for drinking on the railway. Now you'd have the sack if you're seen going into a pub, which is right. There were thousands of rules and regulations on the railway and the first rule was that intoxicating liquors must not be consumed on duty, but nobody took much notice of that.

As you were approaching a place called Little Mill Junction there was a cottage where a ganger[19] lived with his wife. When the driver of a goods train went by this cottage he would blow his whistle and the lady would come out and when the guard's van came along she came out into the garden and pulled her clothes up. All the train crews knew about this.

---

[19] Someone who oversaw a gang of workmen.

On the way to Abergavenny there was a falling gradient and the goods guard's job here was to walk down the side of the train and put the brakes on each of the wagons. Usually the guard would work his way down the train and get back into the guard's van, but one night the driver was going too fast and I couldn't get back on the train so it went on its own down to Abergavenny. So I went to the signal box and the signalman said, 'Where have you come from?' I said, 'I'm on that train and it's gone without me. I couldn't get on.' So then they had to send what they call a bank engine from Abergavenny to pick me up.

I was on a goods train one night going to Pontypool Road and I knew there was ammunition on it. After we left Abergavenny I could see blue smoke coming out of one of the vans, so when I passed the next signal box I showed the signalman the red flag and we stopped at the next station. I walked down the train and what had caused it was a glass containing acid had burst and all the acid was burning out of the bottom of the wagon. The driver came back as well and put a handkerchief around his nose, because the smell of the acid was terrible. I had to get in touch on the phone to the Newport Control and they said, 'You'd better get this up to the Little Mill Junction yard as quickly as possible.' I said, 'There won't be any bottom left in this wagon.' So in no time a signal came down and we were away.

Opposite Hereford Station was a little café that was open continually, day and night. There were three girls who worked there and on a Sunday morning I used to nip off a bit early. Instead of finishing at six o'clock I used to nip off about five to take one of these girls home. There was an inspector who had reported me twice for this, then the third time he reported me I thought this time I'm going to get the sack, so I resigned and went to work at Bulmer's cider factory. Then at Hereford they formed a new gang called the Mulwell Gang and I went back to the railways to work on that. There were five of us and our job was putting up fences at the side of the railway line and digging holes for the posts. I really enjoyed that, the outdoor life, but me and a friend of mine transferred to London to the relaying gang in West Ealing. I did that for a while and then I applied for goods guard at Old Oak Common in London and I got the job.

While I was there my aunty, who lived in Birmingham, wrote me a letter and said, 'I've met a very nice girl I'd like you to meet.' Her name was Daphne Staime. I used to be a devil for the ladies when I was young, so I arranged to meet her and I took a liking to her, so I applied for a transfer to Birmingham and I got a job as a guard at Small Heath. Eventually we got engaged, but she gave me the ring back about four times because I was drinking too much. We did eventually get married on 1 March 1952 and we had two sons.

When I was foreman at Small Heath there was a signal box and the signalman there was known as Rock and Roll Dave. One day it was very quiet so he went home. But somebody rang up saying that a train was coming in from Weymouth with tomatoes from the Channel Islands. I'd got Dave's phone number and when I rang him he started to panic. I said, 'Don't get panicking. Just tell me what levers I have to pull to get the train in and where do you keep the key?' He told me and I let that train in the sidings, then I ran down from the signal box and detached the wagons myself.

They had these diesel shunters they brought in after the steam engines and I could drive these – they were ever so simple. A young driver came in one night from Birmingham New Street and he said, 'Hey, Reg! You can drive one of these, can't you?' I said, 'Why?' He said, 'I've got a woman coming down tonight and I'm taking her to the old disused cabin.' So he was in the cabin with this girl and I was doing his job driving his shunting diesel. We'd have had the sack if they'd found out about it.

When I was in Birmingham I started doing a signalling course. It was a correspondence course and after about twelve months you had to do a written examination and you were there all day long doing it. The money wasn't very good on the railway; what made it up was all the overtime. If you could work overtime you made a lot of money. But if you didn't work any, the money was very poor. A lot left the railway and went to work as postmen where the money was more and at Hereford a lot of the young firemen left and went to the police force.

*

Besides Lancashire and the West Midlands there were many other manufacturing centres throughout Britain, producing a wide variety of goods. Leeds, which had built its reputation on wool, clothing manufacture and engineering, was typical. The city had a long history of involvement with the wool trade and by the middle of the nineteenth century had over a hundred woollen mills, employing more than ten thousand people. The demand for machinery for the mills created opportunities for engineers and during the nineteenth century many engineering companies were established in the city to produce and export textile machinery, steam engines, locomotives, traction engines, cranes and other heavy engineering products. By 1900 engineering was the biggest employer in the city, providing work for 20 per cent of the male population.

Hunslet, an inner-city area of Leeds about two miles south of the city centre, was home to large mills and factories built in the nineteenth century for the manufacture of wool and flax, and there were also chemical works, glass manufacturers and potteries. With a good supply of coal from nearby mines, it became a centre for all branches of the iron trade, including the production of iron, locomotive and traction-engine building and boiler-, machine- and tool-making. Many railway locomotives were built in the Jack Lane area of Hunslet. By the 1920s the population of this small place was around eighty thousand, packed into narrow streets of terraced houses which remained in use until the neighbourhood was redeveloped in the 1960s. Today it is carved apart by motorways, but for most of the twentieth century several engineering companies were based here, including the locomotive builders the Hunslet Engine Company, and John Fowler & Co., who manufactured traction engines and steamrollers.

John Grant was born in Goodman Street in Hunslet and spent his early years there. Although he moved to a new council estate on the edge of Leeds he spent all his working life at a Hunslet engineering firm, where he became a shop steward.

When the houses were pulled down we were the last ones to move out of our street. We got a brand-new house on Broadway Brook in Moor Grange and it were a good estate. But I still spent my life up in Hunslet, because I worked there and I was involved in a boys' club there as well. So I've never really left Hunslet. Even going for a drink, I very rarely went in the pubs up Moor Grange – I always came to Hunslet.

It sort of hits you when you leave school – all your mates have gone. I got right bored and a kid in our street had just joined the boys' club. I'd never even heard of it, even though it was probably only half a mile from Goodman Street where I lived, but he took me down and I were there for forty years! There was all sorts of sport there: football, rugby, table tennis. We had several players played for Great Britain Rugby League that came from the boys' club. Everyone that's born in Hunslet is a rugby player if they're a boy, so we never struggled for players. Just knock on somebody's door and somebody will come out with some rugby boots. The club leader was a brilliant man called Cliff Goodyear, and we were brought up to behave right. It were probably a bit stricter than schools at some stage, but it were right to be like it was.

All my family were tailors. My dad worked at the top of Government Street at a place called Fielding's and it were like a shop that cleaned suits. He was the hand-presser, the one who put all the neat pleats in your trousers. I can remember as a kid people coming before weddings and things to our house, and fetching their suits for my dad to spruce up. But he didn't have his own press at home. He just had an iron that was on the fire. He used to get it all hot on the fire and clean it on a rag and then put a damp cloth over the clothes he was doing and then press them. But people in our street, if they were going anywhere special at the weekend, they'd come down and give him threepence to press things for them. This was good because he was very badly paid.

My two brothers worked in tailoring, my mother and dad worked at tailoring, and I were destined to go to Burton's. But I just kicked up and said I didn't want to. You see, the firm I wanted to work for was in the same street where I lived: George Mann's. It belonged to Vickers-Armstrongs and they made printing machines. They did most of the machines for the Bank of England at that time – all your banknotes were done on their machines. I'd met some people who worked there, when us kids were playing football in the street. They'd have a bit of fun playing with us as they were coming past and so I got to know some of them. They used to do a lot of work away from home and they told me this was an experience, going working away; it sounded so exciting – much more exciting than Burton's. But first I had to get the backing of my parents to go there. They wanted me to go into tailoring; they didn't think it would work for me to do anything else. You see, when I first went to school I were very poor and they didn't have all the classes they put you in now if you were behind. At that time, if you got behind you were behind for ever, all the way through school. So my record wasn't good. Anyway, I went down to George Mann's. It was just after the war, in the early 1950s, and it was just getting booming again. They actually wanted thirty-two apprentices and they could only get twenty-eight, so you couldn't fail to get a job, really.

Starting there was the biggest shock of my life. I went down on the Monday to start and there were twenty-six of us in this big office. Two didn't even bother to turn up. One by one and two by two somebody would come up, probably foremen from different departments, and take them away. So the group was getting less and less and I was still there. Eventually there were just four of us and someone came for two, so there was just me and this little lad and somebody came for him! Then this bloke said, 'Oh, by the way, you've got to wait for personnel to come.' Well they didn't start until nine and this was half past seven. I really thought, 'I haven't got a job here. There's something gone wrong and I haven't got a job.' The personnel manager came in eventually. He frightened me. He was a bit like a headmaster to me. He said, 'I'm sorry to tell you, young man, you're not old enough to start.' I was only fourteen at the time and he said, 'You can't start until you're fifteen.' It wasn't a great problem because I was fifteen the day after, so he said, 'Come back next week. You'll be all right.'

My first job was with the guy in the time office

called Bill Marsden and I were his runabout if he wanted owt – sandwiches and cigs and stuff like that. They had a butcher's bike and I fell off it going round the corner to the fish shop and a car ran over the back wheel. They took me back to work but I never did that job again. Then I moved into the main offices. I was like an office boy, which was quite good because one of the bosses in there was a staunch Leeds United fan. He found out that I liked to go and see them and when they played away two or three of them used to go and they used to take me and it didn't cost me anything because they used to treat me. I played football for the firm's team as well.

The thing that impressed me when I first started was that they all wore white shirts and ties in engineering. And when I saw photographs on the walls of people fifty year before that, they were all wearing flat caps and white shirts. I can remember when I were eighteen I used to go out with a tie on a Saturday night and all my mates did. When I first started work Saturday was part of the working week and, even though as an apprentice you weren't allowed to work on Saturday, you had to put your forty-four hours in. So I started at half past seven in the morning and finished at half past five.

You could always smoke in the factory, which I couldn't believe, and two lads got £25 for putting a fire out. Little did the company know, though, that they had started it when a cigarette end set fire to some paper under the machine. But because they'd been quick and got the extinguisher and put it out, they got awarded £25 each.

I were so shy at that time it were unbelievable. But I went out on to the factory floor and I went into the oil-grooving department where they put grooves in the castings so oil could get around all the cylinder head. I did about three months there, then I went into what we called the fitting shop, where all the small parts were assembled. There were thousands of them, so you'd be doing something different every other day. It was a big fitting shop and there was a sort of harmony in there.

[As apprentices] we had to go to night school three nights a week. It was at Coburn School and it were half past seven until nine. I never missed a session in the first year, but because my education wasn't very good I failed, so they said I'd have to re-sit it. I were getting a bit down and knew that I couldn't do it again. By this time I had moved into the main erection shop that built the printing machines and I was eighteen. The two bosses, Donald Bury and Tommy Pye, had me in the office. 'You're going to have to go to night school, John, or we're going to have to finish you. We've just finished two in the machine shop,' they said. 'All right,' I said, 'I'll go.' I went about twice, but I knew I couldn't do it so I went to the under-manager and said, 'Don, I just can't hack it. Honest I can't. If you're going to sack me, you'll have to sack me.' So he said, 'How do you fancy going to Newcastle? De La Rue[20] are moving lock, stock and barrel to a trading estate in Gateshead and we're going to send a team up to fit all

[20] Printers of banknotes.

the machines up for them. If you're out of the factory, you're out of sight and you're out of mind. You'll be all right.' George Mann's made all the machines for De La Rue, so I went there, which finished my night school.

I were there for just short of a year and by the time I came back I was nearly nineteen and I was one of the lads. By that time we'd moved to Moor Grange and I used to get the bus down to work with the guy who was the work's convener – that's the head shop steward over the whole factory. He said to me on the bus one day, 'How do you fancy being junior shop steward?' I said, 'I can't do that. I can't get on the stage and talk.' But he said, 'Look, I promise you that if you do it we'll only ask you if there's anything that apprentices are struggling with. You're not going to talk on stage or anything like that. Just listen to what we all say and we'll move on from there.' Anyway, he talked me into doing this apprentice shop steward job and I did that for two years until I were twenty-one. It was good, because it brought me out of my shell a little bit.

Every four years they used to have a printing-machine exhibition at Earls Court, and you really were star man if you got on that as an apprentice. I went when I were twenty, so I knew I'd got a job for life then. For the exhibition we used to build a machine in the factory, take it to pieces and trans-port it down to London. We only had a fortnight inside Earls Court to rebuild it and normally it took a lot longer than that to build one of our machines, but we took this one down in bigger parts. We'd work day and night on it to get it up and printing. If you were going out on a job like this you needed three or four different types of spanners. To get these we had a tool club where they took two shillings or four shillings [10 or 20p] off your wage and you'd go to a place called Bruce's where you got 20 per cent discount to buy your own spanners. Later on, though, the company provided them.

When I went in for my indentures, when I were twenty-one, they give you this book to say that you'd passed your apprenticeship, shook hands and then they actually sacked you! Then they'd reinstate you because they wanted you. Of course they offered it to everybody who'd been there for five year, because those who didn't stick it would've left well before that. When I got my indentures they wanted a shop steward in the fitting shop, so I thought, 'Here we go again.' No one would do it, so Alf said again, 'John, we need you. You've been doing it two years. You're all right.' I'd come out of my shell by then so I took the job on and I was shop steward almost until I packed in. I finished up as the works' convener after Alf retired.

I found the men in the fitting shop were very much together on most things. We all thought roughly the same way. In the machine shop you got favourites and the foreman would give some people better jobs and so they made more money. But in the fitting shop I'd like to think that happened very little. In the end we came up with a system that we'd share all our bonuses with everybody in the shop. So if you were on a job that you were struggling with and you didn't make as much as you should, it all went into the same pot and was divided up between everybody. Everyone had to come into that system – it weren't an option. We did it for years and it were great. There were times you'd make a mistake maybe, and there were times when everything went right and you were dozens of hours in front of yourself. I had one or two people in that shop who were getting older, and as a result they were getting slower, but we could handle that. I didn't mind working with them and doing that bit extra to make up for them, because just listening to tales of where they'd been, Timbuktu and Afghanistan, used to fascinate me and I wanted to go away myself more and more.

My very first job going outside was at a place called Harrison's in Low Road in Leeds. The problem they had on a machine there was just a little spring. It must have fallen off and gone through the machine. It had done no damage, but they couldn't find the spring so I was asked to go and put a new one on. I was shaking because I'd never been out on my own. They took me there in the firm's van, but by the time I got there I'd lost the spring and had to come back for another one. You could have just put an elastic band on it, quite honestly, and it would have done the same job, and if people at the printers were a bit more savvy that's what they did. I went once or twice repairing machines up at De La Rue's and if you looked around at the machines there half of them had elastic bands because springs had fallen off.

I could have got a job at the *Yorkshire Evening Post*,

because we did their machines, but it would have been too tying. Where I was I could do what I wanted with the boys' club; I could take time off any time I wanted. Sometimes I'd go into the office and say, 'I've just had a phone call – something's cropped up. Do you mind?' And they'd always say something like, 'Just put in a dentist appointment when you come back.' I've been single all my life, so I didn't need the money that married men needed. The wages I got were more than ample for me and the benefit of being able to take time off now and again when I wanted was worth a lot to me. I didn't do a lot of overtime because I didn't need the money and anyway we always made way for anybody who really needed it, like a youngster who had to get married or had a family. We made sure they got in at the weekend for overtime. That's how good it were in the fitting shop.

In the late 1960s George Mann's merged with Crabtree's, who manufactured newspaper printing presses for Fleet Street and often I went there to work on the machines. Fleet Street kept Crabtree's going for years. If you worked in Fleet Street there were no better restaurants than those in the printing houses. It were twenty-four-hour working, so the canteen was there all the time. For £1.50 you could go and have a chef's meal; the food was brilliant in Fleet Street. Most places we went to had a canteen and if it were a small firm they'd say, 'Do you mind coming when everyone else has finished? There'll be something left and if not we'll make you something.' The machines we were working on were really big, like three floors going up. The paper reels would go on the bottom, then the people who put the ink on and looked at the print and all that would be on the next floor, and then the sheets would come off at the top. Some people at the top would never meet the ones working downstairs, even though they were on the same machine. The very first machines when I first started used to run at 2,500 sheets of paper an hour and when I finished they were running at 10,000.

[I was in] an installation team. We were a team of guys that never came in the factory – about ten engineers who worked out all the time, but if they needed twenty for a job they would take ten from the shop floor. We got well paid on expenses. We used to get something like £12 a week when I first started working away.

George Mann's had a tremendous name wherever you went up and down the country. If you worked at George Mann's you knew your job and you were good at it. There were no half-measures: even if it took you a lot longer, a job was always right when it was finished. Machines always had to pass a test in our factory and there were no comebacks when they went out into the world. So I never wanted to leave there.

Irene Wharton was born and brought up in Hunslet. She had worked in tailoring from the time she left school, but during the war women worked in all manner of production, from making ammunition to tanks, aircraft and electronics. Hours were long and much of the work was heavy. When war broke out Irene left tailoring and went to work for Clayton's boilermakers as a rivet-heater.

I used to warm [the rivets] red hot, take them out of the stove and throw them up to this old lad we used to call 'dumb lugs'. He'd been in there years and years. There was a big platform and there were all these long rails on it and he were on top of that. A crane would come and put one of these rails on top of the other then he'd have to rivet it together. There were two holes in the rails and he'd line them up and I'd say, 'Here you are, dumb lugs,' and throw the rivet to him. He'd have his cap ready and he'd catch them in that and hold them in it. I'd be on this stove and it would be all red inside, and I used to have to keep it hot with a foot pump. But if there were no rivets about and you had no work to do you used to let it die down. It were a man's job, but I enjoyed it and we used to have some good laughs.

After that I were on welding. We used to have whatever it was we were making on a dais that you used to twist round to weld the parts together. You'd have three parts, but you welded two of them together and then the other part used to be like a screw lid. It was easy enough, but for things that needed gas welding we used to have to go to Garnett Road where they had a big shop. We used to do them up there because the place we worked was under cover and it was dangerous to do it there. It used to blow up in your face. At Garnett Road it wasn't under cover so it was safer. I used to go up there with some jobs, but it were cold. A fella used to go up

there with you because you always had a man working with you to make sure that everything was all
right.

I had what they call 'eye terror'. You would get it
when you were walking out of the welding shop and
you'd get a flash from the welding that nearly
blinded you. You used to put your hand up to shield
your face. When you were doing the welding you'd
have a face mask on to protect your eyes, but not
when you were walking round the welding shop.
Without the mask the flashes from the sparks could
blind you. I'd wake up during night and have to put
milk on my eyes to soothe them.

Then I went on to work on these big buoys that
they used to send out to sea. You had this welding
tackle in your hand and then you'd have some steps
to climb up to get into the buoy and work inside it.
The lads there were all right. They said to me, 'Irene,
would you like to go working in the forge?' If there
was snow on the ground they'd say, 'Go on, you'll be
lovely and warm.' But it were really red hot in there
and by God did they earn some money.

I think I did everything at Clayton's. I went in the
fitting shop and you used to have to take your rings
off in there. That was the only time my wedding ring
came off. Sometimes they'd ask you to work until
seven if they were busy. But it was poor money. I had
£2.10s [£2.50] a week. What I used to earn in sewing
before the war was a hell of a sight more than what
that were. I could earn good money in sewing,
always have done.

After the war I was going to go back into sewing,

but the sewing they were still doing was khaki and hospital blues so I decided to try something different. My brother-in-law said, 'Irene, would you like a change from sewing? They're just opening a new shop up Woodhouse Lane and it's Somnus Bedding, where they make mattresses.' So I went there and the woman in charge said, 'I'll put you in the chippy room.' They're the little things that go through the mattress that hold it together. We didn't actually put them through, we just made them. They got put through by machine. There were a hundred in every bundle and you could do a bundle in about twenty minutes and it were good money. She put me in charge of the downstairs cellar, but I was worse than the lasses. She said, 'I don't know if I'm doing right putting you down there. You're always singing and dancing.' We used to have round chairs with wheels on that swivel, because you used to move around a lot. Anyway, I was on this thing and I was singing 'We put a nickel in the telephone. Dial my baby's number, ooh ah'. She came and she stood there and everybody was killing themselves laughing because I hadn't seen her. This was because there were a big window that looked on to a yard and I was waving to somebody while I was singing. She said, 'I'll ooh ah you if you don't get down off that chair. You're going to break your neck.'

I stayed there for a bit, but then I went back into sewing at Mickey Appleton's and I was there for twenty-five years. I were one of these that's a floater. If there was somebody away I used to go on their machine. There was only one thing I wouldn't do and that were trousers. I used to hate trousers because when it came to sewing a long length I couldn't do it. I had to do it by hand – I hated sewing a long length by a machine. While I was there Mick said, 'Will you do me a favour? Will you take all the alterations on for me please?' So I said, 'Oh, on one condition: that they're unpicked before I get them.'

I enjoyed it there. We used to smoke at the machines and he never used to say anything other than if inspectors were coming round. When they did he used to say, 'Will you promise me you won't have a cigarette in view?' I used to say, 'He must think they're blind.' But he were well in with the inspectors. He said to me one day, 'Irene, what's in that ladies' toilet?' I said, 'Nowt really. It's just an ordinary toilet.' He said, 'Well they're going in to have a look round.' When they'd gone he said, 'Come here you. You didn't tell me there were bloody flowers in the fire bucket, did you? That's supposed to be full of sand. It's a fire bucket, not a bloody flower bucket!'

He were a good lad, though. He went in partnership with Jack somebody or other and the two gaffers used to go to America and bring all the styles over. I used to love working there – you got some really good styles to work on. But Jack parted with him and opened up on Hunslet Lane and he tried to get some of us to go with him. Our gaffer went mad when he found out. 'If he takes one of my bloody lasses,' he said, 'he's got me to deal with!' He got hold of me when I was just out at dinnertime and said, 'Come here,' and he took me in a corner. 'You're leaving, aren't you?' he said. I told him I wasn't and he said, 'I was playing golf yesterday morning at Moortown and somebody said, "You're going to lose one or two of your girls, aren't you?" I couldn't put them bloody golf clubs away quick enough to get on to my solicitor.'

When I was fifty-nine I took early retirement. They asked me if I'd go back. But me dad had had two bad strokes; he couldn't talk at all and he were at home. And me mam was looking to him and she said, 'I can't manage your dad, Irene. He'll have to go in a home.' So I said I'd pack in work. She said, 'Aye, but you're going to lose your wage.' I said, 'It doesn't matter. I'll help you.' Anyway I packed it in. Mickey said to me, 'If owt happens to your dad, Irene, God love him, will you come back?' I said I would, but he'd already sold up before I could.

Leeds had a long history of involvement with tailoring. The city developed as a centre of the woollen industry but as it began to decline in the face of competition from towns like Bradford and Halifax in the second half of the nineteenth century, the ready-made clothing industry grew to take its place, often in the mills that had been abandoned by the woollen manufacturers. The industry flourished and companies like Burton's and Hepworth's, which were soon to become household names, were established. By the start of the First World War a quarter of women workers in Leeds were employed in the industry and it remained a major employer until the 1970s. Enid Rice from Leeds started work in the industry as a machinist in the 1940s. Over the years she was employed by a number of different companies, but her first job was with a tailor called Sid Field.

I left school at Christmas when I was fourteen and I started work the day after Boxing Day at this tailor's. They taught you every aspect of cutting and sewing and putting the clothes all together. I used to make trousers and waistcoats. I liked machining, so I did a lot of that, but I also did hand-sewing. The lapels on the jackets all had to be done by hand. I used to do pockets as well and all aspects of the linings.

Mr Field's father had started off the business with Marks & Spencer's when it was just Marks in Leeds. He used to tell me a lot of stories about his father. They were Jewish and all the family helped; even the little kids used to come on a Saturday. They used to come and take all the tacking seams out and his father used to do all the pressing. It were very much a family thing. It were nice working for Mr Field because he used to say, 'Put your tin hats on and I'll tell you a war story.' You were also close to girls you worked with and we always went to each other's weddings.

I also worked at Burton's, but I didn't like it there. I wasn't used to that atmosphere. You had to do your quota every day and if you didn't they wanted to know why. Burton's used to look at everything you'd done and if it wasn't right you got it back and you had to re-do it. And if it wasn't right then, you'd get it back again and again and again. There were these lines that you worked on and everybody had a different job. You just did your own bit of it and it was very repetitive. You just did a little bit and then somebody else on another line would do another little bit. They had men working there, but most of the men were cutting. I didn't see any men doing sewing.

When you're on a machine the worst thing you get is going over your finger. That happened on my first job – the needle went straight through my finger. But you've got to do that before you're a machinist. You'll hear that a lot.

Working in the clothing industry suited many women, particularly when they had families to bring up. Hours were flexible: they could work part time and in a lot of cases they were able to work at home. Marjorie Griffin from Leeds started as a machinist after leaving school when she was fourteen in 1945 and later, when she had a family, was able to carry on from home.

When I was fourteen I left school. My birthday were in January and I think I left at Easter. You left on Friday and you started at Monday. You'd go down to the job centre and there were always plenty of jobs in dressmaking and tailoring in them days. I chose it because I had two older sisters and they were in sewing. I used to watch my sister sewing at home; I used to sit for hours watching her, so I really knew how to go about it.

In my first job after school you had to learn how to use a machine and then practise doing lines. Then they'd give you something like a blouse to sew and you'd practise on it. I worked at Marsden's and I was there for about fourteen years. Then the lady that were over me left and went to a place called Blackford's where they made swimwear [so I went too]. Marsden's was a big place and we were on piece work there, but the second place was a lot smaller with only about fifty people working there. We'd work forty-eight hours to start with but then in winter, when orders were not so good, we used to have to work three days a week and then sign on for two days.

I did work at home when I had family and I couldn't get out to work. I had three girls and there were no nurseries in those days so you just sewed at home when they went to school or went to bed. Just to earn a few pounds. Then when the children went to school I went to work in the factory that I used to sew for at home down in Armley. I worked there school hours – nine until three. It was a noisy place with all the machines going at once. It was really warm in the summer when the sun was shining because it had a glass roof and windows down each side. We used to talk a lot and have a laugh. You could talk as long as you kept working, but we were on piece work so we had to keep working. If you stopped working your wage stopped. We used to get blouses to do in sixes and you'd go and have them booked in by the manageress. She'd write it all down what you'd got to sew and when you'd finished she'd book it out again. The time it took used to vary because we had different styles to do. There were easy styles and fancy styles that were more difficult. They used to come and time us for all the different styles. Somebody would come and sit at the side of you with a stop clock and time you doing it. Then they'd work it out how long it took you and how much an hour you were getting.

Throughout the 1950s and 1960s Britain was still making things. From sewing ladies' dresses as an outworker at home to manning an assembly line at a huge car plant like Longbridge, a large part of the working population was involved in manufacturing in one form or another, or in producing the raw materials that were used in the manufacturing process. At a big engineering firm like George Mann's in Leeds they made all their own parts, right down to the smallest screw. But many companies bought in components and parts from outside suppliers, so a lot of work was created in ancillary firms that supported the main industries of the area.

In any industrial region there was a lot of work making small tools and pieces of machinery, or doing repairs for local mills and factories, so every industrial community had its blacksmiths. Neville Wilkinson from Halifax started work as an apprentice blacksmith when he was sixteen years old and later became a welder.

When I left school I worked in a shoe warehouse for twelve months because I wasn't old enough to go into the blacksmith trade, which is what I wanted to do. They said, 'You've got to go into the world and get some experience.' So I did this, then got a job at a blacksmith's as soon as I was old enough. The first day I went there I was stood there for quarter of an hour waiting for the owner to come and open up. When he got there he showed me how to light the forge, which were a big brick-built one. It was about nine foot wide – massive, so big that the whole building it was in wasn't much bigger. There was just enough room to get three horses in, the double forge, anvil, a mechanical saw, a small drill and basically that were it. They were all hand tools.

The first job I had was mending shovels. There were a pile of broken shovels there with their shafts snapped off and once he'd showed me what to do with them he said, 'Right, I'll see you later,' and disappeared. It went on like that for about a week or so till I found out that he were a bookie's runner. He used to go round all the pubs picking up his bets all day.

We made horseshoes and we shoed horses and we did a lot of repairs for local mills, and after three or four years I were more or less running the place. I've always been practical, so I picked up things like that pretty quick. I were there about nine years. But then it were coming up to one winter and I'd just had an accident on my motorbike and my leg were aching a bit. I'd chipped something in my knee and I couldn't do the shoeing. It was no good, because shoeing were half of the work, so I said, 'I'll have to go and get a job somewhere else.'

I got this job [welding] and it were about double the pay and a lot more tackle to work with – five-ton cranes and stuff. It were great. That was at Crowther's Engineering in Halifax. It were a private firm – Fred Crowther owned it. His son at that time had just come into work. Fred came down to me one day, in the plating shop, and he had his son with him. I was welding some tanks at the time and he said, 'Neville, can you just show him how to do these tanks?' I showed him what to do and he got started, but he was so bad I had to say to him, 'Look! You're just wasting my time. I'm going to have to grind all of them out.' So he went off in a huff. Anyhow, I didn't end up in trouble. Fred said I'd done the right thing. After that we got on pretty good, me and the son. Graham Crowther he was called. We used to go off in the three-ton wagon now and again to do jobs. We shared the driving and if it was a long way away like Scotland we'd stop overnight.

I were there about fifteen years, but I was having a lot of trouble. The tanks we made were thirty foot long, nine foot diameter, and you'd put the two halves together and weld them all up. You didn't have face masks. If you wanted fresh air, you'd put an air pipe in from a big compressor and just stir it up. I went in a tank one day, painted some special paint on, and I felt funny. I went outside and were vomiting, sick, and I had to go home. About a month later this other guy went outside and dropped dead. I was getting bad migraines myself because of the etching primers we used to use and I said, 'I'm going to have to leave for a while.' So I left for four months and it cleared up as soon as I left. By this time Graham were in charge and he sent me to a specialist. When I went to see him he said, 'I'm being paid to keep you at work, but privately I'll tell you, leave that place. It's that that's causing your problems.'

Graham came down to see me regular while I was off and one day he said, 'I've got this problem. We've got some conveyors to build. Can you come back and sort it out for me?' So I went back and sorted it all out, then said, 'Right then, I'm off again.' This time they gave me a car to keep me on. I was one of the top earners there, so I carried on another five years but eventually the migraines started getting me again. By then I'd got married and the wife said, 'Just leave it.' So I said 'Okay!' and went off to be a gardening handyman.

In Lancashire and Yorkshire the textile and mining industries spawned a wide range of ancillary industries. Engineering firms manufacturing everything from small parts to massive mill engines and boilers grew to support the factories and coal mines by providing the machinery and parts that they needed. Harry Meadows grew up in Atherton, a small town between Bolton and Wigan, and worked there at Prestwich Parker Nuts and Bolts Works. He says he really enjoyed working there and talks about some of the pranks the workers used to play on each other. But what he remembers most is how primitive the machinery was.

The round metal bars that the bolts were made from were each put into a hole in a metal frame. This was put into the forge. When the end of the bar was white hot you took it out of the frame and put it into a clamp. Then you placed it in a press which shaped the bolt. The machine that I worked on just worked off a big pulley on the left-hand side. Running round the pulley there was a belt and this was fastened to a cam. This turned it round and made the press go up and down. There was nothing mechanical about it, basically. It was just so simple. You'd go in each morning and put plenty of oil on the cam. Then you pressed a treadle on the machine to operate it. But when you took your foot off this treadle it didn't always stop straight away; it might do another couple of rotations and so you had to be careful what you were doing because there was no guard on it. You had to be especially careful when you had to put your hands in the machine to change the dies or the hammers. You'd have to keep your eye on that because it would just turn round a little bit, free-wheel. On this machine I would take the metal out of the fire, put it in the machine which would turn it round and chop the end off, then drop the finished bolt off on to a chute. You needed to work about twelve rows of bolts a day to make your money.

All the machines we worked on were so basic it was unbelievable; they were primitive. But they were making some ginormous bolts on these machines. There was one fella in the shop where I worked who was making bolts with a shaft that was probably eight inches wide, and he probably only made twenty a day. They were ginormous and when he was making them the whole floor shook. There was one machine that four people would work on – it was massive. You'd have one fella on the fire, which had a circumference of about four metres, and he would heat the metal bar up in the fire; another would put it in the machine, crop the heated part off and it would run down a chute. Another fella were there waiting; he had a pair of tongs and he got hold of it with these and put it in the die, then pulled it out when it had been pressed. He threw it back on the chute and then there was another fella put them under another press that cleaned all the edges up.

They were doing that all day and when the tins were full, they'd drag them out and start to fill another.

On a Monday morning, when we went in, we would go down to the warehouse where all the sacks were kept and we'd get a sack and tie a piece of string on two of the corners, then you put this round your overalls because when you were stood up working with this iron, you were just about in the machine. If you had a sack on, it would wear the sack away before your overalls. When you put that hot iron in that machine and pressed that pedal and the water was running on it, it was hit or miss whether you got a bang or not. It could be like a firework going off, so you had a piece of leather or an old glove on the palm of your hand that gave a bit of protection.

There was a water supply dripped on the dies to keep them cool, but you had no guard against getting burnt. They wouldn't stand for it now. You had no wrapping over your mouth or goggles or anything like that, no helmets. And everything in there was belt-driven, so you'd have a motor in the corner, a motor with a belt on, and it would be run across the shop with no guard on it, driving all the machines. They were happy times, but the work wasn't without its dangers and there were many accidents. Lots of men lost fingers in the 'cropper machine' – a guillotine that cut the metal.

I used to take a lot of time off work. I'd get stuck in for four days and then I wouldn't go in on the fifth day. The manager would always get on to me about it. He'd say, 'Right. You've made forty-eight gross last week of bolts. But you're having a lot of time off.' So I just used to say, 'Well how many bolts did Mr Whittaker make on the next machine?' 'He made forty-five gross,' the manager might reply, so I'd say, 'Well I made forty-eight gross and I've only been here four days so I'm having a day off.' He didn't agree with me, but he wouldn't get rid of me because I could flit about on different machines. I could make, say, a ³⁄₁₆ bolt or I could go on and make a 1½-inch bolt.

Friday was pay day and we'd always stop work a bit earlier to get our wages. When we queued up for our pay there was one fella we called Plunger who used to sing for us. He'd start singing and some people would throw coins to him, a halfpenny or a penny. But half of them threw in washers out of the stores at him, pretending they were coins.

I used to like the job. The money wasn't brilliant and I knew I could get the same money window cleaning. So when we went on to short time, first of all four days, then three days a week, I went window cleaning. I finished there on Friday and started window cleaning the day after and I'd never cleaned a window in my life.

I don't think there's any bolt works in Atherton now. And at the time I'm talking about there were five or six. Since then the industry has just about disappeared from round here.

In the 1950s and 1960s working-class people doing manual jobs were still by a very considerable margin the predominant group in British society. The world of work they experienced, however, varied massively, from the sort of small, primitive, family-owned, back-street workshop that Harry Meadows worked in to the huge car factories where processions of car bodies moved relentlessly along the assembly lines. In moving from job to job, 'following the money' as he put it, Ray Barrett saw the extremes.

The machinery changed massively during my time at work. Cummins Diesel Engines was my last job and the machines there were so advanced it was unbelievable. You didn't need to touch them; you were just a machine minder. Before this, when I first started, you were actually operating them so you knew the machine you were on, you understood it. With the modern machines now it's remote control. You could sit and read a book all day. I said to them, 'All you need is my thumb to press the button.' I think I was much more interested in setting up a machine than just operating it. It was boring but at least it was safe there – not like some of the places I worked in. One place was the Birmingham Metal and Battery Company. I wasn't there long, maybe a year in the 1960s. It was known locally at the time as the Blood Tub because the accident book was always full. There was a huge machine there, an extruding mill, which was really a horizontal press. A billet of solid brass or copper went in at one end and the power of it forced out twenty or thirty feet of tubing, like the fifteen-millimetre tube you use in plumbing. The billet was heated up by a furnace man before it went in, and the tube was still hot when it came out. Then it was straightened out and rolled. We didn't make the billets there. They were done in a rat-infested Victorian building in Selly Oak that was still there in the 1960s. It was a huge building but there were only about a dozen people working there. If there was a fault in the copper or brass billet, like an air bubble, it would explode in the extruding machine and fire out like a cannon ball. I remember a little fifteen-year-old lad walked into the extruding mill waving his first wage packet and one exploded and took his head off. Nobody had ever thought there should be a safety device at the end. It was a horrific place.

That was a particularly bad incident but, Ray says, cuts, bruises and burns were the norm. The horrific environment of the Birmingham Metal and Battery Company that he describes was typical of the world of work as experienced by many working-class people. There were plenty of jobs, but a lot of the work was heavy, dirty and dangerous. Conditions for workers, particularly for those employed in the many family-owned, backward-looking manufacturing enterprises that filled Britain's industrial heartlands, were still almost Dickensian and would be illegal today. It was a time when the country could still quite legitimately be regarded as the 'workshop of the world' not just because we were still good at making things, but also because a lot of the jobs that people used to do, the conditions they worked in and the dangers they faced were closer to life in a Victorian workshop than to the second half of the twentieth century.

3

Where Cotton Was King

IN THE 1950s nowhere in Britain had a greater concentration of industrial sites or a wider spread of industries than Lancashire. The majority of the towns in the county were by-products of the Industrial Revolution, with terraced streets, towering mills and soot-stained chapels. Manchester and the towns of the region generated much of Britain's nineteenth-century wealth and pioneered many of its ground-breaking technological achievements.

Above all, Lancashire cotton dominated the world market in textiles and by the middle of the nineteenth century the county had become Britain's major textile-manufacturing base. It was the ideal region for the development of the cotton industry: the climate was damp and there was an ample water supply to turn the water-wheels of the new factories. From the 1750s onwards, as textiles became established, the industrialization of the many small villages in central Lancashire had been rapid. By the middle of the nineteenth century spinning, weaving and dyeing had become fully mechanized, mass-production methods were gradually being introduced and productivity was at an all-time high. As the burgeoning factories needed expanding labour forces, mass migrations took place from agricultural Lancashire into towns like Manchester, Salford, Darwen, Blackburn, Burnley, Oldham, Rochdale, Accrington and Haslingden. When the steam engine replaced water power the county had good reserves of coal to fire the boilers, and as the demand for coal increased the mining industry flourished alongside textiles.

By 1912 the cotton industry was at its peak, and that year the UK produced around eight billion yards of cloth, but the outbreak of the First World War brought the first setback for Lancashire's textile industry. During the war cotton could no longer be exported to foreign markets and those countries, particularly India and Japan, set up their own factories. Not only did these countries produce their own cloth, but they were able to do it more cheaply and consequently the demand for Lancashire cotton went into decline. In these newer textile industries one company would buy in raw cotton and take it through all the stages of production – spinning, weaving and finishing – on one site, ending up with a finished roll of cloth. In Lancashire the trade was as intricately fragmented as it had been in the nineteenth century. Spinning mills bought cotton and turned it into yarn or thread. Weaving mills in their turn bought yarn and produced cloth, which was then finished by independent dye-works, bleachworks and printworks.

Historically, spinning was based in south-east Lancashire around Manchester, Bolton, Oldham and Rochdale, while weaving was concentrated around Blackburn, Burnley and Preston in the north of the county. Around 60 per cent of cotton operatives in Lancashire were women, but spinning – which was more skilled than weaving – was mostly done by men. They worked in bare feet, walking up and down behind long mule spinning frames which ran backwards and forwards on wheels. It was noisy, dirty, dusty, and very hot and humid, with the temperature kept artificially high at around 80°F. In Bolton's mills, which specialized in fine spinning, temperatures could be up to 98°F. The warmer the mill, the finer the spinning, they used to say, because cotton is softest at high temperatures. The weaving sheds were very different. As many as five hundred looms would be packed tightly between narrow alleyways on a vast floor. They were not as hot as the spinning mills but they were even noisier and the weavers, nearly all women, had to learn to lipread because it was impossible to hear each other above the racket of the looms and the belts and line-shafting that powered them. Each weaver would have four looms to look after and supervision was in the hands of men, the overlookers.

Although many of Lancashire's mills remained active and profitable until well after the war, the 1950s was the start of a period of rapid decline as British companies found they were not able to produce cotton as cheaply as their competitors in Asia, and by 1958 the unthinkable happened when the country that had given birth to the textile industry became a net importer of cotton cloth. The same Manchester merchants who for nearly two centuries had bought Lancashire cloth and yarn and exported it now made an abrupt about-turn and switched to importing foreign cloth. The Cotton Industry Act of 1959 was intended to modernize the industry by providing grants to mill-owners to enable them to replace outdated machinery with modern, up-to-date spinning and weaving

Miners at Burradon Colliery,
Northumberland, prepare for the
last shift at the pit in 1975.

Mining was dirty, dangerous and hard, from descending in cramped lifts and wedging in pit props to drilling at seams that were sometimes no deeper than eighteen inches.

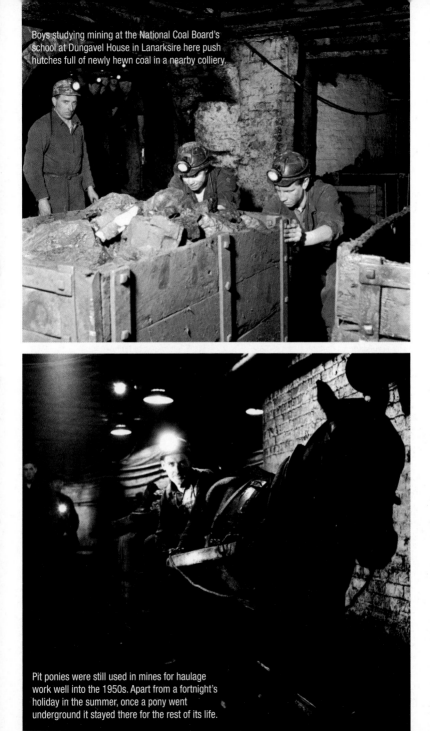

Boys studying mining at the National Coal Board's school at Dungavel House in Lanarksire here push hutches full of newly hewn coal in a nearby colliery.

Pit ponies were still used in mines for haulage work well into the 1950s. Apart from a fortnight's holiday in the summer, once a pony went underground it stayed there for the rest of its life.

Above: Miners in the lamp room at Merthyr Vale Colliery. The only lights in the mines were around the pit bottom. Further into mine, workers had only their own lamps.

Below: Pit baths made a big difference, especially if you had a family; they meant you could bathe and go home in fresh, clean clothes.

Above left: Weekly production totals as miners worked hard to help out during the coal crisis caused by Arctic weather conditions in 1947.

Above right: A Friday-morning scene at the pay desk at Ellington Colliery, 1951. Miners were struggling to produce enough coal to satisfy the needs of Britain's homes, industry and export markets.

The year-long miners' strike, which ended in March 1985, exposed deep divisions in British society and caused great bitterness within the mining communities, which remain to this day.

As many as 500 looms could be packed tightly into the hot and noisy weaving sheds in textile mills. Conditions improved marginally as time went on: machinery was re-spaced and the aisles and alleyways between them were widened.

Above left: Teenage girls on their way home after working a shift at the Lily cotton mill in Shaw, Lancashire in 1957.

Above right: Many of the workers learned to lip-read because it was impossible to hear one another above the din of the machinery around them.

In addition to spinners, weavers and engineers, thousands of managers, administrative staff and designers were employed in the mills.

Above: The cotton crisis. Diversification and cost-cutting did little to improve profits in the 1950s. During the 1960s and 1970s mills were closed down across Lancashire at the rate of almost one a week.

Below: Lancashire cotton workers protest about the use of cheap imported cloth, which decimated their industry.

machines, but it failed to increase either the efficiency of the industry or its competitiveness and could not reverse the remorseless decline. Countless mills were closed down.

Although the decline had already begun by the time the subjects of this chapter were at work in the textiles industry, people's memories of Lancashire in the 1950s are of a landscape full of cotton mills, coal mines, steelworks, canals, railway lines and locomotive sheds. In mill towns like Bolton and Burnley, mighty centres of filth and fume, steam would be hissing and smoke scowling as hundreds of chimneys belched forth day and night over the tightly packed terraces of small Victorian houses. This was a region that truly lived under the cloud of the cotton industry.

The great cotton-spinning town of Rochdale had some of the biggest mills in Lancashire, including some of the last mills to be built in the county. Opened in 1913, Dunlop Mill was once claimed to be the largest cotton mill in the world and it represented the way forward for the Lancashire textile industry. Unlike the smaller specialist family concerns that concentrated on just one part of the trade, Dunlop employed three thousand spinners, weavers, carders, doublers, doffers and winders and stretched for half a mile along the Lancashire and Yorkshire Railway. 'Carders' operated the carding machines that prepared the cotton when it came into the mill by breaking up knots and clumps of fibre. 'Doublers' operated machines that twisted two or more strands of cotton fibre to form a thread. Then, as bobbins on the spinning frames filled with thread, 'doffers' replaced them with empty ones. The 'winders' were the operatives who wound the thread on the weaving looms.

Freda Swarbrick was born in Rochdale in 1922 and

went to work at Dunlop Mill when she left school in 1936.

Dunlop were one of the biggest mills in Rochdale, but it were one of my neighbours that worked there and she got me on. When I started I was learning to double, doubling the yarn. You put four bobbins on and you doubled them up; two to one bobbin or four to one bobbin. You'd to learn how to do it in a week or you were out. You started off laying bobbins on a frame for the doffers. They were the girls who used to come and take the full uns off and go to the winders with them. So that was the next job you did, then you worked your way up. After you'd been doffing you got on a frame, where you had two machines to work for £3 something a week. I've still got me payslips. I always wanted to go winding but my mother said, 'It's not for you, you haven't the patience.' But I thank her for it now, because winders were always on piece work and they'd to make their own wage.

I worked there from when I was fourteen till I got married when I were twenty. Because I was one of the youngest in our family I never had nothing to do as we were growing up. The others did all the work and I used to play out; they used to do all the washing-up and making the beds, so I'd nothing to do. So of course when I got married I were thick; I couldn't even boil water. I always used to be like, 'How do I do this?' But you learn. My husband couldn't cook either, but we learnt together. He was on shifts so when he were on early shift he'd make my tea and when he were on late shift I'd make his tea, so we'd work together.

When I got married I went working at Era Mill on Woodbine Street, doubling. While I were there it was taken over and we had to go to Croft, another mill. You either had to go or lose your redundancy, so we had to go. They were happy times though. At dinnertime we used to go out and sit on the fire escape at Croft having a fag and the boss'd be with us. He used to take us in for pie and peas and half a bitter on a Friday and we used to say, 'We're not going yet, are we?' and he'd say, 'No, have another.' Then we'd go back and bloody hell – you'd be a bit tipsy! Then in the 1950s that shut, so we'd to finish then and we got our redundancy.

Glenice Carpenter was another Rochdale mill girl from a later era than Freda. Glenice was born during the Second World War and started work in the late 1950s, in the dying days of the industry in Lancashire. But by this time working conditions had improved and she would have found things cleaner, safer and more pleasant than Freda had when she started. To make more room in the mills, machinery was re-spaced and the aisles and alleyways between them were widened. Machines were made safer, canteens were introduced and proper washrooms and lavatories were put in. What hadn't changed was that there were still a lot of big families in the mill towns in the immediate post-war years, and Glenice came from one of them.

I've got seven brothers and sisters and I were the little one. I were a twin, but we lost the other when she were two. There's thirty years between us all, from my oldest sister to me. I was the forgotten one. There were that many of them they forgot about the little one. There were always fights going on in the family about one thing an' another. I remember once when one of my sisters hit the other one with a frying pan. She broke her glasses and cut her nose. My father died when I was little and my mother was really strict. She'd never let me go out and I was never allowed to wear make-up. I think it was because she'd had that many problems with all my other brothers and sisters she were making sure she didn't get any with me.

When I was fifteen I left school in the July and the week after I were in work. I started in the warehouse at Shaw Mill. Sometimes the cloth turned over at the edges when they wove it on the loom, so it were sent to me and I had to iron it and I had to do that all day long. I hate ironing, but that was the job I had. The pieces of cloth would get sent down to me and put on the table and I'd have to stand there all day just ironing these edges out. But after I'd been there for a bit I went to be a weaver and when I qualified I went to work in the weaving shed where I got my own looms.

In spite of the improvements in working conditions the mills could still be dangerous places to work and Glenice hadn't been in the weaving shed for long when she was caught in a frightening incident that was all too common in Lancashire's cotton mills. Fire was a constant hazard and there were more fires in cotton mills than in almost any other industry. The inflammable nature of the raw cotton fibre, oil-soaked floors and woodwork, friction from bearings on shafting or machinery or from the rubbing of belts against woodwork, or pure carelessness on the part of employees were all contributory factors, and it would take only an hour to burn down a six-storey mill. Glenice experienced two fires while she was working in the weaving shed at Shaw Mill.

One was where the machinery at the back of me and all the cotton that was on it set on fire and we all had to evacuate. We were very lucky to get out of the shed at all, it went up so quickly. Then one of the looms I was working on set on fire. I was setting it on [up] and it went up in flames. Because of the cotton that was on it the fire just spread very quickly. In no time it was surrounding me; all the looms around me were on fire. It was very frightening. One bit of cotton got hold and all the rest went up. Altogether about fourteen looms were destroyed in that one before they got it under control. But the mill never closed down because of the fires. You just worked round them; you struggled with the rest of the looms that were left. As soon as fires were out you were back at work. The firemen were the mill workers. They call them technicians now, but they were called 'tacklers' then and they used to look after the looms. But they also volunteered as firemen and they got paid extra for this. As soon as you shouted 'Fire!' you've never seen as many people running towards you to help you, because fire was the big thing when you were weaving – either that or being hit with a shuttle.

Many a time I got hit with a shuttle. They'd come

flying off the loom into your side or your stomach or your ankle. You were surrounded by looms so they could come from anywhere and there was nothing you could do to stop them. It was just a fault with the loom, one of those things. It could just be a bit of dust in the warp and if the shuttle caught it, it would send it out. My mother got hit in the stomach with one and she got really bad with it. In fact they actually put that down to why she died of cancer; they said being hit by the shuttle was the onset of it.

But that wasn't the only danger. You had to take your own rolls of cloth off the machine and put another roll on, and as I was taking one off one day it fell on my foot. Now I had clogs on but it still damaged my foot. My toenail will still not grow on that foot and I was seventeen when that happened and I'm sixty-five now. If you were in the carding,[21] the belts were always snapping so you had to be careful because if one of them snapped and caught you, you'd know about it. In carding the belts were always going but we didn't have that problem in the weaving shed.

I worked at Shaw Mill till I was eighteen, then I went on buses for three years until I had me daughter. When I had me daughter I went back weaving. I went to Fothergill and Harvey and I worked there for eighteen years. I worked on cotton when I first went, then I went on fibreglass, then I went on carbon fibre. If they brought a new product in they took the most

---

[21] The mechanical process that breaks up locks and clumps of fibre and then aligns individual fibres so that they are parallel with each other.

experienced person and put them on to that product and I've actually woven asbestos with wire in. One thing about them was when you went on carbon fibre, fibreglass or asbestos you always had full kit on. When I was on it I had a mask on and overalls, completely covered. I don't think they knew how dangerous it was; they were just making sure. One thing I can say about them, they always made sure people were safe. In its heyday there must have been two or three thousand working there. But it gradually got smaller and smaller over the years, especially over this last fifteen years, and it's gone down to making practically nothing now.

In their heyday the bigger mills used to work round the clock. All of them had big Lancashire boilers and the fire-beaters were the men who kept the boilers stoked, shovelling tons of coal into them each and every shift to keep up the steam pressure for the engines that powered all the machinery. There is a story about an engine that had to be repaired during the night to have it working for the first shift the next morning. The chief engineer and the maintenance men thought they'd ironed out the problem and decided they would give the engine a trial run in the middle of the night. They started it up and the next thing they knew was that there were about twenty people outside the mill gates. They'd been woken up by the noise of the engine and thought it was seven o'clock in the morning and time to go to work!

Kath Dunne worked at Moston Mill, close to where she lived in north Manchester, before the war and remembers how the sounds of the mill acted as her alarm clock.

*

You used to have these massive big belts going round that worked the machines, so when you heard the engine starting up in the morning you knew it was time for you to start work. That was at half past seven. If you ever overslept, which wasn't very often, the carder would come and knock you up or he'd send one of the bobbin-carriers. They were the men who used to move all the bobbins in these great big tubs.

The carder used to walk round the card room every so often and if you had any what they called 'big end' – that was cotton on the floor – he'd just make a sort of sweeping movement with this sweeping brush; in other words, get it swept up. I was in the card room and there were massive big frames in there and you had to do all your own cleaning, sat underneath the machines, and you had to oil all the machines. It was very rare for you to take time off work sick in them days. It was always a case of 'Oh, you'll be all right when you get there' if you didn't feel well, and you usually were as well. It was just days we worked when I first started, half past seven till half past five, and you worked Saturday morning as well up till twelve o'clock.

The tenters were the women who looked after the machines and we were working on the frames for whoever was tenting; we were just under tenting. We had to help with the top part and then we did all the cleaning underneath. At first I worked with one tenter and then after I'd been there a while I worked for about three different ones, but then your wage

200

went up to fifteen shilling. You had to be fast, though, and you couldn't sit down. The woman who had the frames was the tenter and she'd be sat down on a little stool at the end of her frames and if she thought you was a bit lax in your work she'd tell you. You had to go and brew up for them as well. Then later on you got your own frames. The one that had the frame, the tenter, told me everything what you had to do, like 'laying on', which was putting your new bobbins in and taking the full ones off. But I hadn't been doing that long when the war started and they closed that mill down till the end of the war and you had to go on munitions, so myself and my sister that worked in the mill with me went to Ferranti's at Hollinwood.

I worked at Ferranti's till the end of the war and then they opened Moston Mill again, so I went back to the mill. All the machines had been oiled and covered during the war and when we went back we had to clean them all before they could put any cotton in again. There were a lot of Polish people came to work in Manchester at that time just after the war and a lot of them used to work in the mills, so they started to bring in shift work when they had all these extra workers. But there were a lot of people like my sister that were very particular. Her machines always had to be perfect. So you'd do all your work and make sure it was right before you went home and then when you come in next morning, if they'd had the shift workers on it and it was all a mess and all untidy she used to go mad.

When they used to come round with the wages they had a little trolley and you had a number and your wages used to be in a little tin. You had to tell them your number and your number would be on top of the tin, and they used to empty it out on your hand and you had to make sure it was right. There was some couples that worked in the same mill and the woman always handed the wages over to the man. You could tell that the man was the boss then. They also had a nursery at the mill and some of them that worked in our room had children in the nursery. Once a year we went on a day trip, usually to Blackpool. They used to have a Lancashire Cotton Queen and the final always used to be at Blackpool.

In the years after the war there was a feeling of optimism in the cotton industry. A poster campaign told the cotton workers that 'Britain's bread hangs by Lancashire's thread'. Order books were full and there was plenty of work for everyone. W. T. Taylor's Victoria Mill in Horwich was the biggest manufacturer of terry towels in the world at that time and after a spell working as a self-employed builder Stanley Bolton got a job there as a maintenance man.

They had their own dye house and bleachworks and there were three weaving sheds, where I had to peg all the looms down. I had to drill the flag floors and fasten the looms down and do the slating and roofing. Another regular job I had was rebuilding the gateposts because the wagons going in with high loads of bales of cotton used to take the bend too quickly and knock the pillars down, and

I had to rebuild them and lift the gates on again.

At twelve o'clock every day the mill would come out. The gates were opened on a rotary mechanical winder and a chap called Josh, who used to be in the gatehouse, would be watching the clock with his hand on the roller that opened the gates. There would be a thousand people all waiting at these gates and they were all chanting, 'Come on, Josh. We want to get home. We want to meet the children from school.' Then the second the clock went on to twelve he started to open the gates, but everybody was in such a hurry to get out that they used to pull them open themselves and they used to break, so repairing them was one of my regular jobs.

I remember going into the weaving shed with some visitors who were being shown round. One of them was a young fella. I was going round with them and before we opened the door to the weaving shed we told them to prepare themselves for the noise in there and to put some cotton wool in their ears if they wanted. There were about three hundred looms in the shed and when we were showing them round I could see this young chap and he was looking at all the ladies working on the looms. There were sixty-year-olds, who'd brought the family up, got bored at home and gone back weaving, and there were also fifteen-year-olds, lovely young women, weaving there. When their ends broke, the girls had to lie on their looms to fix them and when they did they were showing all their legs and everything. I could see this young chap looking at them and while we were walking round he came to me and shouted over the noise

of the looms, 'It won't do for me to work here.'
'Why?' I said. 'Because of the noise?' 'No,' he replied.
'Look at them young women there. I could show
them a thing or two.' Straight away one of the
weavers who was four looms away left her loom,
walked across to him and said, 'Oh no you couldn't.'
'Couldn't what?' the chap said. 'You couldn't show
me a thing or two,' she said. This young man hadn't
realized that all the women in there could lipread
and that she'd been able to see exactly what he was
saying about them.

During Wakes Week the mills would shut down for the
annual holidays and everyone had a reminder of how
dirty the towns really were. This was the only week in the
year when the skies were clear. Blackpool was the mecca
for the holidaymakers, but some stayed at home in the
empty towns, while their friends 'blew in' a year's savings
by the sea. Wakes Week was also the time for maintenance
work in the mills. Boilermakers would come in to carry
out any repairs to the boilers, and these also had to be
cleaned. All the soot used to fall to the bottom and you
could go for twelve months without cleaning them, but
then during Wakes Week the flues would have to be swept.
For this the 'Black Gang' would come in. Stanley Bolton
was in the Victoria Mill's Black Gang, which included all
the maintenance men, the tacklers, the mechanics, the
drivers – a lot of the menfolk who worked at the mill.
They used to pay sixpence or a shilling [2½p or 5p] a week
into a club and then once a year they'd decide what to do
with their savings. 'For four years on the trot,' Stanley
recalls, 'we went to the Isle of Man. We flew from

Blackpool, did a tour of the island and come back home again that night and that was what they called the Black Gang's outing.'

Looking after the engines and the machinery in the mills was always done by men. Bill Hayward was an engineer from Heywood, a small town between Bury and Rochdale that had twenty-seven cotton-spinning mills in its heyday. He spent much of his working life servicing and maintaining the machinery in the local mills.

When I was fifteen I left school and started work at Unity Mill in Heywood. That was in 1951 and I was there till 1954 when I was called up for the army. I hadn't finished my apprenticeship but I chose not to have my call-up deferred – I wanted to go in at eighteen and get it done with. So I went in as a theatre assistant in the Royal Army Medical Corps. There was no choice, I just got put there. When I'd finished my National Service I went back and worked at the mill from 1956 to 1959 when it closed down.

What I was doing wasn't the sort of apprenticeship you'd get in engineering; it was more like being trained to go through the mill on various jobs and you'd work up to City and Guilds standard by going to night school. The first job I did was what was called a roller coverer. On the spinning machines and carding machines they had rollers that were covered in felt with a leather outer cover on top and it was my job to look after these covers and replace them when necessary.

When the bales of cotton came into the mill they had to be broken up. The bales were full of seeds and other waste material so they had to go through a breaker to start separating it. From that they went on another breaker and they ended up on what we called 'lats'. These were like big spindles that the cotton was wound on to before going to the carding machine. This was a big drum that was covered in wires and as the cotton was fed in, it pulled it and got all the fibres lined up and running the right way. It also took out a lot of the dust and seeds and what they called 'nap', which was like little balls of cotton. After the carding it became what was called a 'slider' – that was a cotton rope that was very soft and it was coiled up in a can. After that it went on to the draw frames where they started to draw the fibres out more and with process it just got thinner and thinner until it was cotton thread. All these machines were run by line-shafting which was all connected up to the main mill engine.

Sometimes the main engine would break down and then there'd be panic. It would stop for various reasons, but one of the main ones was because there were big ropes connected to the engine that drove pulleys on different floors and if one of these ropes broke it could snag somewhere and cause a lot of damage. To prevent this there was a safety bar just underneath the flywheel up at the top of the mill and when it hit this it shut the engine down automatically. If the safety bar didn't work and that rope did snag on anything, it became a danger and they'd have to stop the engine. The engine drove the whole mill, so whenever it had to be stopped it would bring the whole place to a standstill. We had an incident at

Unity Mill when somebody got at the big engine and put iron filings in the main bearing. It caused so much damage that the whole mill was stopped for a fortnight. The police were involved and the bloke responsible got prison for it.

There were a lot of people involved in keeping a mill going. There were rope-splicers for when the ropes broke. You had to get a rope-splicer in to piece it all together again and that was a skilled job – it was a job on its own. Some of the bigger mills had their own rope-splicer, but we used to call one in. He was kept busy most dinnertimes because that's when the mill was stopped. If a rope broke during the morning he'd come in and put it back on during the stop time at dinnertime.

Everyone would stop for dinner at the same time. It used to be twelve o'clock till one. Most mills had canteens which were very good and the meals were cheap because the mills subsidized the canteen. Then at the end of the day you walked back home because most people lived local. Where I lived there were a weaving mill down at the bottom of the street. My father worked there, my mother worked there, my uncle worked there. Most of the street I lived in worked there. And you knew everybody in the street, not like today.

But conditions were different then. When I started we were on half seven to half past five and Saturday mornings half seven to twelve. Saturday morning was part of the working week – it wasn't overtime. We only got one week holiday then – Wakes Week. We didn't go on foreign holidays. Most of the people from Heywood went to Blackpool on excursions on the train. Heywood station during Wakes Week was absolutely packed with people waiting for the excursion coming.

Throughout the 1950s, with the industry going into decline, mill-owners tried to cut costs to improve profits, but Lancashire couldn't compete with growing foreign competition. In 1958 the government agreed to support the industry's efforts to secure restrictions on imports from the main Commonwealth suppliers and the following year acceded to its request for a state-supported scheme to scrap out-of-date machinery. The Cotton Industry Act of 1959 was intended to modernize and streamline the industry by eliminating 50 per cent of its spinning capacity and 40 per cent of its weaving. Two thirds of the cost of scrapping surplus machinery was met by the government, with a levy on the industry providing the rest. In addition, a re-equipment subsidy was given to firms that installed new machinery, particularly automatic looms and ring spindles. The Act accelerated the rate of scrapping surplus equipment, but expenditure on modernization was much lower than the government had anticipated, mainly due to continuing uncertainty over imports. The tide of mill closures throughout the county couldn't be stemmed because investment in new machinery only made sense if the Lancashire mill-owners knew that they would be able to use the new equipment intensively and that would have required an expanding demand for long runs of fabrics, which did not exist. Unity Mill in Heywood was one of the many mills that closed down.

When Unity Mill shut down in 1959 there was a bit of a mass exodus. The directors had five mills in Heywood and they shut all five. You can imagine the sort of impact this had, and it weren't just our company that were going. I often wonder what happened to all the people that were made redundant at that time. There weren't redundancy packages like you have now. I didn't get anything. Whether you got anything and how much you got was based on your age and at my age I didn't qualify for anything. I was fortunate, though. I actually got another job before the mill shut. They put the notice up on a Friday and I'd heard about this job, so I went down on the Monday and got it. It was at a place in Bury called John Dale's and they manufactured toothpaste tubes. My job were just the pressing and the trimming of these tubes, setting the machines up.

Bill stayed at the toothpaste factory until 1971 and then decided to get back into the textile industry. He went to work for a Swiss firm that manufactured textile machinery.

This firm had their machinery out in textile mills in the area and there were four fitters at the Rochdale works who went out to maintain it. One of these machines was a carding engine which had to be set up. My job was to replace all the wire on these machines when it had got damaged or blunt. If the machine was already taken down for us in pieces this would take three days; if it hadn't and we had to do the dismantling ourselves you're talking about a week. It wasn't very often we were without a job because the mills that were left by then were running round-the-clock shifts – they were doing twenty-four hours so the machinery wore out a lot quicker, which meant more work for us. Where at one time we might have gone to one machine every three years, we were doing it every year.

I came out of textiles when I finished with this Swiss firm [in 1990]. I still had eleven years left to do so I went to work at a spring works. It was a small family business up in Whitworth. We were a member of a large group, but at that time we were just a small factory. I made springs there and I did some spring-setting and general maintenance. I stayed with them until I retired [in 2001]. By that time we'd moved into bigger premises; five different places had been brought together, but I didn't like it from day one to be honest. We lost the personal touch and you didn't get the same co-operation.

Bill kept in touch with the engineering and mechanical side of the cotton industry after he retired. He works as a volunteer at Ellenroad Engine House next to the M62 motorway at New Hey near Milnrow. Here he helps to look after one of the grandest of mill engines in preservation, but that is about the only point of contact he has with the Lancashire he remembers when he started work.

When I was growing up you knew everybody, not like today. I don't even know my neighbours today, because people come out of their houses, get in their cars and go, and you don't see people like you used to. Going to work you'd see the same people every day, but not now. At one time Rochdale centre was heaving with people getting buses to work every morning. But you can walk through Rochdale centre now and rarely see anyone in the morning. I don't know what happened to all these people when the mills started to close. What did they do? I ended up going out of town for work as I suppose a lot of other people did, but they were all mill people trained up in those jobs, and when they got to forty or fifty what else were they going to do?

*

Burnley in north-east Lancashire was known for its weaving. During the Industrial Revolution it became the world's largest producer of cotton cloth and there were dozens of coal mines in the town to provide the fuel for the engines that drove the machines. By the 1950s both industries were in decline but they still provided employment for the majority of the populace and in Burnley there were more weaving looms than there were people.

Jack Procter was born in Higham, not far from Burnley. His mother and father both worked as weavers and for many years they sat next to each other. Jack left school at fourteen in 1946. He had originally wanted to be an electrician, but one day he went to see his mother working in a weaving shed and spotted somebody doing a job that he liked the look of.

I went into the mill and I saw this chap doing a job that looked interesting to me. I asked my mother what he was doing and she said he was a tackler and, for whatever reason, from that moment on I wanted to be one. I jacked in the idea of being an electrician and I went in the mill as a weaver. That was in 1946. Then they called me up for my National Service. I wanted to go in the RAF so I signed on for three years because they paid a bit more for three years and you could also choose which of the services you went into.

When I came out I went back in the mill as a weaver, but I could see there was no future for me there. So I left that and went to work for Horrocks in Preston, the biggest weaving firm in the world at that time. The job I went on first of all was beam-gating, which was setting up the looms, and within a very short time I could do that with my eyes closed. So it wasn't very long before I was offered an apprentice-ship as a tackler and I was put on a part set of looms with two tacklers looking after me. But in less than a fortnight I was helping them. It just came straight to me – I had no trouble at all and there was no look-ing back. I never went back to weaving after that but I could obviously re-set and run looms when needed after fixing them.

At this time they were getting the newer looms in, automatics. And without any warning they just told me I was going to go on the automatics. So they sent me for a course to Blackburn, which was a waste of time. I was there a week and all you were doing was helping the fitters build the looms; you weren't learning anything. I came back and within a month I was at home on these new machines. They were automatics so you had a battery-filler who kept the battery full of bobbins. It was a little bit more complicated than the basic looms, but to me it was child's play.

The stuff we were making was all poplin, all shirts for America. Sea Island cotton it was. But the trade started going down. Too many people had started weaving cotton poplins, because there was money in it. So I could see the writing on the wall for that particular trade. They started bringing in some heavier cloth, which the looms weren't capable of, and though you could tell the management that parts were breaking left, right and centre because they weren't strong enough, they weren't interested. So I moved to another mill because they had a bit more fancy work and I'd never worked on these machines before. It was what they called 'dobbies' and it was something I wanted to learn. Basically it was a machine on the top of the loom that moved what we called staves up and down in different sequences so that it made patterns in your cloth. And I went on them and learnt them. You needed good-quality yarn and a good weaver to create good-quality cloth. I worked with silk, rayon and wool and on lots of different types of looms, including the Lancashire,[22] which was my favourite.

[22] The Lancashire loom was a semi-automatic power loom invented by James Bullough and William Kenworthy in 1842. It was the mainstay of the Lancashire cotton industry for over a century. Its main drawback was that it had to be stopped to recharge empty shuttles and it was eventually superseded by fully automatic looms. Reference to its use here in the 1950s illustrates the antiquated nature of much of the machinery still in use and the need for modernization.

When Jack started work he was paid £3 a week as a weaver, but by the time he was twenty-five in 1957 he was being paid £9. The good times were not to last, however. As the mills began closing down all over Lancashire, the workers had either to look for other jobs or be prepared to travel further afield.

I got the chance to go to South Africa in the trade with the firm that I had just left [Horrocks]. They were closing down because all that machinery was breaking, so they sold their rights as Horrocks to this mill in South Africa called Berg River Textiles near Cape Town. So I went for an interview to see about going. It was a three-year contract to help set up this new factory and get everything running, with an option of either coming home or staying out [after that. I ended up getting the job and] I went out to South Africa for three years by ocean liner – Union Castle line. A fortnight on the sea. Beautiful.

I was still single then, but I was courting and before I went out I'd told the girlfriend that if I liked it I would send for her. Well I did like it, and I thought how do I go about getting her out here? So I went to my manager – out there it was a different kettle of fish, because you could talk to the directors on first-name terms – and I told him I would like to get my girlfriend out because I wanted to marry her. 'Leave it with us,' he said. About a month later he called me and said, 'I've heard on the grapevine that a certain young lady will be leaving England on such and such a date.' So she arrived on the Thursday and we married on the Saturday and we set up home.

But I hadn't got the bill for her coming out, so I went in to see the manager about it. He brought in the managing director and he said, 'Right, Jack. As you got married straight away we've decided to class you as a married couple coming, so there will be nothing to pay for her.' But then on top of that he said, 'Would you accept this as a wedding present?' and he gave me a hundred quid, which in them days was a lot of money.

Jack came back to Britain at the end of his contract in 1965 and worked in a number of different mills on the borders of Lancashire and Yorkshire. He wanted to be close to the Yorkshire Dales National Park because he was a keen pot-holer and was also in the cave-rescue organization. Eventually he got a job as night-shift foreman at a mill in Pudsey, but he lost it because of a cave rescue.

I was on a rescue and the police asked me to stay on. I said, 'Well if I have to stay on will you ring my firm and get permission, please?' and they rang the firm and the boss turned round and said, 'No. He has to work.' But when I got to work he sacked me. By that time there were mills closing down all over, so I thought I'd go back to South Africa. I flew out, found a job back on the floor as an overlooker[23] and brought the wife out once I'd got settled in, and we stayed out there. I moved from that mill to another and all the time I was looking to climb the ladder,

[23] When working on Lancashire looms you were called a tackler. When the automatic looms came in you were a loom overlooker. Later, when high-tech looms came in, the job was called textile technician.

not on the managerial side but in knowing more machinery. But then my health started failing as a result of a bad back injury I got when I was in the air force in 1950, so we sold up and came home.

When I got back in 1971 I still had to work and I got a job as night-shift manager at a mill in Preston [then] eventually I ended up going to a mill in Blackburn working with jacquards. Now these were the real fancies, so I had to learn how they worked and I was in my element on them. More in my element on the jacquards than I was on the actual loom because you could set the looms up by the book and they'd run and run. But that wasn't my style of things – I used to like to make my brain work a bit more, so I ended up doing most of the work on the jacquards at the top of the machine while a partner looked after the bottom. By this time they were calling us 'textile technicians'. The job had gone up from tackler to over-looker and now to textile technician.

Eventually I had to leave because of my back. I had reached a stage where I came into the drive at home after work and when I got out of the car I was coming down the footpath on my hands and knees. But just before I left all the jacquards were taken down, and they started putting new ones up. These were all computerized. I never got the chance to learn them, but they were all going to computerized.

It was only in 1992 that they found out what damage I'd done to my back: four vertebrae had broken and two discs collapsed and the doctor said it had been like that since 1950. Once they found that out I got an 80 per cent disability pension and retired.

Men maintained the machinery and did the technical jobs, but most of the weavers were women. Dorothy Pomfrett grew up in Padiham, near Burnley. Like most of the other girls from the town she found work as a weaver when she left school.

> The first job I had was delivering papers. I used to get up about half past six and take papers, which I enjoyed. When I started work proper I was fifteen. I went to work in a sewing factory in Burnley, where I made some good friends, but the wage was very low. I was only earning about £2 a week and out of that I had my lunches and my bus fares to pay for and of course I gave all the rest to my mother. I didn't have spending money. So my dad, who was a winding master at a local mill, said they were looking for winders at his mill and did I want to see if I liked it. It was shift work – six till two and two till ten, but the wages were a lot better than what I was getting. So I thought I'd have a go at this Fir Trees Mill at Higham and see how I went on.

Fir Trees Mill was a small weaving shed that had opened in 1851 with 138 looms. The workers lived in terraced houses built for them on the lane next to the mill. By 1860 it had two hundred looms and it was modernized in the 1950s when Dorothy was working there. When she started she got £3.10s (£3.50) per week.

> When I went there I wasn't winding machines right away. You've got to learn other things, so I went in an attic in the mill on my own and I was up there all day

for days pirn-stripping. The pirn was the spool of the shuttle. It went into the shuttle but there were always little bits of cotton left on it and these caused snags in the weaving so they had to be cleared. To do this you'd put the pirn in a machine that took all the bits off and when it had been cleaned you just chucked it in a box, and you did that for hour after hour. It was very boring, but then when I'd been up there a while they found other jobs for me to do. So I was going through the mill learning all the different jobs. One of them was battery-filling. What I had to do was go trundling around the weaving shed with a box full of the pirns and cones[24] and fit them on to the end of the loom. The weaver would carry on working the loom while you did this. I didn't like that. First of all there was the noise – clackity clack, clackity clack, clackity clack. Then there was the dust. You couldn't have a conversation with anybody because you had to concentrate on filling a small circular space with the pirn which fed the shuttle which fed the loom. If the loom was running all right, the weavers could have a 'mimo' conversation with their neighbours – that was lipreading.

Eventually I said to my dad I thought I'd prefer it up in the winding department, doing the pirn-winding. The pirn was like a bobbin and the job involved putting it on to a machine that wound the

[24] Yarn or thread was wound on to cone-shaped cardboard. In the weaving process these cones were placed on a platform above a pirn-winder. The yarn was unwound from the cones and on to the pirns by the pirn-winder. The pirn itself was a tapered bobbin that fed the yarn into the shuttle of the loom.

thread on to it. When it was full it stopped winding and dropped into one of the boxes that I used to take round the weaving shed to feed the looms.

I liked it a lot better up there, but I didn't like the shift work. The one I was on started at six so you had to be up about quarter past five. We had a knocker-up and he had a long bamboo stick that must have been ten or fifteen foot long and he'd walk round and tap on your window. When you put your light on he knew you were up and moved to the next house. He would have a round of about fifty or sixty houses so he had to be quick. The knocker-up used to be paid by people on the street at the end of each week. At Christmas you would always give him a tip, like the paper boy.

There were some cold mornings. We had no central heating and my dad didn't like lighting the fire. He used to put the oven on and then he'd put my shoes in the oven to warm them so I had warm feet when I went out. A taxi used to come and pick me and my dad up. It was a bit of a luxury going to work in a taxi, but it was because Higham was a little village about two or three miles up the road from Padiham and there were no buses at that time of morning. Four or five of us went in this taxi and then when we finished at two o'clock it was waiting outside for us. It was only a small mill so everybody knew the boss. He used to come round checking that everything was running all right and he would always say hello to us. But apart from that he didn't talk to minions like us. The winding master and the tackler would talk to him and he'd communicate with us through them.

For Dorothy life at the little mill in Higham was pleasant, but she left because of the shift work.

There was no shortage of work at that time and I got a job at Raymaker's velvet factory. I'd been told they were earning good money there and it was day work as well. So I went down there and said, 'Give us a job,' and they said, 'Yeah, come on. Start on Monday.' I worked there until I was pregnant with my first child. Velvet weaving was much more skilled. You could only work two looms, where a cotton weaver could work up to eight, but velvet weavers got paid a lot more. Some were earning £14 a week, which was a lot of money at that time. We started at half seven there and worked till about half five, with an hour for lunch. [At first] I had to go to a little school where a lady taught you what to do and then they put me on two big looms. They had a razor going across the cloth that was being woven all the time cutting the pile.

Like all the other mills we shut down for Wakes Week, but I had no money to go away because I just used to give my mother all my money. I got a bit to spend so for a night out I used to go to the Empress in Burnley and saw some well-known people there, like Johnny Dankworth and Cleo Laine. Then there was the Nelson Imperial. It was called a ballroom and I saw Johnnie Ray there and Humphrey Lyttelton. I loved him. On Sunday night I used to go to a place called Joe Mortimer's at Accrington. That's where I met my husband and where a lot of my friends met their husbands too.

I got married in 1960. My husband was in the army doing his National Service, one of the last ones to be called up. I said, 'I don't want to get pregnant while you're away,' so we made sure he only had six months of service left before I got pregnant. He said, 'On the day I come out I'm coming to the mill for you and you're leaving that day.' So I told the boss I'd be leaving on the day my husband got his discharge. When that day came I was waiting for him and all the mill was too. He came into the mill and said, 'Stop your loom,' so I stopped my loom and he just picked me up and carried me out and everybody clapped.

Fir Trees Mill, where Dorothy had her first job, shut down in 1965 when closures were gathering pace across the county. It was sold to an engineering company and eventually demolished in the 1980s; the site has since been used for housing. Dorothy recalls the decline of the industry as a gradual process. She realized after twenty years that all the factories were gone.

A lot of women employed in weaving did highly skilled work, particularly when there were patterns to be woven into the cloth. Like her brother Stanley Bolton, Mabel Ryding worked at Victoria Mill in Horwich and was trained to work on jacquard,[25] which is weaving patterns into the cloth. She recalls how they could do any pattern that anybody required.

[25] A mechanical loom invented by Joseph Marie Jacquard in 1801 designed to manufacture textiles with complex patterns. The loom was controlled by cards which punched holes, each row of which corresponded to one row of the design.

I even saw, during my time there, when England were doing pretty well at football, they brought a jacquard out of a bulldog and they printed quite a number of towels with this on. I was on the jacquard, but I was doing little baby-feeders with 'Good Boy' and 'Good Girl' and little chickens and little animals on them. The loom I was on was one of the old Northrop looms. It was the largest loom they had at that particular time but they only did about a metre wide. I used to get four or five bibs to every metre width. When you'd finished them you would have to take them off the loom and fold them up. Then you'd throw them on your shoulder and carry them up to the warehouse in a great big pile. They didn't have lifts, so you had to walk up steps with all these towels, and then we went in the warehouse and they examined them. Up there they used to cut the individual bibs from the roll and do the finishing on them. It was so noisy in the weaving shed I worked in that you had to learn to lipread. You couldn't hear anybody, so you had to lipread to see what they were saying. Immediately you opened the sliding door to go into the shed, it were deafening. But it was good working in there – like a big family, a shed full of family people, where everybody got on well with one another.

The scope of the textile industry in Lancashire was very wide in terms of the jobs associated with it. As well as the basic preparation and spinning of textile fibres, the weaving of these fibres into fabrics and a wide range of bleaching, dyeing, printing and other finishing processes, it extended to the manufacture of made-up textile articles, including clothing, soft furnishings, household textiles, carpets, specialist workwear and healthcare products. Other firms developed out of the need to service the industry with small parts and consumables. Margaret Taylor from Rochdale worked in several different textile-related industries. Her first job was with a firm that made the paper cones on to which cotton fibre was wound in spinning mills.

I was grinding the end of the small cones. There used to be eight of us sitting round what they called a belt and each of us would have a little grinding machine that took the edge off the paper before it went into the machine that made it into the cone. It was a very quick process – each one only took a second so we'd do thousands in a day.

It was quite relaxed in terms of what the bosses were like. You could go to the toilet and make a brew if you wanted to. But you had to clock on and clock off and you had to be on time or you got quartered. That meant if you were quarter of an hour late you got quarter of an hour knocked off your wages; if it was half an hour, it was the half an hour you got knocked off. It was all younger ones on that job, all school leavers. Then you got moved up on to actually making the cones, but I didn't stay there that long.

I was about twelve months in that first job and a friend of mine got me working at Bescoats where they made household goods like oven gloves, ironing-board covers, dishcloths and dusters. When I first went the machinists were making the things and we just had to cut the ends off, fold them and take them into a warehouse in a little truck. In there they got wrapped up ready for being sent out to the shops. After a while I was put on the machine. There was about eight girls on a belt and we made oven gloves.

My wages were about £6 then, but when I got engaged I went to work at a small firm called Lockhead and Eccles where they made pram bags and carrycots and their flat wages was £9 a week. I was seventeen then and we were saving up to get married. In them days you could walk out of one job and straight into another, so it was always a case of knowing who paid better. I knew a friend who had gone working there and she told me what it was like and how much you could earn. When you had been there for a while, they let you do piece work to make your own wages up and then I could earn £14 a week. It was better doing the piece work, but you had to work for it. It was a small family firm with no more than forty working and I was quite happy there. You could make a brew and take it up to your machines and you could smoke at your machines as well. We always had a Christmas party at the Masonic Hall in Rochdale and we had food and drinks free; it didn't cost us anything.

I got married when I was eighteen while I was work-ing there and I left when I was pregnant. You all got a carrycot and a pram bag given to you when you finished work if you was pregnant. Part-time work was quite easy to get then so after I'd had my children I got an evening job at a local mill, battery-filling. I worked till about nine or ten o'clock each night.

The decline of the textile industry that had started in the 1930s meant that by the Second World War many of the cotton mills had been converted to other commercial and industrial uses. Those around Ancoats and Ardwick in Manchester, which had heralded the birth of the factory system at the start of the Industrial Revolution, ceased textile production and many of them were taken over by clothing manufacturers. The area around here, stretching up to Cheetham Hill, became the heart of Manchester's rag trade. Connie Brown was born in Ardwick and lived on Pin Mill Brow off Ashton Old Road. She got her first job at a firm just across the road from where she lived called Hallets and Company where they made shirts.

Actually I didn't want to be a machinist at all; I wanted to do office work. But my mother was a weaver and she said it wasn't a trade working in an office; you need to have trade in your fingers. So my mother took me over and I didn't come home. My sister worked there and she was a good worker so they snapped me up. I just sewed labels on for about a fortnight. I was fourteen when I started and there was plenty of work, because the war was on and we were doing shirts for the Wrens and the army so we had big orders. You worked on a conveyor then and you had your own section of it to work on. A shirt would come down to you on the conveyor and you took it off to do your bit of work on it, then you put it back on the belt when you'd done it before the next one came along. They had two elderly ladies to teach the young ones and if you just happened to stop and have a talk, one of them would poke you in your back to get on with your job. During the war we worked eight till five with a break for lunch. Then you'd go back at six o'clock till eight and you worked Saturday mornings as well.

We worked there till some time in the 1950s and then for some reason they moved the firm from there to Deansgate. It was in a basement there – you went down some spirally steps. It eventually closed in 1959 but there were still plenty of other places you could go to; you were never out of work. So I went to another place just off Blackfriars Street. I worked there quite a long time, but somebody else took it over and he decided to move into Salford. I still stuck with the same job, but by this time I was married and I'd gone to live in Oldham. But with travelling all that way I had the key to open the place up of the morning. I was doing the collars there, but in 1978 I was made redundant, so I got a job at Brownfield Mill on Ancoats Lane. It was handy for my bus from Oldham but that only lasted twelve months. In the shirt trade places were shutting down all the time by then because all the imports were coming in that were cheaper.

So I got another bit of a job in the same mill, but it was on children's and I hadn't done those and the boss was not very good with the money. By this time I was on my own so I had to earn a wage and I got a job at a firm that made ladies' coats called Snugcoats. I did parts for them, like doing the collars or working on the sleeves, and it was quite good there at that particular time. They had Miss England working for them there, modelling the coats. The company made their own brand but we also got work for Marks & Spencer. Anyway, we had about five years of this, then the directors all wanted to go their own way so they closed the firm down and that was the only time that I went to the dole. But it was only for a week, because one of the directors, whose father had started Snugcoats in the first place, wanted to hang on to the firm, so he had to close it for a week while all the legal things were being sorted out, and he re-opened a week later as a new firm. He kept all the same staff on because he prided himself on his group of machinists; they were all pretty good. He was really good to work for, but he developed cancer and died in 1985. When he was ill his son took over and he was on the arrogant side. Quite a few of us were pensioners and at Christmas we all got called to the office where we were given a letter telling us he was getting rid of us. And in the rag trade you got nothing at the end. He'd had a couple of factories built in Romania and now he has all his work done there.

I'd spent all my working life in the rag trade and when I finished and looked back on it I thought I never liked my job. I'd always felt as if I could have done something a lot better for myself, particularly in a financial way. I got no extra pension for anything, so I've just got my state pension now. When some of the ladies at the club speak about when they retired and they got a gold watch, I think we got nothing at the end of it. I still speak to one or two of the ladies I worked with and we always say 'Didn't we work hard?' because it was all piece work and if you stopped to have a talk you were stopping your wages.

At one of the places I worked we were doing jackets for Next, and they brought in a new machine for doing them. Of course I had to learn it, so I started off on it and the more I got used to it the quicker I got. They gave me a price for the work I was doing, but as I got quicker the supervisor kept dropping my price. It didn't matter how much work I did, she'd only let me earn so much a day. Yet there was a certain little group that just threw the work together any old how and they were earning big money. But I blame the supervisor. This little group would be on £150 a week, but she wouldn't let us earn £100. I have a friend that rings me. She was good at her job and she did it properly but she didn't earn big money, so I've said to her many a time, 'I think you and I were a pair of mugs. We did the work properly but we didn't get the money for doing it.'

Towards the end there was a lot of part-time work. If they had children and they had to get them to school, some of them did part time, but I didn't have any children. All those that had daughters said they'd never let them come into sewing because it was too much like hard work. Some people left sewing altogether and went into something else. When I was in my thirties I just felt as if I wanted to get out of it, but I didn't feel as if I was qualified to do another job to earn a wage, and earning a wage was my first priority because I have more or less always had to look after myself and I don't think I was ever confident enough to go for something else.

Wigan was another major mill town where sewing provided employment for women when its mills started to
close down. Coops was a big clothing manufacturer near
the centre of the town making a range of garments,
including trousers, suits, jackets, vests and Crombie overcoats. Kathleen Boyle from Wigan got a job there when
she left school in July 1955.

I finished school at fifteen and got a job at Coops,
but I had two weeks off because it was Wigan Wakes
Week and the place shut down. So I started the
third week. There were about thirty girls started that
day. Coops was a big building. It had four storeys
with four sides on each storey. We went up these
stone steps and they looked gloomy and I thought,
'Oh heck. What am I going in to?' We were taken up
into this little room which was divided off with glass
panels that you could see through, and this was the
training room. We went into this and I always
remember all the machines all set out in lines. When
we went in we had to clock in and we were given a
pair of scissors, an unpicker – which was like a long
needle that was thick at the end – and a piece of
white tailor's chalk and we were told we hadn't to
lose them. If the chalk broke, you still had to use it
and you weren't given another piece until it was
really worn and thin.

When we first went in they gave us sheets of paper
that had purple lines on them. They showed us
round the machine and where everything went and
then we were told we wouldn't be threading it up; we
were just going to sew along the lines on these pieces

of paper. We had to sew without any thread down these lines and then we did half circles, three-quarter circles and zigzags and, until we got this right, we couldn't thread the machine up. They weren't going to let us loose on the cloth when we first went in, for sure, so for about a fortnight we were given these sheets of paper. Some were quicker than others at getting it right. Once we'd got it right we were shown how to thread the machine, which was easy enough. They were industrial machines and we were given pieces of paper again, but this time we had thread in to sew along the lines and then we got scraps of material to do.

As you got better at it [they used] to bring you actual pieces of work from one of the floors where you were going to be working and that would be your allocated job when you actually went on the floor. But they wouldn't let you go until you got it right. Until then you stayed in that training room.

We were shown how to measure and to a certain degree they showed us how to cut, but the scissors they gave us weren't adequate for cutting; they weren't proper cutting scissors, they were only little ones. If we wanted proper cutting scissors we had to buy our own and I'd say they were a fiver a pair at that time. I was only fifteen and this was 1955, so that was a lot of money. Our wages were only about £5, so it was a whole week's wages for a pair of scissors. You had to get good ones because of the cloth. It was very good-quality and there were a lot of different types we worked with. You had tweed, you had summer cloth and then there was very fine cloth. We also had mohair cloth, but we weren't allowed to cut this because it was so expensive; only the more experienced people were allowed to cut the mohair.

I was in the training room for about four months before I went on the floor. Working there was really good because all the girls had a laugh and a giggle, but they were very strict, especially on timekeeping. You had to clock in and out and nobody could do that for you. That was instant dismissal. Next to the training room there was the personnel officer. She was something to be dealt with, she really was. Her name was Mrs Allane and she was about six foot three, like a pencil. I always remember she had beautiful blonde hair but very sharp features. She was in her mid-forties and it was always whispered that she was married to a black man, which was unusual then. I used to say, 'So what?' It never bothered me. She was a very modern woman for her time and she ran that place with a rod of iron. If you misbehaved or you did anything wrong, you were straight in the office, no messing. She really kept the workers under control, but it was always the best work that came out of that factory. You used to concentrate on one particular job. It could be pockets or what they used to call welts, which was a collar. I did trousers, I did jackets, I did Crombie overcoats, which was very heavy work, and I did pressing as well on a Hoffman presser, but I ended up on the best section, the waistcoat section. That was my last job there.

You didn't really have a lot of choice in where you worked; it was just where they put you. They said, 'Well we need somebody up there' and they used to come round and say, 'Are you willing to go up and learn that?' When you were allocated your job, whichever section you went on, what they used to do was to start you off with the shape of the garment. Say it was a jacket, you'd get the shape of the jacket and the first girl would put the darts in. Then it would go to a presser, who was over on the other side of a big table. She had a little hand-press and she would press the darts out. Then she'd pass it on to the next girl, who would cut it and put the welts in and the flaps.

There were supervisors who checked everything and if anything was wrong they'd wazz it back at you. What some of them would do, which I thought was very, very wrong, was let you work all day, then if it was wrong – even though nobody had come and said, 'You're doing this wrong' – you'd have all the work you'd done back. You'd have to unpick them and do them all again, even with Crombie overcoats which were big and heavy. And you wouldn't get any money because you were on piece work. We also used to have work study and they'd come to the job you were on and go to the woman who had been on that job longest. She'd be quicker than you and everybody else. Then they'd calculate her timing and use that to set the rate for the job.

What struck me as funny when I first went to work there was that all the women used to wear rollers in their hair. You could smoke, but they didn't like it so you had to go to the toilet if you wanted a smoke. They were horrible little toilets, very claustrophobic. I had a larder at home that was bigger than these toilets were. But the factory itself was a big place and every floor had a canteen. The canteen ladies used to bring a trolley with tea and sandwiches round and you'd have a ten-minute break in the morning, ten minutes in the afternoon and an hour for your lunch when you went to the canteen. And they were wonderful meals – always nice, good food and it was very cheap. At Christmas you got a free dinner and I always remember the men got boxes of Senior Service cigarettes and the ladies got a box of Terry's All Gold. I used to swap mine with a man called Jack Rigby who used to go round putting fresh covers on the presses when they were all worn. He didn't smoke and my dad did, so I used to swap over and he'd have the chocolates for himself and his wife and I'd put the cigarettes towards a Christmas present for my dad.

In the end making clothes in the UK just became too expensive. By the 1970s manufacturers producing private labels for large high-street clothing chains were being forced out of business as their customers found cheaper suppliers overseas where labour costs were much lower. Some, like the company Connie Brown worked for, dealt with this by opening their own factories overseas. Other UK manufacturers started to send cut pieces abroad to be made up and then re-imported the garments for sale here. Whatever policy they adopted, it didn't help the machinists who relied on the jobs to supplement their family incomes as the work dried up.

Besides the spinners, weavers and engineers, the mills provided employment for thousands of administrative staff, designers and labourers. Tony Cummings worked in personnel and production control. He was born in Burnley and grew up surrounded by the town's mills and he got his first job in the office at Brierfield Mills when he was fifteen. It was, he recalls, an immense place, and it was quite unusual because it had a spinning plant and five weaving sheds as well.

I started work on 19 July 1965 as a trainee and I remember that on my first day my mother made me wear a hard-wearing, uncomfortable green suit that made me feel like an Irish comedian. I worked in personnel for a couple of years and one of my jobs when I started there was to prepare the labour reports every week for each department: hours worked and absenteeism rates, etc. They were on shifts there – they worked a six to two shift and a two to ten shift, and people used to alternate on these; there was also a permanent night shift. The mill was working twenty-four hours, but there was not a lot of weekend working. It would finish at six o'clock on a Saturday morning, then re-open again Monday six o'clock.

While I was in personnel I was out in the factory all the time because they were always recruiting people and I used to take people round to show them the jobs that they were possibly going to get. Then after two and a bit years there I went into the production-control department where me and my boss loaded the factory every day. By 'loaded' I mean we planned what the production would be, determining how many rolls of cloth would be made. Some of this would be made to meet orders we'd got, but a lot of it went into stock. Most of the bosses I dealt with were OK, but just down the corridor from me were the directors and they were on a different planet. Everybody was very deferential to them.

The mill was part of the Smith & Nephew Group and they made surgical fabrics and dressings. We made a lot of the fabric for Elastoplast and a massive amount of crepe bandages. These would be woven into huge rolls which would be cut and packaged so that they were ready for distribution to hospitals and to chemists. But it wasn't only this. We also made a lot of denim and polypropylene, which is a sort of plastic-backed hessian. A lot of the material they wove, like the gauze that was used for surgical dress-ings, wasn't as valuable as other more sophisticated products in the textile world. This meant that, whilst in some mills a weaver might be responsible on your more sophisticated cloth for a dozen looms at the most, in there you'd have a weaver who'd be respon-sible for in excess of sixty looms and it was more of a patrolling thing.

In the main weaving shed we made a lot of fabrics for Marks & Spencer on Lancashire looms. It was very noisy in that particular shed and one of the dangers was that you could get shuttles flying out of the loom and people would get whacked with them. More commonly people lost finger ends on the various machines they were operating on. My memory of that firm was that it had a strong welfare ethos. People were still seen as people rather than human resources. There was a lady whose full-time job was welfare officer and she would go and see people if they'd been off for a while. There were always baskets of fruit going out to people who were off. It was caring but it was also quite clever, in that when the welfare officer went to visit people to see how they were it prodded them into realization that perhaps they should get back to work.

But textiles wasn't historically well paid and that's probably one of the reasons I left the industry, if I'm truthful. The training they gave you was good and I went through college with them, but then the first opportunity I got after I'd done certain qualifications I cleared off because I didn't see any future for me in textiles. The thing was that as we got into the 1970s the area had gone through a transformation. It had moved from the staple industries of coal mining and textiles to newer, lighter industries, and as the mills and the mines closed down a lot of the textile workers and the miners found work with these other employers. I'm not saying the transition was easy, but Burnley people were used to working and at this time they showed they were adaptable. I went to work in production control for Michelin at the tyre factory they'd opened in Burnley. When I got there I found the whole working environment very different. At Smith & Nephew it was all about reserved parking spaces and a chauffeur for the boss and all this carry on; status corresponded to the size and plushness of your office. When I went to work at Michelin, which paid a lot better money, it was a different firm altogether. There were no directors and the whole place was far more egalitarian, far less status conscious. I'm not saying it was perfect, but things like that were less important. The only person to be called 'mister' there was the boss man, the chief executive of that plant. When I left Michelin I went to work for another French company called Damart, who made thermal underwear. It was like being back at Smith & Nephew, because they too had this really hierarchical kind of set-up where, if I'd had a forelock to touch, I'd have had to touch it with some of the bosses there. I had a reasonably good job there in management, but they were from a different century and ultimately that's why I left.

After Damart Tony worked as deputy manager on a government training scheme run by the Manpower Service Commission running practical courses for the unemployed. He did this for eighteen months before starting a teacher training course and taking a job in higher education.

Tony had got out of a dying industry. By the time he left Damart in 1983 countless mills had been closed down. Some were taken over by clothing manufacturers and the rag trade flourished briefly, taking advantage of cheap, imported cotton cloth before it too became a victim of cheap clothing imports. Some of the bigger spinning and weaving companies attempted to adapt by moving over to the production of nylon and other synthetic fibres but diversification and cost-cutting did little to improve profits and during the 1960s and 1970s mills were closed across Lancashire at the rate of almost one a week.

Eric Beaghan from Rishton near Blackburn was a textile designer who saw at first hand the changes that were taking place in Lancashire's textile industry as he moved from working with cotton to man-made fibres and finally on to carpets.

My father worked in a big engineering company in Accrington and he said he'd like me to become a draughtsman, but I thought that wasn't for me and I certainly wasn't going down the mines. Every day you saw the miners in Rishton when they'd finished their shift going down to the pub and sitting outside on a nice day, black as the ace of spades, and I thought I don't want to do that. So I decided that textile designing would be an interesting start to a career. The wage in those days for an apprentice working five and a half days a week was fifteen shillings [75p], which was all right. I worked out that if I became a designer I wouldn't need any tools for the job; a fiver would buy me all I needed in the way of paintbrushes, pencils, magnifying glasses and so on. So I started on a seven-year apprenticeship at a firm in Great Harwood, Whittle Studios. It was a small design studio but it did work for all the big mills in Blackburn, Burnley, Darwen, Colne, Ramsbottom and Nelson, and it was only two miles away from home so was easily reachable by cycle.

Basically the designer's job involved coming up with a design, then working it up into a pattern that would fit a loom. A drawn paper design could be as big as a whole room.

The studio was split into two sections, the designing side and the cutting part. The designing was straightforward. The way it worked was that someone would give you a pattern and say we want that producing as soon as possible. And you had to start from scratch with a plain sheet of graph paper, draw the design freehand on to the graph paper and then paint in the patterns that they wanted. That sheet would be covered in tiny little dots and each dot meant something to the people downstairs in the card-cutting department who transferred the large images on the graph paper on to cards with holes punched in them.

There was so much work involved that you'd be working on a design for perhaps a fortnight at a time. It was very rare that you got away with a design that you could produce in a week. When you'd finished it you had to check that every dot was in the right place because the next department had to visualize what you had done and then stamp a hole in the card to represent the design. If you were slightly wrong in what you had done you would get a piece of fabric back from the mill that was full of mistakes. The boss would not be pleased, so the next time you were a lot more careful. You got so careful in the end with practice and improving your techniques that you could produce something that was almost fault-free and when the finished fabric came back you could sit there and think, 'Yes, I did a good job.'

The way Whittle Studios worked was that the boss would tour the mills in the area looking for work. The people who ran the mills also came to Whittle to have a look at what we could do. Most of the customers were from Blackburn or Darwen or Bolton, but we'd sometimes go as far as Bradford in

Yorkshire or down as far as Manchester or even Macclesfield. Sometimes you would go out to these mills with your equipment to either correct or modify the designs when the customer wanted something changing. It was always nice to go out to one of these places because they wanted to see the people who had done their designs. And of course it also meant that you got to know people and you got to know the mills in the area.

Most of the bigger mills had their own designers who were with them for life. When I was doing my apprenticeship the designer at the mill opposite us was a doddery old man in his fifties or sixties. At the age of sixteen or seventeen I would think, 'What is that old codger doing for a living?' It turned out that most of the time he was buying our designs, not really designing anything himself. But that was the way that large companies worked. They had a designer but still employed the studios to produce designs for them – I won't say by the hundred, but certainly a dozen at a time, which kept the studios in fine employment. They would bring a piece of material in and say 'Can you reproduce that?' and the answer was always yes. But it was a long, drawn-out process working from material back to a design sheet, card-cutting and then back to weaving. We had to take the material, look at it through a magnifying glass and reproduce it and it would take a month. By the time you'd worked out the combinations of the weave, your eye felt like it was coming out like Popeye. And I thought at the time, 'Is this doing my eyesight the slightest bit of good?'

There was no such thing as health and safety at that time. They scream now about watching computers all the time, but to have an eye glued to your magnifying glass in one hand and a paintbrush in the other going dot, dot, dot, dot, dot had to be a strain on your eyes. There were only a specialist few doing the apprenticeship who could do this, or even put up with doing it. Nowadays they wouldn't do it. They'd say, 'I'm sorry, health and safety say I can't work for a fortnight or three weeks with my eye glued to a magnifying glass,' and that would be it. But they were happy times. There were no misery-guts about.

Eric's apprenticeship lasted for seven years, including two that were taken up doing his National Service, during which he learnt to drive. When he returned to work he was the only younger member of staff who could drive, so he went out on all the errands and even sometimes went out in place of the manager when he couldn't go. Although Eric's apprenticeship gave him a broad experience of textiles, for a young man it did have its problems.

The drawback was that I was doing three nights a week and a half day at Blackburn technical college. You thought, 'Three nights a week – what are the others doing? They're out playing football in wintertime, they're out playing cricket in summertime, and you're slogging away writing notes after notes after notes.' When you got to the third year and you passed, you got the National Certificate in textiles, which was quite something. Then you thought, another two years for Higher National, three nights a week. Okay. Yes. Do it. So you spent another two years and eventually you got your Higher National. By this time I was married and the next step up was the Textile Diploma of the Institute, which was four nights a week. I said to my wife, 'Look, love, I've just spent five years, three nights a week, trying to fit life in. There's no way I'm going to carry on for another two years, four nights a week.' So that was the end of my textile apprenticeship.

An advert came in the local paper for a job in the Blackburn area as a textile designer and I got it. The wage here was fabulous – £9.10s [£9.50] for a five-day week, compared to the fifteen shillings [75p] a week I'd been on as an apprentice. And I was on staff status, which to me was quite something. Once you got to that level, plus the fact that you'd got the various certificates from the tech, you were into the start of a career.

But it didn't last very long. It lasted two and a half years, then in July 1955 I got the dreaded notice which said, 'Dear Sir, you are no longer required. The mill is closing down. Everybody at the mill is being made redundant.' It was just before the annual holidays, but because I was on staff I got four weeks' notice. I was due to go away on holiday so I gave my details at the labour exchange and went away. When I got back there was a letter for me from a firm in Great Harwood offering me a job as a designer. It was good because it was much nearer to home and I'd be among friends.

As well as designing I could do almost anything

that was required in the weaving department there because of all the qualifications I had from the tech. It meant there was always something happening. You were never bored; you were always up to the eyes in work, thinking about work, trying to be one step ahead of what might happen.

The decline of the cotton industry in the 1950s was in part a result of the wartime disruption of world trade routes that had encouraged the development of textile industries in India, Japan and China, and exports of British machinery ensured that they grew rapidly. Lancashire was beginning to find it increasingly difficult to compete on price in these, its traditional export markets. Eric recalls the way the mill-owners responded.

When I was [at Great Harwood] it was a time when things were changing from the old-fashioned system of one large engine that would run an entire weaving shed or an entire spinning shed to using electricity to run the machinery. The next thing that happened was that two-shift working started. Now this was the newest thing in textiles. It sounded good at the time and the large companies could afford to do it. They re-equipped with the latest Northrop looms that were produced in Blackburn in great quantity, and because of the expense involved they had to start two-shift working. Now this was good for a while. Everybody was happy. People that moved from the single-shift system to the two-shift system were pleased with the working conditions, and also with the extra wages that they earned. But it was only the large companies who were able to do this because it went against what I would describe as textile tradition. The single-building enterprises, run usually by brothers and family, could not afford to re-equip with this new machinery, so they kept working with the old Lancashire looms in the way that they had done for the past forty, fifty or sixty years. Later on the three-shift system was introduced. Now it sounded good on paper, but it was a nightmare in practice. The wages went up again, of course, and we employed anybody with textile experience. And there were endless problems [because] the people that were employed only came for the money. Production didn't soar and the quality went down. It also made life more difficult trying to keep tabs on a three-shift system. Two was bad enough, but three was difficult. So eventually I came to the conclusion I'd sort of had enough so I thought, well, what else is there in textiles?

In the 1960s, nylon, which was produced by warp knitting, was becoming popular. So I changed jobs from working in Great Harwood to working in Rose Grove, Burnley, at warp knitting. It was a good time to move from textiles because more or less over the next three or four years textiles just went down a step, another step and another step. But we were booming – things seemed to be going very well. Nobody seemed to want to stop using this new thread. I wasn't happy with it, because I think nylon itself only has a limited use. We were mostly in production for Marks & Spencer, shirtings, lightweight fabrics and things like that. Warp knitting was a nice, easy employment. There was no need to juggle anything. It was a lot faster than standard weaving and it was fairly straightforward because the yarn came on bobbins. We had the preparation department and the knitting department within a minute's walk from the [design] office, [so] I could sort things out to my satisfaction.

The warp-weaving mill that Eric worked in changed owners several times while he was there.

After I'd been there about four or five years, we were taken over by a Mansfield-based company. No problems, just a new boss with the same staff. After another three or four years another big clout came – Courtaulds were taking us over. And they said yes, the staff are all right. I thought that's unusual, because when a big company takes over the first thing they do is bring their own men in. And then all of a sudden Courtaulds said, 'Your turn next. We're shutting up shop.' They were good to me, though – they gave me time to look around and in three months I found a job in Rishton.

This time it was carpet weaving. I thought, well, if I don't like it, after a period of time I can look round and see if there are any other vacancies, preferably in textiles. The trouble was that weaving textiles in those days was really going down and the reason for that was India. When Mr Gandhi did a tour of Lancashire mills he knew that, providing he could get skilled people to relocate to India, he could beat

Lancashire all ends up, mainly because of the wage situation. Wages were reasonably high here and Mr Gandhi knew how much lower labour costs were in his own country. So he really put the dagger in the Lancashire textile industry.

But the quality of the wares that came in from India then used to make us laugh. There were so many faults in it you thought I don't know how they can sell this material. You couldn't look at a piece without saying there's a great knot there, there's a bit missing there. Who is doing the checking before the fabrics are put on to rolls and then re-exported to Lancashire? But other countries have to live, and the skilled people that went out from here to places like India and Peru to set them going meant that after perhaps five years the quality slowly improved.

And of course the machinery went as well. What happened initially was that the big company in Blackburn, British Northrop Loom Company, were producing the best looms in the world, and they were exporting looms to all these up-and-coming nations. Their people were out 365 days a year, somewhere in the world, installing new, up-to-date weaving machinery that was better than what we were using, because ours were ten years old. And every few years a new model came out that would be faster and easier to run. But management here couldn't afford to invest in new machinery. With the decline in the industry here, no one was prepared to re-equip a shed with four hundred brand-new looms. They could have done it in stages, but I think the bosses had realized that the end was near and the government was always nudging a little bit about redundancies, closing down and this, that and the other, so it was just out of the question.

The days of the large textile-manufacturing companies employing hundreds or even thousands of workers are long gone and nowadays the industry is made up of small- to medium-sized firms specializing in technical textile products such as flame-retardant fabrics, coated textiles and breathable materials. In 2010 there were estimated to be 4,300 employees working in this sector in Lancashire and a further six hundred working in the clothing industry, manufacturing, in the main, specialist workwear and uniforms.[26] Most of the companies they work for are based in clean, modern industrial units – a stark contrast to the monolithic mills with their towering chimneys billowing out smoke and fumes that once dominated the landscape. Many of the terraced houses that clustered around the mills remain, but new housing and industrial estates have now sprung up on the sites of a lot of the mills themselves.

[26] www.lancashire.gov.uk

4

North East Shipbuilders

THE INDUSTRIAL LANDSCAPES in which people lived and worked throughout Britain each had its own distinctive character. The river, the docks and the cranes of the shipyards on Tyneside, the flames from the melting shops in the steelworks lighting up the night sky in Sheffield, and the winding gear of the collieries strung out along the narrow valleys of South Wales – what they all had in common was noise, smell, dirt and a strange sort of monumental grandeur that symbolized power. Robert Hunter was brought up in the little mining village of Mansfield Woodhouse in Nottinghamshire. He had family on Tyneside and he has vivid memories of the train journeys he used to make through much of England's industrial heartland when he went to visit them.

> My mother had a sister in South Shields, so from the end of the war onwards we used to go there for the family holiday and stay with them. So my introduction to heavy industry was coming on holiday to South Shields on the River Tyne. I still remember how we used to get the bus from Mansfield to

Nottingham and the train from Nottingham to Grantham, where we changed to one of the great steam trains like *Mallard* or the *Flying Scotsman* to take us on to Newcastle. The last stage of the journey was the electric train from Newcastle to South Shields. One of the early recollections I have was of the train coming out of Darlington and passing all the industrial forges that were still busy at nine o'clock at night. And I can remember the smell of the forges and the heat from them as the train went past. It excited me because Darlington was very famous for the construction of the Sydney Harbour Bridge and the Tyne Bridge in Newcastle, as well as the Wear Bridge and the Cleveland Bridge. And these engineering companies were based in Darlington and the train used to pass their premises at nine or ten o'clock at night. That to me was the signal that we were in the North of England, and we were going to this huge industrial complex at Tyneside and Wearside. And that's where I was going on my holidays.

My brother was six years older than me and my treat on a Saturday morning was for him to take me from where we were staying down to the market place in South Shields. From there we used to get the vehicle ferry across to North Shields. Over there we always used to buy a packet of black bullets sweets from the shop in the little wooden shack that was next to the ferry landing and then go for a walk along the Fish Quay. We used to go back on what was called the 'ha'penny dodger', which was the passenger-only ferry and that was more direct. It cost a halfpenny or a penny. What I remember about that was going across on the ferry through all the shipyards and the ship-repair yards. They were all working on a Saturday morning because in those days it was a five-and-a-half-day week. The terrific noise of the riveting that was going on is one of the things that I remember very clearly. It was bedlam.

From the ferry you could see all the shipyards and see the ships in the docks. You could look down and see the water hull form[27] of the ship when it was in the dry dock when the water had been pumped out. At that stage there were probably thirty or forty ships of different sizes on the quaysides and in the dry docks of South Shields and North Shields at any one time. All were being repaired, or waiting to be repaired, or loading coal for the power stations on the River Thames. Others would just be loading coal into their own bunkers for their own consumption because a lot of them were steam ships in those days with coal-fired boilers.

For two or three years after the war we came here on holiday. But my father was a civil servant and he was moved to Newcastle, so we sold up in Mansfield Woodhouse and moved to South Shields. The house we bought was on the sea front and my brother chose the front bedroom so that he could watch the ships coming in and out of the harbour. I chose the back bedroom because there was an old coal railway line with steam trains taking the coal wagons

[27] Shape of the hull that would normally be below the waterline.

backwards and forwards from Whitburn Colliery to the washery and then down to the coal staithes[28] to be loaded on to the colliers that took the coal down to the London power stations.

The rivers Tyne and Wear in the north-east of England developed as major shipbuilding centres in the middle of the nineteenth century. Prior to that traditional wooden shipbuilding in Britain was concentrated in the south and south-west, but the development of iron-clad steam ships in the mid-nineteenth century changed the geographical nature of the industry. The new ships depended on a ready supply of iron and as bigger, more fuel-efficient furnaces produced cheap iron in the country's industrial north, it was towards the estuaries of the great northern rivers that much of Britain's shipbuilding gravitated. By the end of the nineteenth century Britain had the largest shipbuilding industry in the world. At its peak, around the turn of the century, the country's shipyards built eight out of ten of the world's ships. On the Tyne and the Wear, on the Clyde and on the Mersey, and in Belfast there were hundreds of small, family-owned shipyards which before the First World War built the most advanced steamships in the world. In the early 1930s, however, the greatest casualty in world trade was the ship-building industry and in Britain over 60 per cent of shipyard workers were on the dole. Between 1930 and 1935, thirty-eight yards were permanently closed down. At one point only two out of seventy-two building berths on the Tyne were in use, but when the Second World War broke out every usable berth in the country was occupied. Much of the

[28] Stages or wharfs equipped to load and unload coal.

work was repair work. The war was followed by a short boom and for ten years the yards were busy and jobs were as plentiful as they had ever been.

In the 1950s conditions for shipyard workers were almost unchanged from before the war; it was still cold, heavy, dirty and dangerous work. When it rained everything was mud and the sheer brutality of the working environment, with its hours of hard, physical, dirty graft, made the yards some of the toughest, most primitive workplaces in Britain. Much of the labour was brought in on a casual basis, and in *Making Ships, Making Men* Alan Mackinlay[29] quotes a worker who was used to the daily call-on:

> There used to be a daily market. If you were a riveter or whatever you used to go down in the morning and wait outside the foreman's office and he would say, 'You, you, you', and give you a start. Sometimes the foreman would walk up and down the line of men waiting for work without saying a word, not even a grunt – which most of them were capable of. That meant that there was no work for you that day. They were just reminding you that they had the power and you had none.

At the heart of the shipbuilding process were the riveters, who were paid according to the number of rivets they hammered in. Riveters fastened plates and beams together by hammering red-hot metal rivets into pre-drilled holes to make a watertight connection. Many of them had to work high up on wooden planks beside the hulls on the

[29] *Making Ships, Making Men*, Alan Mackinlay, Clydebank District Libraries, 1991.

building berths and the work went on in all weathers. Each riveting squad was made up of two riveters – one left-handed, one right-handed – one holder-on and a boy who was the heater. The worker quoted by Mackinlay described the process:

> You had a furnace and the boy to put five or six rivets in the fire, he had a bag of rivets at the side of his fire, he throws the hot rivet to the holder-on and he picks up the hot rivet, sparking hot, and puts it through the hole, rams it through with a back-hammer. The riveter drives it in with alternate blows on the outside of the shell, and that way you fill up every hole with rivets. In the bulkheads you could be bent nearly double and riveting heavy beams and plates. That was twice as hard as ordinary shell riveting. You had to work just as fast because the rivet had to be hammered while it was red-hot. Men would be riveting eighty to a hundred feet up, sometimes higher. We would be working – swinging hammers – on two wooden planks, sometimes only one, without any guard rail. The plank would be bouncing as they worked. We'd have been safer trying to work on a tightrope.

In the North East, shipyards dominated both banks of the Tyne from North and South Shields at the mouth of the river past Newcastle and Gateshead and on upstream to Elswick. As far back as the thirteenth century there are records of a galley being built for the King's Fleet at Newcastle and by the beginning of the nineteenth century there were about a thousand shipwrights on the River

Tyne and five hundred on the Wear. Most were engaged in the construction of small wooden vessels used in the coal trade to London. By the 1830s Lloyd's Register[30] recognized Sunderland as 'the most important shipbuilding centre in the country', but the real growth of the industry in the North East occurred in the 1850s following improvements carried out to the rivers, including straightening, narrowing and deepening by dredging. A yard was established at Jarrow on the Tyne and the first iron collier was built there in 1851 for shipping coal to London. This led to the establishment of specialized construction facilities on both banks of the river, and within ten years there were more than ten yards building in iron on the river, employing over four thousand men. Change was slower on the Wear, but by the end of the nineteenth century Sunderland found fame as the largest shipbuilding town in the world.

This period of rapid growth in the second half of the nineteenth century was fuelled by a dramatic increase in coal and iron production. Iron was replaced by steel as the major shipbuilding material well before the end of the century and Teesside and Consett developed as centres of steel production. In the early 1900s Sunderland's yards employed over twelve thousand men, a third of the town's adult population. On the Tyne communities based on shipbuilding developed along both banks of the river: in Hebburn, Jarrow and South Shields to the south; Elswick, Walker, Wallsend and North Shields to the north. The birth of Hebburn's shipbuilding industry was the result of one man's vision, Andrew Leslie. In 1853 he arrived in

---

[30] Maritime listing and classification organization founded to inspect and examine the structure and equipment of merchant ships.

Hebburn from his native Aberdeen with £200, determined to take advantage of the opportunities the River Tyne offered for shipbuilding. Between then and his retirement in 1886 the company he founded built 255 ships. He also built several hundred houses for his workers, provided schools for their children and partly financed the building of the town's church. On his retirement a new firm of Hawthorn Leslie was formed from a merger with Hawthorn's marine engine builders. Improvements were carried out to the yard, adding two new berths and extending the dry dock. During the First World War and in the 1920s the company continued to be profitable, but the Depression of the 1930s meant a reduction in orders and the workforce fell from five thousand to 1,400. The Second World War saw the workforce rise again to over four thousand and the yard was kept busy building and repairing casualties: 120 warships and 112 merchant ships were repaired, including the destroyer HMS *Kelly*,[31] which had been built at the yard in 1938.

Cicily Horspool was born in Hebburn and recalls growing up surrounded by the sights and sounds of the industry during the Second World War when her father worked at the Hawthorn Leslie yard.

My father was a fire watchman when the war was on and during that time he lived in the shipyard; he had his own little cabin there. We lived in Hebburn New Town at that time, which was about twenty minutes'

[31] The Royal Navy destroyer was twice damaged on active service during the early years of the war. She was towed back to the Tyne for repairs, before being bombed and sunk in 1941 during the evacuation of Crete.

walk away from the yard. My dad worked twenty-four hours a day because during the war they worked round the clock in the yard. In his cabin he had a bunk to sleep in and a bowl to wash himself. He also had a little pot stove and he had his kettle, and he just loved it. I don't think he ever wanted to come home. He loved being in the shipyard. I don't think my mam was bothered about him being away, to be honest. She used to walk down to take his food, or sometimes he used to send apprentices up to my mam's to get stuff, clothes and things like that. On a Sunday I used to take his dinner on two plates – that was my job, to run down the bloody shipyard with his dinner. He'd be waiting at the gate and I used to go to his little cabin while he ate his dinner, then I used to take the plates back.

He was there when HMS *Kelly* was brought in for repairs. Lord Mountbatten brought it back to Hebburn and it was repaired there. It was badly damaged and there were bodies in it and my dad was one of them that took the bodies out of the ship. Louis Mountbatten was the commander of HMS *Kelly*, so he was in the shipyard while it was being repaired and my mam used to see him every day. She said he was a very friendly man. They called my mam Dolly, but he always used to call her Dorothy. He was a gentleman – it was lovely.

I was fifteen when I moved from Hebburn New Town down to Hebburn Quay, right down past the shipyard entrance, and lived in the Hawthorn Leslie's flats. My father had worked for them from leaving school. He was a rigger, but if there was no work going he also drove the mid-Tyne ferries if they were a man short. It was like a bit of overtime for him. In fact, he worked more times on the ferry than in the yard. [The shipyard] had a little ferry called the *Happy Wanderer* – that was his little launch and he used to take all the managers and that up to Newcastle, or wherever they had to go. If they needed somebody to go across the water during the night when the mid-Tyne ferries were off, they just used to go across the road and knock my dad up.

Where I lived I looked out from my bedroom window and I could see the ships getting built. Just imagine – there was my house, then the street, then the shipyard wall over the other side of the street and they were building a huge ship just behind that wall, right practically in front of us. Being so close to the yard, you got all the noise, twenty-four hours a day. On the night shift the ship was all lit up. All through the night they had the lights on and they'd be riveting all night long, and they had what was called a windy hammer and it went boom, boom, boom all the time. But after a time you just didn't even notice it was there.

It was lovely just to watch the ships getting built, and then when they were launched they used to invite people to the launch. All the shipbuilders would be there and all kinds of visitors and dignitaries and local councillors and what have you. And the whole works were there – nobody in the shipyard worked. [At every launch] they broke a bottle on the bows, and on the bottle they had red, white and blue ribbons. I don't know how he did it, but my dad always got the ribbons. We all had plaits in them days and I remember cutting the ribbons into lengths for my plaits so when I went to school I always had red, white and blue ribbons in my hair. Sometimes in among them there would still be the glass off the bottle.

I remember once we had a ship in from the West Indies and it was called the *Queen of Bermuda* and they had a steel band who used to stand on the ship and play for hours. They were brilliant.

My dad was in the shipyard from when he was fourteen until he died when he was fifty-eight, of lung cancer. He worked really hard. He was a very unassuming man, very quiet, but he could do any job in the shipyard. He used to take me on the ships and sometimes there wouldn't just be one in the yard, there'd be maybe two or three and you'd have to go across the gangplank from one to the other. I went down to the engine room – I think I was about twelve then – but I wasn't a bit interested. What I did like there was that they had a multitude of kittens in the rigging loft; they had them because there were a lot of rats there. My dad was a lovely man, but if they were tomcats he used to kick them in the river. He always had to keep the tomcats down because they didn't want too many kittens. But I couldn't believe it that he'd kick them in the river and drown them.

My husband worked in the shipyard as well, but he was just a labourer and he hated it. He did some dirty jobs like tank cleaning. They had to clean all the rust off the inside of the ships and he used to come home in some terrible states. He's got emphysema now through working in all the dirt and dust. I was only eighteen when I was married, and when I was nineteen we moved away from the river into prefabs.[32] But I loved every minute of the years I lived down on the river.

Each of the towns along the Tyne had its own yard and in the years immediately after the Second World War each one was independent. South Shields, at the mouth of the river, was dominated by John Readhead's yard, which, like many others, had its origins in the middle of the nineteenth century. As well as building ships, two dry docks capable of accommodating vessels up to 450 feet in length enabled the company to carry out repairs to all types of vessels. Rows of terraced flats built next to the yard at the end of the 1800s still housed many of the workforce. Kenneth Moore got a job at Readhead's when he left school and served his apprenticeship there as a shipwright.

It was just after the war, 1946, and to get an apprenticeship then was hard, but my dad used to run the South Shields football team and one of the players was the foreman shipwright at Readhead's. With him being a friend of ny dad I got an interview and he said, 'Start on Monday. You'll be starting in the stores till you're sixteen, then you can serve your time on

---

[32] Prefabricated houses manufactured off site in standard sections that could easily be transported and assembled. The word is usually associated with a specific type of single-storey house built in large numbers just after the war as a temporary replacement for housing that had been destroyed by bombs.

the ships.' I remember on my first morning I was wearing one of my dad's old blue boilersuits that had to be turned up for me. When I got to the yard all the men were standing in what was called the market place, [which was where] all the shipwrights gathered to find out what jobs they were being put on. Every trade had a different place where they gathered each morning and the foreman would come and tell them which ship they were on.

I ran errands for people for a year, then I started my shipwrights' apprenticeship. At that time apprenticeships at Readhead's were huge. They would start maybe a dozen or so each year. That year they started three shipwrights, and three started as joiners, three as fitters and there were three plumbers. Every apprentice worked with a full-class tradesman and you stayed with this man for your full five years. Most of them were top tradesmen. It wasn't like nowadays, with people trying to do ten different jobs. A shipwright apprentice would just do what a shipwright did and a plater would only do a plater's work; you wouldn't do anything else.

The shipwrights were the original shipbuilders in the days of wooden shipbuilding, making and fitting the frames, beams and planking. With the introduction of iron and steel and subsequently prefabrication of large parts of the vessel, their job changed to give them responsibility for the erection and alignment of the ship sections. When I first started it was all made up of plates. Everything was riveted except the actual join of the two plates. These plates already had holes in them and when they were put on the frames they were paired up equally with the holes on the frames and you were left with a butt joint. Now that joint might be tight or it might be open a little bit, so what you would do was to put a brass piece at the back of the join and that was the only thing that was welded in my time. The brass would go on the back side right inside the ship.

There was always some of this brass went missing. People who worked there and knew where it was used to come in the night time and raid the place. It was known about, but they didn't clamp down on it because money for building ships was no object then.

I worked on the shells of the ships for about five years. There might be five hundred or even a thousand shell joints to weld and me and a lad called Jimmy Wilson did all of them. Once the staging was up Jimmy worked on one side of the shell and I worked on the other. We put the staging up. All the way round there were steel ladders and what we called bars that we put the planks on. You'd be standing on one plank, or maybe two, fifty or sixty feet up and you didn't have a harness or any protection whatsoever. But when the welder came, he wouldn't work on one plank – he wanted two or three, and he wanted a back rest.

The riveters had three planks to work from. Everything had to be done properly for the riveter because he was always seen as head man. He was on the outside of the shell and on the inside somebody would throw the rivet up and a lad – a holder-on – would catch it in a bucket. He would put it in the hole and hold it in place on the inside while the riveter riveted it from the outside. They were really heavy the machines they used and you had to be really strong to hold one of them all day. They were very clever because they had a little Morse Code to communicate with the people they were working with on the inside.

I had to wear glasses because I used to get these terrible flashes from arc-welding. What would happen was that you would feel your eyes go watery and you've got no idea what the pain was like in your eyes by the time you got home. It was like a really hot burning. You used to put apple or cucumber on your eyes to try and keep them cold. That used to last about fifteen to twenty hours and you could get it twice a week. The welders themselves were covered up and they had protective glass, but it was people like the platers and the shipwrights who used to suffer. You might just walk in a door and get a flash that would mean a day off work. Conditions generally were horrendous. People were tough, though; they were hard as nails. The engine rooms were the most dangerous part of the ship. A lot of men would be working down there and they'd have other men working maybe two hundred feet above them and anything could come down on them. I had a good friend who had a bar came down on him and split his head. But he survived.

There were no clocks and you had no tea breaks. You weren't allowed off at all, so if you needed a break you had to go and hide. You weren't allowed anything. You were only allowed to be late twice in a month. If you were late the gates would be closed. Mind you, everybody had a way in. Apprentices would get over the wall so we wouldn't get caught. We used to sneak out to the canteen to get cups of tea and if the foreman came in we would go out the back way into the boiler room and hide there, then the woman who worked in the canteen would knock on the door when it was time to come out. Sometimes we'd climb over the wall and go for a walk in Shields and then climb back again. I remember one time there were six of us on a flat roof all shouting at the gaffer and he didn't know where we were.

Very rarely you'd have a night shift, but there would only be a few people working. Men worked Saturday mornings and then went to the club when they finished, so the clubs used to be packed. There used to be four or five hundred in every Friday, Saturday and Sunday, and every afternoon the clubs were open because men worked different shifts. I always used to call in and have a couple of pints.

I loved my time at Readhead's – the best time in my working life, because what I did I enjoyed. It was a steady job, but the money was better elsewhere so I decided to move on. I worked in a number of different yards and always found it easy to get jobs. If you were good, word got around and people would always send for you.

By the time I was forty I was working as a 'liner-off'. When you were a liner-off you were separate and didn't mix with the rest of the men; you had your own cabin and you had your wireless. You were a bit important. The job involved setting out the positions of the main sections of the ship and its equipment, using plans, tape measure and chalk lines and taking into account the camber of the decks, to ensure everything was lined up correctly. There might be a bulkhead here and some steel there, and we would line it off to make sure that it was in the right position before it got welded. Every ship had to come in line. If a plate was a quarter of an inch or half an inch out of line what you would do was reduce the welding. It was a bit of a cover job, but everything in the ship had to come in line. Otherwise by the time you got to the front it might be ten or twelve foot out. When the Board of Trade used to come and check them, the inspector used to be on one end of the tape and you would be on the other. Sometimes I knew beforehand that it was about half an inch out because I'd already measured it, so I'd shift my end by half an inch so that it would be right for him at the other end.

Everything was done with single plates. They didn't have heavy-duty cranes, so only one plate went on at a time. It was only in the 1970s they started to build five-ton, ten-ton or twenty-ton sections, especially things on the upper decks like the wheelhouse navigation bridge. These were completed in the yard inside a massive workshop and taken to the ship, and as liner-off you would be responsible for making sure that they went where your marks were. Any error would only be found once it got taken on board and they found that everything wasn't working to plan. Then whoever had lined it off would be in trouble. As time went on more and more things got partially made like this.

Located on the banks of the Tyne, Jarrow was a major shipbuilding centre from the middle of the nineteenth century until the 1930s. Charles Palmer established a ship-yard there in 1851 and the firm's notable firsts included a seagoing screw collier and rolled armour plates for war-ships. Palmer's was a major employer in Jarrow and neighbouring Hebburn, but it didn't survive the Depression and the closure of the Jarrow yard in 1934 was one of the events that triggered the Jarrow March against unemploy-ment two years later. In 1934 Vickers-Armstrongs took over the site and set up the subsidiary Palmer's (Hebburn) Company Ltd. The new company invested heavily in the yard, concentrating during the Second World War on naval repair work. Because of the size of its dry dock it was able to handle some of the largest naval vessels and during the war the yard had over 4,500 employees.

In a shipyard workers didn't identify themselves as shipbuilders but as members of a particular craft. They were riveters, caulkers, platers, shipwrights, drillers, fitters, blacksmiths, plumbers, electricians and joiners. Most of the trades were represented by a union which guarded entry jealously, as well as protecting the 'trade rights' of the work their members did. Fitters battled with plumbers about their rights to handle iron pipes as opposed to lead pipes, and platers fought with ship-wrights about who should erect sections. Ken Goss from Jarrow secured an apprenticeship at Palmer's as a sheet-metal worker but he soon found it didn't suit him and moved on to another of the crafts.

I just wanted to leave school and get a job. There was plenty of work around but it was almost all manual: shipyard worker, mine worker and engineering. I had no real ambition, but I got a job at Palmer's ship-repair yard with a view to becoming an apprentice sheet-metal worker. The apprenticeship didn't start till you were sixteen, but I left school at fifteen and went into the sheet-metal shop as a boy labourer. I was overwhelmed the first day I went there. The sheet-metal shop was very, very noisy and full of fumes from the welding. The din and the racket in there was so great I couldn't make head nor tail of anything.

I was doing odd jobs at first, making the tea and going to the canteen for bits and pieces. There was a brazier working in there who used to make pots and pans and all sorts of articles like that for the ships. He had to have a fire and one of my jobs every morning was going to get firewood. The thing is they all had little empires in the shipyard and the foreman joiner wouldn't allow the foreman sheet-metal worker to have wood, so I had to go and pinch it. It was absolutely barmy. It was the same making the tea. There was an unofficial nine o'clock tea break and the shipyard virtually shut down. But if you were caught with a can of tea, the foreman would come and kick it over because it wasn't an official tea break. Every now and again the foreman and the manager used to come and have a purge, and anybody with a can of tea could either be sacked or they would just kick the can over. [Usually it] was kicking the can over, but if you persisted in doing it you'd get the sack. You had no comeback. It was just accepted.

I started to work with the welders and began to learn how to weld. But I had fairly bad eyesight at the time and I kept getting flashes off the welding equipment. It's like a severe burn in your eyes that makes them stream and you can't see. It was getting really bad for me, so I got a transfer to the electrical department when I was sixteen. I was lucky, really, because to me it was a far better job. It was much more interesting and there was more scope. As an electrician I would be able to work in the shipyards, go down the mines, go to sea or work on building sites, and during my working life I did most of those things.

There was no sort of formal training; they just said, 'You work with Geordie, keep an eye on him and see what he does,' and that was the way it was done. We had to go to evening classes as well and I went for a few years, but I couldn't see any relevance between what I was learning in the evening and what I was doing during the day. There was a lot of mathematics involved, which I was hopeless at.

In the shipyard you started to build up a tool kit. Every tradesman had to provide his own tools in those days, so you got a toolbox and that was something you treasured. It might be something you got for Christmas or for your birthday. Spring-roll tape measures were starting to appear and if you had one of them you were really good, and you had to have fancy pliers and they cost about £10 a pair. You also had to have an assortment of screwdrivers, hammers, chisels and bits and pieces like that.

When I started the apprentice's wage was less than £1.10s [£1.50] for a forty-four-hour week, but I soon settled into it and enjoyed working on the ships. After the age of eighteen you started to get more responsible jobs to do yourself that were bigger and more difficult, and your money went up every year. I can't remember exactly how much I got when I came out of my time, but it would be round about £5 or £6.

The big thing for me was repairing ships that came from all over the world. There was crews on the ships of all nationalities – very interesting people – and I enjoyed that side of it. The other side of it, though, was that it was always cold. Shipyards are always cold, even in the summer, and in the winter it was horrendous. The ship would be classed as 'dead', which meant the engines weren't working, so there were no boilers to heat it up. There is always a wind blowing down a river and if you were working on the deck of a ship you were surrounded by steel in water. If you were stationary, connecting up a fusebox or something like that, and you weren't using any energy, you used to find a bit of wood to put on the deck to insulate yourself from the steel. We wore thick socks and heavy boots, but in those days industrial clothing wasn't what it is today. You just used to wear your old clothes for work. You also had a boilersuit, but you had to buy that yourself. It wasn't until the 1960s or 1970s that industrial clothing started to be provided by the employers.

One of the big jobs was installing cable trays.[33]

[33] System used to support and carry electric cables in a building or on the ship.

Sheet-metal workers used to install them in some yards, but in others it was the electricians who ran the cables that went on the cable tray and this led to a lot of friction. Then when it came to welding the cable trays on to the bulkheads and deckheads, although the sheet-metal worker was quite capable of welding the lugs and the brackets to hold them, he wasn't allowed to do it because that was the welder's job. On shore in your own shop you could do virtually anything, but when you went on a ship there was this rigid demarcation. There were disputes between sheet-metal workers and shipwrights and platers as to who should make a certain item. They were always protecting themselves and their jobs to stave off redundancy because that was always the big fear.

While Ken Goss worked in the yard, Ken Findlay from Jarrow also got a job at Palmer's when he left school in 1951 and after a year working as an office boy he started serving an apprenticeship as a draughtsman.

I was an eleven-plus failure, mainly I think because I didn't see much point to what we were doing, but when I was at secondary school there was a teacher called Ernie Stinton and whenever we used to do essays he always used to encourage me to illustrate them with little drawings. When it came to school-leaving time, unknown to me, he mentioned me to a guy he knew in the shipyards and I went for an interview and was offered a job in the drawing office. To be honest, I didn't really know what it was all about at the time. The day I turned up for work I went there with my new charcoal-grey trousers and Harris tweed jacket and a pocket full of pencils, expecting to be drawing *Queen Mary* and *Queen Elizabeth*, but the reality was quite different and I started as the office boy. I gradually worked into doing little jobs in the office, but the main thing was I had to prove myself as being a good printer. My most important task, though, was to keep the more senior guys stocked up with cigarettes and things like that and my job every morning was going out with a haversack and getting pork pies and packets of crisps, but most of all their favourite brands of cigarettes. That might seem an easy task today, but then it was like looking for bars of gold in the street because it was just after the war and there was a shortage of everything because lots of things were still rationed.

I started work in 1951 and I was office boy for one year, which took me to sixteen when I started serving an apprenticeship. In the drawing office they had a slightly different scheme to the one for the lads who worked in the yard. The apprenticeship scheme in the yard was five years, but for a draughtsman it was different because they didn't consider you good enough or well enough trained after five years, so there were another couple of years after that where you were called an 'improver' and it was only after those two years that you were considered a time-served draughtsman. During my apprenticeship I had to start attending evening classes and that went on for quite a few years, but I always did fairly well because, unlike my school work, I could see the tuition was related to my work. I could see why I was doing it and that made me take a greater interest.

When I first went into this drawing office I was getting twenty-five bob [£1.25] a week, and you do talk about these things. There was a whole range of ages working there and I found out that in the past the job I was doing had been a premium apprenticeship, which was like an indenture and parents had to pay for their sons to be trained. It had been that sort of situation with some of the older guys in the office and of course you come along as a young lad and you are being paid. I would say at least half of them at one time or another said, 'You're bloody lucky – you're getting a wage and our mothers and fathers had to pay for us to get this training.' So there was a big social divide there. They were all gentlemen, but the shipyard labourer's son could never afford to be an indentured apprentice. I wasn't middle class; I was working class. My father was a shipyard worker and it was purely by luck that I'd got in there. The schoolteacher who recommended me must have taken a shine to me or recognized something in me which I didn't recognize at the time.

During my apprenticeship I had to go out and work in the yard to get experience. I did six months in the blacksmith's shop, six months in the mould loft, six months with the platers and six months with the shipwrights in the dry dock; all invaluable experience. The bottom of a dry dock is always wet and it's standing on twenty-five feet of solid concrete because they had massive foundations to take the weight of the ships. In the winter it was a good job we finished at five o'clock because you used to feel the cold rising up through your body. But one of the things that I can remember was that, without exception, whoever I worked with always looked on me as a softy from the drawing office and what is the most awkward thing we can give him to do that will show him up? If there was somewhere that was tiny that you had to struggle to get into, or if there was something awkward to do, it was always given to me. When I was working with the shipwrights they did a lot of things with hammers and wooden wedges, but the hammering was hard slog and the puny frame I had at that time wasn't up to it. So that created great laughter among the guys who were strong enough to do it. So if there was some hammering to do, they would look around and say, 'Let's have a laugh.'

The biggest hammer was called a Monday hammer and the story was that it got its name because after the weekend you hadn't enough strength to use it. The fitters used that one and it probably weighed about half a hundredweight. They used it for tightening bolts on ships' engines. A lot of the equipment was primitive and a lot of the processes were more primitive in the early days. A lot of things were achieved by hammering and it's said that in the past, when people in the town were starving, if there was any food in the house the mother would ensure that the father got the good meal and then the kids came next, and very often she would do without herself. But that was a necessity, because in the days when they did heavy work, when the father would be maybe a riveter hammering away on hot rivets, he could only keep that up if he was well fed. So very often the mother would do without.

Palmer's was one of the best-equipped repair yards in the world, I would say. It did very well and it was a profitable business. You quoted a price for the particular job, then when the ship came in it was discovered there were other problems and once there were extras to do, the company seemed to be able to charge what it liked, especially if it was a warship. The government didn't mind what they paid. Rebuilding and repairing was a hire-and-fire business. When the yard was busy you were expected to work all the hours that God sent and I would say that was the cause of any industrial unrest in the industry: the fact that a man would be expected to work like hell and get a job finished, but the harder he worked the more likely or the quicker he would be paid off if the yard didn't have a follow-on contract. My situation was a little bit different. In the drawing office very often we weren't working on the jobs that were in the yard. We would have done drawings and ordered materials before the ship came in. Then when it did come in the yard would work on that job but by then we were attempting to get the next job and when a job finished we were always working on trying to get the next one.

By this time, though, Palmer's was a subsidiary of Vickers-Armstrongs Shipbuilders and the industry was changing. It changed on the Tyne when Swan Hunter gradually took over everything. I think there was pressure from the government to standardize and for Vickers-Armstrongs to get out of shipbuilding on the Tyne and concentrate only on their Barrow yard. That was when the decision to close Palmer's was made. When I first heard that the yard was going to close I couldn't believe it, because just a few years before that the firm had spent millions and millions of pounds building a brand-new dry dock. It's still there at Hebburn and it's still the most modern dry dock in the country. I think the general feeling was that it would never close after they'd spent so much money on it, but it was all part of a process of rationalization of the industry. This led to the Swan Hunter Group being formed and Swan Hunter taking over all the yards on the River Tyne and on the Tees, which led to nationalization and eventually the failure of nationalization and the disappearance of the industry.

There were some strange things happened at that time. For example, for every ship that has to be launched they use enormous amounts of wood and wood is expensive, so when Swan Hunter amalgamated all the yards they thought they could save money by shifting the wood around to wherever they were building a ship. To supervise this they made somebody a manager and he was called the berth controller. Of course that guy was always known as 'the Pill' for the rest of his working life.

The yard closed in 1982, but in actual fact I was never made redundant. I got a bit of an indication that things were going to end so I wrote after a job with Lloyd's Register of Shipping. It did mean that I had to leave Tyneside and go and live in London and work in an office, but that's how I kept in employment when the yards started to close. Lloyd's Register set the standards for ships to be built and to be repaired and my job was to check with Lloyd's rules that all the steel sizes and all the pipe sizes and everything were all correct on any ship that was being built or repaired.

The Tyne and its shipyards brought a wide range of jobs to the communities that had grown up along its banks. Tommy Procter from South Shields grew up by the river and from an early age he set his sights on getting a job on it.

Because I lived on the river and always knocked about down by the river I always wanted to work on the tug boats. My father wanted me to be a draughtsman because I was very good at drawing, but I didn't want that. I wanted to be close to the river. But when I left school there were no jobs on the tugs so I started to serve my time as an apprentice fitter. I started in a little shipyard called the Tynework Engineering Company, which was also known as the Market Dock or the Pawn Shop Dock because it was close to the pawn shop. I was an office boy first and the only thing I can remember about it was that there were a lot of typists and you could smell their perfume and their make-up. It was pretty daunting, all that red lipstick.

From the office I went down into the general store dishing out nuts and bolts and rivets. They had two small steam cranes working in the yard and you could always smell the smoke off them mixed in with the smell of all the smoke from the river. Then there was the noise. There was always a lot of riveting going on so the noise was continuous. Sound carried a long way over water so you would hear it coming from all the other yards on a continual basis, especially when the river was busy.

After I'd spent some time in the stores I should have gone to the fitting shop, but I didn't get that far because, when I was sixteen, a job came up on the tugs and I took that. I got it because [the tug crews] used to come through the shipyard to get to the tugs so I was pretty much in constant contact with them. As well as that I'd put my name down at the tug office, so I was on the waiting list. When I started on the tugs I was an apprentice deckhand. You did this until you were twenty-one, then you came out of your time and became a fully qualified deckhand. As an apprentice you did all the menial tasks like the cooking, so one of the first things I had to do was learn to cook. We had a coal fire so I had to light the galley fire and we had fires in the cabins, so I used to have to light them as well. There were seven crew members, six men and a boy, and the boy was the mainstay – he did everything. I had to trim lamps, then there was brasswork to polish and I had cabins to keep clean. I had to scrub all the floors and wash lots of dishes. I didn't have a sink with taps and hot and cold running water; I had to go and boil a kettle or use condensed steam. I was still known as 'the boy' when I was twenty-one years of age. 'There boy,' that's how they used to talk to you.

The tugs used to moor out at the buoys about a

quarter of a mile off the shore. Each one had a little boat and I had to go out to the tug in that by myself first thing in the morning before the crew to light the fire and put the kettle on, because if the kettle wasn't boiling when they were coming on board you got your lug kicked. There might be another two or three lads in their boats going to their tug because there might be four or five tugs ready for that time in the morning if there were two or three ships coming in. You climbed aboard the tug by yourself, made the boat fast, did your business, got back in the boat and went and picked the men up. When you made the boat fast to the buoys you had to lower the boat into the water from the tug as it was still moving, get down into it and row to the buoys. The buoys were massive and when I got to one of them I had to get a runner and climb up on to the buoy to attach it. I couldn't swim, so I had to be extra careful not to fall in. And surprisingly, nobody was ever lost. I used to take the oar home with me just in case someone else pinched it. If they did I wouldn't be able to get back out to the tug.

Two men and the boy worked on the deck and when you had to get the ropes and cables in you had to pull them in by hand. In the winter it was very cold and that was when it was good to be on a steam tug.

One of the fond memories I have is how we used to cook for ourselves. We used to pay 2/6d, which is 12½ pence now, for the food and I used to have to go and get the stores. I used to buy the meat every day and I used to get the vegetables, and one of the crew used to cook and then he taught me how. I learnt how to make mince, potatoes and dumplings – good old stodgy food. And you needed it, because you were working long hours. It was all fresh; no frozen stuff. I always remember the smell of the cooking. It used to be great. Prior to lunch I went to shore again with a couple of haversacks and got bottles of beer from one of the local pubs, because they liked their bottles of Brown Ale to drink at lunchtime. Screw-top bottles it was – none of these crown tops or cans. You used to get them in a wooden crate that had four big bottles in it. If you took them back you used to get a penny on the bottle. I used to have a bag full of empty bottles to take back and woe betide you if you didn't get the penny. Any time the crew could get drink they would drink it. [After dinnertime] if the tug had no work the crew would go and have a siesta and the boy would be left to get on with his work. I washed the dishes, scrubbed the galley, polished the brass, polished my kettle and blackened the stove, and I would keep an eye on the three fires to keep them alight and keep the steam up while the rest of the crew were snoring.

We didn't stop work on Christmas Day. Ships still came in on Christmas Day and New Year's Eve. I have sailed myself on Christmas Day, because it's one of those industries you've got to keep going twenty-four seven. If a ship was in a yard and work on it was finished, it would sail whatever day it was. The shipyard would not hold it up because that would make it late and they would have to start paying the ship-owner. The hours that the tugboat men worked were long. Often it was 120-odd hours a week, so you're looking at eighty-odd hours' overtime. We used to work all through the night, because ships came in all hours of the day and night. We used to go two and three days and nights round the clock. I can remember going aboard on Monday morning and stepping back on shore on Thursday dinnertime. The wage was poor but the overtime made up for it and this is one of the reasons why so many went to work on the tugs.

I wanted to be a tug skipper, but when I was twenty-one and I came out of my time, the ship-repair yards were declining, which meant less work for the tugs, so six of us got paid off. I was married by then, so I took whatever work I could get. I was young and fit so I worked on building sites and in the shipyards doing tank-cleaning. I did various other little jobs, at that time including working in a factory, which I hated because I didn't like being indoors. But you do these things because I had two kids by then and you had to provide for your family. I worked on dredgers on the river and then I got a job back on the tugs when I was twenty-four. I was relief master, which meant I was acting skipper when I was twenty-five. But it was dead men's shoes. I was qualified but I didn't get a skipper's job until eleven years later.

By then there wasn't the work here on the river. What we felt as river workers was that the shipyard workers and the dockers didn't help themselves. Basically they did themselves out of their jobs by too many strikes and asking for too much money. As the work on the river went down I did a little bit of sea-towing – that's not just the river, that's taking things from the river, towing barges and ships around Europe. Then I went wherever I could get the work – Scotland first, and then I went to work abroad for more money. I ended up working all round Europe, West Africa, the Gulf of Mexico, around New Orleans, and I even worked on the Caspian Sea. But it was a big step to leave the River Tyne.

The whole period from the beginning of the 1950s to the end of the 1980s was a time of great change for Britain's shipbuilding industry. The pneumatic riveting hammers had begun to be replaced by welding during the war years. At the same time there was a revolution in shipbuilding, starting in the United States, where the advances in welding and developments in prefabrication techniques led to greater standardization and the idea of mass-producing ships on a flow-line basis. After the war other countries called on the American experience to rethink their approach to shipbuilding. Again, as in other industries where Britain had led the world, the UK shipbuilding industry found it difficult to adapt and change. The new techniques called for a higher degree of mechanization than the traditional British system did and could only be applied in yards that specialized in a narrow range of ships. Some yards were too small to turn out the larger vessels that were now in demand and yards that had always prided themselves on their ability to produce a wide variety of different ships on a one-off basis couldn't adapt very easily to specialization and mass production. As the technology changed, the British shipbuilding industry went into decline and the great shipyards began to struggle in the face of foreign competition.

In 1965 shipbuilding became something of a pre-occupation of Harold Wilson's new Labour government and a committee was set up to look into ways of re-structuring the industry to make it more competitive in world markets. The resultant Geddes Report's recom-mendations included the separation of shipbuilding and engine building, and the streamlining of shipbuilding through the amalgamation of the many small shipyards into five large groups in order to strengthen skills and expertise. As the industry was restructured, shipyard workers had to move from yard to yard to stay in work. Traditionally there had been great rivalry between the workers from the Tyneside yards and those on the Wear, but that now had to be put aside as men had to move from one river to the other. Kenneth Moore had spent all his working life on the Tyne until in the early 1970s he got a job at Thompson's yard in Sunderland.

It was only about five or six miles from South Shields and I used to bike it because there were no buses. Because South Shields was right on the beach they used to call the people from there Sand Dancers. At Thompson's they used to call me Little Sandy and my mate Big Sandy. The Sunderland lads were called Mackems and they never liked the Sand Dancers. When eight men had to get paid off the foreman come to me and my mate Graham and asked us if we were happy there, because he didn't want to lose us. We said we were, because we were earning good money there – £20 a week, and this was in the early

1970s – [but] the men had a meeting outside the gates of the yard and said the Sand Dancers have got to go. We went to see the shop steward and then got the manager down. The manager asked the shop steward where he was from and he said he was from Hartlepool. 'Well,' the manager said, 'these lads only come from four miles away from here and you are from thirteen miles away, so you're the stranger. Not only that, I've asked ten different shipwrights to do the job they're doing and there's not one of them that can do it. I've asked these two lads and they can do it with their hands tied behind their back, so I'm not finishing them.' I was there for thirteen years and because I was a Sand Dancer it took me about ten year to get accepted and make friends there. You'd go to the clubs with them at night time and you'd get certain men who were okay, but you always got some, mainly old-timers, who had been there a long time – and they didn't take to a Sand Dancer coming in and doing the job better than they could do, so there was a lot of animosity. People were watching their backs and thinking other people were coming in from outside and taking their jobs. They would say, 'We don't do things like that here; you've got to do what we do.' But what they were doing was crap and I'd tell them it was.

The state-directed modernization and rationalization of the industry after the Geddes Report in 1965 was followed by nationalization in 1977 by a Labour government, then a swift return to privatization after the election of the Thatcher government in 1979. Throughout this time the industry was contracting, but yards were also modernizing and bringing in new technologies in an attempt to compete more effectively in the international market. John Bage, who was born in South Shields in 1947, began his working life at Readhead's and finished up on the Wear at Sunderland Shipbuilders. He trained in the drawing office and throughout his career witnessed a transformation in the way a draughtsman worked.

When I was at school in the early 1960s one third of my lessons were related to technical subjects. Whilst my classmates dreamed of sailing off to distant shores in the Merchant Navy, I was quite happy to do what I liked best, and that was Technical Drawing. I wanted to be a draughtsman and I never considered doing anything else.

When I left school a friend of mine, who wanted to become a welder, was working as an office boy at John Readhead & Sons. He mentioned this to me and I thought I would send them a letter. These were the days when there were plenty of ship orders around and the yard was a hive of activity, offering excellent prospects. I got an interview with a Mr Chisholm, the personnel manager, and I was offered a position as an apprentice draughtsman. So just three weeks after leaving school at seventeen I started in the outfitting office. That was 17 August 1964 and I was very pleased to have what was considered in those days to be a good job with a reasonable salary and conditions. For my first week's pay I proudly took home £3.8s.8d [£3.43], half of which I gave to my mother for my keep.

The office I worked in was in a very old building.

It smelled of stale tobacco smoke, but that was acceptable in those days as nearly everyone smoked. The walls were all wood-panelled and there were only a few sash windows that gave very little natural light. Large canopies with fluorescent lights in them hung down on chains from the ceiling over every drawing desk. These desks were large, heavy wooden sets of plan-storage drawers with horizontal tops to which the drawings were pinned. Everybody in the office was required to wear a suit and tie and polished shoes, but it was okay to take your jacket off when you were working. Respect was to be given to older staff and management, and when the managing director came round the place was so quiet you could hear a pin drop.

The drawings were done in ink on a waxed linen which had to be pinned and stretched out on the desk top and then rubbed over with powdered chalk. One job the apprentices had to do was to scrape a block of chalk to ensure sufficient powder was available for everyone. We also had to make the coffee twice a day for everyone in the office and I remember one morning an older draughtsman said the coffee tasted like chalk. He was overheard by one of the trainees, who made the afternoon coffee for the complainer with a dose of the powdered chalk and he drank it without any comment or complaint. The office turned out to be very friendly and in fact was more like family – something I haven't really experienced in any of the many drawing offices I have worked in over the last thirty-six years. My years there were a pleasure and I met some very fine people who became a source of encouragement for me for the rest of my life.

It sounds crude now, but when I started we used to have italic nibs on the pens we used and we got the ink from a dipper. It was a very slow process. All the printing on the drawings was done with an italic pen and I spent my first few days just sitting using this pen on the special waxed material to see if I could get the hang of it, because you could easily blotch it or smudge it. It used to take a while for the ink to dry. We used to have to bring the lamp over on top of it and that would dry the ink. A very slow process and extremely expensive.

In those days the plans weren't a set size like they are now. They were a general arrangement for a ship and they could be the length of one of the desks, which was about ten foot. Most of the actual drawing was done by the older guys who had been doing it for many years, since long before the Second World War, and they were very skilled at it. It was almost as if they were artists and the younger people who started, like myself, used to admire the work. They used to do the better plans and drawings, like the side view of the ship. They used a ruler and set squares and compasses to draw the thing, but they were also filling in more detail, like an artist would do, to create a beautiful finished job. They always went into great detail and in the older ships they even used to draw in the coal. If the ship's galleys had tiled floors they'd actually draw each little black or white tile. They were beautiful. When the ships had been built and they were finished with the plans they used to go down into the vault and later on they became collectors' items. As time went on the materials changed and everything had to be produced a bit more quickly, but in those days they were doing drawings that were works of art.

During my apprenticeship I had to go to college one day a week and one night a week to study naval architecture. In my first year I passed the exams and did well and I got put into the design office, which was in the same building but with less people. The work in here was much more interesting, designing the ships and doing calculations for launching the ships and for their stability. There were no calculators then, so everything had to be worked out longhand.

There were three or four offices where all the design work was done. The outfit office was all the furniture, the furnishings and fittings and the machinery on the decks and lots of other stuff. Then there was one that did the steelwork for the whole of the ship. And there was a separate building where the engineers did all the engine side of things. In our outfit office there were only about seven or eight people, which wasn't very many to produce the drawings. It used to take about a year to do all the drawings for one ship – about a hundred drawings would be needed. For each ship there would be one guy who we called a section leader and the rest of them were just draughtsmen and an apprentice or two. Some of the drawings were quite complex, but a young apprentice would do smaller drawings, detailing say lamps or lights.

The ships always started off in the same way. Somebody who ran a shipping company would be wanting a ship, or several ships, and they would put feelers out around various places. Our company, along with others, would put in an estimate and we would do a small version of a general arrangement drawing, maybe about two foot six long with plan views. We would just do simple arrangements of what was required and then that would be submitted to the people who were interested and they would make their comments on it, say if they wanted more crew on board or more cabins or more space to carry cargo. Estimates generally would be done in a hurry, so there was always overtime then. It would be all hands to the pump to get the drawings done, work out all the necessary volumes and capacities of the holds and that sort of thing. Then if the order was placed we'd be elated; everybody would be over the moon because that meant there was another year's work for the yard. It would hit the headlines in the local papers – always front-page news when we got an order. Exciting times they were. You were doing something you liked doing and you were with people you liked and it was a reasonably good wage and a secure job at the time, we thought.

The yard started at 7.30 in the morning and finished at 4.30. In the office we started at 8.30 and finished at five, with an hour and a quarter for lunch. It was a five-year apprenticeship but we continued going to college for another two years after that, one day a week and one night. You were expected to go to college for the full seven years and try to get the relevant certificates in naval architecture. Some people went on to take degree courses and became naval architects, or went on to Lloyd's Register as surveyors. You tended to get the upper management in the shipyards by that process. There was rarely a plumber or a joiner who made it up to director levels. They tended to come through the drawing office. They often became shipyard managers as well.

Exactly opposite Readhead's was a shop where everybody from the shipyard used to go for something to eat and for cigarettes. In those days just about everyone smoked, so they made a lot out of cigarette sales. It was like a café and they used to make sandwiches up, so people used to go across at break times and get buns with eggs in and beefburgers and all the unhealthy stuff. Then there were two pubs up the road and on a lunchtime men from the yard would go out to the pubs. From the office we didn't go in every day, but on a Friday lunchtime we used to go to the pub and play darts or dominoes. Readhead's had their own social club too, about a mile from the shipyard. It had a bar and a couple of lounges and they had snooker tables and darts, and we even had karate lessons there. Everybody used to pay so much a week out of their wages for it, but it was just pennies.

When apprentices started at that time someone would always have a bit of fun with them. They'd maybe ask you to pop down to the stores and get a bag of nail holes, and when you were a young apprentice, brand new to the place, you'd just go and do it. Or you'd be sent to get a bucket of steam. You knew it was impossible, but you'd take an empty bucket and go in the stores and say there is a man up there who says 'Can I have a bucket of steam please?' But these things were never done to hurt your feelings or give you an inferiority complex or send you crying for a psychiatrist. It was just good fun and you just took it. And when we were apprentices we had good times there. A group of us would go out quite often at lunchtimes. One day we'd go to the swimming baths, another day we'd go tenpin bowling. It was great. We also had interdepartmental football teams. I used to play on our team even though I couldn't see the ball without my glasses because we were always short of people to play in the drawing office. There was some real rivalry between the departments. Usually the welders won the tournaments every year because they had the toughest guys. But the good thing wasn't the football; it was afterwards, we used to go in and have a good drink.

There were only a few apprentices in the drawing office, but I was fortunate because my friend was going to be a welder. I'd been friends with him for years and we used to go out drinking in the town and clubbing and that sort of thing, so through him I got to know a lot of the shipyard apprentices of all the trades. But I do remember whenever I met a new one I always tried to avoid telling them where I worked to avoid any sort of stigma about 'them and us'. If they said, 'Where do you work? I haven't seen you round the yard,' I'd just say, 'I work in the office.' I didn't say I was a draughtsman. But I got on well with most of them. I went to one or two of their weddings and we always used to have stag parties for those getting married, and birthday parties were regular things.

The changes in the shipyards on the Tyne that followed the publication of the Geddes Report saw Readhead's become part of Swan Hunter Group, along with Hawthorn Leslie and the Vickers yard at Walker. For John, the changes meant a move.

Once the decision [to merge] had been made over a period of about a year, they gradually moved office staff up to Hebburn shipyard and we worked there. At first there was a separate office for Readhead's and we were still designing Readhead's ships, but gradually we became absorbed into the bigger company. Everything became centralized and Swan Hunter's design office started to make all the big decisions. Even though Readhead's still had some of us in the design office, it was Swan's management that were actually discussing it with us. So slowly over a period of a year or so it all gelled together into one company – the Swan Intergroup.

I was there for a while, but then I went to the Wear to work and I had twelve great years there. In the 1960s and 1970s the unions were very strong on the rivers and people were not allowed to move from the River Wear to work on the River Tyne and vice versa. [But in] 1975 there was a bit of a shortage of draughtsmen, so I was able to get into the drawing office of the newly formed Sunderland Shipbuilders. It was a brand-new shipyard, the most modern in Europe, purpose-built and everything under cover. They got lots of orders in the first few years and built lots of beautiful ships, all under cover without the rain and snow on the workers, so there weren't any stoppages for bad weather. It was great. I loved it there. We had brand-new offices with a fantastic entrance, all marble and wood. In those days we didn't have any stoppages because we got ship after ship after ship, so the work was continuous. I was often called a Sand Dancer because I was from South Shields, and I'm sure there was one or two of them there weren't keen on people from South Shields working on the Wear, but generally I got on okay with most of the people there.

By this time my work as a draughtsman was changing. I'd started off with the waxed linen and Indian ink and then they brought out a pen like a fountain pen for us to use. It held cartridges with ink, so you no longer had to use an inkwell. Then they brought out a translucent sheet of plastic that we could draw on with a pencil. It meant that if you made a mistake you could rub it out and generally it speeded the job up quite a bit. That went on for a good number of years, then they started bringing computers in and that completely turned everything upside down. The office I was in had around seventy people, but at first they only had six or eight computers and they had them in a separate room because they were such big, cumbersome things. You had a keyboard, but you also had a box at the side, which was called a 'function box', and you also had a light pencil, so you really needed three hands to operate the things.

You used the function box to select a shape, like a circle. Then you had to touch the screen with the light pen where you wanted it to go and then use the keyboard to type in the measurements you wanted for it. But that was the way forward, we'd been told, and they were promising that we would all have lots of leisure time and that the hours in the working week would go down drastically. But it never happened. Computers were more accurate than the old ways of doing things, but [they] tended to drag you into detailing more than was needed.

All of those computers that we had at first were on a mainframe and if it crashed everybody was stopped doing anything. I remember one time we had two days off because something went wrong with the hard disk in the mainframe and they couldn't get it replaced for two days, so nothing got done. Gradually they got more and more computers in the drawing office, but they still didn't have enough for everybody, so they introduced shift working – six o'clock in the morning till two, and another shift that started about one o'clock and went on till eight, and eventually they put about six or eight people on night shift. I was a supervisor by then, so I was the one who was actually organizing the shift rotas and I did see changes in personalities. Shift working had a bad effect on some people. They were coming in unshaven, obviously falling out of bed and coming straight into work. Some people fell asleep on night shift and had to be moved back on to day shift straight away. It was a big change. A lot of people liked it because there was an increase in salary, but some of the older draughtsmen struggled;

they couldn't adapt as well as the younger ones. I felt sorry for them.

By this time I was working in an air-conditioned office, sitting on a padded swivel chair at an ultra-modern desk and using a state-of-the-art, powerful computer to produce drawings by creating 3D parametric models. We have come a long way from the conditions of that first office I started in. But there have been changes in people too and how they relate to each other. Nowadays people sitting within a few metres of one another often communicate by internal email. The lunchbreak no longer features a thriving card school, but instead individuals play games by themselves on their PCs. That 'family' feeling so apparent in my first job doesn't seem to have a place in modern times. Our society has advanced tremendously in terms of technology since I first started work in the shipyard drawing office, but it is so very sad to see how people's relationships have deteriorated in just thirty-six years.

Fortunately for me, I have fond memories of that first office and my first job in the 'grown-up' world. And I will never forget the sights and sounds of the shipyard as the steel plates were formed into magnificent ships that would go on to sail around the world to so many different places for years to come. We were so proud of every one of them. The people in the North East's shipyards were unique – this has been said many times by many people. I can confirm that they were very special from my years working with so many of them in and around the shipyards of the Tyne and Wear.

In the final years of the industry one of the most successful yards in the North East was Austin & Pickersgill, a
medium-sized firm on the Wear that had traditionally
built general-purpose cargo vessels. The yard was exten-
sively rebuilt at this time to concentrate production on a
standard bulk carrier which would meet the needs of the
yard's customers at low cost. The new ship, known as the
SD14, was first launched in 1968 and proved to be a great
success. Robert Hunter grew up in South Shields and was
taken on as a management trainee at Bartram's yard in
Sunderland. He went on to be fitting-out manager there
and was involved in the construction of SD14s that were
built under licence from Austin & Pickersgill, but he will
never forget his first impressions of the industry.

> Suddenly here I was in an industrial environment
> where, to my horror, the men in the shipyard started
> at seven thirty in the morning! That was the time I
> had been just getting up in the morning, but to be at
> the yard for seven thirty they had to be up at six.
> There was this hierarchy about what time you
> started in the morning. I was classed as office staff
> and they came in at eight thirty, or quarter to nine,
> or, if you pushed it, nine o'clock. The directors
> didn't come in till nine thirty or quarter to ten. The
> foremen should have been there at seven thirty with
> the rest of the workers, but a lot of them didn't come
> in till quarter past eight.
>
> Part of the management trainee scheme involved
> going to university to do a degree in naval archi-
> tecture. But I spent the first of the five years working
> in the planning office because the university degree

course didn't start for me until after twelve months. Because I was well qualified in pure and applied maths, part of my task was to calculate the weight [and centre of gravity] of all of the units of the ship so that before a crane picked up a unit we knew exactly what the weight was and could work out whether it was a one-crane lift or a two-crane lift, or even a three-crane lift. I was very quickly given the responsibility of working out all of the weights of these units, five or six units a day.

One particular lift we had was the four-pick unit, which meant you picked the unit up with a combination of a twenty-five-ton crane and two fifteen-ton cranes. We used to have to lift it up, rotate it through 90° and offer it up to the ship. And all of that had to be done in such a way that none of the cranes were ever overloaded. It was a hairy experience for me during those first twelve months, always wondering whether I had got the calculation right, especially as my immediate boss, the planning manager, hadn't got the time to go through my calculations to see whether I had got them right or not. It was an intricate task that needed method and precise discipline in order to do it properly.

After twelve months doing that I started my university course and then I had to work in the shipyard in all of the different departments during the vacations. So whereas a lot of my friends at university were going off to pick grapes in the south of France in the summer, I was having to work in the shipyard with the shipwrights and the platers and the welders and all the different departments – the drawing office, design office, commercial department, production control, plumbers, painters, fitters, joiners and electricians. During the five years of my training I got hands-on experience of every aspect of shipbuilding. [I might be told to report to the] head foreman plater, who would give me a lecture about being on time for work at seven thirty with everybody else. I wasn't a staff member any more in the summer, and because I was working with all the other men in the yard, I had to behave as they did and be at work at seven thirty. I had my leg pulled – but what young man doesn't get his leg pulled, particularly when he's working in an environment where he is going off to university and college to train in an intellectual activity like naval architecture and at the same time he's being trained in what actually goes on in a shipyard.

Towards the end of the five years I was given real responsibility. At times we had possibly two or three ships in the water for outfitting.[34] The outfitting manager couldn't cope with three, so I was withdrawn from my normal training programme to take over as assistant outfitting manager and have the responsibility for fitting out one of them until he became free to finish off. So at the age of twenty-three I was responsible for the fitting out of some major ships. I had a team of foremen under me, so suddenly I had gone from being the trainee under them to being their

[34] The processes associated with outfitting or fitting out a ship include the installation of engines and boilers, completion of super-structure and deck equipment, painting, plumbing, electrical installation and the fitting of furniture.

immediate boss! They were very supportive of me, though, because they had been part of my training programme and they were proud of this. But I was still only getting £5 a week and the foremen who were working under me were getting £25! They used to pull my leg a lot because I was very naïve and unworldly. I hadn't been exposed to street life at all. And this was heavy industry where there was trade union activity and there was occasionally a bit of trouble there with me. At one stage I was accused of being the management spy, which was untrue. So there was occasional animosity, but that was part of life in the yard and the more sensible guys were all right.

By the time his management training had finished in the mid-1960s Robert was working in the planning and production-control department. It was a time of change in the shipbuilding industry and the management at Bartram's were, as Robert recalls, in the forefront of bringing in new technology and changing the way the yard was run.

It was a time when pressure was being put on our department by those who were in financial control. The yard got stage payments for building a ship, so they were involved in working out different ways to get some of the stages completed quicker. Basically it involved getting more of the work done prior to the launch in order to minimize the amount that needed to be done once the ship was afloat. From a logistical point of view this speeded the job up and cut costs, because the cost of doing a job when the ship was afloat was significantly higher than the cost of doing that job if the ship was still on the stocks.

As a result of all the changes that were made at this time we were successful in building ships that were significantly more complex than our little yard should have been capable of and we were building rather sophisticated ships for the Blue Star Line and the New Zealand Shipping Company to bring meat from New Zealand, Australia and South America to the UK. They were fully refrigerated and had high-quality accommodation and sophisticated engines that enabled them to travel at twenty knots, which was fast. But the design was an old one. They were basically Liberty ships, which were the cargo vessels of the Second World War. Over two thousand were built in the US during the war, but the basic design was a modified version of a British tramp cargo ship.[35] We were struggling to build four a year. Then in 1965 another Sunderland company, Austin & Pickersgill, came up with a new design to replace the old Liberty ships. Most of them were run by Greek shipping lines and Austin Pickersgill's had good connections with them, so they designed a replacement so that the Greeks could scrap all their twenty-five-year-old ships and buy new from them. That design was called the SD14, and we started building them under licence at Bartram's in 1967. By that time I was fitting-out manager and I was involved in the construction of the very first SD14 that was launched.

[35] A ship which does not have a fixed schedule or timetabled ports of call.

Things were going well at Bartram's, but the British shipbuilding industry in general was in a mess. It had been the largest industry in the world, one that used to build 40 per cent of the world's ships. But the Japanese and the Koreans were taking over. They were building much bigger ships in more modern shipyards – huge new complexes on green-field sites. [In Britain the] industry was locked into narrow river estuaries that were just not large enough for huge complexes like that. They were small establishments and they couldn't expand. We were still looking for lucrative contracts from British ship-owners, but the owners started to get much better contracts from overseas where [the shipbuilders] were getting government support. But then things changed dramatically.

Bartram's was an independent, family-owned company, but following the publication of the Geddes Report they were put under pressure by the government to merge with Austin Pickersgill's. What it meant in practice was that Bartram's were taken over by Austin Pickersgill's and I was appointed manager of the Bartram yard at the age of twenty-seven. I was the only member of the Bartram management team who got promotion out of all this. All of the others, unfortunately, had to play second fiddle to an Austin Pickersgill man. But it was a very successful time because the true benefits of standardization for building repeat ships one after the other and the sophisticated planning and production-control system that we had really started to be felt. Previously our throughput of tonnage had been little more than two hundred tons a week and when we started the SD14 programme it was thought that we would only be able to build about four SD14s a year. But with the young team that we then had in the yard we forged ahead and increased our production to over three hundred tons a week, which was six SD14s a year.

For me it was a wonderful experience. The management said they weren't going to interfere with the work I was doing. They were good bosses who trained people properly then gave them their head, delegating responsibility and allowing them to get on with it. Although the companies had merged, both the yards had been kept open, which was good because there was friendly competition between the two. The Austin Pickersgill yard was producing about 430 tons a week and at the smaller Bartram's yard we produced about 330. We had a blackboard in the yard and each week it would be brought up to date with the production figures from both yards so we could compare what was going on. We made use of this friendly competition and it worked very well.

During this time I came to the attention of the senior management because of the production figures and they decided I could do with some formal management training, so I was sent off to the States for six months to Harvard Business School in Boston. The upside of going away to Harvard was that I was exposed to what was going on in the rest of the world. I was one of 150 students on this course; a hundred were from America and fifty were from other locations in the world, and suddenly I realized there was this whole big wide world out there full of opportunities. But the downside was that I knew I was running the risk of being side-tracked when I came back, and that's exactly what happened. It was a very chastening experience for me. I was only thirty-one and I was being frozen out of a senior position in the company. I had a period when I thought, 'Do I stay here and try and challenge this? Or do I look elsewhere?'

It was 1971 and at the time I was aware of the growth and development of the oil and gas business in the UK, so I wrote a paper and presented it to the directors of Austin Pickersgill's, proposing that we should be developing a subsidiary and starting up a new yard devoted to construction for the oil and gas business. This was a brand-new industry and I could see small companies, like William Press on Tyneside, starting to develop offshore fabrication yards, so that's what I advocated for Austin Pickersgill's. The only response I got was, 'We've got a full order book for ships for two years. How can we possibly do any-thing else?' So I decided to leave. It was 1973 and when I went to see the managing director of Austin Pickersgill's he was rather critical of my decision to go. He said, 'You shouldn't be considering leaving the industry that has trained you.' But I said, 'Hang on a minute, I am only thirty-two now and when I am forty-two I don't believe you will be in business.' They might still have had a full order book then, in 1973, but they had become complacent. In spite of the reorganization of the industry – or maybe because of it – they weren't as sharp and commercially aware as they had been in the late 1960s. They were resting on their laurels. The yard did eventually close down ten years later, just as I had predicted.

The decline of the industry meant that for the ordinary shipyard worker and his family times were often hard. The men were in and out of work all the time as Win Currie from Hebburn remembers.

I was married to George for forty years. He served his time in the shipyards, but it was hard for him because he was on deck in all weathers and there was no protective clothing so he used to get soaking. He was a fitter so he was working all over the ship from the deck down to the bilges below. I'd go looking for old boilersuits to patch his because you never bought a new one. They'd bring their overalls and boilersuits home and you'd be washing them and the washing machine was full of oil and filings.

He was made redundant quite a lot. We hadn't been married very long when he was first made redundant from Swan Hunter's, but then he got work at Palmer's and he was there for quite a while. But then there seemed to be big pay-offs all the time and after that he was a casual worker, in and out of work all the time. When one was out, they were all out of work. You didn't go to the dole looking for jobs; it all went by word of mouth. You'd find out there was a ship coming in, so you'd ring up and get taken on in that sort of way. You'd have the phone number of the charge-hand and he'd say, 'Oh it's you, George. Can you get in touch with your mates and tell them we're taking on?' They were all well known. There was a squad that went from yard to yard. That's the way it was, rather than going to the dole. We were just starting off with the family then. So it was hard but we always managed to keep our heads above water. We all had to be good managers.

When they were out of work it was hard for the women. You'd no sooner got the benefits sorted out and he was in and out of work again so you had to sort it all out again. You were getting further and further behind with your rent. Benefits would take you on, but then it would stop when he got a job, but you wouldn't get a wage for the next fortnight and it was a case of in and out all the time. I looked after the money. He used to come home and give me his pay packet, which was unheard of then, I think. I'd give him a bit of pocket money and then everything was worked out to the penny what we had to pay out. And even when he was on the benefit I'd get all the money, but he wouldn't have the pocket money when he was out of work. It was a case of making do and mend.

He was out of work once for twenty-six weeks. That was the longest and that was really bad. Debts were mounting up – not that we had a lot of debt because we did without. If you couldn't afford it, you didn't get it. But it was the rent that was the hardest. It got worse as the yards were starting to close because more men were vying for fewer jobs. The shipping was declining and more men were out of work. And he wasn't trained for anything else; he didn't know anything else. Sometimes he had to travel away to work where there was a boat – Southampton, Liverpool, wherever. And sometimes in brief spells when he was off he'd go cleaning in power stations. That would see us through a little bit. That's how we kept our heads above water. But he never liked to be away from home. When there was a boat in, say, for eight weeks he'd work all days. He never had weekends off because you knew when that was finished there would be a lean time to come. So when the work was there he worked all hours. He worked on a Chilean destroyer once that was in for two years. It was a complete overhaul, refit and that was great. We knew it was two years' work and we could plan. We even had a holiday that year; we took the kids to Butlins.

Win got married in 1967 and her husband, George, was first paid off in 1971. 'Really,' she says, 'from then for about thirty years he was in and out of work.' The industry was in decline throughout this whole period and in spite of rationalization and state-directed modernization, nationalization and privatization, the decline could not be halted. The industry was unable to compete with lower-cost yards, principally in Japan and South Korea, and by the end of the 1990s there was very little left of an industry that had once ruled the world.

5

Men of Iron

A S WELL AS building ships and making everything from
the smallest nuts and bolts to the largest steam locomotives, Britain produced the raw materials that were
used to make them. Her prowess as a manufacturing
nation was built on iron and steel. The country was
blessed with good reserves of iron ore and in the seventeenth century the iron industry thrived in the Forest of
Dean and the Black Country. Early blast furnaces smelted
iron twenty-four hours a day, requiring a continuous
supply of raw materials. As well as the iron ore itself, wood
was needed to produce charcoal and limestone and clay
for the furnaces. By the end of the seventeenth century
there was a huge demand for wood and large areas of
forest were being cleared to provide the timber that was
needed, particularly for shipbuilding. This meant that
wood was becoming too expensive to be used as fuel for
the iron industry. A cheap and plentiful alternative was
needed. The breakthrough came in 1709 when Abraham
Darby of Coalbrookdale mastered the process of using
coke rather than charcoal to smelt iron.

The widespread adoption of coke as the fuel used in the

smelting of iron was a watershed in the history of industrialization. In the second half of the eighteenth century further technological breakthroughs in the field of ironworking and experiments in the use of steam power resulted in the invention of machinery that revolutionized the various processes in the manufacture of textiles. The application of the new technology to transport with the development of the world's first successful railways in the first part of the nineteenth century saw Britain change beyond recognition during the reign of Queen Victoria. As well as seeing the country linked by railways, she saw sail give way to steam at sea and industry spread its smoky cities all over Britain. The availability of vast quantities of coal and iron ore, along with the technological breakthroughs made here, transformed Britain during the course of Victoria's reign, turning it from a land of farmers to an industrial giant dominating the world and ruling over a vast empire.

In the first half of the nineteenth century Britain's iron output soared and demand from engineers and railway builders seemed unlimited. Then Henry Bessemer and other metallurgists made a series of breakthroughs that allowed cheap steel to be made in large quantities. Bessemer patented his revolutionary steelmaking process, the Bessemer Converter, in 1855. The process is a highly economical and efficient way of making steel in which the carbon, silicon and manganese impurities in cast iron, which is what makes it brittle, are oxidized and then removed by blowing air through molten cast iron in a furnace. Iron could be converted into steel at a fraction of the previous cost and the process only took between twenty and thirty minutes instead of ten days!

Iron and steel became the giants of industry, involving production on an epic scale, and they played a major part in Britain's nineteenth-century industrial growth and dominance. Steel brought railways, bridges, ships and armaments and a revolution in mechanical and light engineering as techniques were developed for turning large masses of the material into something that could be used by engineers. The age of iron and steel, together with advances in engineering, was seen as a new technological age, with Britain at the forefront of progress.

By 1900, however, iron and steel had become the first major industry in which Britain had lost its lead, as first the United States then Germany overtook British output. For much of the twentieth century Britain fell further behind. The root of the problem lay in the fact that the industry remained dominated by the nineteenth-century tradition of small, fiercely independent ironworks located on the coalfields where iron ore was also found. By this time many of these original supplies had been exhausted, leaving the plants trying to operate in locations that had become uneconomical. A lot of these original sites also lacked sufficient space to allow steelworks and rolling mills to be integrated, and as a result the industry was fragmented, with costly transport implications between ironworks, steelworks and rolling mills and a more expensive, complicated production procedure. In contrast, the Americans and Germans, although they had begun later, developed large plants where iron ore could be taken right through to finished steel on the same site, never allowing the metal to cool.

Matters were made worse during the First World War when, to meet munitions demand, money was spent on upgrading and enlarging old, inefficient steelworks, many of which should have been scrapped. During the Second World War British steelworkers turned out seventy-two million tons of steel, but outdated plant meant that in an industry in which the work was always demanding, working conditions were tougher than they needed to be.

Despite a lack of investment in new plant, in the 1950s South Wales, Sheffield, Teesside, Scunthorpe, west Cumbria and central Scotland were all still major steel-production areas. South Wales had been one of the earliest centres of the iron industry. As the demand for iron built up in the second half of the eighteenth century the industry came to dominate the landscape. All the raw materials needed for making iron – limestone, wood (charcoal), coal and iron ore – were found in an area known as the Heads of the Valleys and ironworks sprang up from Aberdare in the west to Blaenavon in the east. The counties of Glamorgan and Monmouthshire contained abundant seams of coal and iron ore, and immigrant workers from Ireland, Scotland and the English Midlands flocked there in search of work. In 1801 the population of Monmouthshire was forty-five thousand. A hundred years later it had increased to four hundred and fifty thousand.

In 1750 Merthyr Tydfil was a small rural village, but its proximity to large supplies of iron ore and coal made it an attractive site for the eighteenth-century ironmasters and the first ironworks there was opened in 1759. Others soon followed and by 1784 there were four large works within a two-mile radius of the original village. One of these was the Dowlais Ironworks, which by the 1830s had become the largest ironworks in the world. In 1845 it had 8,800 employees and eighteen blast furnaces producing

88,400 tons a year. In the 1850s it took out the first licence to use Henry Bessemer's process to produce steel and constructed the world's most powerful rolling mill. The first Bessemer steel was rolled there in 1865. The Dowlais works' early conversion to steel production allowed it to survive into the 1930s, but, largely as a result of the Depression, the main works ceased steel production in 1936. The iron foundry and engineering works in Dowlais, known locally as the 'Ifor Works', continued for some years under the name of the Dowlais Foundry and Engineering Company, but was transferred to the nationalized British Steel in 1973.

Ron Jenkins joined Dowlais as a metallurgical assistant after leaving grammar school at seventeen and when the company became part of British Steel he was manager of the general casting foundry. He was there until the works closed in 1987.

Before I started in I didn't even know what a foundry looked like. I remember [those early days] as a time when there was no discipline in the works. I was classed as an errand boy. It was always 'Go to the shop for something' or 'Go to the pub and get me ten fags.' I was an apprentice really, but I used to think we were just lackeys, and the workers would give you a thick ear as good as look at you. It was dirty there, but the best thing about it was that the foundry had a shower block. Every day I had a shower and washed my hair. Where I was living it was a bath one night a week on a Sunday night, shared by my three brothers and sisters. Also the works had a canteen block subsidized by the company and there were three canteens, workers, staff and management.

I worked in three different types of foundry [at Dowlais]. One was called a general castings foundry, one was an ingot-mould foundry and one was a non-ferrous foundry. All of them made equipment – or what we called furniture – for the steel industry at that time. Whatever a steelworks required in cast iron, I was involved in it. We made the ingot moulds that they poured the steel into to make a slab that went to the rolling mill and then came out as a sheet. Some of the ingot moulds were big; the biggest I've made was forty-five ton and that was six foot high. The weight of the mould was the same as the weight of the ingot.

Then I worked on the furnaces, which were called cupolas. As a metallurgical assistant I ensured the right material went into them in what we call the charge. In the melting process in a cupola you put a sand bed in the bottom to create a slope and the metal came out of what we call a tap hole. I wouldn't make the tap hole; that was the job of the furnace man. I would make certain that coke went in to make the bed. This had to be a certain height. You'd then ignite the coke through gas burners. Then you made sure the fire was a certain height above the holes all round where the blast of air goes in. Then I would check the charge going in. You put coke in as a fuel, limestone as a flux and any other addition that had to go into the furnace such as ferromanganese or ferrosilicon. My job was to check it going in and record the weights. This was pre-computers so I monitored all this manually. Then I would go down-stairs and check it as it came out for temperature when it went into the ladle and I would check that it went into certain castings.

Dowlais was good to me. There's no way in modern industry that you can start off at the bottom and get to the top inside the same works. I started in 1959 and became a superintendent in 1976 and manager two years later. I was lucky. I loved what I was doing and I only lived a quarter of a mile away. I was staff straight away. I earned £1.10s [£1.50] a week at the age of seventeen for a forty-five-hour working week. On Saturday morning I [also had a job] delivering suits for a local outfitter and I was getting ten shillings [50p] for that. So for forty-five hours in the foundry I was getting £1.10s and for four hours I was getting ten shillings! The man in the clothes shop offered me more money to go and work for him, but I loved what I was doing at the foundry.

At that time my father had a car and I was taught to drive. So that meant I could give lifts to people like the bosses. In those days rises were given by the managing director. He'd look down the list of names and think, 'Oh, Bill Jones – I don't know him. Give him five bob [25p]. Ah, Ron Jenkins – he's all right. Give him ten bob!' I might have been useless at work but they knew the name, so that was my first stroke of luck. Also because I had a car it was easy for me to get to [night school in] Cardiff three nights a week after I had finished work at five o'clock. They also allowed me to go to our parent company, Guest Keen Iron and Steelworks in Cardiff, for one of those days. So I went down there and if anyone wanted some-thing done between Dowlais and Guest Keen I was the one to do it. As I went up the ladder, working long hours didn't bother me so long as I could play my football on Saturday.

I was staff so I was somebody different: you had to set an example. I always wore a shirt and tie. There were certain people like directors that I called 'mister' from the day I started till the day I finished. There was also one of the older workers, lived round the corner, that I always called mister. People asked me why, and I said if my father was here and he heard me calling him by his first name I'd have a thick ear. It was a matter of respect.

You could never become a metallurgist unless you were qualified. You had to have a degree or HNC or HND. So as well as night school they sent me on courses. I went to Birmingham in 1964 and they put me up in the Grand Hotel, me and my cardboard case. I went in the revolving door and the doorman went to take my case. I held on to it fast – no way do you take it! At the desk the man said, 'What paper do you want in the morning, sir?' I looked at him and thought, 'Who are you calling "sir"?' '*Daily Mirror*,' I said and I thought the dog had done something on the floor the way he looked at me. I'd never seen anything like the room they put me in, [with] my own bathroom. But I learnt quick – the hard way but the right way. People used to talk about the working classes. I used to turn to them and say, 'I came from a slum. Cold-water tap, no hot water, didn't know what a bathroom was till I was twenty-four.' You'd see their faces change. People don't choose their environment, but they can get out of it. I was lucky and I was taught manners.

I left the works for two years and went first of all to work in a local college as a technician, then I went to work on open-hearth furnaces in Port Talbot Steelworks for eight months. After that I went back to Dowlais as a foreman on the modern hot-blast cupolas. With no drop bottom in them you had to keep a fire lit all the time and they'd run them for eight weeks. You had to see how many tons you wanted every day, clean the furnace out and maintain it, then on the night shift you started the cycle over again. The trouble was, if anything started to go wrong you couldn't see what was happening inside; you could only guess.

If you go anywhere you'll find all the blast furnaces are given women's names, the reason being they're all bitches. And that's the polite way to say it. Because they performed yesterday doesn't mean to say they're going to perform today. You can do identical things but you don't always get the same result in getting the metal out.

I was in charge of that on a three-shift system, seven days a week. It was a position of responsibility. If you made a mistake, everybody knew about it. There were no assessments then, no reviews. If your boss liked you, he put you forward. I got promotion to become a superintendent and moved to be manager of the general casting foundry. It was where I had started from, but it was not what I was actually trained for. I'd been on metal but this was where moulds were made from patterns in sand and it was a new learning curve for me. All of a sudden I was in charge of a hundred men, with four foremen, and [by then] the place was going to the wall. I wasn't a tradesman – I hadn't served an apprenticeship, and so the unions were up in arms about it. They even sent a letter to the managing director. I was on a loser, particularly as they were going to shut it down anyhow.

The first people I sorted out were the foremen. Apart from playing football on a Saturday I never socialized with them, but I told them they were with me or against me. And I was lucky. I made some major mistakes at first but then I did my homework. I read the union rules and I learnt the union set-up, because in those days the unions were strong. I don't decry the unions. Give me a good union man or a good shop steward and everyone progresses. A good shop steward is the best asset any manager can have. Somebody with a bit of sense. You can talk to them and they can talk to you. Anyway, I pulled that place round. I dragged it up by its feet, kicking and screaming. I couldn't set myself up as an expert, but I made people work for me and in the end we had a common goal. When I [became manager] that foundry was going to close in a month, then we started making money so they shut the one in Swansea instead.

I was adamant about the way I did things there. If I said I was going to do something I did it. [The whole place ran on] custom and practice, which meant they'd always done it that way. One example was that they used to have union meetings every day – it was far easier talking than working. I came home one day and said, 'Joe Bloggs has really got me down today.' My wife said, 'Joe Bloggs from round the corner? He's down at school every morning, taking his little boy, and he's there at dinnertime as well.' I thought he was in work all the time, so the next day I went to the security lodge where you had to clock in and out. When I asked if he went out every morning they told me he did, but he had permission from the previous superintendent. The following day I got him and he told me it was custom and practice. When I told him he must clock out whenever he left the works he said that meant he would lose money. I explained that it was a question of health and safety: if he was outside and had an accident, guess whose insurance it would be and who would be in court saying why he was out there without permission? 'From now on,' I told him, 'you clock out and you clock in, and I'll be checking.' Funnily enough, he didn't take his child to school any more after that.

I loved my work. I could sit down with a man and give him hell, we could have a real up-and-downer. Then he could go out and come back and say, 'Can I have an early finish today?' And I would say, 'Yes, I'll sort it out for you.' That was the understanding. I could go round and give them a row and then they'd still make me a cup of tea. I'd always tell them that I'd got a boss as well so there was always somebody telling me what to do. And I had a few rollickings myself.

It could still be a dangerous place to work. There was dust and noise everywhere and overhead cranes were a constant hazard. You didn't wear rings there. I've been suspended on a crane, and also on a ladder, by my ring. I didn't think it was possible, but it happened to me. I got a spillage of hot molten metal on my foot and I have been blown up three times. I saw all sorts of accidents, bad burns, two deaths. One was a suicide, the second was somebody doing a job at a height. He didn't strap himself in and he was throwing things down. As he did he caught his over-all and took himself down too. I've seen people gassed and I got gassed myself once. It was the worst half hour of my life.

One day we had something wrong and I had to go up a ladder to check what it was. While I was up there everything went black. I thought somebody had switched the lights off. We were fifty foot up, but my training held me in one spot. There were two of us up there so I shouted, 'Stay!' When I turned round all the roof had gone from the plant. There was a leak in the system and gas had ignited. Carbon monoxide and oxygen had combined and bang, it went up – £100,000 worth of damage. One thing you find when something like that happens is that nobody tells you the truth. We'd say to people, 'Tell us the truth, then we can try to prevent things happening again.' But you never got the truth. People omit certain things or somebody might say they've done some-thing even if you know they haven't. You've got no way of proving it. It's only later that pieces of the jigsaw come up, but this could be six or twelve months later. Also you don't always know what you're doing. In this case we were injecting oxygen into our system to enrich the coke and save on our fuel costs. In retrospect I realize we were putting pure oxygen into that plant, so any spark – boom! But we learnt.

We put new procedures in all the time, but whatever you do there's always something catches you again.

Later on in 1980 I became superintendent of the two foundries that were left at Dowlais. The brass foundry had shut down by then. There was the foundry workers' union, the AEU,[36] the ETU,[37] the boilermakers' union, the patternmakers' union and the staff union, so there were six unions altogether. I used to deal with all of them. My fight was usually with the foundry workers' union. They consisted of moulders and labourers and they had very old traditions. The personnel manager told me that in any situation it's never black and it's never white: it's 1 per cent black and 1 per cent white and you work inside the other 98 per cent. When I was dealing with the unions I always did my homework and I learnt to sit and listen. Let them talk long enough and they'll cut their own throat. I could do a lot in Dowlais at that time that in other places you would not be allowed to do. I could make a deal and I also used to try to keep it local all the time. Once the full-time union officials come in you lose control. I worked during the steel strike in 1980, which was a farce, because the day they went out we knew when they were coming back and for three months before that strike every plant supplying steel to the trade was flat out making stock for while they were out.

It was a time when great advances were being made

[36] Amalgamated Engineering Union.
[37] Electrical Trades Union.

in the industry, with processes like continual casting coming in, and the Japanese were way ahead of us. It was all coming down to manning – how many men per liquid ton. The most expensive commodity you can have is a man. [The industry was] progressing, getting more production, but in doing so needed less manpower. People had to go. I was good at that, but I was never popular. My father was as proud as hell that I was somebody in the works, but he couldn't understand how I could make people redundant. I was classed as Tory by everyone. I still had my locker till the day I finished, but I was resented going in there at finishing time.

As the Dowlais works closed bit by bit, Ron became second-in-command and was part of the management team fighting to keep the plant open. But it was to no avail. He finished there in September 1987 and in December of that year Dowlais closed down completely. Little remains now of the works that once sustained the local community, employing nearly five thousand people. That's nearly as many as the total population of Dowlais today. The community revolved round its largest industry, as was the case with the other major steel town that developed twelve miles to the east of Dowlais along the Heads of the Valleys road. The huge steelworks at Ebbw Vale was regarded as the flagship of the British steel industry. It dominated the town and, in the 1950s and 1960s, ten thousand people were employed there.

Ebbw Vale's history mirrored that of Merthyr Tydfil. Until the late eighteenth century it was an insignificant village in a valley in rural Monmouthshire with a population of around 150. Then in 1778 the Ebbw Vale Ironworks, later to become the Ebbw Steelworks, was established. This was followed by the opening of a number of coal mines near the village around 1790. The first iron produced in Ebbw Vale was made in 1790. From the middle of the nineteenth century the Ebbw Vale Steel, Iron and Coal Company ran the Ebbw Vale works, but in 1929 economic depression and lack of orders finally shut down 99 per cent of the business, throwing many skilled workers on to the dole. By 1934 unemployment in Ebbw Vale stood at 54 per cent of a population of thirty-one thousand, and many able-bodied workers had to move out of the valley to find jobs elsewhere. The following year the government decided that massive help must be given to the district and encouraged a tinplate manufacturer called Richard Thomas to buy the entire site and redevelop it. Thomas imported the latest technology and transformed the site into a new, modern, integrated steelworks, which had a new steel plant and strip mill[38] on the same site. It meant that all the parts of the process, starting with the blast furnaces, were on one site. At the forefront of this redevelopment was the introduction of a continuous hot-rolling facility, developed in the USA, producing hot-rolled coils instead of bars, billets[39] and plates. This changed the way steel was worked in the UK and production was massively boosted.

A new era had been born in Ebbw Vale. Many people returned to the area with the promise of well-paid labouring work. Many immigrant workers also arrived from less

[38] A rolling mill for producing long continuous strips of flat rolled metal.
[39] Freshly made steel in the form of a bar or rectangle.

fortunate areas of the UK, creating a huge workforce. At its height, in the late 1930s and 1940s, the works was the largest in Europe, attracting attention from German bombers during the Second World War; the deep valley proved difficult to bomb, however, and the plant survived. After the war production continued to increase and actually surpassed a target of six hundred thousand tons annually by 1948 to create one of the largest companies in the UK. That year Richard Thomas & Co. merged with tinplate manufacturers Baldwins and the first continuous tinning line[40] was introduced. The new firm, Richard Thomas and Baldwins (RTB), became a major iron, steel and tinplate producer.

The success of the company was part of a post-war boom in steel production throughout the UK and a time of increasing government intervention in the industry. In 1946 a steel-development plan was introduced by the new Labour government with the aim of increasing capacity, and the Iron and Steel Act of 1949 led to the national-ization of the industry, but fifteen months later the Conservatives were back in power and kept their promise to denationalize. The industry, however, remained under close government control and an Iron and Steel Board was set up to supervise it. It was made clear to the owners that in return for government help they would have to modernize, but progress was slow.

Despite the fact that the industry had become a political football, the 1950s saw some improvement and, with increasing government intervention, the capacity of the industry expanded rapidly. From eleven million tons

[40] Production line for tinplating.

produced at the end of the Second World War, production had risen to twenty-seven million tons by the early 1960s. The pressure of demand was great and the number of steelworkers went up from 296,000 in 1950 to 326,000 in 1960. But the relocation and expansion that was needed didn't happen and there was a limit to what outdated plant and machinery could do. Eventually the key processes of steelmaking began to be automated in the 1960s. Even then, however large the plant, production in many places still depended on the skill and judgement of the men who ran the furnaces and the muscle power of the men who handled the white-hot metal in the intense heat of the melting shops.

In 1967 the industry was nationalized for a second time by Harold Wilson's Labour government. The new British Steel Corporation that was created was one of the largest steel producers in the world, but apart from new integrated plants that had been built at Llanwern in South Wales and Ravenscraig in Scotland, its inheritance still owed much to the nineteenth century. Twenty years of political manipulation had left the industry with serious problems: a complacency with existing equipment, much of which was still outdated; plants operating below capacity; higher fuel costs; lack of funds for investment; and increasing world market competition, especially from Japan, where enormous new works employing the latest technology had been built. By the 1970s the industry was in serious decline but the government adopted a policy of keeping employment high in the increasingly depressed iron and steel regions.

Throughout this period the Ebbw Vale works was a major employer, but rationalization of the industry brought an end to steel production on the site in 1974 when it was transferred to Llanwern in Newport. The tinning line remained, so this was achieved with very few redundancies. When the industry was nationalized the works became part of BSC and with the return of privatization in 1999 it became part of Corus. It closed down in July 2002 with a workforce at the end of just four hundred.

Noel Evans is from Ebbw Vale and was at the works for thirty-eight years. He started with Richard Thomas and Baldwins in 1964 when over ten thousand people were employed there.

When I was growing up the town was thriving again after the Depression of the 1930s. My parents had both left the town at that time to get jobs, because they couldn't find them round here. My father went to London and my mother went trainee nursing in Oxford. But come 1936, when all the contracts were signed to rebuild the works and start it all off again, they both came back. That happened to a lot of people.

When the works got going a lot of smaller service-industry factories grew up and shops opened to service the town. The people who had the best jobs moved to live in Abergavenny, which is only twelve miles away but is a totally different country as we're a thousand feet above sea level and they're about three hundred. So they have better weather down there and it's an old market town with a castle, very posh, so people aspired to live there. Here it was very smelly. We lived beside the works and every now and then the smell would drift over us. I grew up wondering why we lived in such a dirty, noisy place. Because we lived so close to the works there would be the sound of jungle drums when the wind changed. It was all the women running to get their washing in, otherwise it would go bright orange on certain days and black on other days. You'd get them in or your neighbours would climb over the fence to get them in if it turned that bad. It was a lovely community and everybody knew everybody else.

I went to Ebbw Vale Grammar School and the only jobs available were at the steelworks or down the pit. I tried to get in the navy but failed because I've got scars on my eardrums. So I joined Richard Thomas and Baldwins in 1964 as a clerical apprentice. I didn't understand what that meant but I thought, well, it's a job. I tried to become a fitter but I was first reserve. At that time there were two intakes a year, up to about sixty-odd people. There were electricians, boilermakers, fitters or turners, and about half of them always went to sons of union people. If your father was a fitter you had a better chance of getting the job you wanted, but my father was a crane driver. I could have got a job as a crane driver but my father wouldn't put my name down because he didn't want me working shifts. Practically everyone at the works was on shifts, except the main office. When I joined there were nearly twelve thousand people working there, plus the contractors on site who never worked anywhere else. There were about 3,500 of those workers, so over fifteen thousand on the site in total.

When I started at the works I didn't know what it was all about. I didn't even know I was supposed to go to college once a week to do Business Studies. The first week was induction where they took you all over and showed you the different processes and where you could end up, [then] after the medicals and talks about what to do and not to do we were all given different offices to go to. You had two years where you had to move round, three months in a different office. I ended up straight down on the plant, because I was the scruffiest. From there I went all over the steelmaking end. During the induction the place I didn't fancy was the main office, because it was very strict. You had to have a white shirt and a tie and a jacket, and you couldn't take your jacket off in the summer unless you had permission because any visitors or clients came through there.

The office where I spent my first three months was underneath the blast furnace. It was deep down in the bowels of the steelmaking, which was a bit frightening. The furnaces were built up high and the molten steel came out of the bottom. You were told that all you were there for was to answer the phone and, if he was needed, to go and find the manager. The first time I was asked to find him I wanted to know where I should look. I was told that he was often with the engineers, but he wasn't there so somebody said, 'Come with me then.' We went on to the blast-furnace floor where they were taking off 'slag' – that's molten iron, about 2,000°C. It had been poured into a channel and was running along it. 'He could be over there,' I was told, but this was over the slag. 'How do you get over it?' I wanted to know. 'Well you just step over it,' I was told. I didn't really fancy this but I had to do it and it was all good experience. You had to be able to find your way round the place.

We had a steel plant and three blast furnaces which made iron. It was very hot around the furnaces as well as dirty and dangerous. The molten iron was taken from them and carried very quickly to the steel plant. There it was put into a huge mixer where it was kept molten. Then eventually it was tipped out of the mixer into Bessemer converters for bottom-blowing, where air was blasted through it and impurities blown out. Most of the carbon was blown out – you didn't want it in because carbon made steel brittle and then it became malleable. The process eventually changed from bottom-blowing to top-blowing with oxygen in the converters, which made the process quicker. We also had a system of open hearths, which were massive gas furnaces like giant ovens. We had thousands of tons of scrap and that would go straight in there. The scrap would come in from all over Britain, mainly by rail. Old cars and all sorts of things; we even had unexploded bombs in there. They were there by accident, but thank God they found them, otherwise there would have been a few deaths around the place. Quite a dangerous place!

Then we had a hot mill. In the old works they used to beat the steel to get length and width out of it, but this was the first hot mill where it was rolled. When you finally made your steel you poured it into an ingot mould, so you ended up with an ingot of steel that was allowed to cool off. Then you reheated it up to white heat and put it through a system of rollers, six giant mangles. Each one would reduce it till after the sixth you got it to the gauge you wanted. So where it was about two foot thick going in, it would come out about an inch wide but an awful lot longer.

These rolling mills took up massive floor space. The hot mill was a quarter of a mile long. This was to try and get things through in one go. When it comes out between guides the steel strip rides up into the air. But it's still pretty hot. If it went right up and hit the ceiling everybody ran, because you had no idea where it was going then.

One of the main things was the gauge of the steel – the thickness, the width and the length. A lot of our product was sold as coils. As soon as we had hot-rolled it, it became a coil and it then went through the entire system being coiled, uncoiled and coiled again. Ebbw Vale was the first steelworks in Britain to be able to work with coils. It made the steel so much easier to transport. But not all our customers could handle coils, so it all had to be cut up into sheet for them.

After two years of wandering about all the different offices, they decided to send me back to the one I started in, which was production planning and control. That involved scheduling the entire works. There were forty-two different units, all working different speeds, different tonnages and all working shifts, and you had to keep them all going without blocking any of them. And of course this was all pre-computers. Everything was manual; computers only started to appear in the 1970s, very basic ones. By 1976 I was on shifts and I thought it was wonderful because they gave me a 30 per cent rise. When I started I was put in charge of seven units directly and forty-two indirectly, which meant I had to sort out their sickness, holidays, days off and all of that.

We had an annual shut-down the last week in July and the first in August. It was never the same time as the miners. Even in that fortnight off they couldn't let the furnace go out. That was because all furnaces are lined with bricks and they would break, which meant you'd have to re-line the furnace and that was very expensive. So they'd just damp the furnace down without letting it go out. That's when everything would close down. Most people would go to Porthcawl, about forty miles away. At that time the works gave you a bar of carbolic soap every month and a new towel every six months. Do you know, you'd go to Porthcawl and every bloody towel on the beach would be the same!

RTB was a fabulous company to work for. They looked after everybody's welfare. When you joined the company you had to join the club and institute, and there was rugby, cricket, football, golf, sailing, model engineering, you name it. If somebody wanted to do it, RTB would put some money into it. They were very good.

Unfortunately steel was nationalized in 1967 and we became British Steel. But to be fair, it was still the same, still the same managers there. We had a big problem in the early 1970s when Michael Foot, who was our MP, was Minister of Employment in the Labour government. He had to come and announce the shutting down of the steelmaking and that there were 4,500 jobs going. It took them a while to do it and they came back with a plan saying they were going to extend the tinplating and they gave us a new tinplate line. But things were not good. Michael Foot said no man with a man's job would come out of the steelworks without a man's job to go to. That was his promise. But the first little factory that opened here was a marshmallow factory and the second was a fur factory. To be fair, the men just took the work. My father came out. He had £400 redundancy and he'd been there since 1937.

Since the works closed Noel has been helping out with the Ebbw Vale Works Archival Trust and Museum and learning about the two hundred-plus years of history of the works. Through the museum, which is helping to keep alive the memories of the industry on which the town was based, we met Mel Warrender, who started at Ebbw Vale Steelworks in January 1955 when it was still Richard Thomas and Baldwins.

I left school early because I hated it there, but there were plenty of jobs around then. I could have had one at ICI fibres and I was offered a job at the local colliery, which I didn't accept. My headmaster said there were jobs going in the steel industry – he knew I had an interest in chemistry – so I started as a helper in what was then called the metallurgical department. [Because] I had left school prematurely they paid for my education. I was told I could get a day off to be educated and get paid.

It was all a big shock after leaving school. I spent a period of six weeks getting to know just a part of the plant, because it was about 2½ miles long. It occupied the whole valley. After six weeks I went on to shifts which were eight hours, weekends and all; there was no stopping, it was a continuous process. I walked into a laboratory atmosphere where it was polished floors and people in white smocks – they were the senior people – but I was also exposed to the rough and tumble of the plant itself. It was noisy because of the machinery – it was about ninety-six decibels, which today you wouldn't be allowed to work in. The area I mainly worked in was the finishing end of the plant and the high-speed processes there contributed to the excessive noise. There was also a smell of rancid oil and chemicals. It was a totally unforgiving atmosphere, beyond description. People have to experience it to appreciate it. It was one of those environments that was totally unacceptable by today's standards, but it didn't seem so at the time.

There were several products that came out of the plant: tinplate, which was used mainly in can-making, oil cans and drums; galvanized material, which was used in agricultural machinery and certain components for automobiles; and there was also sheet steel, which was used essentially in the automotive industry for building cars. In those days we used to build a lot of cars in this country – Austin, Morris, Vauxhall, Ford – all made with steel supplied from Ebbw Vale. There were other products that were made at the works too. Halfway through the process you would produce hot-rolled coil and that would be sold as a product. The plant also manufactured silicone steels that are used in electrical components.

So it was a range of products with a variety of widths and thicknesses and they would have different surface characteristics, different dimensional and metallurgical characteristics. Some needed to be very malleable, some needed to be very stiff, very hard, very strong. It was a complete range manufactured at this one plant.

There were lots of people at laboratory level – you'd call them technicians today. Your responsibilities involved going out and picking up samples and preparing them for further testing. If you lifted a big, long sheet, two of you would need to handle that sheet to obtain samples out of it. You'd have to take that sheet to a big hydraulic shearer because it was so thick and heavy. But it wasn't only testing the materials; you had to test the solutions with which the product was manufactured. There were oils for protective and lubrication purposes and lots of chemical treatments like chromic acid. Most of the time you'd be out in the plant collecting these things, not sitting in a laboratory. The process involved a gaseous element where you heat materials up. For this you had to have protective atmospheres and they had to be analysed because you couldn't afford to contaminate the product, so you'd actually carry out gas sampling. There was a whole range of tests, not just of the product itself but also the process. You'd be involved with a process operator. He'd say what had to be done and you'd report the results to him so he could do something about it. You were involved in it all and none of this was laboratory based. It was all out on the floor of the works.

[Then there was the laboratory itself.] You can't really call it a laboratory – it was just a room with a sink in it for washing chemical equipment. There were block floors that had all suffered through water leakage, so you couldn't walk in a straight line because the blocks had all expanded. Doors and windows were smashed. It was terrible. To get from the main laboratory to the satellite laboratory you had to walk through the plant, finding your own way through. Down in the cellars there were large tanks of oil or chemicals. It was dark, dirty and slippery and you'd have to go down there on your own. I can remember my first walk through the works. The noise was tremendous – overhead cranes, gantry cranes, tractors driving up and down, the clattering of equipment. It was an incredible experience. There was an element, not of fear, but of amazement. Before I went in there I didn't realize this was what industry was like – the noise, the dust, the general activity, everything going on around you while you were trying to get from A to B. It was frightening at first because it was unfamiliar. Then you moved from unfamiliarity to contempt, so you dropped your guard and that's when you got accidents.

The rolling mills were electrically operated, but they weren't automated. The operator would feed the mill. He'd set it up manually and press the buttons to speed it up, but that strip would be travelling at 1,800 metres a minute and it was as thin as a razor blade. If that broke, it would be all over the place. The most dangerous department, though, was the old pickling department where they used sulphuric acid to burn

the rubbish off the top of the coil of steel. It involved
taking in a hot-rolled coil from the hot mill and processing it through a pickling bath. These were
virtually open baths and there was a lot of leakage
and smells. The coil was covered in oxide which
would become dislodged during part of the process,
creating dust. The acid that was used would create
fumes, so you'd have respiration problems and skin
complaints that came from handling the materials.
You'd walk in there and your eyes would start blink-
ing because there was literally acid in the air. There
were men down there with no hair and no teeth, but
they wouldn't come out of there; they would work
there until they finished. About 1973 we went to a
brand-new hydrochloric pickler that was a lot more
contained and they did away with the sulphuric acid,
thank goodness.

People tend to think of the steel industry as hot
metal, but there are many other aspects of the process
which were equally dangerous. I've seen people run
over by tractors carrying coils. There was a guy standing where he shouldn't have been and he was cut
virtually in half. There were accidents all the time – it
was absolutely shocking. This was why they had
medical centres and surgeries scattered around. You
were surrounded by an industry that was immense in
terms of the size and scale of things, and you took a
lot for granted. You'd think nothing of walking across
a conveyor. I used to catch plates that were coming
out of a shearer and they were like razor blades.

I worked all over [and I studied part time for six or
seven years]. As time went on I became more distant

from the actual process of the product and went into more of a managing role. I went on to be production manager and manager of the galvanizing department. Basically, I went right from the bottom to near the top. The opportunities were there to develop your career in the industry, but whatever you did you still had to walk through the plant, to communicate with process workers. Eventually in 1988 I became technical manager liaising more with customers, suppliers and plant managers.

Like Ron Jenkins, Mel took the management route. In a works the size of Dowlais or Ebbw Vale, where groups of workers were anxious to protect their own crafts, a great deal of management time had to be spent on labour relations and dealing with the unions. By the 1950s the unions had won recognition almost everywhere and there was a broad acceptance that organized labour had permanently arrived as a force to be reckoned with. Their strength brought collective bargaining and pressure for better wages and conditions. Lyn Humphries was a branch secretary at the Ebbw Vale Steelworks, but union work was not something he had in mind when he started there.

I left school at fifteen and went underground because it was the only place you could go at that age. You couldn't get into the steelworks because the minimum age for that was sixteen. I stuck [the colliery] for a month then I went home and said to my mother that I was going to finish and there was murder! I joined the Royal Air Force, but then my father was killed at Ebbw Vale Steelworks [and so] they felt obligated to give me a job. So I left the RAF and came home because my mother was left with two young children.

When I went to the steelworks my first job was a pen-pusher. You did all of the pencil work, the recording of what was being produced. You'd do things like fill out a stoppage report to say the reasons why the mill had stopped, and the lengths of slabs they were cutting. You'd go to the weighbridge where they were weighing the coils as they came off the strip mill and you'd be recording all the weights. Every time you got promoted you went to a different job. You started off first in the slab yard as a spare boy, then you became a 'number boy'. Every single slab had a different number and that number would go back to the furnace where it was produced and it would follow it right to where it came out at the tinning lines. They could trace everything through that one particular number, so if there were any inconsistencies they could trace it back. They'd be producing different grades of steel all the time. Every twenty pieces would be a different grade. So at the beginning of the day each machine would get a list of what was going to be produced and they'd have an addressograph machine with metal plates [on to which] they'd type the numbers then stamp it on to the slab. That's what the number boy would do. Then you went to the strip mill as a strip-mill runner and from there you went back to the slabbing mill.

At the start of the process you'd have your smelting shops and your convertor shop that would be producing steel ingots and these would be twelve ton in weight each. They would go from the smelting shop to the slabbing mill where they would be put into soaking beds and reheated. They would be rolled in the slabbing mill and turned into slab where the ingot would be thirty-six feet long and, say, six inches thick. It would be cut in half to eighteen feet, then they would go over to the slab yard and from there it would be put back into the reheating furnaces and be taken up to 2,300°F. Then they'd be rolled through a strip mill, getting longer and narrower as they went through each mill until they come out at the other end as a twelve-ton coil.

In Ebbw Vale it was all done by locomotive. The ingots would be brought from the melting shop back to the slabbing mill by rail and the coil would go up by rail up to the coal mill. It was very noisy, so there'd be a sign language. And there were the hooters as well. You'd blow a certain number on the hooter, like five for a foreman, three for a fitter, two and a half for an electrician to come, and everybody understood.

In the late 1950s you'd have as many as fourteen double-decker buses converging on the works from all directions at six o'clock in the morning, two o'clock in the afternoon and ten o'clock at night. It was a twenty-four-hour operation, because once a furnace is lit you can't put it out until it falls down. And it's 365 days a year. The furnaces would be going all the time, but the mills themselves would have to go down for maintenance. That was usually done at the weekend – they'd stop rolling on Saturday morning and recommence on Sunday afternoon. This is when you could work your overtime. It would be dirty work, clearing out the corridors and such like [for] the full twenty-four hours, from two o'clock on Saturday to two o'clock on Sunday.

Come grub time we would pool our food. We had this guy working with us who always had cheese sandwiches – 365 days a year he'd have cheese sandwiches. So we composed this letter: 'Dear Mrs Mudie,' it said, 'Why is it Dai is working like a horse and you are feeding him like a mouse? No more cheese please!' We put it in his grub box and Dai didn't even know the letter were there. He came into work the following day and come grub time he opened his box and there was a letter on the top: 'To whom it may concern,' it said, 'I reckon my Dai is looking all right on his cheese.'

Another character that springs to mind was Jimmy Hennock. He was a friend of the old age pensioners in Ebbw Vale, and he used to take them firebricks. He would wrap up a firebrick in a towel, put it under his arm and go out through the main gate. The pensioners used to put the brick in their grates and that meant they weren't using as much coal. Jimmy was walking out through the gate one day and there was a patrol man on the gate, a fella by the name of Trevor Whitston. Now as Jimmy walked past, the bloody brick fell out and he turned round as quick as a flash and said, 'See that, Trevor – some bugger's throwing bricks at me!' Trevor said he was so surprised he had to let him go. But, do you know, he probably had got through enough firebricks to build a house! But he wasn't making anything on it. He'd do anything to help out. But he could drink. I'd say to him, 'How much pay have you got this week, Jim?' and he'd tell you in pints!

After I'd been there a few years I became a [union] branch secretary at the works. I didn't set out to go into the union, but I got into trouble so many times with management and had to go into the office with the union official that I got interested. I used to be in trouble about all sorts of things. In those days, in the 1950s, men would think nothing of giving you a clip. People above you, I mean. If you answered somebody back they'd box your ears. And in my eyes it went too far and I wanted to get something done about it.

When I first became interested in the trade union movement I used to attend branch meetings and sit and listen to the old generation talking of what had gone on and I took it from there. My aim was to become a full-time union official. I got myself elected on to the branch committee and then I put in for the secretary job and [at the second attempt I got elected]. I became the youngest branch secretary of one of the largest industrial branches of the Ebbw Vale Steelworks with about a thousand branch workers under my jurisdiction. In the steel industry the branch secretary was always the number one man. There was the chairman, the representative, then the branch secretary, but it was the branch secretary who ran the branch.

The first experience I had [came on my first day in the job]. It was about seven o'clock in the morning and the mills hadn't started rolling. A lad by the name of Alan came over to me and said, 'You'd better come over. The lads in the slab mill are going out on strike.'

First day of being branch secretary and I've got a bloody strike on my hands! 'Well why?' I said. 'Well they've found out the staff members who were stock-taking the same time as them were having double time and a day in lieu.' I was terrified, so much so that I took the longest way round [to get to the slab mill], thinking what am I going to say to them? Well when I got there they'd gone! I took so long getting there to sort things out that they'd gone home.

We had a wonderful relationship with the manage-ment; it was never them and us. And I soon found there were some perks to the job. When I first started there was just a shed for tea and toast, then they built a brand-new canteen with fantastic facilities, every-thing you could think of. For 1/9d (about 9p today) you got egg on toast, bacon, tomatoes and a mug of tea. And if you were branch secretary like me and those girls were in the branch you didn't pay anything, or you had twice as much on your plate as anyone else!

[As a branch secretary you learnt a lot about people.] We had a welder's mate by the name of Jim Davis. He'd been working on a shift on a cold night, him and the welder, and [Jim's ribs got cracked in an accident that was the welder's fault]. Jim was off work for about three to four months and when he came back I filled this accident claim form in, saying the accident wasn't his fault. I wrote to our solicitors say-ing I didn't think he had made a full recovery [and] they wrote to Jim's own doctor for his opinion. They sent me a copy of the letter from the doctor, which said Jim had a bronchial condition before the accident which had been aggravated by the accident, but his ribs were fully recovered. I went to find Jim and gave him the letter. He sat down, put on his glasses, looked at the letter, put it back in the envelope and said, 'Well that's a good offer. Tell them I accept it.' I stared at him and didn't know what to say. I couldn't believe it. He couldn't read a word of it! [He and a lot of other workers] were people who'd left school when they were thirteen or so. They were quite proficient at their jobs, but they couldn't read or write.

Another character was an Italian chap. The day he started work the branch secretary [at the time] went to see him. 'It's thirty-eight pence to join the union,' he said. But this guy said, 'No, I don't want to join the union.' Well it was just at the time they were trying to stop the closed shop[41] so you didn't have to be part of a union, but [when I became branch secretary] I kept going to see him [all the same] and he kept saying, 'I no want join your union.' He used to call me 'communist bastard'.

I went to see him one Saturday morning and asked him if he was working the following morning. When he said yes, I said, 'Well let me tell you what's going to happen in the morning. When you clock on at six o'clock I'm going to take this mill out on strike. We're not going to work with you no more. We don't work with blacklegs.[42] The mill manager will come to see

[41] Union agreement under which the employer committed to hire union members only and the employee had to remain in the union in order to stay in his/her job. Closed shops were made illegal in the UK in 1992.
[42] A worker who is opposed to trade unions. Usually used to describe a strike-breaker or 'scab'.

me and say "Why are you out on strike?" and I'll say "We're not working with a blackleg." They'll come down here with a patrol and they will drag you off because they're not going to have one man stopping this mill. And they'll put you on the road.' He put his hand in his pocket and threw some money at me. 'Have your money, you commie bastard,' he said. So I bent down and picked up 38p out of his money and left the rest on the floor. I said sign here and he signed.

It turned out to be the worst day's work I ever did. Wherever I put him to work he'd cause trouble. He'd fight at the drop of a hat. He'd scream and shout and intimidate people. Then I thought, I've got somebody in the roll shop with exactly the same temperament. So I put this Italian to work there with him, with the consent of the management, of course, because they'd had enough of him as well. But one day the Italian chap went to the list of men signed up to work overtime at the weekend and crossed off the other fellow's name and put his name on instead. I got a message, 'You'd better go up the roll shop.' These two men were up there fighting – there was blood on the walls, there was murder. By the time I got there the Italian was on a stretcher with the doctor and the nurse. He had his arm up in the air, all swathed in bandages, and he said, 'Humphrey, Humphrey, my finger gone, top of my finger gone.' So I walked up to the stretcher, kicked him in the ribs and said, 'You glad you joined the union now!'

[Losing the top of a finger was a common accident, so I made a claim for him and when] he came back to work I gave him a cheque for £3,000 on the Monday or Tuesday. [On the Friday evening] I heard a bang at my front door, ran out and there was a brown envelope inside the door. There was £50 in it. So I opened the door quick to see who was there and there was a bottle of whisky. I couldn't see anyone at all. But it had to be the Italian fellow. He was the only one I'd paid out. And he never mentioned it and I never mentioned it to him. My daughter knew his daughter from school and she used to visit his home. He used to say, 'How's your communist bastard father?'

When I first became branch secretary it wasn't a full-time position; I was still working in the mill. What I wanted was to become a full-time union official because then you automatically went on to the parliamentary B list for the Labour Party. In 1968 Ron Evans, who was Michael Foot's agent, came to see me. Now I was a member of Plaid Cymru at the time and he said, 'They tell me you want to be a full-time trade unionist. Forget it, because as long as you're a member of the bloody Plaid you'll never make it. Now here's a membership form for the Labour Party.' So I joined the Labour Party. At the time the WEA used to run weekend courses in Porthcawl for budding politicians and trade unionists, so I used to go on these courses during the winter months. They used to put you up in the Esplanade Hotel or some other hotel and you'd have invited guests who would come along to lecture. I was friendly with Rhodri Morgan, who became the First Minister of Wales, and Neil Kinnock who used to come along. But they all had their careers planned, knew exactly where they were going. Kinnock went to where he knew the candidate was getting on [in age] because he knew if he made a name for himself he'd get the nomination for the job. It was the same with Rhodri Morgan. I thought if I could become a trade union official and get in the number six division, which covered the Ebbw works, I would have a good chance. It was what was called a 'steel seat', sponsored by my union. But in 1972 I had a stroke, so all my plans of becoming a full-time trade union official stopped then.

After 1972 I took stock of myself. I knew steel was coming to an end and I applied to go to Coleg Harlech, which is a college of second chance in North Wales. I was due to finish in the steelworks, but then I got a call from the general manager and he said, 'I believe you're leaving us, but I'd like you to re-consider. We're setting up a counselling department where we will be interviewing and counselling all the people who have been made redundant and we'd like you to be one of the counsellors. The wages are £3,000 per year.' Well at the time I was earning £26 per week and I didn't know what £3,000 a year meant! When I got home and worked it out it was £60 per week. So I became a works counsellor. We were sent to York University for an intensive counselling course and that was brilliant. Three months in York. And when I came back, what a fantastic job it was.

I was put in charge of all the people who'd been away from work for long periods of time. The situation was, if you'd been away for more than two years the company could dismiss you – no pension, no compensation, no redundancy. There was a place in Tredegar where I had to go to see this fellow who'd been away with his nerves. When I got there, there was a policeman on the door. I said who I'd gone to see and the policeman said, 'He's in custody. He's just murdered his wife.' There was another fellow in the same place [whose] two years was coming up. So I went to see him, explained everything to him and said I could arrange things so he'd get his pension. I said I'd go back the next week but when I got back he'd committed suicide.

By this time the works had really gone into decline. In 1961 they had revamped the whole of the works, and Ebbw Vale was the most modern fully automated steelworks in the world. But then in 1966 the government wanted to build a super-steelworks and there was so much pressure being put on by the Welsh and the Scottish that they split it. In Scotland they built Ravenscraig and in Wales they said Ebbw Vale was too far from the coast so they built the new one at Llanwern near Newport. They called it Macmillan's Folly because it brought about the demise of Ebbw Vale. Twenty miles from the coast, I ask you. There was a rail link there and it was used all the time.

The first part of the closure at Ebbw Vale came in 1978, but the works itself didn't close till 2002. They were still importing coil and finishing it in the top end of the works. It was the longest closure in the history of the British steel industry! Some people stayed employed till the very end and actually finished their working lives there. They were the fortunate ones.

In 1988 the British Steel Corporation was re-privatized as British Steel. The company embarked on a radical re-organization programme backed by massive capital investment in an attempt to become competitive in the world market place. But thousands lost their jobs as the workforce was cut dramatically as part of the restructuring. One of the places to be hit was Llanwern. Steelmaking there ceased in 2001 with the loss of 1,300 jobs. It had been the opening of the Llanwern works that was seen by many Ebbw Vale workers as the beginning of the end for their jobs. That view was shared by steelworkers in Scotland, where some of the old established works were similarly affected by the opening of Ravenscraig.

*

As in South Wales, the history of the iron and steel industry in south Lanarkshire dated back to the second half of the eighteenth century. In common with much of central Scotland, there were deposits of coal and iron ore at Cambuslang and here, on the banks of the River Clyde a few miles south-east of Glasgow, the Clyde Ironworks was opened in 1786. In 1828 the works was the first to use the hot-blast process invented by Glasgow engineer James Beaumont Neilson. This involved pre-heating the air blown into a blast furnace and resulted in a substantial reduction in the amount of fuel consumed in the process – a breakthrough that transformed the cost of iron production, bringing it down from £8 per ton in 1811 to £2.12s.8d when the hot blast was in full operation.

Lanarkshire's iron industry grew rapidly and by 1839 there were thirteen ironworks in the county with a total of forty-five blast furnaces. The growth of the industry led to the simultaneous expansion of the region's hitherto insignificant shipbuilding and by the 1870s more than twenty shipyards on the Clyde were producing half of Britain's tonnage of shipping. Firms in Glasgow itself made the engines, the boilers, the brass, copper and wooden fittings, and the frequently lavish furnishings. Forges and foundries abounded as the Scottish iron and steel industry grew to meet the demands of the shipbuilders.

The first steel ever produced in Scotland in commercial quantities came in 1873 from the furnaces of Hallside works at Cambuslang. The works, owned by the Steel Company of Scotland, had the Clyde nearby and ample local supplies of coal and pig iron. In the early 1870s nine ships out of ten built on the Clyde were made of iron, but the directors of the company believed that steel, though costing half as much again and not always reliable, was the material of the future. They began to produce steel plates for the shipbuilding industry and so successful was their move that ten years later nearly every ship built on the Clyde was built of steel. In no other British shipbuilding area was the switch from iron to steel so rapid. By this time the company had so high a reputation for its boiler and ship plates, and so great was the demand for its steel – not only for shipbuilding but for bridges and construction work as well – that Hallside could not take all the orders it was offered, as a result of which, from the 1880s, many other steelworks installed their own plate mills and new works opened.

Clydebridge Steelworks, also in Cambuslang, opened in 1887. In 1931 the plant was integrated with the adjacent Clyde Ironworks and by 1939, with hot-metal working from Clyde Iron, Clydebridge had become one of the largest integrated steelworks in the UK, setting world records for the production of sheared plates used in many of the most famous ships built on the Clyde, including the *Lusitania, Queen Mary*, HMS *Hood, Queen Elizabeth* and *QE2*. It reached its maximum size with the addition of a new plate mill and shearing facilities in the early 1960s. Throughout the 1970s the works continued to provide steel plate for Clydeside shipbuilders, including John Brown, Yarrow Shipbuilders and Fairfield Shipbuilding. Peak output was reached in 1977, but by this time the yards were beginning to wilt under foreign competition and demand slumped. The Clyde Ironworks closed down in 1978 after operating for 192 years and after this Clydebridge's supply of cast-iron slabs came from nearby Ravenscraig, the integrated steelworks that was set up near Motherwell as a result of government intervention in 1958.

After attaining a record output of 3.3 million tons in 1970, the Scottish steel industry went into rapid decline, with the demise of shipbuilding on the Clyde, high manufacturing costs and overseas competition all being contributory factors. By the late 1970s its losses per ton were higher than the UK national average and Ian MacGregor, chairman of the British Steel Corporation, believed that the entire Scottish steel industry needed to be closed down. Clydebridge rolled its last plate on 12 November 1982 and the last shift at the last works to stay open, Ravenscraig, was worked on 24 June 1992. The closures had a knock-on effect on the surviving small iron-founding firms in the area, nearly all of which were forced out of business, leaving nothing of the industry that had been so fundamental to the prosperity of Clydeside for nearly two hundred years.

Peter Phillips from Cambuslang started at Hallside in 1969 when he was fifteen as an apprentice electrical engineer and was there for just under two years before moving to Clydebridge, where he too got involved in union work.

At that time the steel industry was booming. Hallside had just been through a total refurbishment about ten years before. It had included a lot of new technology and a hundred-ton furnace, the largest furnace in Scotland. It produced high-quality steels. I was in the drawing office for two years. I worked as a junior operator apprentice and I did all the printing – things like the blueprints and a wee bit of tracing. My first wage was £4.19s.6d a week. It was good money, without being great. But that was the time of plenty; you could get a job anywhere. They were advertising in the steelworks every week: twenty men wanted, thirty men wanted. So people were starting and stopping. At that time it was common for a man to take a job then after six months chuck it to get his holiday pay. That gave him a lump sum – his wage and his holiday pay would give him the equivalent of a month's wages and that was a lot of money to people at that time. Clyde Alloys owned Hallside and Colvilles owned Clydebridge, so there were two different personnel officers and that's how people could swap and change. Somebody who'd left Hallside would be taken on at Clydebridge because he had experience. So there was a regular flow of people between the two plants. For getting jobs there

I think they favoured Protestants more than they did Catholics. When I was born they called me Patrick at first, after my grandfather. But he said, 'Don't call him Patrick. He'll never get a job.' At that time it was quite difficult for Catholics to get into the steelworks and if they did get in, it was for menial tasks.

I did two years in the drawing office then I left and went to Clydebridge. There were roughly 2,500 men worked there. The Clyde separated us from the Clyde Ironworks, which was also owned by Colvilles. They had 3,500 men over there, so there were six thousand in total and the only division was the river. Although they were on separate sides, they were integrated and one fed the other. The waste gases from the ironworks fed the furnaces in the steelworks and there was a bridge that brought the iron over for the steelworks.

I started off in the cogging mill and it was good money there. I went from £4.19s.6d [£4.98] to over £8. In the cogging mill slab was taken and reduced to a smaller slab. I was a lid-lifter boy. I lifted the lids off the furnaces to allow them to take the white hot slabs out. These slabs were either seven ton or fourteen ton, depending on the sort of plate they were doing, and they'd be in the furnace for maybe three or four hours, so they got the heat all the way through them. In the bay where I worked you'd have two lid-lifters, a gasman to check and make sure the gas in the furnace was at the proper level, a checker who would make a note of the number and the identity of the slabs and a crane operator. I had to climb up on to this lid-lifter, which was about eight or ten feet off the ground, and lift the lid. Then a small overhead crane would come in to take the slab. It had a set of dogs on it, which were like a big pair of scissors, and they gripped the slabs and took them out and carried them on to the cogging mill. While this was happening the lid was still off, because after the crane had taken one away it had to come back to put another one in.

In the cogging mill the slab was made into a smaller one and then transported over to the Harvey bay, which was named after the Harvey furnaces they had in there. There they heated them up again to get them up to another high temperature – about 1,000°C – and then they'd go into the mill to be rolled. The total process from actually lifting the slab out of the furnace, cogging it, putting it straight into the Harvey and then on to the mill would probably take about two hours. That would produce mother plates that could be taken to any size or gauge they wanted.

If you look at steelworks buildings, they only seem half built. They're producing all sorts of waste gases in there so they have a part of a wall and then the rest is open to allow the air through and let the smoke and fumes dissipate. The roofs have all got cat roofs on them so the heat can get out. If they didn't have that you'd die in there – the fumes would kill you if not the heat. The conditions in there were pretty dire. I always remember one incident. The lid-lifter was made of steel and I stood on a platform. The machine broke down with the lid off, and the steel slab was about eight feet away from me and flames were shooting out. I got down and got the engineer, who said it was a cog and he fixed it. When it was fixed the manager told me I'd have to get in closer to close the lid, but by that time the platform that I stood on was glowing red. I said, 'If I go up there I'm going to end up on a funeral pyre,' but I didn't say it as politely as that and I got suspended for three days! The other thing was the dogs that lifted the slabs were prone to slipping. They lifted a slab up ten feet above the height of the molten pool and then the slab could slip and fall in. When that happened you'd have molten metal shooting up out of there maybe thirty or forty feet in the air, and you'd have no protection, none at all. You just had to dive under something and hide. And that happened regularly.

The most common injuries were burns. When a plate is red hot you can see it is hot, but when it cools down to 70°C it goes black, so you don't know it's warm. So you get people standing on them by mistake and it burns the soles off your shoes. So the first thing you do is put your hands down to save yourself, and then you burn your hands. The guys who worked in there wore clogs that were wooden-soled for walking on top of the plate. The clogs were given for certain jobs, so if you were seen wearing them for anything else you could get the sack because you'd obviously stolen them.

The health facilities were very poor. When you started there you got a tour of the works with the safety officer, a man called Frank Wright. You all got a helmet and then he'd take you into an office and show you a video. It showed you a bolt that had killed a man the week before. But this same bolt had been killing men for about twenty years! Then Frank would screw off his hand and throw it on to the table and say, 'That's what happened to me. Don't let it happen to you!' And all these boys who were just starting would shrink back. So basic safety was that you got a helmet, but then as soon as you started in the works the first thing you threw away was the helmet. Nobody wore any safety gear at all. You could buy safety boots, mainly because you were getting them cheap.

I left the steel industry for a while and then came back into it in 1971 and went into stock control in the engineering stores. That's when I got involved with the union. I was safety rep for stock control, then I became rep for that area. I was on the safety committee for twenty-five years and I remember in the early days if you wanted a certain sort of earplug that cost a tenner, you'd probably get one that cost £2.50. But in the last stages they went the total opposite – you couldn't go anywhere without safety stuff. You had to wear hat, glasses, ear muffs, no matter what you were doing.

The big thing about Clydebridge was that everybody always assumed the place was going to close. And by 1982 it really was going down. Shipbuilding had died off by that time in the Clyde. No new markets opened here, everything had gone abroad. In the last days before the works closed I'll give them their due – anything that was required for safety, they bought.

Colin Findlay first encountered the Clydebridge Steelworks when he drove there from his home in

Edinburgh for an interview as a Mechanical Engineering graduate trainee in 1972. He went on to work as a plate-mill engineer at the works and remained there until 1981, the year before Clydebridge rolled its last plate.

As I approached Cambuslang on the London Road, my first sight of the industry in the area was the huge clouds emerging from the cooling towers at Clyde Ironworks. I could see the smoking chimneys of the steelworks beyond as I drove down the dusty, rust-coloured road that passed through the middle of the ironworks, underneath huge black pipes that criss-crossed the road. As I was early for the interview I drove round the centre of Cambuslang and stopped in the car park at the back of the 'precinct' – a dreary 1960s concrete wilderness.

My interview was in the blackened red-sandstone main office [at Clydebridge and] my main impression was of being told that, despite the rumours – which I hadn't heard – of falling markets and possible closures, the future of Clydebridge was looking good. I passed the interview and started shortly afterwards.

The day I started I thought I had better wear a suit. However, this was quickly replaced by a boilersuit, as I was immediately dispatched to work with the melting-shop maintenance engineer, Jimmy Cassidy. He was up on a crane at the far end of the melting shop and I was taken to meet him by the melting-shop charge-hand, Charlie Morrison. To get there we walked up a ramp to the furnaces-charging floor. We had apparently arrived at the gates of hell. Charlie was disappearing and a red-hot box on what looked like

Teesside, South Wales and the Clyde Valley were all major centres of steel production, but the name that was synonymous with steel was Sheffield.

Steelworkers generally wore flat caps, neckerchiefs, thick leather aprons and wooden-soled clogs, but they had very little to protect them from the infernal temperatures.

From smelting and fettling to casting and cutting, steelwork was dirty, dangerous but very highly skilled work.

The rolling mill of Peech and Tozer, Rotherham (*top*). Once rolled into sheets, jets of pressurized water help to cool the plate (*middle*). Sparks fly from hot steel as it is cut to size (*bottom*).

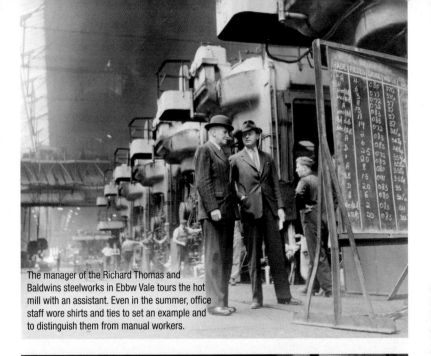

The manager of the Richard Thomas and Baldwins steelworks in Ebbw Vale tours the hot mill with an assistant. Even in the summer, office staff wore shirts and ties to set an example and to distinguish them from manual workers.

A worker hangs out newly silver-plated forks and spoons to dry. Sheffield's unique reputation and dominant position in the manufacture of cutlery continues in Britain to this day.

It took around a year for draughtsmen to produce the drawings for one ship. Liners-off then set out the positions in the shipyard of the main sections of the ship and its equipment, using plans, tape measure and chalk lines to ensure that everything was correctly lined up.

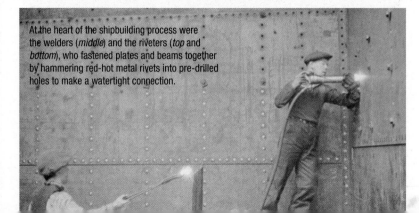

At the heart of the shipbuilding process were the welders (*middle*) and the riveters (*top* and *bottom*), who fastened plates and beams together by hammering red-hot metal rivets into pre-drilled holes to make a watertight connection.

The fruits of their labour. Workers who built the
ship *Uganda* for the British India Company await
the launch ceremony on Clydeside in 1952.

a gigantic jousting pole hanging from a crane was swinging right at me. A row of furnaces, stretching as far as the eye could see, was belching flames as the jousting pole and its box swung on towards a door that was opening in a furnace. The box tipped its contents into the furnace and I could immediately see that something had gone horribly wrong. The roar of flames that shot out of the door completely engulfed the furnace and cranes, and went right up to the roof of the building some sixty feet above. Everything seemed to be in slow motion and I realized that I had been the first to notice the disaster. I was about to warn Charlie, but the box that had been emptied into the furnace, by now red hot, was swinging back towards me. I ran to get out of the way and still no one was paying any attention. By this time the door of the furnace was closing, and as the flames began to die down I noticed that no one was paying any attention because to them this was normal!

As I hurried after Charlie I never knew which way to go to avoid the 'charger' cranes at each furnace as they swung wildly around with their boxes of scrap and mill scale[43] to feed the roaring, hungry furnaces. But Charlie and everyone else seemed to have a sixth sense about where they were. Eventually we reached the far end of the melting shop and the floor ended at a huge drop down to the valve pit and the 'teeming bay floor'.[44] The height from the floor below to the roof above was awe-inspiring as Charlie headed up

[43] Flaky surface of hot-rolled steel produced when the plates come through the rolling mill.
[44] Where molten metal was poured in to make ingots.

an iron ladder towards the cranes above. On the way up, the sun shining in through the vent slats in the side of the building cast long sunbeams in the dust in the air.

When we arrived up on the crane rail at the end of the building, Charlie pointed out Jimmy Cassidy on the nearest crane, about halfway back along the melting shop and high above the furnaces. This was one of the cranes that lift the ladles of molten iron transferred from Clyde Ironworks to charge the furnaces and it was capable of lifting sixty tons. I thought we were going to walk along the girders to the crane, some hundred feet above the ground, but Charlie said we didn't need to as the crane was coming this way. I realized he was right as the massive structure of the building that I was standing on had started to sway. As the crane's rumble and bulk increased I began to think that another disaster was unfolding and the building was sure to collapse. But Charlie wasn't in the least concerned and I realized that the crane and the building had been there for many years, so the chance of it collapsing at that moment, despite the wobble, was so low I might as well just enjoy the experience. As a trainee I spent four months in No. 2 Melting Shop, where eventually I did develop the sixth sense necessary to avoid the charger cranes.

*

Teesside, South Wales and the Clyde Valley were all major centres of steel production, but the name that was synonymous with steel was Sheffield. Even before the Industrial

Revolution got under way, the city was renowned for its manufacture of nails, knives, scissors, scythes, razors, axes and other metal products. It had also established its unique reputation and dominant position in the manufacture of cutlery – a virtual production monopoly that continues in Britain to this day. Originally a cottage industry, cutlery-making quickly grew in scope from the middle of the eighteenth century when a Sheffield cutler, Thomas Boulsover, devised a means of fusing a thin layer of silver to copper to produce silver plate – the famous 'Sheffield plate' that looked like silver but was far cheaper and was to take silver-plated cutlery into the dining rooms of almost every middle-class family in the land.

It was at this time that Sheffield's success as a steel-producing city really took off, thanks to a breakthrough by Benjamin Huntsman, who operated a foundry at Handsworth, four miles to the east of the town. The crucible-steel process he developed in 1740 was a relatively simple method of purifying blister steel by melting it in crucibles and skimming off all the impurities that floated to the surface. The liquid steel was then poured into a mould and left to solidify. This process produced an ingot of cast or crucible steel which had a uniform high degree of purity. High-quality steel like this had never been produced before, and so Huntsman laid the foundations not only of the steel industry in Sheffield but of the whole of the steel industry as it has developed around the world to this day.

But it was the development of steam power and the bulk production of steel that led to the really massive expansion of the industry and the city in the nineteenth century. In 1801 Sheffield's population was 46,000, a figure that had risen to 135,000 by 1851 and 409,000 in 1901. By this time Sheffield had gained an international reputation for steel production and many innovations were made here, including the Bessemer process which enabled steel to be produced cheaply and in bulk. Stainless steel was invented in Sheffield in 1912 and the city stayed at the forefront of technological innovation with the development of modern high-strength, low-alloy steels.

The greatest of all Sheffield's assets was her human resources. The ingenuity of the inventors, the entre-preneurial vision of the businessmen and above all the skills of the workers all combined to create the industries for which the city became world famous. Sheffield's steel-workers were intensely proud of the skill in hand and eye that their jobs required, and melter, roller and forgeman were all prestigious occupations. They were also well paid. When Ian Richmond, who grew up in Sheffield and had his first job at a credit draper's warehouse in the city, started courting 'there was no way,' he says, 'that I could hope to save up enough money to get married on the money I was earning.'

The money in the warehouses was absolutely pathetic. It was like normal shop work, which has always been poor money, so [Pauline's] dad got me a job in the steel industry at a firm called Osborn's and I should think I worked there for four or five years. It was intriguing because it was like a two-storey build-ing on the riverside and you'd wander down there at night and down below on the ground floor would be the forge lads doing the really heavy, tough work. It really was hot and quite dangerous work at times.

They'd have these heavy hammers thundering away with these big ingots. Then when you walked down and had a look at the lads in the rolling mill they'd be taking these steel bars and whizzing them through. You would see them standing there with their steel tongs and these bars would be coming through at a fair old rate of knots. But those guys who worked in there used to be able to knock off early legitimately and go off to the pub.

In those days they all wore exactly the same stuff. They'd all have their flat caps and they all had their neckerchiefs round – they were sweat towels. The guys on the forge used to have these great long hefty leather aprons that were really thick, and huge great metal safety boots, because every time the forge went down sparks and bits shot off. It was heavy and dirty and dangerous, but it was also incredibly skilled work. If you see an old bit of film of it now you see a hammer going down and smashing a red-hot ingot, but what you don't realize is how much knowledge there is in the guy who's controlling that, because he's got to get it to a certain size and he's got to know exactly how much force he wants to put in. And those guys always worked as teams. They used to be turning the metal as they hammered it and each of them had to know his job, because it was dangerous if he didn't. They'd whip it over and then do the hammer again and then whip it over again, and they kept doing that all the time, just whipping it over until they got the right size and shape. And there was no talking because it was too loud to talk – they just used hand signals.

There were some bad accidents there. These sheets of steel that were going through the rolling mill could whip up in the air and of course the smaller they got the whippier they were. Sometimes they'd go through and then all of a sudden instead of coming through straight they'd go all over the place. All the men working there had was a pair of tongs and they'd have to grab it quick or otherwise it went somewhere and did some real damage. I saw a bloke once who had one straight through his thigh. I don't know whether they had to take his leg off in the end. It just came through the mill and he missed it and it cut straight into him. I remember taking him out and that was the end of working in there that night. That was horrible.

There used to be notices all over the walls for the mill workers: 'Don't forget your salt tablets'. They had to have salt every day because they were losing it through sweating so much. They had to go to the ambulance room, which was across the road, to get their salt tablets. The guys who did the real hard work in the rolling mills went off earlier and the first thing that they would normally do was go straight into the pub, because those guys could drink. That was not surprising, really, when you consider the work they were doing. A lot of them were heavy drinkers so they used to have what you might call a beer belly. But the work was a lot heavier then and you just did not have the health and safety regime that there is now, which would forbid almost half of whatever we used to do. There were these young apprentices and they'd just sit with a lever that they'd be pulling down all the time; it was making a massive noise and they were right on top of it. Then there were the poor guys who had what I used to think was the worst job of the lot in there, on what they called the swing-grinder. They used to have to walk on these ingots when they had just come out of the furnaces, and it was almost like shale. They'd have these huge grinders, things on swing arms, and these big, massive ingots would be on the ground and they'd have to use the swing-grinder to take off all the top layer of slag, or 'spelt' as we used to call it. They all had things tied around their mouths because that job was absolutely filthy. It was probably the dirtiest and I should think the most dangerously diseased job you could imagine. It was a horrible job, it really was.

We had to clock on and off every day but it was a fairly informal sort of thing. You all supposedly went through the gates and there was a window with a guy there who was the gatekeeper and he was supposed to watch people clocking in. This was to stop you doing it for your pal, who might turn around and say, 'Can you clock me in for six o' clock?' and he'd not get there until seven. The gatekeeper's job was to make sure this didn't happen, but invariably people would distract his attention and would do that sort of thing. When I was on the afternoon shift, which was two to ten, the work rota was such that you could actually knock off your quota probably between two and six if you really worked at it. Being a football fan I used to like to go to matches, so a friend used to say, 'Don't worry about it. I'll clock you out at ten.' So when I was going out I'd have to keep an eye on what the gate man was doing and get past at a time when he couldn't see me going out. I always remember one guy on the gate who was a bit of a bully if he thought he could get away with it. I remember him wandering into the rolling mill and there were half a dozen of the lads playing cards, playing for money. So because they weren't working he decided that he would help himself to the money in the middle if they wanted him to keep his mouth shut. He went over and said, 'I'm having that.' But one of the lads laid him straight out with a pair of tongs.

When you look back you are not really too surprised some of these companies went out of business, because some of the working practices were so old fashioned. Samuel Osborn's was a private company, still run by the family, and all the bosses came in to work at eight o'clock and went home at teatime. If you were on at six in the morning it was not unknown to go into the cabin on the floor and the guys would be sitting there from six until half past seven reading the paper or having a sandwich and then off they'd go before the bosses arrived and start work.

I used to be what you call the 'reeler' and I used to straighten steel bars ready to be put through a more finicky finishing process, like grinding them or turning them to a really close tolerance. I was quite good at it and I used to do most of Jacky Carnell's work. He was on the opposite shift to me and he was ill. A smashing lad, but he only had one lung. Nowadays they wouldn't employ him, but he'd been there and all his family had been there for a long time so they kept him on. Usually poor old Jacky would be lucky if he'd done half his shift work, but I could always whack it off for him.

Then I was taught how to work the centralized grinder because I could add up and use a micrometer. What I would do would be relatively small-diameter stuff – anything from about half an inch to a couple of inches in diameter. You would work your way through different types of steel in different grades, depending on what it was eventually being used for. An awful lot of it would go to companies like Sheffield Twist Drill to be made into drills. They would come to me, having gone through all the various processes in the rolling mill, and I had a machine which had rollers and I'd feed them through. Because they were whipping around the noise was terrible. They would roll perfectly so that they were dead straight. Then they could go through the grinding process. For this it would be flooded in soluble oil, which would keep it cool, and you'd feed the bars through once, twice or three times, depending on how many passes you needed. This would grind off the rough top surface and get it down smooth and then get it to its final finish. By this time it would leave the place all lovely and shiny and gleaming. Then when they brought in centralized turning machines I progressed and went on to work on bigger-diameter stuff. We worked on anything up to about five or six inches in diameter. This is quite a hefty chunk of steel and again you could work to very fine tolerances. We did a lot of work for the aero-engineering industry for people like Rolls-Royce. I enjoyed doing that because when the bar went in at one end it was all grey, rough and horrible but eventually it came out the other side absolutely silky smooth to the touch and shiny.

In those days everybody was paid in cash; it wasn't by bank account or monthly or anything like that. The staff got it on Friday but the men got theirs on Thursday and some of those guys could shift a week's money and go home with nothing. They could booze it, bet it, you name it. We'd go into the pub next to the steelworks just after nine o'clock and all the rolling guys and forge guys who finished early would be in there. Pauline's dad and I worked in the same building and when we were pushed he'd always say, 'I want you to work Saturday and Sunday this week, Ian, because we've got to get this order out.' So I'd work Saturday and Sunday and say, 'Oh, I'm not going in on Monday.' Then he'd go berserk, because on Saturday you would be on time and a half and on Sunday you'd be on double time, so you'd think to yourself, 'I've made the money, so I'm not going in on Monday.' But when I went in on Tuesday he'd start blistering me, 'I'm not going to give you any more overtime if you think you can take off Monday morning.' But he always relented in the end because he knew that we'd get the work done.

Because I went in on Pauline's dad's say, nobody messed me about. But I would imagine if I had gone in there without the patronage of Pauline's family that would have been a little bit different. They all had their own little cliques. Perhaps a half dozen guys would sit together and have their snack break, and you didn't really break into the conversation too early, until gradually you got accepted. Then you could say your little piece and they would listen to you or josh you or take the mickey out of you. Eventually, once they realized I was interested in what I was doing and I could work on their machines as well if one of them wanted to dash off, you were then regarded as one of the gang. You got used to ripe language there, but there was a tremendous camaraderie – they were a very close-knit community.

There were some rather disgusting habits in the steelworks. Jacky Carnell's favourite was going around and tiddling in somebody's juice bottle. Then they would go and get people's snack and, because it was on the riverside, you could look over the balcony at the side in an evening and see rats by the score. Some of them were not squeamish at all and would think nothing of killing a rat and slapping it in somebody's snack box. The toilets were medieval to put it mildly and in the steelworks proper they were disgusting, because some of the men there had no idea at all about hygiene and a lot of people never even had proper toilet paper. Even in people's houses – you'd go in many a house and they would just have newspaper on a string. In the works they'd wait until somebody was going in to have a wee and they'd get a great goo of soft soap which we used to use in quantity. It was a glutinous mass which they used in industry to wash your hands and it would come in big containers. They would get a great handful of this – or a great handful of grease, because there was loads of black grease around for greasing the drop hammers and the rolling mills – and the guys would shoot off behind somebody to the toilet and the great ball of grease would get wanged over their bits and pieces. Or if somebody was sitting in the loo, hopefully in private, something disgusting would get lobbed over the top at them. Lovely people as they were, one or two of them had disgusting habits because they came from really rough backgrounds. But the vast majority of them were good souls and I did all right there. I didn't have any problems, because nobody would take Pauline's Uncle Frank on – he was a nutter when he was roused. He wasn't very big but he was tough, and her Uncle George was a big lad as well and her dad had quite a temper on him, so I was lucky. They might have just teased me a bit, taking the mickey, but after a while they didn't.

One thing about Sheffield at that time was that virtually every decent works had its own sports ground and they all had their own club house, cricket pitches, football pitches, hockey, netball. As a junior footballer you were always chuffed to play for the work's teams because you got showers and things like cups of tea. When I used to play for a local under twenty-ones team you were lucky if you had anywhere to change and you'd certainly come away from football absolutely plastered in mud because there were no public facilities. Up at Concord Park, which had lots of football pitches, everybody used to get changed in what was called the decontamination shed, but you didn't think anything about it because that's all that there was and you wanted your game of football. Then once you got into the works team you got a heated dressing room and an actual bath or a shower and good pitches.

In those days not many of the firms were international companies or huge groups. A lot of them were family firms. And when there was a vacancy almost everybody knew somebody whose son or daughter would come for the job. In the mid to late 1950s and early 1960s jobs were so absurdly easy to come by that you could just wander in. I walked out of one at lunchtime and got another job before teatime. By that stage I'd moved up from being a labourer to being a centre-bar turner, which was a bit more of a skilled job, but I had a dispute with them at Osborn's because they wouldn't give me the rate of pay for this particular job I was doing. So I decided to go down to Leadbeater & Scott. It was doing the same job but they were paying a better rate. The morning I was starting there I couldn't get my car to go. I had an old 1949 Austin Devon and in winter you actually had to take the spark plugs out and put them in the oven at home, get them warmed up, then hop back out and put them in the car to get it started. It meant I was late starting there so I just didn't get off to a happy start.

From Osborn's, where we worked on some very expensive stuff like titanium and things like that for Rolls-Royce, and everything was perfect, going into somewhere where it wasn't was a bit of a shock. It was a very low building and they used to crane steel bars in there, so they'd come whizzing past your head and I didn't like that. By half past twelve I decided I just could not work in there because the situation was so different. So I walked up and said, 'I'm sorry, I can't stand working here.' This was because I was standing right on top of the soluble oil tank which had a grille over it and I found it was affecting me. Health and Safety wouldn't allow you to do it nowadays. So I walked out of there. I got the *Sheffield Star* in the afternoon and I thought, 'Right, I don't think I fancy any more steelworks.' Firestone Tyres had a depot in Sheffield and they were looking for a van driver, so I thought, 'Oh, I fancy that.' So I went down there and got set on the same afternoon.

I also had a short spell in a cutlery works and, like all cutlery works, they had the buffer girls working in the buffing shop, which was an absolutely disgustingly filthy place. In here they would have the knives, forks or whatever bit of cutlery it was they were working on and they would have a mixture of grease and powdery stuff that buffed it up from being fairly rough to get it smoothed and polished. They had these buffing wheels that went round rather like a grindstone, except they were made of something like a sheep's skin and that rubbed the grease in and got the cutlery smoothed down so eventually they were able to get a nice shine on. They used to say you could always tell a buffer lass because they'd never be able to completely get all the grease and filth out of their hands. The buffer girls had a favourite trick with any youngster who arrived. Any young fella who came to work at the place would be lured into the buffing shop and they would drop his trousers and slap all this grease that they used in there all over him. So you learnt to walk very carefully anywhere near the buffing shop. In the 1950s you had a lot of ladies who had lost their husbands in the war and who had families to look after, so a lot of them would get work in the buffing shop; as I recall there were women working in there from sixteen to sixty. It was very often a job that stayed in the family. If you were from a working-class family, and if your children proved to be not particularly academic, a girl might well follow her mum and go into the buffing shop, and the sons likewise, if they weren't academically minded, might follow their fathers into the steelworks.

The steelworks were Sheffield's biggest employers, but not everybody wanted to work there. Mike Lomas was born and bred in Darnell, which was close to the centre of Sheffield and within sight of all the steelworks. He got a job at the English Steel Corporation but it was more by accident than choice, because he had always wanted to be a joiner.

My friend's dad was a manager in the steelworks and he had said to me, 'So what do you want to do when you leave school?' When I told him he said, 'We've got a joiner's shop where I work.' When I went into a steelworks for the first time on 4 January 1960 I was just fifteen and I think the industry generally had been fairly quiet just prior to that, and then just after I started there seemed to be a boom. The biggest steelworks, like the English Steel Corporation which I went to, all had their own training workshops and they did assessments of any prospective young trainee or apprentice. I remember going in a couple of months before leaving school and I sat an exam. It was in a canteen, full of young lads, and you just did all these tests in English, maths and things like that. The impression I got was that if you were grown up and you scored well you were office material; if you were average you were apprentice craftsman potential; and if you didn't do very well but you had a bit of brawn you were in a melting shop or a rolling mill where brawn over brain was to your advantage. I must have been average because I was given a position of probationary apprentice.

The very first day I started work I went through number one gate on Brightside Lane which leads up to the melting shops and the rolling mills. They had their own private train system, locos pulling wagons with ingots on, and inside two minutes of going into that steelworks on my very first day I turned a corner and a loco was coming up towards me. On a wagon at the back there was a huge ingot that was almost the diameter of a room and it was glowing red hot. The pavement was very narrow and as it came past me I was pinned against the wall and I nearly melted – my clothes were nearly smoking.

The works was a massive place. Over two thousand people worked there in the 1960s. One of the lathes they had there was half a mile long. It was taken from Krupps in Germany as payment for war damages. They just dismantled it and brought it over along with lots and lots of machines that had been taken from Krupps and they were all massive. A guy could use one of those machines to put a cut on a piece of steel that was possibly the diameter of a room and putting that cut on it might take a week. You used to wonder how they did it. And any steel that was taken off all went back to the furnace, to the melting shops to be used again.

Once I started there I found out that you could go anywhere in that factory and get anything. I could take my watch if it was broken to the watchmaker and I could have the watch repaired because every department had a clock – everybody clocks in and clocks out and all the clocks needed to be repaired, so there was a little clockmaker's workshop.

You couldn't start your apprenticeship until you were sixteen, so for the first year we were scattered around the works. I ended up in the machine shop which was attached to the research department. Steel had to be tested, examined, X-rayed and all sorts of things, so we had to prepare all these test pieces. Generally they would be small samples of steel that had been taken from a melt across the way in the melting shop, but I remember one of the pieces that I worked on was Donald Campbell's *Bluebird* after he crashed it on Salt Lake Flats in Utah. Parts of the car had been built from steel that had been made at the company, so they were brought back and went to the research shop for tests to see if they could improve them.

I worked for a year in that machine shop. I did three days in there, a day and one evening a week at night school and one day a week in the company's junior training workshop. While I was in the training workshop using all the machines I absolutely loved working on a centre lathe – it was a joy.

When I finished my time at the training workshop
I had to be interviewed again by the apprentice training supervisor, the RSM. He read out all the marks I'd
attained on all the machines and bench exercises and
machining exercises and I'd done quite well. I'd got
good marks, especially in centre-lathe turning, and
he said, 'I can get you in the machine shop.' But I
wanted to do carpentry. I'd set my sights on that so I
said, 'Sorry, Mr Ayre, but I want to be a joiner.' At that
point he just threw things up in the air and stamped
around, shouting and bawling, 'This is a bloody
engineering firm not a bloody building site. I've told
you that before.' I was quaking in my boots, but I said,
'Well if I can't go in that joiner's shop I'm prepared to
leave. I'll go somewhere else to be a joiner.' He just
said, 'Get out!' and he threw me out of his office. 'Get
back to that bloody machine shop,' he shouted. So I
were there for a fortnight, [but] at the end of it this
foreman in the workshop said, 'Mick, you've got to go
up to the joiner's workshop. You're on interview.' [I
got the job and] I started learning from there.

At first I'd be shafting hammers, shafting brushes,
running errands, sweeping up. Then on Friday nights
you greased all the machines because they didn't
want them going rusty. All the joiners used to push
handcarts. If you were going to another part of the
works there was no lorry or white vans to take you,
you walked and you pushed your handcart. It would
have your trestles on, your timber and your tools. If
you were the apprentice you pushed and the joiner
walked at the side. All the furniture in the offices was
made in the joiner's shop; they didn't buy any of it. I

made tables, chairs, cupboards, units, sets of drawers, everything. In the office block they had vaults and on a couple of occasions I remember going in and building new shelves. They had all the shareholders' papers in there and joiners are nosey, so it was always 'Look at all this lot.'

The furnaces were open hearth and they had a big dome on top. It was made out of furnace bricks, but for the bricklayers to lay the bricks they needed an arch made in wood that they laid the bricks on top of and one of our jobs was to make those wooden arches. The carpenter made the shape first and the bricklayer or the mason used that as a framework. Then it was all taken away. That's called 'centring'.

Steelworkers are rough people and if they couldn't get in a door they'd smash it to get in, so we would have to repair the doors or make new ones and go and hang them and fix them. Then because the steelworkers wore hobnail boots they would slip, so all the steps up to the furnaces were lined with hardwood so that the boots would grip.

The Queen visited the steelworks once. She couldn't go on to the melting-shop platform because it was a little rough, so they broke a big hole in the wall of the furnace and had a special staircase made for her, quarter-turn landings all the way up.

So you were doing all the things you'd do in a normal joiner's shop times ten. They also had a blacksmith there and as a joiner I could go to him and have any hammer I wanted made by him. Hammers in the steelworks were everywhere – lying on the floor, discarded with broken shafts. I once picked up a little hammer locally, took it to a black-smith and said, 'Eric, can you turn me that into a Warrington hammer?' And he just heated the end of it and turned it into the hammer I wanted.

I used to clock on at seven thirty in the morning and clock out at twelve minutes to five. It was a forty-four-hour week if you were on the shop floor. And my wage at the time was £2.2s [£2.10]. So I worked for one shilling an hour – that's 5p now. You used to get a birthday rise. I seem to remember when I was sixteen I was on something like £3.6s [£3.30] a week and I certainly remember when I was nineteen I was on over £9 a week for forty-four hours. That was when I started paying board and I gave my mother £3 and I had £6 a week. I was able to buy a motorbike and the world was my oyster.

I was never a morning person and being a big, long, lollicking layabout teenager at the time I could stop up until all hours but waking up in the morning was not my forte. My mother sometimes used to threaten me with a wet dishcloth to get me out of bed. I was always late for work. I'd get to the factory gates and it was always a run up that yard to get to that clock before half past seven. Everybody in that factory was on production bonus and the main-tenance men had a share in that bonus scheme. So when I was twenty-one, a joiner was on £14 a week but they got £4 a week bonus. If you were late in the morning and you lost fifteen minutes in a week you lost £4. So you made sure you were never late.

All the big companies in this city had their own sports grounds and you could do any sport you liked at the one I worked at. For me it was just about two miles from where I lived and I used to go up at night and for threepence I could play table tennis. Then in the summertime I could run around the track or play shuttlecock.

In that joiner's shop, if it was made on the bench it had to be perfect. There were absolutely no shortcuts. If it weren't perfect it were broken up. Even if it was going to be taken into a machine shop or melting shop or the rolling mill, it had to be perfect when it went through the door of the joiner's shop; there was no second best. Everybody had pride in what they did and it were absolutely brilliant. One of the best joiners that ever drew breath was a guy called Tommy Booston. He was fabulous; he was naturally gifted and he could do anything. I worked on his bench, I was his lad. Old Tommy always used to say, 'Neat, nice and precise.' We used to make these big step-ladders that had handrails, treads and risers. When they were sanded down, you'd have put one of them in your living room. They would even have gone in Buckingham Palace, they were so perfect.

A lot of the joiners who worked there were like refugees from the land of hard knocks. They'd all been outside working for private companies, joiners' shops and on building sites, and they seemed to gravitate to this joiner's shop. Lots of other joiners I've met in Sheffield who worked in the steelworks all said the same: it was like the place to finish their working lives, because it was permanent, it was reliable, it was for ever. On a building site the job might finish next week, but what people want is security and regular employment and that's what they got in the steelworks.

In that steelworks there were loads of women who had been taken on during the war. They were machine operatives and they could work as good as any guy. And they also worked as file-cutters and had a file shop down near Hillsborough, Sheffield Wednesday Football Club. No man ever walked through that file-cutting department, ever. They got debagged, it was as simple as that. The women's language was quite colourful and they could more than hold their own. They were very tough – they had kids and were running homes and going out to work. When you clocked out at night there were just as many women as guys waiting at that bus stop. They were dashing home to get the tea ready for the kids. They'd all have turbans on and overalls on, and it was the same anywhere in town. The cutlery industry in particular was still quite busy and lots of women worked in that as buffers.

At one time there were hundreds of little cutlery workshops all over Sheffield. Mechanization eliminated all but a handful of them, but some small family firms remained to carry on the centuries-old traditions of Sheffield's earliest industry. Vin Malone was born on the Manor Estate in Sheffield and went to St Teresa's Roman Catholic School. After leaving when he was fifteen and working first as an apprentice plumber and then at Firth Brown Tools, he went to work for one of these small cutlery firms in 1962.

[At Firth Brown] I were getting the princely sum of about £2.10s [£2.50] a week, but friends were telling me, 'Oh I get fifteen pounds a week working in cutlery.' So I went to John Donnelly's on Portobello Street and initially it was a Saturday-morning trial. For this I got ten shillings [50p], which was a lot of money, and I was told to start on Monday. Then it clicked that I had got to start at seven o'clock in the morning! But Mr Donnelly only lived on the Manor Estate, which was five minutes' walk from where I lived, and he used to pick me up and take me to work.

When you got there you were stepping back years. It was dirty and it was cold in the winter. There was no glass in the windows and there was no heating apart from an old pot-bellied stove in the middle of the shop and when that was lit in the morning the whole place was just full of smoke; you couldn't see anything there was so much smoke. You were working all the time and there was no talking. If John Donnelly saw you talking he always used to say, 'If I want people to talk I'd employ radios.' He always worked alongside us and if you'd seen him you would have thought he was just a dirty old worker. But he wasn't, he was the man that owned the firm.

It was very hard work. You were working sixty-two hours a week for £15, but I absolutely loved it and I learnt everything I could. I used to stop behind until seven o'clock and we used to take carver forks for shot-blasting down at Darnell and we used to get home at seven thirty at night, but I weren't bothered and I couldn't wait until next morning to get to work. I picked it up very, very easy. Mr Donnelly had two sons. One of them, Danny, was the same age as me; his other son, David, was probably twenty-five. They'd been doing that job for years and within the space of six months I was telling these lads what to do.

Carver forks were the main things we made, but we also made spoons, forks, steak forks, corn on the cob forks – which were actually like a little arrowhead – carver heads, pickle forks and all kinds of things. It was dangerous, particularly if you slipped with a carver fork and the tongue on the fork that the handle fits on to went in your hand. That happened to me three times. And there was no health and safety. The cure, believe it or not, for stopping it bleeding was to get some paper, set it on fire and while it burnt away you got the ashes and put them in the hole in your hand and you just wrapped right round the hand and carried on working. And it worked.

In winter it was hellish. There was just that one pot-bellied stove and it was a large area. You worked on twenty-four-inch wheels and they went round at probably thirty or forty miles an hour and the draught that was created by these wheels going round made it cold. You had to sit on your hands to warm them up; it were really, really cold. And some mornings in winter if there had been a severe frost the forks would be frozen to the bench. There's a story about that. A lad started some time after me and one particular winter morning it were so cold that at dinnertime I went to old man Donnelly and said, 'John I'm going home. It's too cold.' So this other lad said, 'I'm going home as well, John.' Next day I came to work and old man Donnelly said, 'I hope you're warmer now. Go and start work.' But the other lad got the sack because he'd gone home the day before. Years later it clicked that it was because I was good at my job. I didn't realize it at the time. Anyway, it prompted him to put individual electric fires all around the walls of the firm for each worker, which were good. Another good thing about that place was that when my wife Mary was having our firstborn, Sean, she was only across the road. So they phoned across when she'd had Sean and I just dashed across in all my filth.

If you could work at Donnelly's for a month you could work anywhere for the rest of your life; nothing was too harsh after that. And it really set me up. From there I went to several other firms, just going around chasing money. I worked at a place called Dearden's on Liverpool Street; I worked at Cooper Brothers on Arundel Street; I worked at Lee & Wigfall on John Street; I worked at Osborn on Headford Street; and I got a job at Sipple's on Glass Lane, but I was only there for a while. I left because there was a woman in charge and I don't like women telling me what to do. I worked at Gee & Holmes for a week and I left there because in a week all I did were polish six knives. It was just boring. I wanted to be working, so I left. And I came out of cutlery for a year and went working at the Whitbread Brewery. I didn't like that so when I saw a job advertised at George Butler on Sidney Street I phoned the company. 'What can you do?' they asked me. 'Oh, I can do this and I can do that, I can do everything,' I told them. I was just able to watch people and I'd think, 'I can do that job,' and I could do it. It was just natural for me, like walking.

Everybody [at George Butler] worked in a particular section. You got spoon or fork, you got blanks, you got press shop, you got buffing shop, but I was put in a separate section. My one was a section where I could go in any of those shops and just ease any pressure off that was building up. On my first day in Butler's I actually met the man who trained me at Donnelly's. He was a brilliant man, John Mannion, and he was working there so it were great. I was experienced, John was experienced and between us we turned some good carver forks out of that place, some of the best in Sheffield. On these particular forks, instead of just getting steak handles which were imported from India, a lot of them were getting silver handles put on. Then the works manager asked me if I'd like to do a bit of bolstering. 'There's a shop up there with some lads in it who don't know what to do,' he said. Bolstering entails cleaning the back of the blade up and the bolster that the handle sits on. I'd never done it before but I'd seen it done so I went up and I did it and production went up straight away. I ran that shop for about five years and the lads I had in there were great. There were some good characters, and strangely enough you'd see people, pardon the expression, who weren't a full shilling, but as soon as they started work, honestly, it was just beautiful. I enjoyed training all these young lads and my wife worked with us as well in the warehouse. Just below this bolstering shop some buffers worked. By that time the bad reputation that buffers used to have had more or less gone and this lot were really gentle women, lovely people.

One day I was sent for by the works managers and one of the directors and they asked me to go on the staff because they didn't want me to leave. But soon after this George Butler's was bought by another firm from Birmingham and we moved down to Vulcan Road. We had two units and everything was open-plan. It was terrible working like that. The old buildings were like rabbit warrens with little shops here and little shops there and everybody loved them, but these new open-plan places were absolutely wicked. We were there for a couple of years and then they moved to Ecclesfield into another old cutlery firm. This was Lloyd Roses, but a French firm called Garde Grande bought that and we were all made redundant. I were out of work three weeks and I got a job at British Silverware down Ealing Bank Road by the side of the railway track. I was in charge of issuing the blanks, but I was only there for a year and I were made redundant again.

I were out of work probably another three or four weeks and I saw a friend I'd been working with at British Silverware. He told me that he'd seen this job advertised at David Mellor's. I knew it would be a very basic job and I didn't really want to get it, but it was work and I applied. They must have opened my letter and phoned me straight back. I went there the next day and got the job. I've been there for nine years now and I don't like it. I don't like it simply because it's like a child's job which I've trained people for. I can do better than what I'm doing. But I just can't get another job anywhere else.

Generally, though, what I really like about my time in cutlery is being able to take a rough forge piece of metal and take it through its stages and it comes out to be a thing of beauty. You get it and you can see your face in it. Mr Donnelly taught me, 'When you are putting one piece down, you're picking another one up at the other end. You've got to keep doing that.' So you pick a speed up and you cannot get rid of that speed all of your life. That's how I've learnt and all the people that worked at Donnelly's have always been like that. They could get a job anywhere. One of the best things about working in cutlery for me is knowing that a lot of things I've touched have gone all over the world. I've done cutlery for Stanley Matthews, and Lulu has got some cutlery from where I've worked. And I don't like admitting it, but I've actually done work for Maggie Thatcher when she were in Downing Street.

Unlike other major steel-producing centres, where the industry has been wiped out, Sheffield is still Steel City. But the industry has changed. While heavy steel production has now all but ceased, the actual output of steel in recent years has been greater than ever. However, it is now mainly stainless and specialist steels that are made here and the industry has also become highly automated and employs far fewer people. The city still has an international reputation for the finest-quality cutlery products and the words 'Made in Sheffield' are an assurance of the best-quality cutlery that can be found anywhere in the world. Many small cutlery manufacturers still operate in the city, including David Mellor's where Vin still works. He says, 'I'm working alongside people a lot younger than me and I'm doing twice the amount of work what they do and it's a lot better. I'm not bragging, but that's just how it is.'

6

Driving the Wheels of Industry

IRON AND STEEL supplied the materials for making things, but it was coal that provided the power to drive the machinery in the mills and factories where those things were manufactured. The country's vast coal reserves provided the energy to drive the machines that turned Britain into the world's first great industrial nation. The rise of manufacturing, mining, trade and transport brought a big increase in national prosperity and transformed the appearance of the country as the pithead winding gear of coal mines began to appear all over the country to provide the fuel for this great industrial expansion.

The areas in which Britain's massive industrial advance took place in the nineteenth century were determined by the presence of large seams of coal. The coalfields of Lancashire, Yorkshire, the North East, the Midlands, South Wales and central Scotland became the great centres of industry and by 1914 there were over a million coal miners in Britain – more workers than in any other industrial activity – with numbers continuing to rise until the 1920s. The work was heavy, dirty, dangerous and unhealthy. Seams could be as low as eighteen inches, making it necessary to dig out the coal lying down. Some of the deeper mines were very hot and there were ever-present dangers from gas, flooding and rockfalls. Accidents were frequent and in the 1920s around five hundred miners were injured every day.

By 1932, when the full Depression in world trade had hit the industry, over four hundred thousand miners were out of work. Nevertheless, the 1930s saw the introduction of mechanization: coal-cutters, mechanical picks and conveyors to take coal from the face began to come into general usage, speeding up the pace of production. A further stage in modernization began during the Second World War with the introduction of large power-loading machines that both cut and conveyed coal in one auto-mated process.

After the war coal still dominated the economy, fuelling not only steel production, engineering and textiles but the newer electrical and chemical industries as well. Coal was needed for the railways, gasworks and power stations; it was still the main resource for domestic heating and remained one of Britain's greatest exports. In 1946, appealing for between seventy and a hundred thousand men and boys for the mining industry to bring the work-force up to the required figure of 730,000, Hugh Gaitskell, Parliamentary Secretary to the Ministry of Fuel and Power, said that the industry was going to have a new deal. 'This nation,' he said, 'would indeed deserve the doom and disaster which would overtake it if the mining industry were allowed to languish and fail through neglect.' Higher coal production was seen as the key to Britain's whole industrial recovery and on 1 January 1947 coal became the first British industry to be nationalized. A national plan for coal was drawn up. When it was published in 1950 it assumed that demand would rise to reach 250 million tons in 1960. The target was to be reached by modernizing the old mines and opening new ones in the Midlands and Yorkshire. It was a time when Britain's consumption of coal was still rising and in 1951 Geoffrey Lloyd, the Minister of Fuel and Power, said, 'In peace and war alike, King Coal is the paramount Lord of Industry.'

In Lancashire large coal deposits were one of the most important contributing factors to the development of the cotton industry. The steam engines that provided the power to drive the machines in the mills needed plenty of coal and it was the unlocking of Lancashire's coal seams that turned the county into a great manufacturing centre. Many of these steam-powered mill engines were used until the 1960s and steam locomotives continued to be built and operated on the railways until the same time. And as transport and industry turned more and more to electrical power, it was still steam that was at the heart of the generating process, with coal needed in vast quantities by the power stations to raise the steam.

The Lancashire coalfield covered an area of some 550 square miles from Stalybridge in the south-east and Burnley in the north-east to Ormskirk in the north-west and Rainhill in the south-west, and it was one of the most prolific in England. In 1907 there were approximately 320 collieries operating in Lancashire producing some twenty-six million tons of coal per year and employing 94,300 men. Many of these were small collieries, but after nationalization in 1947 many of them ceased working and the coalfield was consolidated into a relatively small number of large mines. Some of the last of Lancashire's private mines survived on the lower slopes of Winter Hill near Horwich. As well as coal, seams of clay were mined and supplied local works making bricks and pipes. Crankshaw's Pipeworks, whose mine was known as Klondyke, was open until 1961 and John Garrity from Horwich got his first job there.

When I came to leave school in 1957 I couldn't get a job. I went to different places for jobs but I was only fifteen and everywhere I went they only wanted youngsters at sixteen because it was all shift work and it were against the law to put somebody at fifteen on shift work. My dad worked at the pipeworks and they had a mine where they got coal and clay out. My dad was a fireman and he worked on the Lancashire boilers there and just·above the boilerhouse was the entrance to a tunnel where the trucks full of coal and clay came out of the mine on an endless chain. We had a distant relative who worked there and he used to come into the pipeworks for supplies for the mine. My dad must have seen him and asked him if there were any jobs up there at the drift mine. 'Aye,' he said, 'the lad on the tip is ready to go underground because he's sixteen, so tell your lad to come up.'

The place was called Wilders Moor Colliery, but locally they called it Klondyke Tunnel. So I went up and saw the manager and I got the job. I started on the jig with the tubs, where the full ones came off down a brew [hill]. The lad who showed me was a right beggar and he made it really hard for me. Anyway, eventually he went in the pit and I was left to it. What I had to do was catch the full trucks as they came up out of the mouth of the tunnel. There were bell posts like telegraph poles all the way from the bottom of the mine right up to the tunnel mouth. These posts had copper wires attached to them. To ring the bell you had to touch the wires together. My job was to scrape the empty trucks out, coal on one side, clay on t'other, because you can't mix the coal with the clay. There were two bunkers; one were for coal and one for clay. When the tub came off at the end of the track, I used to jump behind it and turn it round with Frank who I worked with. He would push it backwards and it would go over into one of the bunkers. Then he'd pull it over and give it to me so I could clean it out and put it back on the empty return track. Every twenty yards apart these tubs were, so by the time I cleaned one out another one were coming off – you had to be really quick.

In winter the place we worked was open to snow and I had to go up the track with a spade, clearing in front of tubs. We had no waterproofs, so we were wet through in the winter from first thing in the morning and the tubs were wet, so your pants got wet and that meant your whole body would be wet through all day in the freezing cold.

I did that till I was sixteen. Then I went underground. There were two mines, the big mine and the little one. The men in the big mine were on piece work but in the little mine they were day men, th'older men, so they used to put you in there to start with and if you weren't a good worker they'd leave you in there. But they didn't show you anything – you had to watch and pick it all up yourself. So I'd watch while they were laying a set of rails or to see how you filled a tub. Anyway, I was in there for a bit and they said, 'Right, you're in the big mine next week.' I was only about seventeen or eighteen, but the manager was a good manager and I've realized since that he saw I was a good worker and he thought, 'We'll have him in the big mine and he can go on piece work and earn more money.' So they put me in, but it was cold in there. There were two ways to get to it: you could walk over the top of the moor and go in through an air hole to get to it, or you could go in all the way along the tunnel. Sometimes when the weather was bad I'd go up the tunnel thinking, 'I'm not walking over the top – it's a blizzard.' But if you went underground all the way up it was hard work because it was so low you were crawling and crouched down all the time.

When you got to the face they were pillar and stall workings[45] and you went in a place, six foot wide by about six foot high, and that was your face. We used to call them 'places'. It was just before it closed in January 1961 and they put me in a place and when I could do enough tubs to earn a wage they said, 'Right, we'll pay you now,' because I was only getting haulage pay while I was doing this training. The training period lasted for two or three months, but nobody came and trained you during this time like

[45] In pillar and stall workings coal was removed from large areas underground, but large amounts of coal were left unmined. These were the pillars which supported the roof of the mine.

they did at the NCB where I went to work later. You had to pick everything up along the way and you didn't ask. You just got a pick and a spade and you went in, and you used to scar all your knuckles raw digging the coal out by hand. We'd drill it and then go and shout for the fireman. He'd come in and sort the powder out. This was sticks of gelignite and they smelt like marzipan; if you kept smelling them they'd give you a headache. While the fireman was putting a det [detonator] in I was what we used to call 'making pills'. To do this you'd get a handful of puddle clay and roll it and then the fireman would put it into one of the holes you'd drilled. When he put the rest of his sticks of gelignite in he used to ram the holes up tight with this clay. If he didn't the gelignite would just shoot out. But it was old fashioned; they used to call it Klondyke and it was just like a cowboy mine. Anyway, then the fireman would put his fuse in and that was like a clothes line that would go in with the det. Then he'd say, 'Reet, firin', and he put a light to it and you'd got to go round and find a corner to get behind. When it went off everything shuddered and you couldn't see a thing for smoke, and the cordite used to get on your chest.

The only lights down there were candles, but if you were on haulage you had what they called a carbide lamp. It was split in two and you'd put water in the top part and a handful of some things like white pebbles in the bottom. This was the carbide. It came from Germany and it stunk. Then you used a clamp to put the two halves of the lamp together and tighten them up. And when you turned the water on with a butterfly tap it would wet the carbide, which would cause a gas and when you put a light to it this would light up really bright.

Half a crown [12½p] a tub was what the colliers got, whether it were coal or clay, and you could do at least a dozen in a day. But before I got paid a proper wage they said they were closing. The seams we were working at the time were very near the surface. The farther you went into the workings, the nearer you got to the top and it ended up just about twelve foot from the surface. Just before we finished some diggers came along and took the top off the workings and started to dig the coal and the clay pillars out. There were times when you'd be going to your face and you'd see the diggers outside, just above you. One day I heard this mighty noise like a vacuum and I thought, 'What the hell's that?' What had happened was that it had 'fallen up' – that's a miner's term for caving in. It had all come in from the surface, so Tommy, the fireman, said, 'Reet, get your spades and get out on top.' We went outside through the air holes and got on the surface and the hole where it had fallen in was about as wide as a room, so we had to get in there and keep digging it all out.

After that John got a job with the National Coal Board. He was eighteen and when he started he had to go to Sandhole Colliery at Walkden to do three weeks' training.

We used to do half a day in the classroom then go down the pit for half a day. But we only went halfway down the shaft into what they called the

Black Mine, where they used to train you for the haulage. When they said you're going down, I'd never been down a mineshaft before. I was used to walking in along the tunnel into the hillside so I'd never been down in the cage. I was stood on the bankhead next to the shaft and I went and looked over. If I hadn't done that I probably wouldn't have been so bad, but when I saw the pit bottom it were [so far down it were] like a sixpence and I thought, 'Oh heck! Oh that's a long way down!' So I stepped back and thought, 'I don't know what to do here.' It was really hard – one part of me were saying, 'I'm not going down here,' while the other part was saying, 'Well you have to. It's going to be your job.' Anyway, they must have seen one of the other lads getting nervous and I heard them say to him, 'You know, if you don't go down now, you'll never go down.' So when I heard this I thought, 'I've got to do it or I'll be the same.'

So the cage came up and there was a gap you had to step over to get into it, but I got in and the cage itself was quite solid. It held twenty-two men. In a way it was easier for me than for the others because, although I'd never been down a shaft like this before, [at least] I had more experience of working underground. The others had never been near a pit before. They were all new recruits. Anyway, we set off in the cage and I thought it would be slow – but it went faster and faster and it was bouncing about and my guts felt as though they were coming up into my throat. I thought, 'Oh – I'll be glad when this stops.'

We stopped halfway down and they opened the

gates and pushed a little bridge out across the gap, and you had to step out on to this to cross the great void between the cage and the training gallery. It was pitch black in the shaft but as you got into the inset there was lights there, but they were only round the pit bottom. The further you go in, there's no lights. You've just got your cap lamp.

After his training John got a job at a colliery close to where he lived. Like a lot of young lads just starting with the NCB, he was given a job on haulage.[46] He left the mine and went to work in an engineering works for a couple of years but he didn't like it as the job he was doing was very repetitive and he found it boring. The pay wasn't good either, so he decided to go back down the pit and he went on to spend the rest of his working life as a miner, first back on haulage, then as a face worker. He worked at a number of different pits in Lancashire. The last was Parsonage at Leigh, which was the deepest pit in Europe. It was a mile down the shaft and John recalls 'they used to drop you down at fifty foot a second'.

In the 1950s the Lancashire coal industry was still in full production as most of the county's mills were still operating on steam power. By this time, however, a lot of small mines had been closed and the coalfield had become consolidated into bigger companies working a relatively small number of large mines. Bolton was one of the places that had lost its coal mines, mainly because they were small and not very profitable, but there was still plenty of work for miners in the surrounding area. Many men from

[46] Transport of mined coal from working faces to the surface.

Bolton travelled each day to nearby places like Leigh, Atherton, Tyldesley, Westhoughton, Walkden and Wigan to work in the mines there. Alf Molyneux is a Boltonian who was employed at several of these, working his way up from picking up paper to pit deputy.

My dad worked at the pit, so when I left school when I was fifteen it was just a natural progression for me. He travelled to Mosley Common, which was a fair distance from Bolton, but each of the pits had their own buses and they were very good services. That is if you could get on them, because most people hadn't got cars then so it was quite common to go to the bus stop and three buses would go past you full when all the workers were going to work. Different buses would have the pit name and headcode on them: Mosley Common, Astley Green, Parsonage or whatever.

I started at a training colliery, which was St George's in Tyldesley. You did six months' training there, which involved a bit of schooling in the class-room and underground trips at various collieries. One of them was Newtown Colliery at Swinton where they had a special training gallery. Then after that six months you went to the pit you'd chosen: Mosley Common in my case. You then did twenty days' training with an old collier who just showed you round the pit, basically, and then you'd be allocated a particular job.

My first job was going round with sacks picking paper up. They would give you two or three small sacks and tell you to go to such a place to pick the paper up. Now you wouldn't know where such a place was, so you had to ask somebody where it was and they would guide you. In that way you got to find your way round the colliery. I remember my first day of picking paper up I was sent up what they called Durkins Brew and I was about halfway in on the top road of a coalface, where the return air comes out, when they fired the 'top ripping lip'. This is where they blow stone down in the mine roadways to increase the headroom for traffic and ventilation. That was the first time I'd heard an explosion go off underground and it frightened me to death. I'd never heard a sound like it before. Then after the explosion all the smoke comes out, and the dust, so you can't see anything and you can hardly breathe. When you got used to it you learnt to pull your shirt over your face or put your helmet over your nose and mouth, but on my first day down there I didn't know what to do.

When I started [in the mornings] it was a waste of time waiting for a bus where I lived, so I used to walk to Great Moor Street bus station in the centre of Bolton [for the bus]. I had to get up about half past four and if I overslept my dad wouldn't wake me, even when we were on the same shift. I remember my mum used to say, 'Why don't you wake Alfie?' and he always replied, 'He'll get up when he's short of money.' And it worked.

I think I did the litter-collecting for about two weeks and then I got a job on the main rope haulage, where it's very busy, with empty wagons going in and coal coming out all the time. The track was laid so it ran slightly downhill from the face so the coal free-wheeled out. They used to run about fifteen tubs at a time and they were controlled by what they called 'squeezers'. These were placed at intervals on each rail. Basically they were two pieces of rail about eight foot long on the inside of the track and they were worked by compressed air. As the wagons came along the track the squeezers would trap the wheels and slow them down. Operating the squeezers was my first job. Haulage was the job that most of the lads would start on when they first went down the pit. They would always have a responsible collier who'd probably had enough of face work and he'd oversee you all. He'd make sure things kept moving, but at the same time he'd be watching out for you because there were quite a number of accidents.

The trouble was the place I was working was very cold. You were in the main intake where air comes down the pit from the surface – it was the main ventilation for all that part of the pit. If you imagine a very cold winter's day with a wind blowing at you as well, that is what you were working in. You'd have to wear a vest, a shirt, a pullover, a jacket, a donkey jacket, a balaclava, gloves, two pairs of pants and you were still cold, even though you were working hard. I were on that for a month or two and I thought, 'This is no good – it's freezing.' So a chap told me to go to the doctor's and get a sick note to say I was having problems working in the cold. So I went to the doctor's and I told him the tale I was working in water and freezing cold. I got the note from him, sealed in an envelope, and it cost me five shillings [25p]. Back at the pit I went to see the manager, Manny Marland, gave him the note and briefly explained the situation. A couple of weeks later nothing had happened and I was still working in the same place. One day the manager came past me so I said, 'Excuse me, Mr Marland, I came to see you a couple of weeks ago and gave you a note about working in the cold.' He said, 'Yeah, I remember. It's all in hand. But where's all this bloody water?' There was no water there because I'd made that bit up and I didn't know the doctor had put anything about it on the note! Anyway, he did move me a couple of days later to a place where it was a lot warmer. It was haulage again, but it was better.

I did various jobs when I was on the haulage, including belt-repair work, and this lasted until I was eighteen, when I applied for coalface training. At Mosley Common they had a coalface specifically set up for trainees. On it you'd be instructed by an ex-collier who knew what he was about. You did 120 days on that, so many days on each face operation. There'd be coal filling, which was basically all pick and shovelling; setting roof supports; packing, where you retrieved stone from waste ground they were leaving behind and built stone pikes which were three or four yards long; and then there was ripping, which was enlarging roadways. There was also moving conveyors over and there was coal-cutting. They were the basic jobs. Then when you'd done your 120 days you'd be allocated a job on a coalface or, if there was no job for you, you'd be what's called a 'market man' or a 'spur man' so if somebody had a day off you'd fill in for him.

My first job when I left training was packing and ripping, mostly packing. They hadn't fully mechanized in them days so it was almost all hand stuff. As the face moved forward what they left behind was called waste. That was left to collapse and you had to retrieve that. With the stone and rubble you retrieved you'd build three walls and then you'd fill it with small stuff with your spade – but not coal; you couldn't put coal in. It were pretty hard work. You worked in twos and if you couldn't get enough stone out of the waste you had to drill the roof and get enough stone from there to make your pack. Then towards the end of the shift the fireman would come round and he'd pull part of your pack down to make sure you'd put no coal in, because that was a mortal sin. He'd also make sure there was no wood in; it all had to be stone. If he pulled it down you'd have to build it again. If you didn't build it you didn't get paid, simple as that, and if he didn't like you he'd pull yours down more often than somebody's he did like.

Eventually I left Mosley Common to work at Astley Green, on the other side of the East Lancs Road. That was in the early 1960s. I always tended to move where the money was. If the money weren't good and I'd heard it was good somewhere else I'd go, because in them days you could stop work today and start somewhere else tomorrow, no problem. I've actually worked at three pits in twenty-four hours – no problem at all. You'd just say, 'I'm done here,' and go and sign on somewhere else. The money used to vary a lot. At one spell in the early 1960s we were on £2.10s [£2.50] a shift at Astley

Green and at Golborne at that time they were getting £8 and £9 a shift doing the same work. There were various reasons for this. You made your own price with management for one. And the other was that some pits would do the same job with a man less so they shared his wage between them. So if you could do the job with less men, you got more money, simple as that. The danger in that was the next job you went on, you made a contract again and they tried to cut you down.

I went on night shift and we started getting £2 a shift, which was a drop, so I stuck it for a couple of weeks and said, 'That's enough for me.' I packed in and went to Bickershaw on more money for the same work. I was there a while and then I got talking to another guy who lived on the same street as me and he said, 'Why don't you come with us? We're contractors'. He was getting fabulous money, more than double what I was getting. So I went with ATC – Associate Tunnelling Company – and I did a few years with them. And that was good. He was a Polish fellow, our gaffer, and he was a good boss. If you did the work he would pay you; if you didn't want to do the work he wouldn't give you a bloody penny if he could help it.

One habit the tunnelling companies used to have that I didn't like was that there would be so many on a job and they'd be paid different wages. None of us ever liked that. At one time me and a guy I was working with called Paul always compared wage slips. One week I had fifty pence a shift more than Paul, so we went to the boss and said, 'We're not wearing this

– it's not on. We're both doing as much work; we both want the same money.' So he dropped me and put Paul's up so that we were both on the same money. They were the sort of tricks they did.

In the early 1970s Alf moved to Blackpool and left coal mining for a time. He tried some other jobs but, as with many others, it was a case of 'once a miner, always a miner'.

I've worked in quarries and I've been a barman; I've been a bus conductor and worked for an asphalt company; and I worked for a building company, labouring. But I never really settled outside of the pit. The thing about the pit was that if you did your work you got left alone to get on with it. If it were piece work it was all up to your own efforts – nobody on your back; nobody watching you; nobody bothering you as long as you did your work. And that suited me. So about January 1973 we came back to Bolton, got a house, and I said, 'I'm getting fed up of all this moving about. I'm going back to the pit and I'm stopping there.'

So I went to Golborne and a very happy pit it were, with good production. I was with a tunnelling company again, but then in 1975 I thought, 'I've had enough of this. I'm getting older and this is getting hard work.' I had one or two back problems and you couldn't get out of the back problem when you were working with a tunnelling company. You used to wear a thick belt and when your back started aching you put a notch on. When it ached a bit more you put another notch on just to get you through the shift. Although they'd gone on to machines by this time, there was still a lot of hard work to do by hand, like carrying your roof supports. In some tunnels you were going down one in four with a shovel and that is bloody backbreaking work, no doubt about it.

In 1975, early on in the year, I went to see the personnel manager at Golborne and said, 'What's the chance of me coming back with the Coal Board?' Well by this time, because people had been flitting about that much, they had more or less stopped taking people back on, so he said, 'No chance.' But I knew they were always after deputies so I [applied to be one] to get me back with the Coal Board. [After a period at college to learn about safety and legislation, and shot-firing and explosions and so forth, I passed and became a deputy.[47]]

In a pit the size of Golborne there must have been fifty deputies, basically one for each district and for each shift. On top of them you'd have overmen, senior overmen, under-managers, a deputy manager and a manager. When you came to senior overmen you'd come to people who had got as far as they'd get up the ladder without a lot more education. They were like foremen, but the deputy was always in charge – not so much for production, the overman's

[47] A pit deputy was a responsible, supervisory position and the men who did the job had to be qualified and experienced. They were responsible for safety underground. They oversaw the setting of pit props to support the roof and ensured that the mine was well ventilated.

job is production, but the deputy was responsible for
safety, supervision and the fabric of the mine itself.
On his shift the deputy is king. He's responsible for
his district by law. Whenever the mines inspector
would come in he'd come round with the manager
and he'd always call you Mr Deputy.

As soon as my papers came through I got a
district. I decided to go on night shift because
promotion prospects were a lot better. You always
worked with a smaller team than on other shifts, but,
having said that, we always got more bloody production done because there was nobody interfering
with owt. You'd nobody stopping conveyors or owt
like that. Then because we were on night shift and
there were less officials you tended to get a bigger
area, so sometimes I covered for the overman as well
as my own job.

Alf was working at Golborne Colliery in 1979 when ten
men lost their lives in one of the Lancashire coalfield's
worst modern-day mining disasters. On the morning of
Sunday, 18 March an explosion ripped through the
Plodder seam at Golborne. Two of the men who lost their
lives, along with one other who escaped with serious
injuries, were electricians who were there to move some
electrical switchgear controlling the ventilating fans of the
intake tunnel to one of the Plodder faces. The operation
would normally have stopped the fans for two to three
hours, then the tunnel would be de-gassed. But because of
mechanical and electrical faults on the fans in another
tunnel on the seam the intake had not been ventilated for
between ten and fifteen hours and this resulted in a higher

concentration of gas in the area. In the official report by HM Inspectorate of Mines and Quarries on the causes of and circumstances attending the ignition and explosion of 'firedamp' (methane gas) it was stated that one of the electricians used a rectifier – an electrical current convertor – to test circuits. This probably caused a short circuit which led to a spark igniting a deadly mixture of firedamp and air, resulting in the blast.

The Plodder seam had two faces designated as P1 and P2. Alf was the night shift deputy on duty the night before the blast. On his inspection of the seam he found conditions in the P1 return drivage[48] were normal, with fans in good working order. But as he approached the P2 return drivage he realized that the fan ventilating it was stopped. On investigating further he discovered that the fan was damaged and saw signs of damage to the fan cable entry. He traced the cable back to the fan switch, placed the isolator in the 'off' position and withdrew the cable plug. He knew that he couldn't restore the ventilation, so he fenced off the entrance to the P2 return drivage. Continuing with his inspection he found that the P1 intake drivage fans were also stopped and attempted to restart them without success. He found that the circuit breaker on the transformer supplying the switches had tripped and wouldn't re-close, so he telephoned this information to the surface, speaking to the official who was in charge of the mine and the duty electrician. The two officials thought the stoppage might have been associated with the electrical work that was scheduled to be done on the fans the following morning, but Alf wasn't convinced.

[48] Roadway.

I was the man that found all the damage to the fans the night before the explosion. We tried to get them going but couldn't, so I phoned surface and they said, 'Oh, right, I'll tell them in morning.' You know – usual reply. But I were more concerned than he was so I actually rang him and the chap who was in charge of the pit half a dozen times, but nobody would take any bloody notice. I'm no electrician, but it's possible that if that electrician had come under-ground he may or may not have been able to get it sorted out before the gas had built up too much. But he didn't come underground and things went from bad to worse. With no fans working there was no ventilation in them dead-end roadways and gas was building in them. It was when they were trying to get power established back to the main fans that I'd tried to get going that the explosion took place the next morning, and it happened because by that time too much gas had built up.

Three men were killed instantly in the blast, but the other eight survived and for the next few days battled for their lives in Withington Hospital, in Manchester, all critically ill with burns and lung damage. Golborne itself was a silent town. Most of its inhabitants had relatives or friends who worked at the colliery.

Some died straight away, some died after seven days, some fourteen, some twenty-one. Only one survived and that was the young electrician. It was hard because some of the fellows who died in there were mates. Colin, my own district electrician, died and some of the other men, like the Grainy brothers – I'd worked with them when I was with the contractors.

All pits close for a few days after a disaster like this, just to make sure everywhere is all right. Safety is paramount, so the part of the pit that was not affected by the explosion still had to be examined. But that quickly got back to work. The area where the explosion were, if I can remember rightly, was some months before things got sorted and back to normal there. You do a couple of weeks where nobody's allowed in apart from the inspectors because everything's looked at in great detail. With me being involved, I was not allowed near that place. In fact I did a few weeks off work. I was going to the pit every morning, being grilled with the Mines Inspectorate and police there, and by union officials and management. It were a bad time because you'd be in a meeting and somebody would knock at the door and say suchabody's died and I would just burst into tears because I knew these people intimately. I didn't know them socially away from the pit, but they were all really good friends at the pit.

After twenty-one days I was still not working and everybody else was back at work. So I were getting it in my head 'Are they blaming me?' But they weren't. I went to my boss and said, 'Am I suspended?' And he said, 'No. It's been a bad time for everybody. Take as much time as you want off work or start back tonight. It's entirely up to you.' So I said, 'Well, if you don't mind I'd rather come back tonight.' Weeks later, when I was allowed back to the area where the explosion had taken place you could still smell it. You could smell the explosive effects.

The disaster at Golborne showed the true cost of coal. But it was to be the last disaster in the Lancashire coalfield. Within five years the pit-winding engines were to be silenced by the miners' strike and the pit closures that followed it.

The strike didn't affect us too much, and on my shift I always had two or three who worked right through the strike and I don't think they got much aggro. It wasn't as bad here as Yorkshire – nothing like as bad. I remember one thing that did aggravate me about the strike was when there was a ballot for us officials to join the strike. Our area secretary came to the pit for a meeting with us and he knelt down and said, 'I'm begging you to vote for a strike.' Now I wanted to go on strike for this reason: they'd been out then for several months – no bloody wages all over the country. If the officials had come out then, the whole strike would have collapsed that same day. There's no doubt about that, because if the officials are on strike no one can go underground. All the pits would have started flooding and gassing up. So I wanted to go on strike for that reason. It would have finished that strike and then men could have got back to work. When they had that officials' ballot they got, I believe, 86 per cent for strike – but when it came to it they didn't bloody go on strike even though there had been a ballot in favour of it.

After the strike they started closing the pits round here fast. Some never even restarted. We were lucky at Golborne in the sense that we were on the [closure] list but there'd been that many closed already we had at least three or four more years to get used to the idea. It was a very profitable pit and a very happy pit. It were a right family pit as well, because at that time everybody who worked there lived in Golborne or close to and everybody knew one another and knew next door and all the rest of it. It was only as some of the surrounding pits closed and they got an influx of other workers from other pits that that started disappearing.

When Golborne amalgamated with Parsonage and Bickershaw, which were two loss-makers, they all became loss-makers. And the work practices at the other two pits were very different. Bickershaw was only half a mile away from Golborne but you wouldn't believe the difference. [But in the end] I was running all of the pit. I always said I were a bloody good boss, not because I was owt special but because I had a bloody good team. I had two men out of the whole pit who, what can I say, you had to be careful what job you put them on, but the rest of them I couldn't have wished for a better team of men.

Right to the end I loved my job. I did some hard work in my life – wet through, slushy, lying on my belly – but I bloody enjoyed it. I'd do it again if it were the same. I didn't want it to finish, and I would have stayed till I was sixty-five, no doubt about that, if they'd stayed open. I loved it – all them years.

The colliery finally closed in 1989 and Alf took early retirement. He used to go walking with his friend, Jimmy

Crooks from Wigan, who had started work as a miner round about the same time as Alf. Like Alf, he spent time on haulage and tunnelling before working his way up to being an overman, a position he held at Golborne at the time of the disaster.

I started at Wigan Junction pit on Bickershaw Lane on haulage, endless rope haulage. To get to where I was working you had to walk a mile and a half underground. The roadway you walked along was only four foot high and it was always dusty. The faces themselves were only twenty-seven inches tall. After the haulage I went to work on the face at the Junction. It was the old-fashioned spade and fill-in method they used there and if you went in with your spade the wrong way up on that twenty-seven-inch face you couldn't turn it over. You had to come off the face and turn your spade the right way up [and go back in again].

The Junction closed in 1962 and everybody from there went to Golborne. There was no 'You'll be finishing', no notice. It was just 'Come up here Friday afternoon, you're wanted in the office.' We all had to line up and they said, 'Right, you're going to Golborne Monday morning.' It was about seven or eight miles from home and I had to get two buses. By now I was married and we'd just moved into the house that we still live in now and our daughter, Julie, had just been born. We had very little money. I was fetching £9 and a couple of shillings a week home. My mortgage was £5-odd, so I was spending over half my wage on the mortgage. I went to ask if I could go back to school to improve my promotion prospects, but I was told I was too old. I were twenty-two years old then and I was too old.

When the face that I was working on finished, I was told 'I've got a job for you on Monday if you want it, tunnelling.' I said, 'I know nowt about tunnelling,' but the boss said, 'I want you to learn.' He told me to go with a Polish man called John and he'd teach me. Anyway, I did this for a bit and I ended up charge man[49] after a while. I wanted to get back on the face because they were getting more money than me, but the manager said, 'I want you to stop where you are. Stay on the tunnelling and I'll make sure you get more money than they do.' He wanted me to go to Keele University, but I said, 'I couldn't go when I was twenty-two because I was too old, so I'm not going now when I'm thirty-two.'

Jimmy worked his way up to being an overman, which is the position he held at Golborne at the time of the disaster. Alf Molyneux had been in charge of the night shift on 17 March and the following day Jimmy was the overman in charge of the whole mine.

It was St Patrick's Day, 17 March, the day before and we'd also altered the clocks that night. So, Sunday morning comes and I'm ten minutes late getting to the pit and Alf had gone, but he'd left me a note about a fan – one of the fans was off on the Plodder seam. I was concerned because I knew it was a very

---

[49] Man in charge.

gassy mine, so I got the deputy who was responsible for the day shift in the Plodder seam district to go down and let me know what it was like and what was happening there. He went in and got me on the phone and confirmed that the fan was damaged. He also said there was no gas in the main road, but there was a lot of gas in the heading. So I said, 'Right, as long as you fence it off and stop there it's all right.'

Quite a few people hadn't turned up this Sunday morning, including the three electricians who'd been scheduled to do the work on the switchgear. So we got hold of three other electricians to go in and do the work and I told them not to start de-gassing until I got there. I also rounded some of my own men up from my section and sent them with the idea of changing the damaged fan, because we had a spare one. Then I got a message that a rope had broken on a loop winch on my own section, so I said I would call at the stores and get a rope on my way in to supervise work that was being done on the Ince Six Feet seam. When I got down there I was talking to an overman near the face and the phone rang. It was one of my own men down the brew and he said, 'Jimmy are you shot-firing up there?' I said, 'No, John. What's happened?' He told me that he'd heard two thuds, that the air door had just opened and shut and that there was a lot of dust in the air. 'Bloody Plodder!' I said and rang the surface to speak to the under-manager. I said, 'Can you contact Plodder straight away – something's gone wrong. And let me know.' He rang me back and said he couldn't get hold of anybody, but smoke had started coming out of the fan air vent on the surface. So I said, 'Right, let everybody know. Get on to t'other districts and tell them to organize themselves to come out. I'm on my way to Plodder.'

No one will ever know how bad the explosion which ripped through the Plodder seam district was, but for a few minutes the eleven men who were in there must have known real terror. They all knew that fire had ignited, but that wasn't what killed them. They died because the ignition developed into an explosion two minutes later. The concentration of gas in the tunnel was too strong to explode immediately, but it burnt slowly until a weaker mixture of gas was lit by a hanging flame. It's not certain what the men did during those terrible two minutes. They may have tried to fight the blaze or to escape, but when the explosion came it was savage and none of them had a chance. They were so badly burnt that some were unrecognizable. But it wasn't the burning so much as what they breathed into their lungs that did the most damage.

The place where Jimmy was working was at least half a mile from the explosion, but he wasn't too far off a main road, so he jumped on a diesel and went straight out to Plodder. When he got there he got off the diesel and walked in along the level, which was about a hundred or so yards, and then down the hill to where the explosion was, not knowing what he was going into – whether he'd walk into another explosion. As he got close to the scene visibility began to deteriorate as a result of all the dust and on the way in he started to meet some of the survivors and Jimmy just did what he could for them.

I met this lad coming out, no clothes on, not a stitch of clothing on. And skin black, crispy, curling up. So I took my donkey jacket off, put it on to him and I said, 'Now stop here till I come back. I'll go and get some blankets out of the first aid tube.' I got a bit further down and I come across another one. He was walking out, walking up the brew the same, no clothes on. So I took my overalls off and wrapped him up in them, and told him to stop there till I came back. Then I found a couple more. One were dead, a big hole in the back of his head. There was no fire there, but all the ducting that had been on the fans had all gone and all the stone dust barriers had gone. Burst. One of the fans was still running so I stopped it. It wasn't serving any useful purpose with all the air ducting destroyed. Then I tried to get on the telephone to the surface but it wouldn't work. There were pairs of boots standing in the road; no laces, but inside the shoes at the bottom you could see socks. The socks had been burnt down to the inside of the boot.

I'd already been on to my gang, in my own district, and said find all the stretchers and blankets you can. The rescue men were there too and when we went in we got the men we'd found earlier on to stretchers and a young electrician came to me. 'Jimmy, Jimmy,' he said, 'I want to tell you what happened. I kept telling him not to do it.' Then we got him out. He was burnt but he was fully clothed, that young electrician.

A second rescue team found four more casualties, making a total of ten accounted for and one still missing. He was the overman. By this time the manager had come down and an inspector. I said to Joe, who was one of the rescue men, 'Just go round that corner and have a look under that wall – I bet he's there.' And he was, so we'd found them all. Then I went round with the inspector and you could see there had been different explosions, because you'd walk so far and everything had been blown up brew [up the hill]. Then you got past this area and everything has been blown down brew [down the hill]. Then you'd go further and everything was the same again.

When we came up the pit, all the newspaper men were there of course. One asked me to go round the back to talk, but I wouldn't talk to anybody. And then over the next couple of weeks they wouldn't let me go down. They did a lot of recovery work, but they wouldn't let me go down. They kept saying the case was still on. But you've no idea what it's like. You walk into an office where everybody's talking and it all goes quiet and no one speaks till you walk out again. I couldn't sleep. And then for months and months you'd go through everything, and when I did go to sleep I'd start dreaming. From when I first started off, I would go through my life, every job I'd done, everywhere I'd worked. I'd go through it every night. It weren't all in one night, but it would continue in instalments till I got up to that day. And that went on for weeks and weeks. Anyway, finally they let me back down pit. I didn't know it at the time but I had a tail. They had somebody following me round everywhere I went. One day I was fed up of doing nothing, so I went for a walk to have a look in some old workings somewhere, and everybody was in a panic. They thought I'd gone and done away with myself.

Jimmy carried on working at Golborne after the disaster and was given the Plodder district to look after and turn around. He stayed there until 1985.

They wanted me to go to Platt Lane [another colliery nearby] and I kept refusing. Then in 1985 my father persuaded me to go. They offered me twice as much money as I was getting to be in charge there and it was very different. It was 1,470 metres from the surface so it was hot. The deeper you go, the hotter it gets. The first fifteen yards it's constant, like when you go caving. Then it goes up 1°C for every hundred yards you go down. Then you have your idiomatic compression, which is the same: 1°C for every hundred yards you go down. So you've two means of increasing temperature, and working down at that depth it was 47°C. There were many a one got carried out for collapsing. Not the lads, because they were used to it and they always used to take these bottles of water down with them. When I went there I got some fridge-freezers put in the canteen so that when they were going home they'd fill their gallon bottles of water and put them in the freezer, then next morning they were blocks of ice to take down.

When I first took the job there they said the men were no good, but I hadn't been there long before I realized that it wasn't the men that were no good. The problem was that they were getting that many separate instructions they didn't know whether they were coming or going. Generally, though, all the men were okay to deal with. They just had to know who the boss was. There was one bloke I wanted to see, so I told the clerk to put a note on his lamp. 'He won't come,' the clerk said. 'He will,' I said. But he didn't, so the clerk said, 'I told you he'd not come.' 'Yes he will,' I said, and sure enough when Friday came he was there waiting for me, because he'd not got paid. I said, 'I told you he'd come and see me.'

I always made it my business to go round and speak to everybody at least once a week. We'd have a sit down and a chat. And it's surprising what you learn: he's fallen out with his wife, or the kids weren't behaving or whatever. You learnt quite a bit. And I always kept them informed about the work. 'Next week,' I'd say, 'I want to start doing such and such a job. What do you think? How do you think we should do it?' And you'd go and ask the electricians the same thing and the fitters, and then you're all together. Everybody's on your side when you start. So sooner or later it all comes together as one thing and after a while you don't have to argue with them. They just accept what you say. And it was the same upstairs; they didn't argue with me. But we were just getting things right there when they shut it.

At the time of the miners' strike in 1984 seven Lancashire collieries were still open, but within ten years they had all been closed. Jimmy continued to work for the NCB until the end, overseeing the contractors who were closing the mines down, supervising them stripping out the shafts and filling them in. 'But,' he says, 'there's still plenty coal down there.'

*

Just as the presence of large coal deposits turned Lancashire into an industrial powerhouse, so too coal fuelled the development of Tyneside and Wearside as major industrial centres in the nineteenth century. Along with ready access to sources of other raw materials, such as iron, and access to markets via river and sea, it was the main factor behind the industrial success of the region. Coal had been extracted from outcrops or shallow seams in the valleys of the Tyne as far back as the fourteenth century, but these outcrops were quickly worked out and new workings were opened further from the rivers and mined to greater depths. By the middle of the seventeenth century there were between twenty and thirty pits within an area of about 150 square miles. These changes demanded transport links to carry coal to the rivers and Britain's first wagonways were built in the region in the seventeenth century – the precursors of the first railways. Throughout the eighteenth, nineteenth and early twentieth centuries coal production in the North East continued to expand, peaking at over fifty-six million tons in 1913, with a total workforce of almost a quarter of a million.

In the 1950s coal was still a key part of life in the North East and the pit villages of the region were close-knit communities with their own social clubs and community facilities. Typical of them was Brandon, just a few miles south-west of the city of Durham in the heart of what was the Great North Coalfield. Ron Grey was born among the pit heaps of Brandon in 1939 and went to work down the local colliery when he left school.

The railway line that ran through the village was built in the 1860s when the coal mines were taking off. It was on the main drag from Newcastle to Bishop Auckland and it was the supply line for all the coal. They used to fill all the trucks here and they were taken to the coast. Domestic coal was just taken straight to the house or to the local depots and then wagons would take it round. Everyone who worked in the pits got the coal free.

[When I started down the pit] it was just ten years after the war and a lot of the men down there were still a bit traumatized. They got no help then, no post-traumatic stress treatment. A lot of them were very quiet. They'd speak, but not very much, but I admired them. They were real men, real tough guys. They'd been through hell and seen death and blood and they'd come back to an awful place to work.

I started in the timber yard, which was where all fifteen-year-olds started. Then I went straight on to the belts, or the screens, on the pit bank. These were about thirty yards long and they were made in steel sections like tank tracks. They were five foot wide and on them you had the coal that had been brought to the surface. It wasn't clean yet and it still had bits of stone in amongst it, so the idea was that the kids and the old men who couldn't work down the pit in their last days would stand on either side of the belt and pick the stone out to clean the coal before it went into the trucks below. It was boring because you were just standing on a conveyor line and it was filthy work. You can imagine the dust! When it had been cleaned and sorted it would fall down shoots into the railway trucks below and the trains would take it away. There were three different levels and everything was gravity-fed and on each level there would be people doing something to it before it went down. This was called the bank. Women did this work until 1947.

When I first went underground I was a timber lad. This involved getting the timber for the pit props to the face or wherever it was needed. It was a teenage, start-up job and it made you extremely strong because it was just constant lifting and carrying. We would get twenty-five props, two foot three inches long, in a bundle and sling them over our shoulder like a coolie would. Sometimes we'd have to walk through water and get our boots wet. It was hard work and I was only nine stone three.

I was down there one day when I was about sixteen or seventeen and the deputy had a bad accident. He'd been crawling off the face when the 'caunch', which was the overhang of stone above the coal seam, gave way. He was trapped and when they got him out they found that he had two fractured legs. But he was very conscientious and as they were carrying him out on a stretcher he stopped near us to have a word with us about the job we were doing. When he finished he said, 'Is there anything else?' and like a flash I thought to myself he won't have eaten his bait [lunch]. So I said, 'Oh aye, there's one thing. If you're going to hospital you won't be wanting your bait, will you?' The two stretcher-bearers looked astounded and the deputy shouted,

'You're a bugger. Get me out of here! They're like a set of bloody vultures!'

When you worked on the face you'd have a two-hundred-yard stretch of coal, two foot three high and five foot deep. You'd advance five feet every day over the two-hundred-yard stretch and there'd be twenty men on it. There were three shifts. First there were the drillers and cutters whose job was to loosen the coal by under-cutting. A cutter would cut five feet of coal about three inches deep with something like a huge chainsaw and there were two men working each cutter. The drillers made the holes that the shot-firers set their charges in every four feet along the face. The driller was the lone one; he used to drill by himself. He would spend his whole shift going along drilling at the coal and he'd have to do this a few hundred times with a big heavy drill with an electric motor. We used to call it the 'pig's head' because that's what it looked like. Once he had done his holes that was him finished. Drilling wasn't a job for the faint-hearted. Lying on a two-hundred-yard, two-foot-high face dragging a heavy cable with an equally heavy drilling machine took some doing. Strong arms and broad shoulders were required for the job, and a big heart. I remember one driller telling me about a time he'd drilled a hundred-yard face out and he crawled into the tailgate and started to pull the electric cable out. Just as the end of the cable came in sight the whole face closed from top to bottom.

On the next shift the coal was got away from the face by the fillers. This was my job, but before we could get it out it had to be broken up and that's where the shot-firers came in. The holes that had been drilled along the length of the face were filled with powder by the shot-firer. 'There's fire!' he would shout as he twisted the handle to fire the shot. When a shot was fired you would turn your head or put your hand over your face. A shot went off with a tremendous bang and shrapnel would shoot quite a way, sometimes burying deep into props like bullets from a rifle. But as long as you were behind solid coal you were fairly safe. Our shot-firer used to ask us what kind of shots we wanted, 'Jacks' or 'Toms'. Jacks meant that the coal would only be cracked after he'd fired his shots and would need to be hewed and Toms was the sweet sound of a shot that had broken the coal up. Harry was very good at his job. When I was on filling I noticed that most of the other shot-firers would stem the drill holes with bits of coal as they set their charges. Harry was the only one I came across who carried clay which made sure that the shots would be fired properly, making the job a lot easier for the fillers.

The filler's job was to shovel the loose coal away from the face and fill it on to the belt. The belt would run parallel to the face right along its full length. You'd be lying down pretty much flat, using a shovel, and you'd only got two foot three inches to work in so you couldn't lift it properly – you'd just have to slide it. You'd got a man on either side of you ten yards away. To get to the face you had to crawl fifty yards through a deep layer of coal dust. The cutters left little pieces of coal that we called 'curvens' and these lay about eight inches deep. You only had a limited amount of space to crawl, so you had to shift all that before you started and then you'd just crawl about five yards and you'd be completely black. Hand-filling on a longwall face[50] was tiring, especially for the young lads who had not acquired the stamina or the experience to fill ten yards of coal off every day. The older fillers would often shake their heads at us young 'uns as we tried to keep up with them.

At every pit there was always someone who stood out – men who never seemed to tire. 'Crack fillers', they were called, and we had one at our pit. He was always the first one to come off the face while everyone else was still slaving away. After he got something to eat he would always return to the face and help someone else off. He was only nine and a half stone and the thing about him was that he never boasted about his prowess.

When you had finished your section you'd help somebody else because you're all on the same pay-roll. You didn't just get paid for your bit, so if you saw somebody who was getting behind you'd help them. He might have had a bit of difficulty with a timber or some other problem. But if he didn't have trouble and he just couldn't do the job, after a while he'd be told not to come any more because he was a

[50] Longwall mining is a form of coal mining where a long wall of coal is mined in a single slice. The longwall panel is the block of coal that is being mined. Gate roads are driven to the back of each panel. The road along one side of the panel is called the maingate or headgate; the one on the other side is the tailgate.

burden on the other men. There were a fair few old men who thought they could still fill coal but they couldn't. So they would be told, 'Sorry, but you're struggling here.'

As a filler you'd also put timber supports up as you were going along. In a yard-high seam a pitman would sit and knock a prop into place with his pick. To make sure the prop was vertical he would drop a small stone from the roof and wherever it landed would indicate the place where he would set his prop. You could always tell where an older pitman had been working; his props were always perfectly in line. 'Keep thee timma [timber] in!' was pit talk to remind you to set your props as you removed the coal or stone. Old pitmen still use the expression when they part company as a way of saying 'Look after yourself.'

On the third shift the stone men used to retrieve stone from waste ground they were leaving behind after the coal had been filled. With this they built the packwalls which were three or four yards long by three or four feet wide and these supported the roof. The shifts were seven hours, but if you had an easy shift it could be finished in five and a half or six.

For all of these jobs you did training first on what we used to call the training face or training wall. We learnt how to fill and how to work a cutter. The cutter was absolutely lethal. It was about three inches wide and the picks or the blades on it used to be at different angles. On the training face I had to follow the cutting machine to keep the picks clear of cuttings. My instructor warned me not to get too close to the picks with my shovel, so when it started up I gingerly slid my shovel in and in an instant it was whipped out of my hands. It went right round the cutter, underneath the coal, and when it came out it had been shredded. The thing was absolutely lethal so you learnt very quickly how dangerous it was. Everything was about safety.

Just short of my eighteenth birthday I got a job as a filler on the face. I hadn't filled ten yards of coal on the training face, but I had learnt the basics of timbering-up and levering the coal out, so I was thrown in the deep end.

I was on a longwall face, which is a thin-seam method of mining. Up here in the Durham area it's all thin seams. If you get four foot off the ground that's a high seam to us. My friend was working in eighteen inches and I worked in two foot three. Now he was six foot two and I was five foot six, so it should have been the other way round. But a lot of jobs were the wrong way round because you'd have a job lottery. If there were four of us and there was one bad job, everyone said, 'I'm not having it, I'm not doing it.' But so as there was no argument, you'd say, 'Right, put the cavils in.' A 'cavil' was the job or place of work, so whoever was in charge would put four marks on the front of a piece of wood with the numbers 1 to 4 jumbled up on the back. Then he'd nominate a number for the bad job and if you selected the mark that corresponded to that number you'd get the bad job. The word 'cavil' came into general usage around here even on the surface, so if somebody got a bad job to do outside you'd say, 'By God, you've got a bad cavil there, mate.'

Size didn't mean anything down the pit. In fact it was a disadvantage to be over six foot, as you can imagine. The tall ones were the stone men because where they worked they could stand up. What counted down the pit was stamina and strength, especially for the fillers. The best fillers were the smallest, the ones who were wiry and fit. I don't think I knew a big filler. There was a man called George Alan. He was only seven and a half stone, but he had a big heart and terrific strength and stamina. He smoked sixty full-strength Capstan a day and he was always wheezing and coughing. I was a fit young seventeen-year-old but this skinny, asthmatic fella crawled past me on the first day I was filling coal and said, 'Do you want a bit of a hand, Ron?' That was the strength of these guys. Next time I saw him in the club I bought him a pint. I totally respected that man. What a role model he was.

Weaker people were put on menial or light work, like watching the 'gay head'. This was an electric motor that ran the main belt in a tunnel. So they would sit and watch that, or they might be on maintenance, mending things, but not actually on the coalface. But they wouldn't be looked down on by people on the coalface. Pitmen didn't do that. They would respect them. We had somebody on our shift called Tommy and he was a classic example of this. He'd had an accident and hurt his back, so they put him on a light job, but he was always falling asleep because he was taking tablets for the pain. The job he'd been given was to look after the junction of a belt that took the coal up, where it tumbled over down a chute from one belt on to another. Tommy used to sit there and you could see the light on his head from hundreds of yards away. When he fell asleep the beam would drop down, then all of a sudden you'd see it jerk up again as he woke up. One time when he fell asleep all the coal piled up and blocked the tunnel. Me and this other lad were young fillers. We'd finished early and we still had our shovels with us. When we saw what was happening we woke Tommy up and he said, 'Oh Christ! I'll get the sack for this.' So we stopped the belt and cleared the coal and got it all back on the belt. We didn't have any animosity and didn't say anything about it to anybody. Tommy thanked us and bought us a pint next time he saw us. If somebody was lazy, though, that would be a different matter and they would be pulled to bits. The work-shy were looked down on.

On the face it was dangerous. It was noisy as well, but you got used to noise. On the belts we used to scream at each other from five feet away. A lot of pits were hot, but ours wasn't. It was ninety fathoms – that's five hundred-odd feet. It had five seams, like layers of a cake, and each one had a different name. And of course it was dirty as well. Everything you had to eat down the pit you ate with black hands because there was nowhere to wash, and there were no toilets. But the coal was virgin coal so it was sterile, which meant that if you cut yourself it wouldn't turn septic. There's no germs down there, so you can't get an infection. But a lot of miners would age quicker and at fifty-five they'd be old men with walking sticks and probably have arthritis from working in the wet. But emphysema was the worst thing. You couldn't breathe with that.

You were in the mines because that's where the money was. My brother was shovelling concrete, laying floors. That was very hard work, probably harder than the mines, but mining was very dangerous. So I got £24 a week and he got £10.

I was on the face for only a year and a half and then I had a bad accident. I was filling one day when the top gave way and came in on me and mashed my spine. I was only nineteen. That's why I am partly paraplegic now. I was completely paralysed from the waist down for five months. They said if I had any feeling at all to let them know and it did gradually come back. But they were tough with you. I was with the physiotherapist one day trying to walk with the aid of elbow crutches, but I was in a bad way. She said, 'If I took that crutch what would you do?' When I said I'd fall down she took the crutch away and sure enough I fell down. This is what they were like then! I fell down and I crawled back up with the help of the crutches. I was able to do it because I was immensely strong and fit at the time. And I did recover. One day I lifted my left leg up and I was thrilled to bits. I thought I was dreaming at first. The physiotherapist came and I said to her, 'I want to show you something.' So she whipped off the bed-clothes and said, 'What do you want to show me?' When I lifted my leg up she burst into tears. This was the physiotherapist who could be such a cold-hearted monster sometimes. From that first

movement it was very slow, but feeling and movement began to come back. It took two or three years
to get to a state where I could walk again. I have to
use a stick if I walk long distances but I can walk
now.

It is over fifty years since Ron was carried out of the pit
and since then all of County Durham's coal mines have
been shut down. He died in 2011, but he never forgot the
days he spent on the coalface and to ensure that future
generations are aware of the hard work and dangers their
forebears had to endure he wrote and illustrated several
books about his experiences and he used to give talks
about his days as a miner to groups of schoolchildren.

Roof-falls like the one that brought Ron's mining career
to such an abrupt end were always one of the biggest
dangers the miners had to face and the men who had the
expertise to ensure that the roofs were safely supported
were important members of the mining community. Tom
Jackson was a mining engineer from County Durham
who got involved in this work as soon as he joined the
Coal Board in 1947.

I left grammar school with some very good results
and I was sent to do my National Service. I had no
trouble with the medical and when they asked me
what I was interested in I said Royal Engineers. I
wanted to do surveying but they said I'd have to sign
up for seven years and I didn't want that, so I came
home and my father said, 'Pop along to the pit and
have a word with the manager.' [Miners were exempt
from National Service], so I went along to Black

Hole Colliery, about six miles north of Hartlepool, and the manager said they hadn't got anything in the surveying office but they had what they call 'linesmen' who did the underground surveying and there was a vacancy for that. I took the job and started going to night school at Sunderland, three nights a week. I had to do five years underground, of which two years had to be at the coalface, before I could even sit the examination.

Getting all this experience on the coalface was invaluable. It was better than any amount of theory, as I was to find out very early on. There was a divisional strata control engineer in Durham who had a degree in mining. I knew one or two others like him and none of them had done the five years underground that I was doing, so they could not become colliery managers. All they could do was advise. They may have had brilliant brains but they could not say to a manager 'You will do that,' because according to the Coal Mines Act it says the manager shall be responsible for the support of the roof. Anyway, this guy tried this roof-holding at Horton Colliery, which was next door to Black Hole. I went down with him to do the job. When we'd finished it they brought a photographer down from Newcastle and there were four of us standing in his picture, not a wooden prop in sight, just the roof that we'd bolted. When I went down next morning everywhere I looked the roof had collapsed! The whole of the roof we had been standing under twelve hours earlier had collapsed and you could see all the bolts sticking out.

During this time I got married. We came back

from our honeymoon in Harrogate on the Thursday and on the following Monday I was working nights down Easington for about three weeks. I was getting off the bus at half past seven in the morning to go home and my wife was getting on the bus to go to work in Hartlepool. The girls in the factory she worked in couldn't believe it and she got her leg pulled at work.

At this time my grandfather was still alive. He'd been a miner and he used to work in eighteen inches with a hand-pick. When we used to go to see him he'd say, 'What's new then?' He just could not comprehend the way technology had moved on. He used to have an old settee that was quite high off the floor and we went one day and he got down underneath it to show my wife how he used to work. He was a role model for me, a strict Methodist, so there was no gambling and no drinking. The only thing he had was his pipe. He used to go down to the little chapel and it was always packed in those days. And when they sang you could almost see the chapel roof lifting. They sang, 'Oh for a thousand tongues to sing my great Redeemer's praise', and you would think there was a thousand men in there.

I went through all my training and [became] technical assistant to the manager, which meant I got all the dirty jobs and problem-solving he didn't want to do. Black Hole was a big pit [with] roughly two thousand people working there in a twenty-four-hour cycle. We were doing seventeen thousand tons a week normally and in a bull week, which was before Christmas or a holiday week, we were getting twenty thousand tons out. I got a good reputation while I was there. Whatever job came up, the job always came first. Time didn't matter; that was the way I was brought up. They put a new cutting machine in and I was responsible for getting it in and getting the old one off the seam. I knew it would take a long time because we were cutting the old machine out and we had to keep stopping it to put bars in to stop the roof collapsing. I was in charge of this. When we reached a point where the roof was very precarious the men who operated the machine said, 'We're not bloody cutting through there.' 'Oh, get out of the way,' I said, because in my two years in training I had learnt how to cut, so I put the machine through and the men sat and watched. The un-written order was 'Come out when the job's finished, not before,' so I was twenty hours on the coalface, working on a seam that was two foot nine inches high. I went through three shifts of men. After twenty hours of non-stop work I did at last get the machine cut out.

Now one thing about being down the pit is there's no sunlight, so you don't realize the passage of time. It's always dark. My wife had made up a bag for me with a flask of coffee, some tongue sandwiches and some wedding cake. When we'd got the cutter out I rushed out to the loading point and there was my bag hanging on a nail, but when I took it down about six mice shot out. I dropped the bag, smashing the flask as I did, and when I picked it up I found that the little so-and-sos had been in every compartment. So I had nothing to eat or drink; the only thing

I had was water and that was out of the hosepipe.

[Some time later] the area production manager asked me to go and see him and he said, 'You're interested in roof control, aren't you?' I told him I was and he said there were four vacancies in the West Midlands. Did I want one of them? It meant leaving the area, but I was interested so I went down for an interview and to cut a long story short, I got the job.

In the West Midlands I had eight collieries I was in charge of for this roof control, so it was quite a big promotion for me. My job title was Area Strata Control Engineer and I was all over the place doing different jobs in all the eight pits. There was one called Hamstead, which was in the Great Barr area of Birmingham. Next to that was Sandall Park, quite near West Bromwich football ground. I had Baggeridge, which was just five miles south of Wolverhampton, one down in Worcestershire and three out in Shropshire; quite a wide area. I had less collieries than the other lads, but mine were all spread out so I spent more time travelling. I had to get a motorbike to get round.

When I first went down I was involved in putting bolts in the roof to support it. The idea was that above the coal seam was a good solid roof, so you would drill a hole in maybe five foot and put a bolt into it that had a wedge at the end that expanded. Then there was a plate at the bottom with wire mesh. My first job was to go down each of the pits every week just to make sure these bolts stayed tight.

Moving from one area to another I had to get used to different ways of working. In Durham they used to work four shifts and the shifts changed over underground. This meant you had contact with the men on the other shifts and if there was any problem you'd be able to mention it to them. When I went to the Midlands it was three shifts and you would only meet on the surface, if at all. You'd get one chap coming out of the pit early and missing the man who was taking over from him, so communications were not as good. But the Midlands were ahead in terms of technology and it was all what we call longwall – one long face. The first one I went down was Sandall Park and there was the Staffordshire thick coal with seams thirty foot thick. It was a big change for me because most of ours in Durham were five-foots and three-foots. It was the first time I'd ever seen a thirty-footer and it gave me quite a shock, especially when I saw how different their methods were. They would blast twenty-eight feet or so of coal and there was a bucket that used to go up and down scraping the coal out. A man sat there with his controls as the bucket was pulled out and emptied on to the conveyor and no one was actually physically touching the coal. The machine was taking it all out.

Then you realize that the Staffordshire thick coal used to catch fire – spontaneous combustion, which we didn't have in Durham, so there was a tremendous learning curve in dealing with that. We used to get fires in one or other of the pits almost every day, so we used to put sandbag dams on to try and stop the air getting in to feed the fire. But if the barometer rose, air got through the air bags to keep the fire going and when it dropped the carbon monoxide came out. The fires started within the coal seams, but there were always good warning signs because you'd see little drops of condensation appearing on the cold steel girders; that was what was called 'heating' at that stage. The first time I had to deal with it I was the under-manager sitting in the office on the surface when I got a call to say they'd got heating down at the south part of the pit. When I got there you could see steam coming out from the seam and the men were jabbing at it with what looked like javelins. Suddenly hot coal just fell out all over the place, so it was just everybody out and start building the sandbags up. There was never a dull moment. Dealing with these fires was quite a main part of the job in Staffordshire.

When I was acting under-manager at Baggeridge we had a fire and I had six gangs of men working in twos building these sandbag walls in different parts of the pit. Each gang had to have a canary with them, so I used to have to go into a big aviary we had and put the birds into little wire cages. I'd give them to the men and say, 'Keep an eye on the bird and if he gets distressed, come out. It's a sign of carbon monoxide.' It's quite a primitive method but it works. The idea is that because the bird breathes faster than we do, and the heart beats faster, so they have the effects of carbon monoxide before we do. I went round each of the gangs and when I got to the last two men they were both sitting down looking tired and I couldn't see any sign of the canary. 'What the bloody hell's going on?' I asked. 'Where's the flaming bird?' 'Oh, she was cold,' they said, 'so we took her round the corner and put our coats round her cage.' If I had been a bit later those two men would have been dead. By the time I got to them I think they had got past the stage of reason, so I had to take them out, get them to the surface and give them some oxygen. Carbon monoxide is a silent killer. When they started to feel tired they should have realized. This was the annoying thing: I was new to all this but they were used to working in these conditions – they'd been brought up with it.

Although Tom enjoyed mining, once the Staffordshire pits began closing down he decided it was time to get out. He went back to the North East and for a few years he stayed in mining engineering, working for a firm in Durham that dealt in roof supports. Then he went to another company that made mining machinery and equipment, mainly drawing up their patents. He stayed in the mining industry until 1966, by which time many of Durham's pits had closed down. So Tom did a teacher training course and went into a teaching job in the North East when he qualified.

By the 1960s Britain's coal industry was in decline and pit closures were a regular occurrence throughout the country's mining areas. The North East was particularly badly hit. In the two decades from 1950 to 1970 around a hundred North East coal mines were closed, with devastating consequences for the small mining communities that relied on them. One of them was Trimdon, where Jim Grigg was born and brought up.

It was all pits round here. There was Deaf Hill Colliery and Trimdon Colliery. Just over the fields there was Wheatley Hill, Wingate, Trimdon Grange, Thornley and Shotton. There were so many that the air round here was terrible. The collieries all had big chimneys and everything used to get covered in coal dust, including when the women put the clothes up on the line.

I had three generations of my family working the pit. My grandfather first started at Trimdon; he used to cycle every day from Hartlepool, which was roughly ten miles. He used to bike over here, work all day on the face and bike it back every day. He didn't finish work till he was sixty-six. My dad worked there as well – it was a generation thing. Of course in them days it was seen as a job for life. The trouble was that fellows used to finish work at sixty-five and then drop down dead at sixty-six. That's if they reached sixty-five. A lot of them didn't because in them days they had more dust to contend with. They were old men by sixty-five and they didn't live a long time after that.

If your dad worked at the pit you followed him. There were some thick-headed blokes, like myself, who went to grammar school and had a chance of a good job, but still came back and went on the pit. I remember my dad was one of the best-paid guys. He was making canny money and I remember seeing his notes in the early 1950s. There were thirty quid, which was a lot of money then. But it was a hard life.

Some of the faces were only two foot high, so face work was difficult. One of the hardest jobs was one they called 'timberling'. It was taking the supplies in [to the face] and all the young lads had to do it, but it was slave labour. When I started timberling there were no rails going in. We used to have to drag these twelve by eight circular girders in for a third of a mile, with one half of the girder on your shoulder, to the place where the face started. And there weren't even any rails to push them on. We were taking them to build the road in as the face was worked forward. It was so bad for the young lads at Deaf Hill, where I worked, that they actually got ponies back into the pit in 1963 or 1964 and they had been out for years. So much for modernization and mechanization.

One particular face was like a very soft shale stone. First South, as it was called, was so bad that it used to fall in every day. There'd be falls on top of the lines, so you had to clear all of them before you could start to get the supplies in for the lads who were on cutting or the lads who were on filling. So we had the 'Gallows' in there – that's what we used to call the ponies, because they came from Galloway in Scotland – and they had to do the work, because the young lads couldn't manage themselves. They used to say it was horsework and that's exactly what it was. There were some lads who just couldn't do it at all and had to go and find something else, farming, the army or something. A lot of people went in the army and the navy so they didn't have to go down the pit. At the time you had to do National Service, but if you went to work at the pit you didn't.

When they brought the ponies back [into the mine] there were only seven or eight of them. You used to get some lads who just couldn't handle them at all. They hadn't a clue and they used to get themselves aerated with the horses. You didn't always have the same pony. When you went in, the stable-man used to say, 'Right, take this pony or have that one.' And if there was a horse-keeper who didn't like you, you got the bad one. We used to ride the pony out when we could but we'd get fined ten bob [50p] if we got caught. When we were going back in again none of the other men would get in the cage with you, because you used to stink of horses.

But there was worse smells than horses down the pit, especially on a Monday morning. They didn't have any pit baths when I first started. I used to go home and get in the tin tub. The pit baths came in here in 1958 and that made a big difference, especially if you had a family. You could get bathed and come home in your good clothes.

The cages at the pit were still run by steam and they had big furnaces to keep the steam up. There was many a time when you got ten or twelve men in a cage to come up to the surface and it couldn't lift because the steam pressure was too low. So they had to drop the cage and let some out. Half would have to get out and it would come back down for the others.

We did start to get cutting machines in, but [the one we got] at Deaf Hill used to weigh about a ton. Solid steel it was. [It took] twelve men on the front to pull it in on a leather rope and about twelve at the back shoving it in. [It was an] Anderson Boyes cutter which was seventeen inches high and the coalface was only eighteen inches high. It was just old planks keeping the roof up and there's many a time you had to knock them out to get the cutter in. The cutters created so much dust that you couldn't see.

Dust respirators came in later when I went to work in Nottinghamshire. They were little tin cylinders with breathing apparatus in, but prior to that in some of what we call the tailgates it was terrible. When they used to use the explosives to blast the coal and the stone out you couldn't see or breathe. We had a lot of men used to chew baccy just to get the coal dust out, but I used to take snuff because I couldn't stand tobacco. It was horrendous up there on the face. You were lying down all the time and everything was coming into your eyes, all the dust and that. It used to be terrible.

The power of the deputies was enormous. That was a bad thing with the pits. These people were the same as us – done the same work, went to the same school, but they got big ideas about themselves. And there were always bullies. Some lads were working in what was called the Landhill district at Deaf Hill. They had a deputy there called Wilfred Wright and there was an overman called Joe Storey and they were both bullies. Anyway, there were some lads who said, 'We're sick of this.' They were only kids and after they'd had a pint or two they brayed Wilfy's door in. They got reported to the police and this Joe Storey came up to them and said, 'You wouldn't have brayed my door in.' 'No,' they said, 'we would have brayed thy bloody head in!' You had to stand up to these people. One of my main things, all my working life, has always been I used to make sure that they knew that they weren't better than me. You made sure they knew that, because if you ever got intimidated at work that was you finished. I've been sent home a couple of times because I was always bolshie. If somebody did make trouble, you got your own back outside the pit on a Saturday night in the club. You just smacked them. Once they got smacked a couple of times they were all right after that. When we went out with somebody to fight, it was hands. One to one. Then it was finished with. I've seen me go round the back of the pub and have a good battle and gone back in and had a drink together. It was finished.

*

In Durham the coal seams were thin, which made them difficult to work. Geologically the South Wales coalfield was similar to that of Durham and had the same problems, resulting in early closures for a lot of its mines. Although Welsh coal had been known since Roman times and small collieries and ironworks had long dotted the landscape of South Wales, the great period of industrial growth in the valleys began in the eighteenth century. Larger ironworks were built amongst the mines and then, with the discovery and extraction of high-quality steam coal in the mid-nineteenth century, the South Wales coalfield developed rapidly. South Wales became one of the most important coal-producing areas in the world. At its peak in 1913 fifty-seven million tons of coal came up from the mines and the region produced one third of the world's coal exports. Over a quarter of a million men were employed, more than forty thousand of them in the Rhondda Valley alone. The coal-mining industry employed one in every ten people in Wales and a lot more relied on the industry for their livelihood. But the Welsh colliery-owners failed to invest in mechanization and between the two world wars the South Wales coalfield had the lowest productivity, highest costs and smallest profits in Britain. Most of the mines in the valleys had been sunk between the 1850s and 1880s, which, as a consequence, meant they were far smaller than most modern mines. The Welsh mines were antiquated and methods of ventilation, coal-preparation and power supply were all of a poor standard. By 1945 the coal industry throughout the rest of Britain cut 72 per cent of its output mechanically, whereas in South Wales the figure was just 22 per cent. Few mines in South Wales could modernize because the coal seams were too thin for the new machinery to work.

Tom Minard from Merthyr Vale started work at the Merthyr Vale Colliery in 1939 when he was fourteen years old. The first coal had been mined there in 1875 and by 1913 it employed 3,575 men, making it the largest colliery in the South Wales coalfield by over seven hundred men. It was a huge place and Tom soon learnt that there was a lot of walking involved in the job.

I started underground straight from school and I can still tell you what I had in my lunchbox on my first day. Corned-beef sandwiches. I had a new pair of shoes from the local Co-op in Troedyrhiw and a new hat. I was put with a collier and he gave me a 'curling box', which was like a large steel plate with sides on it. He said go up there, fill it up with coal, carry it down and then try and lift it and put it into the tram. Well it was as much as I could do to lift the curling box, never mind fill it with coal. At that time there was no man-riders[51] – you had to walk from the pit bottom to your working place and that was on a slope. It wasn't too bad going down, but after a full shift coming back up the slope to the pit bottom was a real slog. What we used to do was, if there was a journey of coal drams coming from the district up to the pit bottom, we used to get between two drams and stand on the buffers. We used to have to carry big lamps that weighed twelve and a half pounds. And you had that on your belt and you'd be trying to hold on to that and the two drams, with your feet on the buffers. If something had happened you wouldn't have a dog's chance. Looking at it now it was really stupid, but that's what we used to do because it was such a long walk.

It wasn't all hard work underground – there was humour there as well. I used to go out with a chap, Arthur Aldridge, and he had a keen sense of humour. Of course, when you were green you didn't know any better. So you'd be working and he'd send you down to the next stall. 'Go and get a bucket of blast,' he'd say. Now I should explain a bucket of blast is compressed air, like you get in pneumatic drills on the road. But you'd fall for that. So not all hard work. There was a great amount of fun attached to it. There was one chap working in our district who could throw his voice. Now we used to call the waste behind the face the 'gob' and he used to throw his voice from there. 'Help me, help me!' he'd shout. And we would be panicking. He'd frighten the life out of you.

---

[51] Trains used to transport miners underground.

Some of the colliers were good. They realized that you were a youngster and you didn't have a lot of knowledge, so they'd take care of that. But others thought you could do everything; do it or else was their attitude. The collier was your boss and sometimes you might have three different bosses during the week. Now your wages were on his docket. When you came up the pit on a Friday, some of them got their pay and they waited to pay you, but some of them went straight to the local pubs, the Navigation Hotel and the Aberfan, and you had to go up there to get your pay – 8/6d [42½p] it was.

When I started underground it was all horses and drams. In the early stages of Merthyr Vale Colliery I think there were three hundred-odd horses working there and when the horses got back to the stables after they'd worked hard the conditions were good. They were well looked after and if a horse got killed there'd be a big inquiry. If a man got killed they just put him on a stretcher and took him out. They thought more of the horses than they did of the men [in those] private firms. When the horse went underground it was there for the rest of its life apart from its ten days' or fortnight break in the summer holidays. They weren't too bad coming up the pit, but to get them back down they'd be kicking.

A horse has got good instinct. If there's something wrong along the line, you could do what you like to that horse. You could hammer it, coax it, but it wouldn't move. I don't know what it is, but they are very clever and very sensitive. Very often they'd stop when there was no indication of anything wrong at all. I would think over the years they saved many, many lives.

Colliers used to have their own pony. Generally they treated them well, but I remember one man and it was savage the way he treated his pony – that's the only way to describe it. The ponies used to have a feedbag with oats and hay over their head and if this chap had had a bad night, the first thing he'd do if he was in a bad mood would be to take that bag off so the pony had nothing to eat. I've seen him take the food out of the bag and put a shackle in – that was a contraption that joined the two trains together. They're heavy and that horse would have to carry that around all day. We had 'sprags', as we used to call them, which were bits of stick we had to put in the wheels to stop the trams. And what he wouldn't do to that horse with that sprag is nobody's business. But if an official saw him doing it he would be in trouble.

Accidents were frequent and every mining area had its mines rescue teams. Terry Sargeant from Merthyr Vale started work as a miner in 1950 when he was sixteen. He was a coalface worker all his life and was a member of the South Wales mines rescue team.

When I started work I spent two years in Treharris as a trainee. Then I came to Merthyr Vale and worked there until 1986 when Margaret Thatcher closed all the collieries, so we were made redundant then. When I started as a boy in the 1950s there was loads of pit around here. There was Merthyr Vale here,

Treharris three miles down there, there was Troedyrhiw, there was Plymouth, and there was pits in Merthyr. In them days truthfully you could start in one colliery today and, say they sacked you one Friday, you could go and start at another one on Monday. There were so many jobs, but it was only in the mines.

My father had been a collier but he died when I was nine. My mother had five children and I was the oldest. So up to when my father died in the pit we were having a ton of free coal every month. When my father died my mother had no coal, so when I started work I was the man of the house and she could have coal again.

The first time you go down the pit it's frightening. Terrifying. Halfway down your stomach is still up there. But in the end you get used to it. I always remember going down the first day at Treharris. There were six of us and when you came to the foreman he'd say, 'You go with that chap, you go with him.' The chap I went with was called Ken Monkley and as we was walking through the face you could see the colliers pointing at me and looking. 'Look at that poor little bugger there. How is he going to do anything?' At first you don't know what to do. The chap you're with shows you a bit but he can't show you much because he's got to get his coal out and you've got to help him.

I did work in filling drams. You had rails going through the face and you had to chuck the coal into the drams. You had to mark your dram, so say I was A1, all the drams I filled had A1 on them. So when

442

you went up the pit they counted how many drams were yours and that's how we were paid. Every dram was a ton and when they checked them if you had a lump of slag in it they wouldn't pay you for that ton. So you had to make sure it was all coal.

We still had horses down there then and most of the men were good with them. One with us was a chap who had a horse called Charlie and he'd bring in stuff for that horse every day. During the fortnight holidays, he used to take her over to Aberaman and put her in a field there and every day he'd be going over there feeding that horse.

I was a coalface worker all through my life. The dust was terrific. Sometimes you couldn't see the chap next to you. But I've got no regrets for going underground. In fact it was great and the main thing about it was good companions, men without malice. And there was a lot of humour and practical jokes. I remember one thing they done to one chap. He was a fitter called Malcolm Williams and he didn't like to go anywhere on his own. One day the chain broke on the face and because he was a fitter he had to fix it. He had to go back to his box, which was about a hundred yards back up the road, to get the tools he needed. It was all dark and his box was about six foot long. So he went back to it and when he opened it there was a chap lying inside looking up at him. It gave him the fright of his life and he just screamed and ran. But that was the type of humour they went in for.

A lot of miners swore more underground, but once they came to the top of the pit, it was a different world. You never swore in your house. You never swore much in the club, because if you did you were chucked out. If somebody had one too many and his tongue slipped, he'd be put in his place in front of the committee on a Sunday night.

If you fought underground you'd be sacked. It was dangerous and I remember two who were taken to court for it. So it was very rare I ever heard of a fight underground. Sometimes you rowed and called each other rotten and sometimes you would go up and have it out at the top, but never underground. Another sacking offence was sleeping. You had a twenty-minute break for food. The belt would stop about ten o'clock and it would start again about twenty past ten. Sometimes when you were on that break you'd be so tired you'd fall back and sleep, but there were so many of you at the face that if a fireman was coming down somebody would wake you up.

We did have some men taking fags down, even though you would be sacked if you got caught. Imagine a hundred men going down hiding fags in different places. I remember I was on a night shift once with a fireman called Ben Jones and he said, 'Terry, there's somebody smoking down here.' I said, 'How do you know?' 'Well,' he said, 'I can smell it.' It took a week to find him but they did find him. We worked it out – it was in the engine house. It was an engine chap on his own, driving the engine, so he got the sack. One Monday I put on a different coat to go to work. When I was going down to the face I put my hand in my pocket and found a candle there. What had happened was that where I lived was a three-storey house and we only had electricity downstairs, so we had to take candles to our rooms. I had put the candle in my pocket and didn't realize and took it to work. But if I had been caught with that I would have got the sack.

When I was working in Treharris as a boy we had mice, but in Merthyr Vale it was rats. You wouldn't have mice in the same colliery as rats because what the mouse would do was go into the rat's nest and kill the young. I used to be a track layer at Merthyr Vale and I would sit down and be on my own and the rats would come out and I'd chuck a bit of grub down. I wasn't afraid of them. Only one man I ever heard died from a rat and it wasn't a bite. He was a ropesmith and he was working on one of the big steel ropes when a little piece of steel was sticking out and went into his hand. What had happened was that a rat had peed on the rope that had gone in him and he died from rat poison.

I was in the mines rescue team in South Wales. I was part-time and I went to a few big disasters. I went to one at Cambrian, where twenty-eight men were killed. I went in but I didn't see any of the bodies, because by the time I got to the face all the bodies had been taken out. It took us about an hour and twenty minutes to crawl through that district with all our stuff on. It was a hard one. I was in the fire-fighting team as well. The best part of it was I'd have a day off work now and then, and if you were a mines rescue man you'd get £50 a year for it. But it was very dangerous. I've gone into one pit and the whole lot was on fire. For about three hundred yards all the rings holding the roof supports were on fire and we had to walk through them. Then further on was where an explosion had been. It had left a big gas fire and you could hear the ball of gas up above the rings moving backwards and forwards. Men had been in before us and taken hosepipes in to keep the fire down. Our job was to make sure the hosepipes were up and working, but one of them wasn't so we had to get that sorted out. One of the boys went with the captain to put it in its place and as they got there a ball of flame come down on top of them, but the force of the water from the hosepipe pushed it back up. The rest of us looked at each other and we said, 'We're not coming up here again.' What they told us to do was to douse the fire to keep it from spreading. So we were there dousing the rings with all the fire around us and all of a sudden we heard a roar. When we looked up a ball of flame was coming towards us, so I just dropped the hosepipe and ran. My butty then caught hold of it and held it tight and it was like he froze. He held it and he pushed the fire back up with the force of water. He called me chicken then for running. But imagine a ball of fire coming on top of your head. What would you do? But you got used to it and I went to a lot more fires and explosions after that.

We nearly lost one man once. We went into a district and it was all gas, so if you took a breath you were dead in seconds. We were walking in and I could see a chap called Dai Murray in front of me and he was wobbling. I rushed up to him and I could see he couldn't breathe. When I looked at the gauge on his breathing apparatus there was nothing on there, so we had to rush him out. But all of a sudden he started panicking – kicking and going into what was like an epileptic fit. Once we got him in the fresh air he was all right, but if we'd gone in any further he wouldn't have made it.

We had a convalescent home in Bournemouth and every miner in South Wales paid towards it out of their docket every week. If a miner had a really bad accident they would send him there for a week or a fortnight once he started to get a bit better. But they had very strict rules there. During the day at one o'clock you'd all have a rest. And you all had to be in by ten o'clock at night. If you were fit enough and you went for a pint there'd be the sister by the door. She'd have a watch and if it was gone ten o'clock, even one minute past, when you got to that door, she'd give you a row. Then if you did it another time she'd keep you in for a couple of days and if you persisted they'd send you home.

For a boy leaving school and starting work down the mine the prospect of coming face to face with death or serious injury at an early age was very real. Wyndham Jones grew up in the small village of Gilfach Goch in what was West Glamorgan in the 1940s and went to work in the Britannic Colliery. He got a job there as a measuring boy and soon after starting he saw a man lose his life.

On Fridays the face overman or colliery under-manager would come with me through the coalface and I would have my 'measuring book' with me. In it there was a page for each collier detailing the work he had done during the week. Each collier would check my book with the overman that I had correctly recorded the work they had done and would ask for money for extra work they may have done, such as clearing a minor roof-fall. I would have details of all this written down. We would start the 'measuring' at about eleven a.m. and it would take about an hour and a half. When it was finished I would go up to the colliery surface to the timekeeper's office to start totalling the work done by each collier for the week. This would take several hours, so we had to work Saturday mornings to complete it.

One Friday my overman, Glandwr Williams, was late coming to meet me so I set out to search for him. I was told he had gone back in the 'timber road'. There were two kinds of roads or tunnels. The main road in which the cut coal was delivered in trains or 'journeys' [lines] of trams – drams as we called them – to the pit bottom to be sent up the colliery shaft. The journeys were pulled by steel ropes that were driven by a massive electric or compressed air engine. Then there were smaller roads in which supplies such as wooden roof supports were taken to the faces, usually in single drams right to the coal-face. These were the timber or supply roads. They were mostly single tracks except for the 'partings' – short double roads where ingoing drams could pass outgoing drams. The drams were pulled by small engines or horses. I went back along the timber road for about a half a mile looking for Glandwr when I

In engineering workshops apprentices learned to master the precision skills involved in operating machine tools (under the watchful eye of experienced instructors).

After the Second World War, Britain led the field in civil aviation. **Clockwise from above:** inspecting a fine steel aeroplane crankshaft; testing a large propeller engine in a wind tunnel at Bristol Siddeley Aircraft; engineers at work inside a high-pressure vessel; assembling RB162 lightweight lift jets at the Rolls Royce factory in Derbyshire.

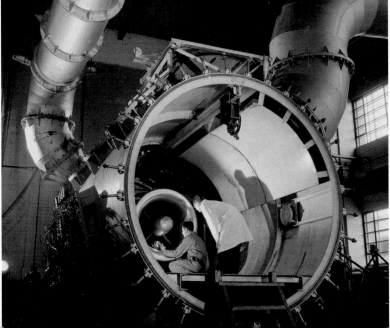

An engineer at work on a ship's crankshaft in Greenock, where around ten marine engines were produced every year.

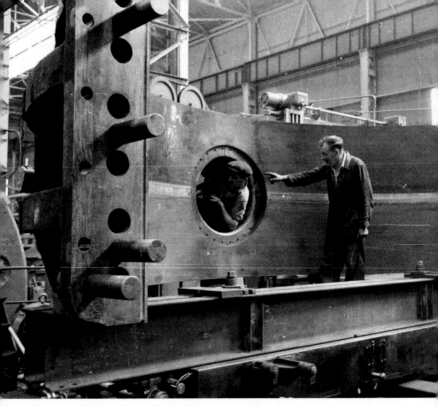

Engineers and factory workers gained satisfaction from investing their skill and energy in making things that were not only needed but also generated wealth for the country. **Clockwise from above:** workers inspect machinery in a factory in the industrial town of Kilmarnock; a worker at the top of the Forth Road Bridge taps the cables into position during construction work; the Wilkins & Mitchell light-engineering plant in Darlaston, Staffordshire.

The West Midlands has always been regarded as the home of the motor industry.
Above: Engine assembly and inspection of the Armstrong Siddeley Star Sapphire, 1959.
Below: Austin A40 cars on the production line at the Austin Motor Company's Longbridge plant in Birmingham.

Britain's automobile industry also catered for overseas markets: lorries carrying left-hand-drive Austins for the North American market are seen here leaving the factory.

A significant milestone is reached in 1965 when the one-millionth car comes off the British Motor Corporation production line at Longbridge.

The 1970s and their associated strikes decimated Britain's motor industry. Workers wait in line to receive news of redundancies.

met two men, George Compton and Idris Hopkins, both men in their fifties, and they were at a parting and Idris was shackling a horse to a dram. I stood to one side talking to George, asking if he had seen Glandwr, when the horse suddenly bolted, with Idris running up the parting stuck between the horse and the dram. George and I ran after him and found him lying on the ground at the top end of the parting. He'd been dragged along and we could see that he was in a serious way, so George ran off to get help. While I was there with him he breathed his proverbial last breath and was gone. These days I would have been off work for weeks for seeing that, but I was expected to go back straight away and complete the measuring. I did this even though I had just seen a man being killed.

On the following Monday I was approached by the colliery police sergeant, who took a statement from me about the accident. Towards the end of the week I was called into the manager's office. In those days, a colliery manager was next to God. They seemed to have the same power as a ship's captain. The only thing they couldn't do in a colliery was to marry people and they probably would have done that if women were allowed underground. I went into his office thinking he would have a bit of sympathy for me for witnessing the death of a fellow worker. But not so. He shouted and wiped the floor with me because I had spoken to the colliery sergeant before I spoke to him. If that accident had happened now there'd be all kinds of trauma experts and one thing and another. Now I can't say I've ever had nightmares about it, but every so often some-thing will trigger off that memory and I can relive it like it was only a couple of weeks ago. And that was fifty years ago.

I remember another time when a man had his arm torn off when he was caught in a roller of a moving conveyor belt. It was on a Sunday morning, so there were not many other colliers about, so he walked about three miles underground to the pit bottom with his arm off and then sent someone back to pick up his arm. They put it in a sack to carry it back out.

There were usually two faces in an underground district, left and right. Imagine a wall of coal about a hundred yards long and on average three to six feet high with a roof supported by wooden posts and a conveyor belt running the whole length of the face. This was to carry the coal that was hewn by the colliers to another conveyor and then to drams, and eventually delivered to the pit bottom to be sent up the pit. One day I and another measuring boy were together in a main road and we wanted to go into one of the coalfaces. To do this we had to step over the main conveyor belt because we were on the left of it and we wanted to go up the right-hand coalface. My friend, Gordon Stacy, stepped over before me and while he was stepping over a small stone fell from the roof and hit him on the back of his neck. It was no bigger than a marble and he completed his step over and was safely on the other side of the belt. But then he collapsed – he just went out like a light. He came round and got up and was fine but if he had fallen on to the moving belt, without a doubt he would have been seriously injured.

We measuring boys – or clerks as we preferred to be known – were also called junior officials, but we weren't the only ones to come under this heading. There were two others who were the same age as us and their job was to ensure on behalf of the management that safety regulations were carried out. Then there were another two who had the job of keeping track of the steel posts that were used to hold the roofs up and ensuring the recovery of them so that they could be used again and again. One of them was Eddie Rogers. He had previously been a deputy, or fireman as they were known, but was too old to continue that job so he became a steel-checker. One morning when I was on day shift I went to my place of work and was told that Eddie, who had started work very early that morning, had been killed by a steel rope which pulled the coal journeys. It was very surprising for a man like that to be killed in such a way, because a deputy's main concern was safety. He had ignored the main rule that was drummed into me from the time I started work in the colliery: if you were walking along a heading or road and a rope so much as twitched you had to take shelter in a manhole at the side of the road and stay there for at least fifteen minutes, only proceeding if the rope didn't move again. This was because when a slack rope takes up tension between the engine and the journey of drams there is a 'whiplash' and the rope can swing from one side of the road to the other with tremendous force. This is what caught Eddie and killed him. Of the four men that were killed in the

Brit while I was there, it was Eddie that I knew best. We both played cricket for Gilfach Goch.

One of the others who got killed was Doug Griffiths. He'd stood inside a conveyor and he started it and it just cut him up. Only his head and shoulders were left. I went down with the inspectors that afternoon myself. We went down to see the spot and they were looking underneath the conveyor. Alan Jones said, 'Oh, look at this.' And it was a bit of flesh. 'Here,' he said, 'put it in the bag.' The older men were very hard people.

While I was working in the Britannic they shut it down, not because there wasn't any coal seams there, but because they had developed the coal in Beddau and they wanted manpower there. They shut all the small collieries to get the manpower. There were seams and seams of coal in Gilfach and they just shut them. They'd spent millions of pounds developing the Cwm Colliery in Beddau and they didn't have enough manpower, so they shut all the small collieries to get the manpower they needed. If the Britannic had still been going I would have stayed there until I retired. It was a family affair kind of thing there; everybody knew everybody else. One of the things that I missed when I went to the Cwm was that no one said good morning to you. In the Britannic if you didn't say good morning to the off-going shift they'd come back to you, 'What's the matter with you? Is there something wrong?'

I worked in the Cwm Colliery at Beddau for two years after the Britannic closed down. After that I worked for nearly forty years in factories. Never once in those forty years was anyone seriously injured, let alone killed like they were when I worked in the colliery. However, the time I worked in the Brit was the happiest period of work for me in almost fifty years of employment.

Between 1960 and 1980, 150 South Wales collieries were closed and around seventy thousand miners lost their jobs. Some of the bigger collieries lasted longer. One of these was Coedely, which stayed open until 1986. Michael Cowdrey from Gilfach Goch had to start work there when his father and brother died and he became the main breadwinner for the family.

I was only about seventeen and I was in lodgings with my mother. There weren't many carpets on the floor, only oilcloth and mats. My mother used to get stuff in the shop and then pay on a Friday and I filled a form in to claim for a load of coal. I worked at Coedely Colliery and I was there until the end when it closed in 1986. When I started over a thousand men worked there altogether. We had a brickworks as well and I worked in there for a time. We had what we used to call 'clod' just above the coal seams. That was like a waste product of the colliery. When it came to the surface, people like me used to sort the clod out from the coal. We used to put it to dry and then ship it up to the brickyard, crush it, put water with it and then put it in the kilns to make the bricks up.

There were forty-two workable seams in the shaft, but when you talk about workable you're talking two foot, two foot six, so it was difficult conditions. It was hard to work down there but there was plenty of coal. We were the last pit to go mechanized. Before that it was pick and shovel. You couldn't mechanize at one time because the Pentre seam had a very soft bottom, so the machine would sink. And the other problem was that there were faults in some of the faces, so you'd have half the face up at one level and six feet lower down you'd have the other half.

I remember working with a fella called Mansell Rees. He was about six foot six with ginger curly hair and he got killed down with us. A big slab of stone fell on him. The whole area shut down for his funeral; two thousand people attended. All of them asked to come out [from work] early and the manager wouldn't let them, but they were all there. There was no sentiment. Not so long ago if somebody got killed they'd just take him home and put him on the kitchen table and that was it. But if a horse got killed underground there was an inquiry.

I was on first aid. I'd never done it before, but you were told to go to a couple of lessons for a couple of hours a week and then you were a first aider. The stretcher boys were big, powerful men. The conditions, even when you were just walking, were terrible, but they had to carry a stretcher with a man on it. The man might be eight stone or he might be twenty, so it was hard work. And they used to get a shilling [50p] a week for doing that.

There was a man I worked with on the belts. Quiet fella, awful nice man, and I was talking to him one night and he said he was in the Cambrian when there had been an accident there. Men had been blown to smithereens and he volunteered to go down to put them into sacks. He never got over it. But people always volunteered to go down. Fighting to go down they were. I was talking to another guy and he was on an ambulance and he said he went down and it was such a mess that they were all being sick. But they just had to put people in a sack, head and everything. And 'Mike,' he said, 'no problem at all. But I went home and cried like a baby.' But the thing is he went in there and did it and he was just an ordinary kind of guy.

If you tried to follow the rules and regulations underground you wouldn't work. With today's health and safety you wouldn't even start. I was on the belts and the foreman fitter, Dick, finished with us and went to the steelworks as a foreman fitter because the money was double. But he came back after about eighteen months. 'It was no good,' he said. 'Here we could mend the belt, cut it, join it in eight to ten minutes maximum. In the steelworks the electrician would come along and knock the power off, a fitter would come along to take the box, then another fella would come along and start a job and it would take about four hours, then you'd have to send for the electrician. So it would take six hours and we do it here in about six or seven minutes. It wouldn't be safe, mind, but we'd do it.'

UK coal production remained at over a hundred million tons a year until the early 1980s, then in 1984 Margaret Thatcher's Conservative government announced plans to close twenty uneconomic pits. Twenty thousand jobs would be lost and many communities would lose their primary source of employment. The announcement led to the year-long miners' strike, which ended in March 1985 in defeat for the National Union of Mineworkers. It was a defining moment not just for the mining industry but for labour relations in Britain in general, and the defeat significantly weakened the trade union movement. The dispute exposed deep divisions in British society and caused great bitterness within the mining communities which remain to this day. Michael Cowdrey recalls those times when the scabs – the men who broke the strike – became figures of hate, shunned by everybody to this day in the close-knit mining communities.

During the strike they were putting people from another colliery to picket our colliery because we had two or three scabs and those men are still scabs today. When we went back and they came down in the shaft with us everybody spat at them. Still to this day I don't think there's six people talk to them. They don't bother with them.

In the strike the neighbours were brilliant. I used to have a black bag of food left every week outside my door. They'd knock on the door and they'd be gone by the time you got there. I knew who it was, but it would be in the dark, in the night, and you could never see them.

I went round to collect tinned stuff at Trebanog. It's a rough area and nobody would go up there. So I took a couple of boys up there going around with carrier bags and we averaged about thirteen carrier bags with tins. The people there were absolutely brilliant. I knocked at this lady's house – she was in her seventies then, awfully old – and when she opened the door you knew you shouldn't have knocked. You could see she didn't have two halfpennies to rub together and she didn't look very clean, she was really grubby. But she asked me in. 'Oh it's all right, love,' I said. 'I'm sorry, I knocked on the wrong door.' 'No, you haven't,' she said. 'You're a miner, aren't you?' So I went in and sat down. And we were talking and she said she'd gone into the workhouse straight from school because she was a bit slow and then people took her in to work as a slave, basically. But she opened her little brown leather purse and I think she had about £2.80 there. She said, 'I haven't got any tinned stuff here, love, but have this.' I said, 'I wouldn't take it off you.' But I had to take it. She said, 'Miners do a good job.' Anyway, after the strike was over I saw she only had some small coal, so me and my butty, Billy Chapel, got a chainsaw and we cut some blocks up at the colliery for her and took about eight bags up to put with the small coal. I went up twice after to give her some blocks, but I went up the third time and the neighbour said they'd put her in a home out of the way. I thought we had it hard, but she really knew what it was to have a hard life.

Coedely only lasted just over a year after the strike. I'd always regarded it as my colliery and at the end I had to go from there over to the Cwm for six months. Although we were joined together the two were a world apart. When I moved to the Cwm there were all kinds of people there. I prayed every day that they'd shut that place because the people there weren't very nice. They were foreign, from Barry and all over the place. There was no comradeship – it was dog eat dog there. It was a strange time. They spent millions of pounds developing the Cwm Colliery in Beddau and they didn't have enough manpower, so they shut it down. We knew we were going to shut but they were still putting all brandnew machinery in. It was crazy, just chucking money away. I was going down the heading on the last shift, having a ride out on the belt, and they had people coming in to put a big cable in. They were setting up a development where they spent £16 million and never got a bucket of coal. But the best one of all was the showers. They had people in the fortnight holidays putting all new sinks and toilets in and doing all the tiling. Then when we started back on Monday we had the bulldozers in to knock it all down. Thousands of pounds wasted. And the machinery left there was unbelievable. When they shut it broke my heart, I'll be honest.

The miners' strike caused coal production to slump to an all-time low. After it there was a brief recovery, but it went into decline again towards the end of the 1980s. More pit closures were announced in 1992 by John Major, who privatized the industry in 1994. By this time the National Coal Board had closed all but the most economic pits. For somebody like Terry Sargeant, who had spent all his working life underground, it is a situation he could never have imagined.

When I was working as a miner we never thought the

pits would close. There was plenty of coal and we thought they would be there for ever. So it was a shock when Arthur Scargill said, 'They are going to decimate South Wales. Every pit is going to go.' We couldn't deep down believe that they were going to close every pit, but it happened in a couple of years – the whole lot.

When the strikes started in 1984 I was the first picket. Me and four other chaps were the first of the flying pickets. I went all over the country and I was picketing right through the strike. Every time they wanted me I would go picketing. My philosophy was you had to fight for your job. And if you don't fight for your job you're not going to keep it. There's no sentiment. It was a beautiful summer, one of the best we ever had, and I remember going to the picket line without shirts on. We had to stop the officials coming through the gate. They'd made a ruling that only four officials could go into the colliery to make sure it was all right, no more. So we would have pickets on the gate making sure only four went through. We had a day shift there, an afternoon shift and a night shift and I was mostly on the night shift. You'd come in about ten o'clock. We used to go to coal tips as well where there were pickets stopping the lorries going in, and to Didcot Power Station to stop the coal going into there. We'd just stop the coal, not the men working there. When we used to go picketing to Didcot, Ruskin College gave us a big room to sleep in and every day a lot of the students would give their grub up for the miners to have their dinner. There was always a big welcome from them – they were great to us.

After the strike any miner could take voluntary redundancy. Most of us had to finish and from then on the best part for me was that I had allotments and that kept me going. There were not many jobs around then, only about four factories. So imagine, with thousands of miners finishing they couldn't all get jobs in those factories, could they? If it hadn't been for the closures I would have carried on. There wasn't much else for us to do. It was hard work down there but if you went into a factory it would be too soft. You'd get so bored I don't think I would have been able to do it. I don't think many men could stick it after being underground, because underground you're on the go all the time.

But I will say this: Maggie Thatcher closed the pits, right enough, but I think she saved my life. I was fifty-one when I finished and I would have had another fifteen years underground if they'd stayed open. But what would I have been like with another fifteen years underground?

With the closure of the pits and the steelworks the whole landscape of South Wales changed dramatically. For most of the nineteenth and twentieth centuries there was no relief from the monotony of the strung-out coal, iron and steel workings that stretched for miles along the valley floors, the belching chimneys and the long rows of terraced houses. Today a drive down any of the valleys gives a very different impression. The old heavy industries have gone and the hillsides are green again. It's hard to imagine that in Rhondda there were sixty-six coal mines giving employment to thousands, or that in Ebbw Vale approximately thirteen thousand men and women were employed at its steelworks as recently as 1956.

The decline of coal mining and the pit closures that followed the miners' strike caused major social upheavals – a situation that was made more serious by the contraction of the steel industry. European community grants have been used to redevelop derelict industrial sites for small businesses and foreign investment, mainly from Japan, has helped to create some new jobs, but, in spite of this, since the 1980s unemployment rates in the valleys have been amongst the highest in the United Kingdom and throughout the region large empty factory units bear witness to the lack of success in replacing the old heavy industries. The main industries now are electronics, engineering and tourism, and many people from the valleys commute to Cardiff for service-industry jobs, but the culture of the mining communities with their sense of comradeship and solidarity has gone for ever.

The last deep mine in Wales, Tower Colliery, closed in 2008, thirteen years after its workforce had rescued it from British Coal's pit-closure programme with a workers' buyout. There are no deep mines left in Lancashire or Durham. The last Lancashire pit to close was Parkside Colliery, Newton-le-Willows, which ceased production in 1993; and the closure of the Wearmouth Colliery in Sunderland in 1994 brought an end to the last remaining colliery in the Durham coalfield. Today the entire UK coal industry is a mere shadow of the great industrial giant that once dominated the economy, with just four privately owned deep mines still in operation along with a number of open-cast mines.

7

A Time of Change

A T THE TIME of Queen Elizabeth II's coronation in 1953 Britain was still responsible for a quarter of the world's trade in manufactured products, but the writing was already on the wall for a lot of industries. During the inter-war years the great staple industries of the nineteenth-century British economy – coal, cotton, iron and steel – had gone into a long-term and what turned out to be irreversible decline. One of the principal features of the post-war years was the speed at which changes took place. In 1950 Britain's share of world merchant ship launchings was 37.9 per cent. By 1985 this had shrunk to 0.9 per cent.[52] In 1954 over half a million were employed in the cotton industry. Within thirty years this had gone down to just over thirty thousand.[53] In coal mining the drop was even more dramatic. From the 1940s to the late 1950s the number of miners employed in Britain's coal industry stayed level at around seven

[52] Lloyd's Register of Shipping.
[53] *Mergers and Takeovers in the Postwar Textile Industry*, Stanley Chapman, Business History, vol. 30, Frank Cass and Company, 1988.

hundred thousand. At privatization in 1994 only twenty thousand were employed.[54]

As the old industries collapsed, new ones rose up and traditional ideas about the natural specialization of a particular part of the country were abandoned. In South Wales the valleys were heavily dependent on iron, steel and coal mining and during the Depression of the 1930s unemployment was high. Thomas Hier is from Merthyr Tydfil, which was particularly badly hit. The steel and coal industries in and around the town began to decline after the First World War and by the mid-1930s they had all closed. The fortunes of Merthyr revived temporarily during the Second World War as war-related industry came to the area, but the revival didn't last after the war. New industry was needed, and Thomas explained how it was government intervention that brought it about.

When the Labour government came in after the Second World War they directed industry to the areas where they were in trouble before the war. Merthyr was very badly in trouble. Before the war there was huge unemployment here because the coal industry was at a full stop and the only plant associated with anything to do with steel was the foundry in Dowlais. Dowlais works shut down in 1935 and about four thousand people went on the dole overnight. It was so bad they were thinking of moving the whole of Merthyr to new towns. When the war was over and people like Hoover's, Lines Brothers, who made Triang Toys, and Kayser Bondor

[54] www.parliament.uk/documents/commons/lib/research/rp99-111

wanted to expand they were given incentives to open factories in Merthyr.

I came out of the forces and I had an opportunity of a job in Triang. I started work in the buying office and wages department. Then I moved more into production control before going into general management. The company grew very quickly. Soon after I started I was buying raw materials and spending more than £1 million a year. That was about 50 per cent of the turnover of the company. We used to make a thousand steel dolls' prams a day and a lot of garden swings. Originally a lot of toys were made out of steel, but by the end even the toy motor cars were made out of plastic. If you were making something out of steel sheet, which is what we were doing in the early days, there's a limited number of companies you can go to to buy steel sheet. We bought from a company down the road that had been set up by Czechoslovakian Jews. They were right there on our doorsteps. We also used to use a lot of tube which came from Aberdare or Birmingham. We used to take people on throughout the year then lay some off when things were quiet, but on average we had eight hundred to a thousand working there.

The creation of these new industries, and a revival of the traditional industries of steel and coal mining after the war, made the 1950s a time of full employment in South Wales. And people now had choices. No longer was it necessary to follow your father down the pit or into the steelworks. Gareth Howells was one of those who found employment outside the traditional industries of the area.

I was lucky to be born in an era when there was plenty of employment. Coal was still king, but I didn't want to go down the mines and my father didn't want me to either. It was hard, dangerous and unhealthy, and there was employment outside the coal industry. There was the ironworks that was a remnant of the old Dowlais Ironworks, but when I came out of school in 1957 there was a lot of new industry as well – places like Hoover, Triang Toys, Thorn Electrical making lightbulbs, a factory making aircraft controls, ICI over on Dowlais Industrial Estate, and a huge place called Kayser Bondor making women's stockings and things like that.

I started work when I was fifteen at Triang Toys, or Lines Bros as they were known then. They were the largest toymaking company in the world. Years ago they used to have big prams for wheeling babies about called Nibbs Chariots and Lines Bros made them as well as the toys.

I was a tool-setter in the wheel shop and that's all we made in that shop: wheels of different sizes and different descriptions. We made them from a coil of metal, spokes and everything. My job was to set the machines, and that could be a few times a day depending on what they wanted. Different-sized wheels would need different settings. The factory was set up into different departments. Next to us was the tube-fabrication department. One of the favourite toys of the time was what they called the gee-gee rocker, which was a rocking horse with a seat on it. We used to do all the welding and all the forming for them there. Then it would go to what they called the paint dips, where they'd all be automatically painted, then into the ovens and out the other side and on to the assembly lines where they'd fit all the bits and pieces together.

They had a huge storeroom at the back by the river and I remember the time in 1962 when it all went up in flames. The story was the storeroom was full of stuff that had been returned and when it went up in the flames they were able to get the insurance on it. I remember it well. It happened in the lunch hour. We used to go up to the park, right by the factory, for our lunch and we could hear all these bangs and see all these flames going through the roof. It looked like the whole factory was going up. We were helping the fire brigade fight it, but in the end we all had to get out. It almost brought down the doors of the shop that made all the dolls' prams. But it didn't affect the actual production; just the storeroom, and that was all the stuff that had been rejected.

You had what I would call a better community spirit in those days. Every year we used to have Sports Day. Every factory used to send a team, and there would be athletics on the field next to Hoover's where there was a running track, and discus and javelin. Then there was the Miners' Gala in Sofia Gardens in Cardiff every year. My father was a miner, so all the family used to go down for that. They used to have a platform there for the guest speaker, like Emlyn Williams, who was secretary of the Welsh Miners' Union. You'd have the political speeches there first of all and then you'd have all the entertainment going on afterwards.

I was at Triang for approximately twelve years, but things were starting to go downhill there, so I went to a place known as AB Metals, which changed its name to AB Electronics, and I worked there for thirty-eight years. We made connectors, mainly for the television industry. Prospects were good there and with the advent of colour television in the late 1960s they took on more people. There were about three or four thousand people working there. Now there's about 150. It was all connectors of various sizes and descriptions. As well as the television industry they made them for the gas industry, the water industry and for trains like the London Underground. At the end of every cable, no matter how long it is, you've got to have a connector and that's what we made. We made connectors for the defence industry, for rockets and tanks. With the defence products you were working in nickel, silver and gold. You'd be making components out of gold strip and it was all precision work. You'd always have a drawing to work to – very different to working in the toy industry where you'd have no drawings at all.

I was union convener for twelve years and shop steward for ten years. I've always been trade union minded; my family were involved with the Communist Party. I was full time on union work and I had a little place of my own on site. It wasn't an office as such, just a little place I grabbed hold of and made into my office. But the company management

467

started to put pressure on the union and people were very reluctant to be seen as militant. I suppose I was the Arthur Scargill and people didn't like me one bit. They sent letters to the district committee complaining about me. The district committee weren't much help because they were what I regarded as right wing. They were yes-men to the employers.

Just as the declining ironworks and coal mines came to stand for Britain's industrial past, the growth of the electrical, electronics and aircraft industries came to represent hopes for its future. John Williams worked at Teddington Aircraft Controls, another of the new companies that came to Merthyr Tydfil after the Second World War.

Teddington's was my first full-time job. The headmaster had the works director, Mr Gardiner, come up to school and I was interviewed whilst I was there. The headmaster was telling him before the interview about my good results in the exams, particularly on the technical side. Mr Gardiner said, 'We haven't got an apprenticeship at Teddington's, but you can come as trainee management.'

So at seventeen I had a job at Teddington Aircraft Controls. They were part of the British Thermostat Group, which was based at Sunbury-on-Thames, and they made specialist valves for aircraft engines. They opened the factory in Wales just before I started there in 1948, but before this they were already making oil-cooler valves for Merlin and Kestrel engines and the other earlier types of aircraft engines that Rolls-Royce were producing. Whilst I was working for them they made about 550 types of instruments to be fitted on to aircraft. We had an experimental shop with various machines: large lathes to small lathes, shaping to drilling machines – whatever machine you wanted to do any metal-turning, they had it there. It was specialist work and it was all men who worked on the lathes and the big machines.

I got married after I started working there and we paid £395 for our first house together at 27 High Street. My wife and I were both working and I remember my aunt asking us one day how much we earned. Anne, my wife, was working as a civil servant in Merthyr and I was working in Teddington's and between us we earned just about £10 a week.

Everything we made had to be thoroughly tested before it was sent out anywhere and I worked in the production test department which made all the test equipment. We had all sorts of temperatures to put things in and we had lots of problems as the years went by, particularly when we got into jet engines and temperatures increased tremendously. We used to do a lot of work with oils and had various grades of oil, and we could work below the flashpoint of oils. You had to be very careful on a piece of test equipment that you didn't go beyond the flashpoint. The testing room could be quite a dangerous place. Every time there was an air crash and you had made a component in that engine, it would be stripped and sent back to us for testing. When you're testing you have alongside you an Aeronautical Inspection Department representative. We had three or four resident AID inspectors at Teddington's who were ministry people.

We had a roomful of instruments that hadn't been checked, because of pressure of other work, so the ministry started pushing, saying you should be checking these instruments. The managing director said, 'We've got to do something about this,' so they formed a new department to do this testing and I was asked to join it. I agreed to take on the job because it sounded great to me. I'd be doing all the testing, and if something failed I would have to strip it down and find out why it failed. We had an AID inspector with us, but basically there were just two of us, Jeff Mason and myself. We got on with the job and we emptied all that room. Then they asked me to go to the production testing department. I was second in command there, then suddenly the boss wanted to move and I was in charge of twenty-three people. As production test engineer I'd write test specifications and design the equipment that was used for testing. Then we taught the people on the assembly line how to use it. You chose the more able people to do this because it was quite a skilled job.

Teddington's employed well over a thousand people in the 1950s and they were good employers. There used to be a marvellous party at Christmas – they'd give everyone the afternoon off for it and they supplied free drink. But then within the departments we organized our own entertainment. In the production test department we'd say we'll have a dance and get somebody to organize it, or we'd go for days out to Weston and places like that.

After a time I told the management the department ran just as well when I went away on holiday as it did while I was there. I said I had some good people working for me who could take over from me because I wanted to do something new. So I tried different things. One of them was technical liaison engineer. The job involved liaising between our drawing office and the accessory-design department in Rolls-Royce who would put jobs out to tender. They'd say, 'We're going to produce this new engine and we'll require an oil-cooler valve and it's got to work at this temperature and that temperature, and it's got to do this, that and the other.' They would produce an accessory design and they would say this accessory is going to work in that part of the engine and it's going to receive this amount of vibration and it's going to get this hot. My job as the technical liaison man was to go up to Rolls-Royce and spend a day with them and talk to the people in accessory design. They'd ask Teddington's to give them a design to do a certain job. So I'd bring this specification back and we'd discuss it in the design department in Teddington's and the draughtsman would draw one up.

I moved on from there to be manager of the assembly department in production, but I didn't like the argument we had there every Friday. I'd go to the works director and he'd say, 'You've got £43,000 of equipment loaded on to the shop floor. What output are we going to get next week?' I'd say, 'Oh, about £10,000, because we've got a shortage of this and that and I've only got so many operatives who are trained to do that particular job.' I'd explain it all and he'd always argue that we could produce more, but I'd walk out of the meeting saying, 'I've given you my figures. You've given me lots of promises saying you'll clear this or that shortage. Unless you do it by Wednesday my figure will stand for the output you're going to get next week.' They didn't like it but they accepted the fact that I was usually right. Eventually they asked if I would join the sales liaison team, but I didn't want that so I went back to look after the technical liaison with Rolls Royce. And that took me to the end of my time at Teddington's. Overall it had been very enjoyable.

One of the biggest new factories that opened after the war in Merthyr Tydfil was Thorn Lighting. Hubert Everson worked there for twenty-six years.

It was a job for life when I started and some people were there for about forty years. There were fifteen hundred people working there, about eight or nine hundred regular ones and then the part-timers. We worked three shifts: nights, days and afternoon shift. My uncle used to call the afternoon shift, which was two till ten, the 'lemonade shift' because you couldn't go out to have a beer – you couldn't drink before or after.

We had about seventy people working in the fila-ments section. I was in there working on a machine called the 'braiders', where we plaited eight wires like lady's hair to make the filament that was put into the lightbulb. The machines were controlled by gears and you made the filaments to the size of those gears. They were made out of tungsten in long strips that then got chopped. They would come off on a drum and the boys on the cutting machines would cut them to certain lengths, depending on what they were for: household lamps, surgical lamps for using in hospitals, landing lights for when aeroplanes are coming in. We made all sorts of lamps and we always called them lamps, not bulbs. We had to measure the filaments and test them, then they went through a furnace. We had a bank of over a hundred machines and I had ten of them to run. They changed over the time I worked there to meet changing needs and to speed up the manufacturing process.

It was a tremendous factory to work at, with very good staff morale. We used to have a shop where we could get a discount on a television or any of the big household machines the company manufactured. There was also a sports club, but most of us were over the hill as far as that was concerned. All the lads would get together and go to a pub or club. It was very close. If anybody was suffering or anybody had trouble, once they knew about it, it was like a mother hen coming round. I had a breakdown while I was there and had a visit from personnel, which was quite something. When the personnel lady came to visit she brought me a box of chocolates. I was treated like a king – the union kept in touch and management kept in touch.

These new industries brought employment to Merthyr and the surrounding area in the 1950s and 1960s at a time when the mines and the ironworks were contracting. As the deep coal mines began to close over this period a number of very large open-cast coal mines were created. David Rudman from Merthyr Tydfil started work at one when he was twenty-six after working on the shop floor of one of the new factories, which he found boring.

I started in 1965 and I had twenty-two years there at Taylor Woodrow. It was four hundred foot deep – a massive hole. At one time it was the deepest in Europe. I had a big wagon to take the coal up to a site about half a mile away where there was a railway station. From there it went on the railway to power stations. 'Sunshine miners' they called us, out in the open all the time. But it's not always sunny. I've been up there when we've worked twelve-hour days, twelve-hour nights and I've been up there most of the time changing ropes. They used to call the earth-moving machines down there 'navvies' and they used to work on ropes, with the bucket to pick the coal up off the dirt or the rock all on rope. Those ropes used to break and you had to change them to keep production going. I've been up there at three o'clock in the morning in a blizzard, up to my knees in slurry, trying to find these ropes to put on the navvies. They were hard times. If there were any stoppages we'd always have to be on top of it. If a navvy broke down it was big trouble because they wouldn't be able to get out the coal. What happened there was that first of all the team of men would go in and drill holes with a big drill. They'd put explosives in there and blow it and that would crack all the rock. Then they would go in with the big navvies and take all the rock off to get to the coal seam. They'd stop then, make it all clear, then get a smaller machine. This would go in and take the coal and load it on the wagons or the lorries that I drove. I didn't know until years later that they called us the Black Gang.

When I first started there we used to go in the morning, perhaps have a mug of tea about six o'clock and at seven o'clock about four or five of us would start to walk. We'd walk the site, a couple of spanners in our pocket, and go to each navvy and ask the drivers if they wanted ropes changing or had any ropes breaking. We'd do bits and pieces there, then walk to the next navvy. We used to walk the whole of the mountain and by the time we got back it was about half past ten and we'd have breakfast. But then they brought the Land Rovers in. The foremen had Land Rovers and they'd take you and drop you off. That wasn't too bad. Eventually there were Land Rovers for the fitters themselves. Then they started walkie-talkies and that was a nuisance because they always knew where you were. When you were on nights they were twelve-hour shifts and, as long as you got the work done that was left there and got it finished, perhaps you'd be finished by half past two or three o'clock in the morning. Then you'd be able to get your head down until seven.

I remember there was a young man of twenty-two worked there and they made him a safety officer. He was married with a young boy. One summer's morning he came in at six, got in the Land Rover and went down what they call the cuts. He got three-quarters of the way down and a boulder came off the top and came pounding down towards him. It landed smack on his Land Rover. It didn't kill him, but he had brain damage. His wife left him after a couple of years because she couldn't handle him. Another young man died back then. They used to have these machines there for dumping all the spoil and he was driving one when he went too far back and went over the top.

In the 1950s and 1960s, as new industries began to take over from the old, chemicals became the most dynamic part of the British economy, with rising productivity that outstripped the rest of industry. On Teesside ICI's Billingham plant had grown out of the need to produce ammonia and nitrates for making TNT during the First World War. In peacetime this was used in the manufacture of nitrogenous fertilizers and by the 1930s Billingham had become the largest factory in the British empire, employing over ten thousand people and covering over a thousand acres. The post-war period saw a rapid expansion in new fibres and plastics based on oil, and a new plant was opened at Wilton on the south side of the Tees to break up oil into organic chemicals. One of the products they could make there cheaply and in large quantities was polythene, while the largest single business of Billingham remained fertilizers. Dennis Carrol worked at Billingham as a rigger.

Teesside had a reputation for being a dirty industrial area and it certainly was. You'd got your steelworks and the chemical works, so there was not much fresh air. I worked at ICI and there were roughly twenty thousand people working there. I think there's less than a thousand now. One of our biggest markets was India and we used to send millions of tons of fertilizer there by boat. Then of course, like the other countries we exported to, they suddenly tumbled that they could manufacture it on their own site and provide work for their own people and still call it ICI, so you got ICI India, ICI Japan, ICI China, wherever. There were factories all over the country but the main board was based in London in ICI House. Each individual works, though, had its separate management structure coming under the main ICI umbrella. The terms and conditions of work were the same throughout the group, so if you worked as a rigger as I did, wherever you worked you would have the same basic pay. That was one of the strengths of the company, because you didn't have the argument 'I can't work there because they don't give enough money,' or 'I get more here.'

Billingham was divided into segments, which were like different companies in a sense. The biggest was fertilizers, but where I worked was where they made nylon. Then next door to us was plastics and they were in a different division to us. The company was very old-fashioned and traditional, very paternalistic. You got a job because your father had worked there, or at least you had a much better chance of one because you had a proven record if your dad was in the family of ICI. Generations from the same families were employed there, from the great-granddad right down to the youngest. They took on predominantly men. Women worked mainly in the canteens or in the offices. But there were also women who worked in the packing sheds. Originally they used to sew the hessian bags for the fertilizers, then later when they got the polythene ones they used to put them through a machine to seal them.

Dennis started work at Billingham when he came out of the army in 1952 and got a job as a rigger. It was a job that was traditionally associated with shipbuilding and it was one of the most dangerous jobs in the shipyards. Riggers set up the rigging that supported masts, derricks and cranes and were involved in slinging and lifting heavy loads. They had to be able to work at great heights in all weather conditions with very little protection. It was not just in the shipyards that riggers were found but on bridges and anywhere that work had to be done or things had to be lifted to great heights.

I didn't know very much about rigging, but I'd seen them working and thought it looked dangerous. Basically, a rigger has the training and the ability to move and lift heavy weights and if you were a rigger you had to be able to work at heights. No matter how clever you were, if you couldn't do that you could never do the job. I got trained by working with them. It was a sort of apprenticeship. You did so much work on each of the plants and you worked with a different rigger on each of them. You wouldn't get the same rate as them because you weren't qualified.

At the end of it you had to do a test and if you passed that you would get the rate and that rate stayed with you wherever you went.

To get to the works there were basically two forms of transport, the local bus service or bicycles. There were a lot of bicycles and we had more discussions about bicycle sheds than about car parks. There were very few cars about when I joined in 1952. Even the works manager of the first works I was in, the nylon works, used to come to work on a motorbike. ICI were very particular really about things like being early for work. One of the biggest sins you could commit was to have a bad timekeeping record. Even if you were only quarter of an hour late, you'd be taken in and taught about it. You could go there quarter of an hour late and do ten times as much work as somebody else who'd been there since half an hour before you started, but that didn't count. You just needed to be there on time. I got into a bit of trouble for my timekeeping. First of all I had to see the local supervisor and he told me to buck up my ideas. The next was I had to see a junior manager and he got all my timekeeping records out. After that I had to see the works engineer and by this time I was getting into serious trouble. I went to see him in his office and he said, 'What's the problem?' I said, 'I can only get one bus.' He said, 'You're going to have to buck your ideas up. You'd better find another method of transport or make sure you get up in time to get that bus. And if I have to see you again you'll be sacked.' That took me by surprise, so I got a bike.

If you were a rigger you had to be mobile because

riggers work all over. Basically, we were a maintenance unit. For instance, if we were doing a big shutdown we would be in there first to do the scaffolding. Then the fitters would come on and we'd be taking the pipes off or vessels out. But, we had to be prepared to go anywhere. ICI had its own construction department, which built all the plant, and when I was in the construction squad I went all over the country. It was always the reason why people wanted to be riggers. When I started most people were getting about £7 a week, but a rigger would be getting nearly £14 or £15 because they worked overtime. They worked two nights – Saturday and Sunday. That was a standard week for most riggers. It was quite a lot more work but quite a lot of pay. There weren't so many of us and there were a lot of people we serviced. We had plumbers, electricians, fitters, joiners and all sorts of people who might want our help to get whatever they wanted into a particular place. They might say, 'We want you to sort that out so that we can work there tomorrow.' So you would work that night for three or four hours.

Job demarcations were very strong, like in the shipyards. People were very particular, especially in the North East, about who did what. To an extent, when you look back and reflect, it was silly. We could lift things and because it was our job we claimed it as our work. So the electrician wasn't allowed to do any lifting. But if there was a lightbulb to change, even if it was only fifteen watt, the electrician would say he had to do that. It was a load of rubbish really, but people were very protective about their jobs and that's what the unions were for, to look after them. The boundaries were very clear, but sometimes if we were putting a simple water pipe somewhere and it was forty feet up you'd do it yourself. The plumber was happy because he didn't have to go up there himself.

If you went to the ICI works you would go through what we called pipe-bridges, which were steel structures made of hundreds of pipes. The product was transferred through these pipes. So the pipe-bridges were an important part of the works and one of the riggers' jobs was to look after them. Anything that had to be lifted for them was our job. We had to decide how to get it there and for this we had to be able to calculate the weight of it. Sometimes things were very heavy and we might have to lift something like six hundred tons. For things like that there were all these different contraptions that used to fit round it. You couldn't just put a wire round it; you had to have proper lifting gear. But for most things you got by custom and practice to find out how you could lift them and how much they would weigh. There was nothing written down, no instruction book like you get for a washing machine.

Sometimes we would have very big vessels to move. They'd say, 'I want it over here,' or 'I want it ten miles away,' and you had to go round and look at it and decide how you were going to get it out. Sometimes you had to lift it by putting rollers down and dragging it over them. One of the things that changed while I was doing the job was craneage.

When I started they didn't have the cranes they have now. They had cranes, but they were all steam powered. Today's cranes can lift three or four hundred tons. We never had them, so we had to put derricks up. A derrick was basically a steel structure which you bolted together and then you put blocks on and wires on and then put the wires on to the steamers and they'd pull it up. So basically you were building your own cranes. We had to do this when we were installing some of the big vessels. Then we had to dress them, which meant put all the pipework on and the doors and the ladders up the side and things like that.

At its peak in the early 1970s ICI Billingham was one of the biggest employers in the North East with about 137,000 employees. The success of an enterprise of this size depended to a large extent on management securing the goodwill and co-operation of its employees and ICI had a long tradition of being one of the more enlightened employers. Before the Second World War this was achieved largely through works councils set up to maintain communication channels between the company and the workforce. These were made up of equal numbers of management and workers' representatives and dealt with issues relating to the safety and well-being of the employees. While the company recognized unions, the success of their paternalistic philosophy meant that union membership was low. Then, after the war, the company introduced new negotiating procedures and agreed to recommend that all workers should join the union. In 1970 a joint consultation system replaced the works councils and workers' representatives in the new structure were now shop stewards. Joint management and employee committees were set up at the level of local works, site and division, and negotiations were conducted on issues such as health and safety, pensions and any areas of potential conflict. Pay negotiations were conducted at a national level between the central personnel department and national union officials. One of the shop stewards at Billingham was Dennis Carrol.

I was a shop steward and for this I went down on courses in Cirencester. The union used to take the agricultural college over in the summer holidays and have courses and if you had ambitions in the union you could apply for a course on public speaking or whatever. You had to put yourself forward every two years to be voted in and all the workers voted for the shop stewards. I then became convener and, once you were elected, you were there till the end. When I was convener I was still, technically, a shop steward for the riggers. But I was the convener for all people – not just the riggers but the fitters, process operators and all sorts of people. Each of them would have a senior shop steward so I wasn't called on every day. Their shop steward would look at a job and it was up to him to resolve any problems. They only came to me if they couldn't.

When I became convener I moved to a different world altogether. I learnt how to speak properly and to listen to people. On Monday morning you'd go in and some fitter had taken something out. It was something he could lift so he did it, but because it was seen as a rigger's job, the riggers objected. They said they could have been out working overtime doing that. So they would come off the plant and you would have to deal with it. The management would say, 'We didn't tell the fitters they could do that.' So it'd be, 'Don't do it again.' But they would do it again and after a while it became simpler to say, 'Look, there are certain things that they can do and certain things they can't.' But you always had to look at the safety aspect of the job. Something might look easy but if anything happened people could get killed.

Of course, people were always suspicious of the management and your relationship with the management. Nobody can kid you that democracy in the workplace is easy, because it isn't. It's very difficult. Instead of saying, 'This is what you're going to do,' you have to say, 'Do you think we should do this?' It takes a lot more time, but consultation is important. ICI recognized that and they made a lot of effort to get it right. Every month the local area would have their own little meeting where things were discussed with all the managers and all the shop stewards. Some of the things on the agenda would be quite minor, but it was still important to air them. If you let little things fester they grow and grow until, bump, you've got a major problem. In the early days of these meetings the men didn't trust the managers. The reason they gave for this was that they didn't know anything about them and they didn't see them as real workers. They thought they went to play golf every day and they didn't have families or anything like that. And it worked the other way. When I asked a number of managers the names of the shop stewards and whether they were married, most of them couldn't tell me. They didn't know what their hobbies were or anything about them. So there was a vast gap between us, there was 'them' and 'us'. They had staff canteens and we couldn't go to them. We had to go to the workers' canteen. You could get somebody's daughter starting at sixteen as a clerk in the office and she'd have more privileges than her dad who'd been there for thirty years if he wasn't on a staff grade.

I used to look at ICI and think of it as a town. That's what it was like – a town subdivided into little villages and each of these had their own cricket teams, football teams and indoor sports teams, like darts and dominoes, and they had a league. This was good because the managers went as well as the lads. It was the only time they'd talk to them. They'd go to the club and have a drink together after they'd played a cricket match or something like that, so that was encouraged. You weren't different – you were an ICI employee. The ICI Club, as we knew it, or the Billingham Synthonia Club to give it its proper name, was a wonderful place. It was always a good night there because people really relaxed. Working at ICI there were a lot of benefits. You had security and reasonable, regular wages. They'd got a good system of work, protective clothing and all things like that. Then there was the camaraderie. Most people came from the same community. A lot lived in the same street so it was like a community within a community.

I was a rigger the whole time I was at ICI. It was dangerous work and there were some deaths, unfortunately. If you worked as a rigger and you fell, the chances are you were going to hit all sorts of things on the way down, so some riggers were killed. There were no harnesses or things like that and a lot of riggers were crazy. They wouldn't have worn a harness anyway, because they thought it was below their dignity. Health and safety laws weren't as strict as they are now, but you did have to wear hard hats. This was very difficult for us because you had to climb in between pipes and structures and you'd catch it and it would get knocked off. You were always more likely to hit your head on something when you had a hard hat on. But if you were down below and something fell on you then it could save your life.

There were a massive number in construction who'd get killed. Sometimes it was their own fault and you'd always find at an accident that it could have been avoided. But that's just hindsight. Everybody says 'I wouldn't have done that,' but we all did it. You know you all take shortcuts to get the job finished. There's always deadlines. Whenever there was a fatality when the day of the funeral came round a lot wouldn't come to work, but not all of them went to the funeral. It was just an excuse for them to go and get drunk. There would always be an investigation and then the factory inspector would come in and sometimes that changed how you were going to work. Then as far as we were concerned with the union, your mind goes to compensation because they had to find someone to blame.

In the post-war years the shop steward became an increasingly powerful presence in the workplace. The motivation for many people to get involved in union work came not just from a desire to obtain better wages for the workforce but to ensure better and safer working conditions. Francis Newman from Dunston on Tyneside had a serious accident at work and this was one of the reasons he got involved with the union.

After I left the marines I got a temporary job at a steel factory. They used to do welding, producing all kinds of steel things for factories and for coal mining, and they gave me a job as a miller. The milling machine took the top off any kind of sheet you put in. My job was to put in these huge steel sheets. It had to go in a press first and then it came to me and I had to put it in the milling machine, and as the sheet went through it milled the top flat. You had to do so many hundred of them in a day. If you wanted to go to the toilet you had to ask permission. The boss would come, look at his watch and when you came back if you were more than a couple of minutes he would say, 'Where the hell have you been? Get this bloody machine going.' I was in a hurry one day and the back of the machine used to get covered with little scraps of steel. I tried to clean it, but the machine pulled my hand in and tore out part of it, taking all the nerves and everything else with it. I went to the guy on the other machine and said, 'I've had a bad accident.' Well he nearly fainted when he saw it. When I looked down I could see a V cut out of my hand. It looked horrific, worse than it was, but I felt really poorly. I was walking along to first aid and it was a long walk. This welder, seeing us looking bad, came running over and got a hold of my arm. He shouted and got another over to help. I'd done some first aid in the marines so I told them where to push to stem the flow of blood a bit till I got to the first aid station. Then it was hospital immediately, where I had seventy-odd stitches.

When I moved from the steel factory I went into the Federation Brewery and I was quite astounded at how it was run. Nepotism was the norm; foremen would give their sons the good jobs. There was no justice. If somebody didn't like your face you were sacked. The shop steward was in tow to the management and so was the branch secretary. Then the shop steward didn't get his own way and said, 'I'm resigning.' As soon as he resigned the lads said to me, 'You put up for it. You know what you're talking about and you're not frightened or anything like that.' I said I didn't want to really, but I would put up and try to get some justice.

Of course as soon as I put up the other one who'd resigned put up and they actually voted him back on. That didn't bother me, but then the branch chairman of the shop-floor union left. So I put up for branch chairman and got elected. The first thing I did was to get stuck into management, telling them that safety measures were needed, like stopping the practice where guys were squeezing past a wall where there was a conveyor belt running round at a million miles an hour. Safety comes first. Get that done, I told them, or the men would be out. They'd never been spoken to like that before and they didn't like it, but they did the job. Then I went to the pay office and said, 'Can you show me the overtime book?' I looked through it and the highest paid were the branch officials of the trade union; all the rest were getting nothing. They wouldn't let me work over-time because they said I was a new starter. When I said I wasn't putting up with this, they said okay, you can come in. I went to individual trade union members, they played hell because I'd seen the figures, and in the end the lads were 100 per cent behind me.

Accidents like the one Francis Newman had remained an all too regular feature of working life in the post-war years. The accident ruined his chances of joining the police, which had been his ambition after he left the marines, but after he had recovered he was able to get another job and lead a normal life. In that sense he was fortunate. Many industrial workers, particularly miners and steelworkers, were less fortunate and paid with their lives for accidents at work. As the reminiscences through-out this book have shown, working in many industries was dirty and dangerous until well into the twentieth century. Accidents were commonplace and injury was so widespread that it was regarded as just part of the job. It was seen as inevitable that riveters would be hit by flying chips of steel, that foundrymen would be splashed with molten metal, miners crushed by falling rock and textile workers hit by flying shuttles. Fatalities were frequent, particularly in the coal mines.

By the 1950s, however, the British workplace was becoming safer. The average number of people killed in industrial accidents each year declined from more than four thousand in the 1900s to just over fifteen hundred in the 1950s.[55] By this time the nature of jobs was beginning to alter. In heavy industry work started to become less physically demanding as new machinery was installed. Throughout industry working conditions improved, and health and safety legislation made the workplace a safer place to be. However, in many firms modern machinery that would have made the work easier and reduced the risk of injury was slow to be introduced because labour was plentiful and equipment expensive. As health and safety legislation was introduced, employers often complained about the cost of implementing the required measures.

Colin Douglas, who left school in 1950 to become an apprentice in the Merchant Navy, eventually moved on to a job as a factory inspector with the responsibility of making sure that the new health and safety legislation was obeyed.

If you served in the Merchant Navy until after twenty-six you were exempt from National Service, so I stayed where I was and [after my apprenticeship I worked my way up through the ranks until] I was appointed master at the age of twenty-seven. But I was married by that time and we had a son, and

[55] *Austerity Britain 1945–1951*, David Kynaston, Bloomsbury, 2007.

I decided to leave the sea. I had several irons in the fire at the time, but the one that I found most attractive was a position with HM Inspectorate of Factories.

I was recruited as a factory inspector specifically because of my seagoing knowledge and experience. At that time the factory inspectorate was a division of the Ministry of Labour and they felt they needed more expertise on nautical matters, particularly the enforcement of docks regulations and also of the regulations that applied to shipbuilding and ship repairing. I was actually the first master mariner ever to be recruited to HM Inspectorate of Factories.

I was based in Newcastle, but the district covered the whole of Northumberland. It was quite busy and hugely satisfying in the sense that you determined your own workload. Every week you had to file a report showing the work you had done, the places that you visited and what you had established there. This went on permanent record. I was sent out on my own two weeks after I first started, but it was to small businesses – confectioners, butcher shops and so on and so forth. There was a tremendous learning curve, but shortly after joining there was an induction course in London. On the training course there were four barristers who had been recruited at the same time as me and another engineer who had a PhD in electrical engineering. So it was a hugely prestigious organization, recruiting pretty high-calibre people. I didn't know anything about the law, but the barristers didn't know anything about ship operation or shipbuilding so there was a certain amount of exchange on the training course.

In the whole of the Newcastle district there were only six inspectors and there was little opportunity for contact with the others because you were out all the time. As a new inspector, when you were in the office doing your weekly report you would take advantage of the knowledge of seniors who were there at the time and discuss with them issues that had arisen in your work and what you should do about them. Of course the work that you had done during that week was scrutinized by the district inspector and you sat down with him as he went through your work report, including the letters you had drafted and action that you had determined to take. He gave you advice and guidance as to what the next step should be. But new recruits such as myself started at the bottom end and then gradually worked their way through.

Factories by definition were everything that produced something. They ranged from a butcher's shop making sausages to a steelworks producing thousands of tons of steel every year, or a company building huge ships. All were regarded as factories.

We were also responsible for inspecting building sites and what they call 'works of engineering construction'. These were bridges and big steel constructions. For a period I was the inspector responsible for the building of the first Tyne Tunnel and for three years I was the inspector regarded as the specialist in compressed-air workings. There were statutory regulations laid down, standards and conditions that had to be applied and observed for working in compressed air. This covered things like the time that workers had been actually working in compressed air, which determined the time that they had to spend in the decompression chambers before they came out again to avoid diseases like the bends. We also looked at the mechanical arrangements in the tunnel, like were there adequate measures to prevent roof-falls.

As a factory inspector you also had to ensure that all plant and machinery that required it had periodic statutory examination to make sure that it was in adequate working order. At that time, health didn't play such a significant part in the legislation as it does today. Nevertheless, there were health standards to be observed – statutory requirements that no one should be exposed to any substance that would cause them harm, such as asbestos. There was a code of regulations for people working with or in the proximity of asbestos, and as a factory inspector you had to be assured that those standards were being met by the employer.

Our working methods specifically said that you should not make a prior arrangement for a visit. Very often if senior executives of the factory were around there was a certain reluctance for the people on the shop floor to show you things or tell you things. Sometimes we would do night visits, knocking on the door of an obscure little factory in the middle of Newcastle at two o'clock in the morning. On a night visit, once I had established myself as the inspector and had a cup of tea and a chat, they came up with all kinds of little snippets about what was going on, which was absolutely amazing.

Routine inspections were only carried out once every four years, but there were requirements for factories to report accidents and dangerous occurrences to the inspectorate. So when you received a report of an accident or a dangerous occurrence you would determine that you would visit, and those visits were generally made by arrangement.

After a time you'd get a bigger case load, with things that were more complex and more difficult, for example steelworks or shipbuilding operations. Some of these were hugely complex and there was no way a new recruit could be let loose in there. But because I was familiar with shipbuilding practice and activities, fairly soon after I was appointed, maybe within a year or eighteen months, I was inspecting shipyards. You started off by doing the accidents, taking the accident report from the shipyard, going to the yard and following specifically on that accident to determine how it had happened. A lot of them were falls, where people fell from staging. Very often men would take a risk and work from just one plank or two planks rather than be bothered to ensure that there was a proper working plank there.

I did this for two or three years, and then I was appointed regional inspector, covering the whole of the northern region. This included responsibility for dealing with any problems that arose on the Sellafield nuclear site and the big steelworks in the region. At a place like Consett Ironworks an inspection would take about a week or eight days. One of the traumatic aspects of factory inspectorate work was doing an investigation of a fatal accident. In heavy industries like steel, construction and ship-building there were fatal accidents from time to time and these required an inspector to examine the circumstances leading up to the accident to deter-mine the cause of it. You also had to determine whether or not there had been a breach of standard regulations, because a breach of statutory require-ments or regulations would very often give rise to a prosecution in the magistrates' court. It was an inter-esting position, where I carried out an investigation and laid information in the magistrates' court and then actually prosecuted the case. The factory inspectorate was an extremely prestigious organiza-tion and there were no more than four hundred of us in the whole of the country.

Later in my career I was made responsible for shipbuilding, ship repairing and marine engineering for the whole of the country. It was a job that involved a lot of time away from home. I was on the road for three or four days a week every week, not just in the North East but all over the country: Vickers in Barrow, Cammell Laird in Liverpool and the yards in the south of England as well. I did a tremendous amount of work on welding fumes, because the shipbuilding regulations said nobody should be employed in an activity which exposed them to fumes that were liable to injure their health. Welders produced a lot of fumes and smoke and other products, which they inhaled. But the diffi-culty was identifying whether or not it was injurious. Nobody could tell me whether or not welding fumes were injurious because nobody could tell me what was in them. We knew that there were iron particles, and we knew that there was CO_2, but we didn't know what came from the welding rods, which had all kinds of material attached to them. So in my capacity as the specialist shipbuilding inspector I commissioned studies and surveys of the fumes from not only the factory inspectorate specialist chemical branch but also from independent industrial-health organizations. I commissioned work from Newcastle University to measure the fume particulars, determine what products were there as a result of the welding and then determine whether or not they were likely to be injurious to health. From that we were able to identify that there were harmful products and what steps could be taken to protect the welders from them. In some circumstances the only other protection they could get would be to wear breathing apparatus.

It was also well known that eye flash was a problem, so a lot of the work that I did led to the kind of situation that you see today where people doing that kind of work are virtually in space suits. People were also exposed to asbestos dust, so I commissioned a lot of work on asbestos to identify the particular size of dust particles from various operations: lagging, applying asbestos insulation and also stripping out asbestos in ship repairing. By collecting dust samples and measuring the particular size of the particles we were able to determine what operations were likely to be harmful. It was that work that eventually led to asbestos being banned.

In the 1960s management began to grasp that looking after their workers with welfare provisions and better conditions was in their best interests. Central to this was health and safety, and Colin was approached by Swan Hunter and invited to join them to oversee all their health and safety requirements throughout the group. 'At that time in the 1960s,' he says, 'the Swan Hunter Group employed forty-five thousand people worldwide.'

We had eight or nine shipbuilding yards in the UK, and repair yards in Trinidad, Malta and Singapore. It was a huge organization. Swan Hunter had always been a very significant shipbuilding company, but after the publication of the Geddes Report [in 1965], which set out that bigger was better for the shipbuilding industry, Swan Hunter became a very significant size and in terms of quality and standard of shipbuilding they were absolutely superb. By that time I was a main board director of Swan Hunter. At Swan Hunter we were fairly unique in that we were building admiralty ships, aircraft carriers and other warships alongside merchant ships. As far as we were concerned it made a good mix, because we had some very profitable work and a lot of our overheads were covered on the warship contracts. That meant we could take merchant-ship building contracts at better prices than most of our competitors.

When I joined my remit was to set up an effective health and safety operation throughout the group. I was virtually given a free hand to do whatever was required to improve the standards. This was against a requirement to reduce the cost to the company of unsatisfactory working conditions that gave rise to accidents with the resulting loss of time and increased cost of accident liability insurance. What I concentrated on was the training and education of managers and supervisors to make them aware of the cost of failing to properly supervise and properly provide the kind of working conditions that minimized the risk of accidents and injuries. Within three years the employer's liability premium was down from over 4 per cent to about 2 per cent. In other words, half the cost, mainly through education and training. So in a company of forty-five thousand people it saved them millions. It was very successful.

The main board of Swan Hunter Group then suggested that we should have a specialist company within the group that would concentrate on selling health and safety standards, and providing nursing and medical support for the workforce. The company was called Swan Hunters Safety and Training Company. It also did all the training throughout the country, and I was appointed chief executive. We employed six doctors and we had nurses stationed at the various shipyards in the medical centres to improve the standard of nursing care available. We also had industrial hygienists whose role was to look at the standards in the yards, and by measurement and evaluation decide on whether or not they were acceptable.

But then came this sad period where we were nationalized, and the nationalized shipbuilding industry was a complete and utter disaster. All that happened was that the hugely inefficient companies that needed subsidies to stop them going belly up became part of the nationalized industry. Their inefficient ship production continued and if they did get orders, the orders had to be subsidized, which meant. there were further losses in those companies and so on. At the time of nationalization we were saying, 'For God's sake don't try and bail out the lame ducks.' The Scottish yards in particular were immensely political. The thought of closing Clyde shipyards was complete anathema to the Labour government, but that is what should have happened. But it meant that the whole industry came down to the lowest common denominator within the industry. The nationalized industry is well documented as unsuccessful. We made loss after loss after loss as an industry.

Everything was nationalized, regardless of either the volume or quality of the work coming from their yard. One big example was Austin Pickersgill building the hugely successful SD14 cargo ship. They were an incredibly successful yard and they invested very heavily in new state-of-the-art shipbuilding facilities in the mid-1970s. In order to ensure that their ships continued to be attractive to ship-owners the new facilities were purpose-built, designed to enable twelve SD14s a year to be produced. Then they were nationalized and what happened was that there were parity claims from other yards and these produced strikes and walk-outs. It meant that the workforce in some yards were demanding, and very often getting, the same level of wages as Austin Pickersgill for nowhere near the volume of work. The Austin

Pickersgill earnings were capped, so what the workers there said was, 'Bollocks to that! We are not going to put ourselves out when we can't earn any more than our brothers in Scotland who are producing nowhere near the amount that we are and getting the same money as us.' The ability of management to balance the workforce to the level of production that they had previously been achieving was taken away from them. So that's just one example of the problems of the nationalized industry.

Come 1981 I was invited to leave Swan Hunter and become part of the British Shipbuilders Corporation, which to my shame I did. At the time I was optimistic. I saw it as an opportunity for me to go to this organization and make a contribution to the industry on a national basis. All kinds of promises were made to me as to what I could do, so at the time that I made the decision it was an attractive proposition. But very shortly after I made the change Mrs Thatcher was convinced that shipbuilding was a dying industry and she decreed that it should be de-nationalized. So I went through all the repeat traumas that we had gone through in leading up to nationalization. We had a similar difficult time, leading to the shipbuilding industry being broken up under the auspices of the Canadian lawyer Graham Day, who was given a knighthood for breaking up the British shipbuilding industry.

The perception at the time was that shipbuilding was a sunset industry and there was nothing that it could contribute to the economy. At this point both Japan and South Korea were continuing with the right kind of organization and slimming down, and with the right kind of support we could have remained confident. The French and the Italians remained confident, and the idea that ship-building was a sunset industry was a complete and utter hoax. The wrong decisions were made for the wrong reasons. My son is a vice-president of Royal Caribbean cruise line and he heads one of the teams responsible for the new build of cruise liners. All that's built into these ships these days is just absolutely unbelievable, and those were oppor-tunities that we would have had if some element of the shipbuilding industry continued. The way the industry was disposed of here was just a pig's break-fast. There were some sales of machinery and equipment overseas, but a lot of the stuff was just scrapped, just destroyed. The last elements of the shipbuilding industry in this region continued until about two years ago when Swan Hunter was finally closed down. And now it's been wiped off the face of the earth.

Robert Hunter left the Sunderland shipbuilder Austin Pickersgill in 1973 and, like Colin, he believes it was a time of missed opportunity for the British shipbuilding industry.

When I left I got six years' experience in oil and gas, managing oil and gas construction projects for Shell and BP. It was a whole new world, with completely different commercial pressures. The operational side of the business was still sticking two pieces of steel together and welding them together, but the whole ambience of the contracting world was so different from shipbuilding. The engineers were all PhDs and generally there were a lot more talented people. My colleagues were all highly intelligent, highly motivated young men rather than the fifty-year-olds who were the directors of Austin Pickersgill. They were open to new management techniques and new operational control techniques. And in actual fact, for a contractor to pre-qualify and bid a job, he had to demonstrate to the oil companies that he was using all of these modern techniques in production control and project management.

Then in 1981 I was head-hunted to take up a three-year contract to advise a Danish shipbuilding company for them to do exactly what I had proposed for Austin Pickersgill. I was to set up a new company, fabricating for the oil and gas industry. They offered me this very lucrative contract for three years and I said yes. It was virtually tripling my pay. I had just been to London to meet up with my new colleagues and sign the contract, and I was feeling very pleased with myself. I got on the train from King's Cross to come north and there on the table opposite were three of my earlier colleagues from Austin Pickersgill, which by this time in 1981 was part of British Shipbuilders. They were all sitting at this table with glum expressions on their faces, so instead of sitting on my own I went and joined them. I hadn't seen them since I had left in 1973, so they asked me what I had been doing and where I was. I was able to tell them that same day I had just signed a three-year contract to do what I was going to do at Pickersgill and it was extremely lucrative. They were all just very glum and I said, 'Well! What's up with you guys? What is the problem? You're not very happy with yourselves.' Well it turned out they'd all been called to London that day to be given redundancy notices.

The thing is, they could have been doing what I was doing for the Danish company. The oil companies like Shell and BP had approached the British shipyards and said, 'We need your industry to develop into a service industry for us. We want you to establish recognizable companies with qualified management and a good labour force, who can pre-qualify and bid to do the work that we want. There's lots of it for the next twenty or thirty years.' And the shipbuilding industry turned away from it. At the time, in the early 1970s, they still had full order books and they said, 'Why should we get involved in this fly-by-night business?' You may say there was some degree of uncertainty about oil and gas exploration, but not very much, frankly. The oil was out there and the gas was out there in large quantities and everybody knew it. The oil companies knew the sort of structures that they needed in order to develop these oil fields and they were looking to British companies to help them and support them in building these structures. The shipping industry in effect walked away from it.

The demise of Britain's shipbuilding industry had been rapid. In the early 1950s Britain was still the world's leading shipbuilder but by 1954, though the country still made most ships in total, Germany had overtaken her as the leading builder for foreign owners and by 1956 Britain was overtaken by Japan in total output, losing a lead she had held since records first began. By the mid-1960s the great British industry that had dominated the world was sinking fast and by the mid-1980s only a handful of British yards remained, making less than 3 per cent of the world's ships.

But it wasn't just shipbuilding. Over the same period the steel industry contracted at an alarming rate. Willie Rae worked in the engineering department at Clydebridge Steelworks at Cambuslang. He got involved with union work and came up against Graham Day's counterpart in the steel industry, Ian MacGregor, the Scottish-born American who became chairman of British Steel in 1980.

I finished up the convener to the maintenance assistants, right up to the partial closure of the works. That's when I had the horrible experience of meeting a guy called MacGregor who told us that he was there to ensure the safety of the steel industry and all he did was do away with the industry in this area. I finished up the chairman of the joint unions in the works, where I met a lot of wonderful guys who were trying to keep some industry within this community. At that time we'd a lot of workers, then productivity schemes came in. And these were words I hated. Because 'productivity' literally means make more with less. That led to a reduction in manpower. When I first became a steward around 1972 there were two hundred maintenance assistants and when I took my redundancy there were six of us. Round about 1978 things started to happen with flexible working practices. That meant I became a forklift driver as well as a maintenance man; I became a cherry-picker driver; I became an overhead crane driver. Then I started making up bits and pieces for engineering that didn't require a great level of skill.

The thing about the works was that nobody was ever made redundant, but management were very cute in getting the numbers they wanted. They didn't sack anybody; they just held carrots in front of people to get them to go. There were all sorts of packages, so if you were a thirty-year man you would leave with about two years' wages. To be honest, you can imagine a working-class guy being offered an amount of money like he had never ever seen in his life. I've seen sights in Cambuslang main street you just would not believe, with people that had money they'd never had in their life. I've seen guys blowing money on me! I'd walk into a pub and because they'd chucked their job, my impression was they thought they owed me, because I'd got them all this money. But it wasn't going to last and there were no more jobs to go to. I compare the River Clyde now to when I moved into the steel industry. Then there were very few fish in the river and now you can fish it anywhere you like. There's an old saying: 'Maggie Thatcher brought salmon into the Clyde. It's just hard luck she stopped all the works!'

Throughout the 1970s the aim of managers in the steel industry was to produce an efficient modern industry that paid for itself. The resulting rationalization brought mass closures and job losses. In 1970 there were 255,000 steel-workers, in 1980 only 166,000. Despite the cuts, the British Steel Corporation made a loss of £500 million in 1980, resulting in their refusal to pay workers a wage increase that kept up with the cost of living. This prompted the first national strike for seventy years. After thirteen weeks on strike the unions lost their fight, new working agreements were pushed through and in the space of the next three years the number of steelworkers was halved from 166,000 to around 70,000.

Among the works where steelmaking stopped was Ebbw Vale. Barry Caswell was at the works at this time and has his views on the reasons for the closure.

There were twelve thousand working here in the 1950s and Richard Thomas and Baldwins, as it was called then, was the flagship of the British steel industry. But with developments in the steel industry, other works began to rival it and the problem here was that the works was twenty-one miles from the coast, up a valley with bad communications. It was natural that one day it would come under the micro-scope and that's what happened. The steelmaking side of the works closed down in the 1970s and grad-ually it became a finishing works. This meant they brought the coils in and we put a finishing coating on it. After that the workforce gradually dwindled down, department by department. Then it came under British Steel. Rationalization, they called it, and that's when the cutbacks started to bite in. Up till then people were very insulated from the outside world. It was a valley and everything you wanted was here. People had been paid very well, but when things started to bite people began to look elsewhere for work. They gradually began to leave the area; that was the sad part. When the works closed in 2002 there were only about seven or eight hundred working here. Of course it had a big impact on the town. Having lived and worked here all my life it's very strange for me now to see that there is no works here any more.

The closure of the works, along with pit closures in the area at the same time, brought misery to thousands. Many could see there was no prospect of any future work and there was very little money to live on. Many redundant miners and steelworkers were forced to hunt for jobs in the new manufacturing and electronics industries, but one of the biggest problems in the area was the fact that a lot of these new factories were closing down too. Hubert Everson, who was working at Thorn Lighting, said,

Even the new industries that had held out so much hope for the future didn't last for long. There was big competition with Philips, but we held our own until we closed down. We found out later it needn't have closed down. They were planning on bringing a road through but it never happened. What they did when we were closing, they came round and asked us would we go over and train people in other countries. That was a little bit naughty. Can you imagine how we felt about that? It's all closed now, though. It was like part of your life gone when the

factory closed. That was one of twenty industries
that left Merthyr within twenty years.

Gareth Howells had worked at Triang in Merthyr Tydfil
since leaving school in 1957 and has his view on why that
company collapsed.

We never had any drawings to work from. All you
had there was samples – things that had been done
before. You'd have a sample on the wall, set up the
machine and say yes, that looks all right. That's
the reason the company collapsed, because when the
Japs moved into the toy industry, their quality of
toys was far superior. When Triang closed in 1974/5,
the whole toy industry collapsed and they had been
the biggest manufacturers in the world. The investment hadn't been put in; they were just living on
past reputation. They didn't have the quality. They
had inspection, but the inspection was at the wrong
end. They inspected on the assembly but they
should have inspected where they were making the
parts.

I left Triang in 1969, then in 1970 Lines Brothers
went bust and closed down. Receivers were
appointed and they sold off the factory. They sold it
to a fellow who was just an asset-stripper. He came
in and all he wanted to do was just cherry-pick, just
take the parts he wanted and sell it off at a profit. The
main factory was closed and the site was demolished.
One guy from there I remember went to work for the
Chinese. They were buying up plants, moving them
over to China and learning how to manufacture. All

that we have here today are small industrial units. All those factories that were there when I left school in 1957 have gone; every one of them gone. At one time Merthyr was the biggest town in Wales, but when all the industry went people moved away. Nobody knew what to do with the town. All that's left in Merthyr now is small tuppeny-ha'penny units paying national minimum wage. I wouldn't like to be born in this era. They were far better days. The quality of life was better, more of a community spirit. That's all been destroyed.

Moving away from the place where you lived and worked, as many did in South Wales, was something that had already started to happen in other traditional industrial communities throughout Britain. In County Durham, extracting coal, particularly from some of the smaller mines in the west and centre of the county, was difficult. By the 1960s a large number of them were exhausted. Others were difficult to work and output at them was low. As a result many of them were controversially declared uneconomic and were closed. During the 1960s the Durham coalfield quickly declined, losing half of its workforce and half of its pits. Many miners and their families had to move to find work in the mines of South Yorkshire and Nottinghamshire, where they were promised security of employment. Jim Grigg from Trimdon was one of them.

Wingate was the first one that closed in 1962 and they transferred men from there to Deaf Hill. I went to work there, but Deaf Hill closed in 1967 and I moved to Bevercotes in Nottingham. I was just married, so me and the wife went down. One of the reasons we went down was that they transferred a lot of the lads from these local pits around Trimdon to the coast, but they couldn't get piece work. Piece work and power-loading were the two best-paid jobs in the pit, so instead of going on to the full grades of pay that they used to get they just got a daily rate that wasn't anything like as good. So that's one of the reasons I moved away, to get power-loading.

When we went down to the Midlands there wasn't a national wage structure. The power-loading down in Nottingham and Yorkshire was about £5 a week more than in Durham – a hell of a lot higher. Up here we were getting about £22, but when I went down there it was about £27. So it was worth moving.

When I went to Bevercotes I worked with people from all over. They're on about immigrants coming into the country now, but I worked with Sikhs, Lithuanians, Estonians, Poles. There was a hell of a lot of East Europeans came over here, particularly around 1956 after the Hungarian Uprising. A lot of them went to the Nottingham area and some of them lads we worked with were great workers. And what a difference it was working there. Bevercotes was one of the biggest pits in the country and it was fifty-odd men in a cage there. The most men you could get in the cage in Durham was twelve. The mine was three thousand feet deep, but the face were six foot high, massive, especially when you were used to working on faces that were no more than two foot here.

While I was at Bevercotes I started to work for British Ropes and when a job came up with them back here I came back from the Midlands. I went to Kelloe pit as what they call one-way rope man. That involved splicing the ropes. I was in the safety team, so I was on call all the time. I lived in a pit house because of that. So I used to come back from the pit at the end of my shift and our lass would put my dinner out, and I'd be eating my dinner and the phone would go: 'Oh, you've got to come back to the pit. There's a rope broken in the shaft.' Or on a Monday night you might be out at the darts and you'd get called to go back in and it might be ten o'clock. The best part for me used to be [when] someone would be knocking on your door at two o'clock in the morning saying you had to go to the pit. I didn't mind that, because you got up, you went to work, did the job, got the job finished and you could go home. Then the next day you had the day off and you got paid at time and a half.

Another Trimdon miner, Bob Willis, went down to Hatfield Main Colliery in Doncaster in 1961. One of the things he soon found out was that when you made a move like this you had to get used to new ways of working very quickly and, as a new man in from a different mining region, you had to be able to stand up for yourself.

I knew they were all going to close up here and I was fortunate because my grandfather went down to Thorn Colliery in Yorkshire in 1926 at the time of the strike up here, so most of my mam's family were

511

down there and my mam's sister's man worked at Hatfield, so I lived with them at first, until my wife sold our house up here. I had one daughter when I first went down and my other two were born down there 1962 and 1965. In Doncaster where I went there were big pits and they didn't have enough men. So you got straight on to power-loading. When I went to Hatfield they had what was called the 'butty system'. One man used to get all the money earned for the full face from the officials and there might be forty of us on that face. Then we went into the pit yard when he got all the money and this man, who was called the butty man, dished it out. And you had to fight for it. There was six of us in this squad working together and when I first went down I said, 'How much have you got, son?' When I found out I said to the butty man, 'Hey, you've made a mistake here. They've got more than me.' He said, 'Here, take it out of that,' and handed some money over. I had no more problems after that, but you had to fight for it. I loved it at Hatfield, but the wife didn't. We were getting more money down there, and in the clubs there was entertainment every night of the week.

From Durham to Yorkshire wasn't very far to go, but, as the certainty of employment in traditional industries diminished, for many British families the search for better jobs and a better lifestyle took them to the other side of the world. 'Ten Pound Poms' is a term still used in Australia today to describe British subjects who migrated there after the Second World War under an assisted-passage scheme operated by the Australian government. It enabled people to go to Australia for £10 to start a new life and career, and in the 1950s and 1960s many British working-class families took advantage of the scheme. Among them was Brian Booth. He was born in Trimdon, but when he was fifteen his family emigrated to Australia.

We started off in Adelaide, but there wasn't much work there, so we went to Perth in Western Australia and my dad got a job in the goldfields. We had not one penny left when we got there, but I was fortunate enough to get started as an apprentice fitter and turner in the power station at the same mine. I was there for just over two years in the power plant, which was above ground, because I wasn't old enough to go down below.

We lived in a really old asbestos house and I walked over a spoil heap to go to work. There was a crust on it and I only found out years later that it was cyanide residue that I was walking on. The first day I went into work I had a pair of winkle-pickers on that had been given to us by a family member in the UK and a pair of trousers and a T-shirt. We had no money for boilersuits and workwear, we were just so skint. But I was made very welcome at that mine and I really grafted there. I used to be working sometimes up to twenty hours a week overtime. They couldn't keep me at home. The foreman fitter lived near us and sometimes he used to get called out during the night, so I used to sleep on his veranda waiting for him to be called out so that I could go in with him. That's how much I loved the job. I have never had a job since then that I loved like that.

Like many families who went out on the assisted-passage scheme, Brian's family never really settled in Australia and as soon as they could afford the fare they decided to return to the North East. Because Brian was enjoying life so much he chose to stay.

At the gold mine I was living in a men-only camp after my mam and dad left. Because workers used to come and go and there was such a high volume of labour turnover, they had this camp where the single men used to live and I was having a whale of a time there. But a sheet-metal worker called Graham, who hadn't been long out from Lancashire, came into work one day and said, 'Wife said, lad, no Englishman is stopping out here on his own. You've got to come and live with us in the town.' His wife Fay had never met me, but she'd heard about me, so I had to go and live with them. I still had a good time in the town. It was a smashing atmosphere, very small like a cowboy town. But I was only seventeen and with my parents back in England I wasn't sure what to do, so I flipped a coin and I came back [to Trimdon].

In our village there was a mine at Deaf Hill and just a few hundred yards away was Trimdon Grange, where there was a mine and a coke works. Every village round there was like that. The coal would go to Hartlepool and then by ship down to London or wherever. Most of these collieries were still working when I came back and because of my experience in Australia I could have got a job, but I didn't want to. My dad didn't want me to either. He'd worked in the coal mines and he said, 'You're not going there.' So I ended up at GEC in Hartlepool.

The first day I went in I was put with a fitter and he took me to a big machine shop where we were supposed to repair one of the machines. I had the toolbox ready to get started, but he said, 'Don't move – don't touch anything. I won't be long,' and he went away. All the other people in there were working away and I was just standing around, so my face went bright red. I thought everybody was looking at me and I wasn't doing anything. When he came back he said, 'I can't get a forklift to lift this particular item off this part of this machine till tomorrow. So we're going to have to look busy.' Then he said, 'I won't be long. I'm just going to pick my winners out. Don't touch anything while I'm away,' and off he went with his paper down the slide-rule pocket on his boiler suit. When he came back he said, 'We'll go and get our hands washed now. It's time for our ten o'clock break.' 'My hands?' I said. 'They're cleaner now than when I came in!'

Anyway, this went on all day. I was staying at my granddad's at the time and when I got home I said to him, 'Granddad, I can't go back there.' He said, 'You've got to go back. You've got to finish your time off. You have to finish your apprenticeship.' And that was how it went on for about two and a half years. Just not doing anything. Well you did work, but not in the way I had been used to in Australia. The unions controlled everything.

When I had been working in Australia I was in the same union and I used to work as much overtime as

I could. As long as I could physically keep going and keep my eyes open I used to work. Then I came back here and I think it was something like six hours a week you were allowed to work over. But as apprentices we were only on about £2 a week, so I asked if I could work on Sundays, but the union and the management both said no. Nobody had ever worked Sundays as an apprentice, they said. That was just the way it was. But I needed the money because I was going to college twice a week. I had to come home from work, get ready and then go back to Hartlepool. So because of bus fares and this and that you did need the money and you should have been allowed the option of doing more work.

In the end I couldn't take any more. By this time I thought my five years was nearly up because I reckoned the time I'd done in Australia counted as part of the apprenticeship. So I went to the union and said my five years was nearly up and I should be finishing my apprenticeship the next month. But they said what I'd done in Australia didn't count. When I told them that it was the same union as in Australia they said I'd have to go to a union meeting. When I went my knees were knocking, but they agreed that I'd worked my time and I got my green card.

As soon as I went back to work I put my notice in. I explained everything to the personnel officer, who was a gentleman. 'But Brian,' he said, 'why do you want to leave? Do you realize the money you are going to get now?' because it was a big jump from apprentice to qualified fitter and turner. He said,

'You will actually be able to get a mortgage.' But I didn't even know what a mortgage was. He asked me if the union had put pressure on me to leave because I was twenty-one. I told him they hadn't. Even so, I had to go to a meeting between the management and the union together. In the end I said, 'Do you know why I want to leave? It's because I've never done a proper day's work in my life since I've been here.' The personnel man said, 'Is that right?' and the union bloke just looked at me as if to say, 'You're finished.' So I left and while I was working my notice nobody spoke to me in the fitting shop or anything.

I was never happy in that job. I was very appreciative of the job, but I hated it, every minute of it. When I left I joined the Merchant Navy and I was actually going to jump ship in Australia if I got a ship that was going there. I joined a shipping company but I didn't know where any ships were going, or anything like that. Luckily I got a telegram to join a ship in North Shields and when I joined it I found out that she was going to Australia. My plan was to jump ship in Port Adelaide and then go from there over to Western Australia to the goldfields, but I was talked out of it and stayed in the Merchant Navy. A few years later I did actually go back to Australia, but I wasn't there five minutes and I ended up in a flying doctor aeroplane. I got injured on a mining site I went to work at and I ended up hospitalized. When I was fit for work again I went back to the Merchant Navy.

At the time there were dozens of shipping companies operating from Newcastle. The company

I worked for was Andrew Weir and they called their ships the Bank line. Every ship was *Margaret Bank* or *Brian Bank* – it was like a suffix. They had a lot of ships and they were all over the world – they were massive. The wealth that just that one company created for the shipbuilding industry in both Northern Ireland and the North East was unbelievable. They were basically tramp ships that would transport anything anywhere. We would take wine, books, coconut oil, animals, the lot, almost like a taxi service. You would take ice cream to New Guinea and then when you were in New Guinea you'd bring all the coconut oil and copper back. We were always led to believe that if we were on the copper run, the copper would pay for the whole trip and everything else was profit.

When I first went in I started as a junior engineer and all you did at first was watch-keeping. Every four hours you went round and did a log, all handwritten. You logged everything, every temperature; every pressure; every indicator in the engine room went into a log book. The vessels were very well maintained and they all had good engineers on board. We would be at sea and we would pull a generator down – and I mean pull it down, pistons out and everything. You did four hours on, eight hours off round the clock, maybe switching a compressor on or keeping the air bottles pumped up that would start the main engine. When you were at sea there were your duties, but there was also overtime when something went wrong and then you were always in at the deep end. When you went into port you reverted to eight-hour watches, just eight hours a day.

We had apprentices on board and they were classed as cadets. They would be on board for designated lengths of time, then they would go to college and sit exams and progress that way. It was all jolly hard work, not like it is now on a container ship. Now they just have a control room and they can do everything and move everything around from there. In my day you were down on the bottom plates and you physically had to get everything out. As engineers, when you were at sea if you were pumping something overboard or something from one department to another compartment you had to do it physically. You opened and shut valves and started pumps up. Now they don't, they just push buttons. It's all automated.

I spent seven years in the Merchant Navy and all that time I planned to go back to Australia, but it never worked out. Instead I came back to Trimdon and bought a little shop. This was about the mid-1980s. It was the time when all the mines here shut, pretty much all at the same time. The whole industry just went. The coastal ones lasted a bit longer than the inland ones, because I think the coal was a bit easier to get there, cost-wise. But for those around where I was from it was just a matter of a click of the fingers and they were gone. So when I got back it was a very different place to the one I had grown up in.

The effect of the pit closures on Trimdon was terrible. It's a totally different community now. It used to be a proper community, but now you can see from the state of my shop through vandalism what it's like. What Trimdon was famous for, and what all the Durham mining villages were famous for, was their community spirit and that has near enough disappeared.

At the time of nationalization in 1947 there had been 127 collieries in the Durham coalfields, but by the end of the 1960s this was down to thirty-four and within ten years of the 1984 miners' strike every pit in Durham was closed. Ron Grey from Brandon remembered those times and the effect it had on the thousands of men who lost their jobs.

The pits around here shut down at different times, but the effect on Brandon was devastating. The closures affected things like the shops and the pubs and clubs because people hadn't got the money. Some people went to work at other pits that were still open, but when they died there was nothing. Most had to travel. Some found work in factories like Black & Decker at Spennymoor, but there were a lot of people, especially men in their fifties, who'd worked down the pits for twenty-five or thirty years and they just never bothered going to work again.

Throughout industrial Britain the pattern was being repeated. Entire working communities like Trimdon used to be based around a particular pit, steelworks, shipyard or factory, but as the industries closed down those communities were broken up. Bob Clark was a miner from Padiham in Lancashire and his experience of what happened there when the last pit closed down echoes that of Brian Booth and Ron Grey.

When all the pits were shut down the younger men couldn't say, 'The pits have shut so I'm not doing anything else.' They were all dispersed wherever they could get a job. A lot of the miners were assimilated into other industries. I was a coalface worker, but you've got to remember there were tradesmen as well. There were electricians, there were fitters, there were men who were multi-skilled. But a lot of the jobs they went into have gone now. Michelin in Burnley closed down in 2001 and we had another local factory that closed three years ago, and they employed up to seven hundred people. We had Philips down the road, making the television tubes, and that's gone, and a plastics factory. These places employed thousands of people, and now in Padiham we have not one major employer. We've no one in Padiham who employs more than twenty people now. It's not a problem for retired chaps like me, but what on earth are the young people going to do?

For those who worked in Lancashire's mills it was a similar story. Bill Hayward from Heywood remembers the devastating effect the mill closures had on the community.

Mills were closing all the time and it was the knock-on effect that was particularly damaging. Round the mills there were always shops – grocers, butchers and what have you. But it wasn't just shops. When a mill shut down you'd got the suppliers of all sorts of things who were affected, and local contractors. People like electrical contractors, sheet-metal workers who made guards for the machinery. So when a mill shut it was not just the people who worked there who were affected; there was a knock-on effect on the whole community. Whole communities became unemployed. When I left school you could get a job almost anywhere and up to the late 1970s you could move about and get jobs easily. We started noticing factory closures when it was coming into the 1980s. Manufacturing was starting to disappear. There was a certain Tory lady who thought we didn't need manufacturing to survive and that was a big mistake.

Throughout his career the mills that Jack Procter worked in were closing down all the time. In total he worked in fifteen different places. He remembers the chimneys disappearing almost straight away because of the extra insurance on them. If they kept a building for use as industrial units, the chimneys went. In some cases, like a factory at Blackburn at which he worked, they reduced the size of the chimney while the place was still running.

Jack Procter was a good worker, but from the time that he started work in 1946 until his retirement in 1992 he faced redundancy at least fifteen times. He says he thinks he may have jumped ship before it sank in most cases. If he saw things were slowing down at the mill he was working in he would always find another job and leave before there were any redundancies. After he'd retired he used to get so upset when he looked at all his tools that he donated them to Queen Street Mill in Burnley with tears in his eyes. By this time the mill, where cloth had been woven for eighty-eight years, was an industrial heritage site.

That seems to be all that is left now. It's all become part of the leisure industry. Johnson's Wireworks, just over the other side of Ashton New Road from where I lived on Grey Mare Lane in Bradford in Manchester, is now the site of Manchester City's Etihad Stadium. Next to it, where the pithead winding gear of Bradford Pit used to stand, there's a supermarket and just beyond that the National Cycling Centre. The former Clayton Aniline factory site has been earmarked as the location for a new Manchester City training complex, with community football pitches as part of a plan to transform this part of east Manchester into a global sporting capital and 'corridor of Olympians' with sports halls, swimming pools and training facilities. It was never pretty around there, but it was a real working community and the grimy works and factories provided employment for hundreds from that community and beyond, as well as helping Britain to maintain its position as the workshop of the world. Today the retail and sport and leisure industries have taken over from the old indus-tries – a reflection of what has happened in the country as a whole. But will the new Sport City provide the jobs or generate the wealth that the old industries of the area did? And will it generate any of the old community spirit of an area like that?

Society has changed too much for that, and in the interviews that were done for this book there was one refrain that constantly recurred. 'Then Thatcher came along and took our jobs, destroyed the communities we lived in and changed the sort of people who lived in them.' Ray Barrett spent the whole of his working life in the sort of engineering workshops that Sport City has replaced, and he summed up the changes. 'The first group of men I ever worked with,' he said, 'were the best. The last men I worked with were the worst. It was a gradual thing, I suppose, but it was all about attitude and selfishness. The first lot were helpful and looked after one another and stuck together. The last lot they were all wrapped up in their own selfishness.'

Acknowledgements

Sincere thanks to the many individuals who came forward to tell their stories. Edwin Airey, John Bage, Ray Barrett, Eric Beaghan, Keith Beckett, Ken Berry, Stanley Bolton, Brian Booth, Jim Bottomley, Clarence Bowen, Sam Boyd, Kathleen Boyle, Connie Brown, Glenice Carpenter, Alf Carr, Amy Carr, Dennis Carrol, Barry Caswell, Fraser Chambers, Jim Chater, Bob Clark, Michael Cowdrey, Alan Crompton, Jimmy Crooks, Tony Cummings, Win Currie, Jim Cuthbert, Bill Daley, John Davies, Roy Davies, Colin Douglas, Les Dunn, Marjorie Dunn, Kath Dunne, Margaret Emerson, Noel Evans, Hubert Everson, Colin Findlay, Kenneth Findlay, John Garrity, Michael George, Ken Goss, John Grant, Jim Grigg, Ron Grey, Cicily Harspool, Jean Harpur, Bill Hayward, Thomas Hier, Ernest Hill, Gareth Howells, Lyndon Humphries, Robert Hunter, Tom Jackson, Ruth James, Wyndham James, Ron Jenkins, Margaret Johnston, Wyndham Jones, John Kelly, Roy Lancaster, Mona Legg, Doris Lloyd, Mike Lomas, Robert McKie, Vin Malone, Molly Matthews, Harry Meadows, Derek Meaking, Billy Melling, Tom Minard, Alf Molyneux, Kenneth Moore, Francis Newman, Alan Perry,

John Perry, Peter Phillips, Albert Phipps, Dorothy Pomfrett, Jack Procter, Tommy Procter, Willie Rae, Enid Rice, Ian Richmond, Pauline Richmond, William Roberts, David Rudman, Mabel Ryding, Terry Sargeant, Reg Sawyer, Harlan Senior, Wendy Simms, Bill Slaughter, Dorothy Small, Mitch Spiers, Freda Swarbrick, Gerald Tarling, Margaret Taylor, Don Thomas, Ivy Thomas, Mel Warrender, Harry Wharton, Irene Wharton, Neville Wilkinson, John Williams, Bob Willis, Tony Willis, Jim Wright, Barbara Yates.

My thanks also to the many individuals and organizations who helped with the research for the book and put us in touch with many of the interviewees. Age Concern South Wales, especially Claire Morris; Age Concern Wolverhampton; Angie at Meadowfields Community Centre, Rochdale; Adam Brown; Moira Black of Pontefract Miners Recreational Charity; Janice Blower of the *South Shields Gazette*; Brian Booth; Dowlais Library; Ebbw Vale Works Archival Trust; Ellen Road Engine House; Jarrow & Hebburn Historical Society; Graham Lewis; Eddie Liddle; Oldham Friendship Club; Sunniside Historical Group; Stuart Whittle and John and Sue Hurst at Horwich Heritage.

Special thanks to my daughter, Kathryn, for doing most of the research for the book, finding the people whose stories are told here and travelling around the country to interview them. Also to my wife, Fran, for her work on the transcripts of the interviews, for helping to make the stories and the processes that are described clearer and doing the Scottish research and interviews. I would also like to thank my agent, Gordon Wise at Curtis Brown, and all at Transworld, especially Doug Young and my editor Rebecca Jones, for their help and encouragement and for the part they played in making sure these stories were told.

Picture Acknowledgements

Pictures are listed clockwise from top left.

Section one

Coal mine, Aber Valley, Wales, 1949: © UPPA/Photoshot.

Housewife, Manchester, January 1954: Getty Images; washing-line, Clydeside, Scotland, July 1954: Getty Images; boy carrying a suitcase, Manchester, January 1954: Getty Images; Manor Estate, aerial view: Sheffield Archives & Local Studies Library; children round a dining table, Salford, Manchester, 1955: Popperfoto/Getty Images.

Working men's club, Durham, April 1955: Getty Images; Blackpool beach, Wakes Week, July 1955: Getty Images; young people dancing the Hokey Cokey, Swansea, 31 December 1943: Getty Images; Saturday night at Byker & St Peter's Working Men's Club, Newcastle, 1973: Getty Images.

Flute band, Belfast, February 1954: Getty Images; works canteen, Lilac Mill, Shaw, Lancashire, 1950s: Bert Hardy/Getty Images; gymnastics team, Sheffield Twist

Drill and Steel Company, 1950: Sheffield Archives & Local Studies Library, courtesy Dormer Tools Ltd; Ollerton Colliery brass band, Nottinghamshire, 1947: SSPL via Getty Images.

A street in Wallsend, 1972: Getty Images.

Section two

Last shift, Burradon Colliery, Newcastle, November 1975: mirrorpix.

Miners, Bold Colliery, St Helen's, Merseyside, 1957: Getty Images; miner, Cwm Gorse Colliery, Pontypridd, Wales, 1956: Haywood Magee/Getty Images; pushing loads of coal, Lanarkshire, August 1951: Getty Images; pit ponies, 1955: Getty Images; two miners drilling for coal, 1951: Charles Hewitt/Getty Images.

Miners in the lamp room, Merthyr Vale Colliery, Wales, February 1974: mirrorpix; miner recording weekly production totals, Kent, February 1947: Popperfoto/Getty Images; pay day, Ellington Colliery, March 1951: Getty Images; miners return to work after a strike, Maerdy Colliery, Gwent, Wales, March 1985: Getty Images; changing-room, Kellingley Colliery, North Yorkshire, March 1973: Getty Images.

Ashton Brothers cotton mill, Hyde, Stockport, April 1947: Time & Life Pictures/Getty Images; girls returning from work at the Lily cotton mill, Shaw, Lancashire, April 1957: Getty Images; workers, Lilac Mill, Shaw, Lancashire, 1955: Bert Hardy/Getty Images; office, Knowles, Peel cotton mill, Bolton, 1957: SSPL via Getty Images.

Empty shop, Lancashire, April 1952: Getty Images; demonstration against cheap imported cotton, London, June 1962: Getty Images.

Section three

Steelworks at night, *c.* 1950: Getty Images.

Foundry workers, Portsmouth Dockyard, February 1950: Getty Images; fettler, United Steel, Sheffield, 1947: SSPL via Getty Images; worker using tongs to handle tin, 1953: Ronald Startup/Getty Images; workers, Walter and Hall steelworks, Sheffield, 1959: Getty Images.

Rolling mill, Peech and Tozer steel plant, South Yorkshire, April 1947: Time & Life Pictures/Getty Images; hot mill, Richard Thomas & Baldwin, steel works, Ebbw Vale, Wales, August 1952: Getty Images; worker hanging newly silver-plated spoons to dry, Sheffield, November 1959: Getty Images; worker cutting a hot steel rail line, Sheffield, 1948: SSPL via Getty Images; rolled steel plate being cooled, Consett Iron works, County Durham, 1959: SSPL via Getty Images.

Ship designer, *c.* 1945: Getty Images; shipyard worker carrying white-hot rivet, March 1940: Getty Images; Welder, Greenock dockyard, Clydeside, July 1954: Getty Images; riveters, *c.* 1940: Getty Images; laying out plywood to the specifications of a plan, 1935: Getty Images; ship-builders consulting a plan, Tyneside, October 1951: Getty Images.

Workers awaiting the launch of *Uganda*, Clydeside, 1952: George Douglas/Getty Images.

Section four

Apprentice using an industrial drill, October 1953: Getty Images.

Worker inspecting a fine steel airplane crank, 1947: Time & Life Pictures/Getty Images; testing a propeller in a wind tunnel, Bristol Siddeley Aircraft, Filton, Bristol, 1959: SSPL via Getty Images; engineers inside a high pressure vessel, Bristol Siddeley Aircraft, Filton, Bristol, 1959: SSPL via Getty Images; engineers at the Rolls Royce factory assembling RB 162 lightweight lift jets, Derbyshire, August 1964: Getty Images.

Working on a ship's crankshaft, engineering workshop, Greenock, July 1954: Getty Images; workers checking machine, Kilmarnock, October 1955: Getty Images; worker laying cable, Forth Road Bridge, April 1962: Getty Images; precision engineering, Wilkins & Mitchell, Darlaston, Staffordshire, June 1964: Getty Images.

Assembling engines for the Armstrong Siddleley Sapphire, Bristol, 1959: SSPL via Getty Images; lorries carrying Austin cars, Birmingham, February 1954: Getty Images; millionth Mini comes off the British Motor Corporation production line, Birmingham, February 1965: Getty Images; production of left-hand drive Austin A40s for the north-American market, Longbridge, October 1947: Getty Images.

Car-workers awaiting news of redundancies, 1957: Jack Estem/Getty Images.

Index

INDEX

INDEX

INDEX

Fred

The Definitive Biography of Fred Dibnah

By David Hall

FRED DIBNAH WON the hearts of millions of viewers with his television programmes about his life as a steeplejack, and his passion for the industrial history of Britain. With his trademark flat cap, enthusiasm and knowledge of the country's steam past, his gift for storytelling, and his cry of 'Did you like that?' as another giant chimney slid to earth behind him, he quickly became a genuine favourite with viewers.

This is an intimate portrait of Fred, from his childhood in Bolton, to his days as a steeplejack – the job he was to love above all others – and on to his successful television career. We discover all the different sides of Fred's personality – engineer, steeplejack, artist, craftsman, steam enthusiast, inventor, storyteller and eccentric. This definitive biography will delight Fred's many fans.

> 'Straight talking, frank speaking – with Fred Dibnah
> you get what it says on the tin'
> DAILY TELEGRAPH

> 'Fred Dibnah, philosopher and steeplejack, has been
> representing the people for nearly 20 years'
> SUNDAY TELEGRAPH

Also by David Hall

Fred Dibnah's Industrial Age
Fred Dibnah's Magnificent Monuments
Fred Dibnah's Age of Steam
Fred: The Definitive Biography of Fred Dibnah
Manchester's Finest
Fred Dibnah's Buildings of Britain
Fred Dibnah's Made in Britain
Fred Dibnah's Victorian Heroes

Sandhurst Library
The Broadway
Sandhurst
GU47 9BL
01252 870161

Bracknell
Forest
Council

09. AUG 14	27. 01		
06. SEP 14	2 4 MAR 2010		
27. OCT 14	1 4 APR 2010		
BBh 2/16			
BSAN 11/16			
31 AUG 2017			
2 1 SEP 2017			

To avoid overdue charges this book should be returned on
or before the last date stamped above. If not required by
another reader it may be renewed in person, by telephone,
post or on-line at www.bracknell-forest.gov.uk/libraries

Library & Information Service

5430000031990 4